Exploring the New Testament

Second Edition

Marla J. Selvidge

Central Missouri State University

Prentice
Hall

UPPER SADDLE RIVER, NEW JERSEY 07458

Library of Congress Cataloging-in-Publication Data

SELVIDGE, MARLA J. [date]
  [New Testament]
  Exploring the New Testament / MARLA J. SELVIDGE.
  p. cm.
  Originally published: The New Testament. Upper Saddle River, N.J.: Prentice Hall, 2003.
  Includes bibliographical references
  ISBN 0-13-099164-3
  1. Bible. N.T.—Textbooks I. Title.
BS2535.3 .S45   2002
225.6'1—dc21   2001056764

VP, Editorial Director: *Charlyce Jones Owen*
Acquisitions Editor: *Ross Miller*
Assistant Editor: *Wendy Yurash*
Editorial Assistant: *Carla Worner*
Editorial/Production Supervision: *Joanne Riker*
Prepress and Manufacturing Buyer: *Brian Mackey*
Marketing Manager: *Chris Ruel*
Marketing Assistant: *Scott Rich*
Art Director: *Jayne Conte*
Cover Image: *The Mother of God or the Blessed Virgin by Hubert Van Eyck (1432),
    from St. Bavo's Cathedral, Ghent, Belgium.*

This book was set in 10.5/12.5 Times Roman by East End Publishing Services, Inc.
and was printed and bound by Hamilton Printing Company. The cover was
printed by Phoenix Color Corp.

The Scripture quotations contained herein, unless otherwise specified, are from the *New Revised
Standard Version Bible*, copyright 1989 by the Division of Christian Education for the National Council
of Churches of Christ in the United States of America. Used by permission. All Rights Reserved.

 © 2003, 1999 by Pearson Education, Inc.
Upper Saddle River, New Jersey 07458

Printed in the United States of America

10 9 8 7 6 5 4 3 2 1

ISBN 0-13-099164-3

Pearson Education LTD., *London*
Pearson Education Australia PTY, Limited, *Sydney*
Pearson Education Singapore, Pte. Ltd
Pearson Education North Asia Ltd, *Hong Kong*
Pearson Education Canada, Ltd., *Toronto*
Pearson Educación de Mexico, S.A. de C.V.
Pearson Education — Japan, *Tokyo*
Pearson Education Malaysia, Pte. Ltd
Pearson Education, *Upper Saddle River, New Jersey*

In memory of

Aunt Thelma Cannon
Uncle Homer Gilreath
Aunt Thelma Gilreath
Jack La Rosa
Uncle Isom Lovitt
Cuma McGinnis
Stephen P. Schierling, Ph.D.
Aunt Emma Stephenson
Cousin "Snookie" Stephenson
and
Muppy Doodle the Second

Contents

1

A Stranger in a Strange Land 1

2

Cultural Heritage of the New Testament   21

3

The Unexpected News of Jesus   49

4

A Humble Community Anticipating a Hopeful Future: The Gospel of Mark   84

5

A Traditional Community Facing Change: The Gospel of Matthew   85

6

A Diverse Community Engaged in Social Reform : The Gospel of Luke   105

7

A Troubled Community in Search of the Truth:
The Gospel of John   125

8

Christianity, a World Religion:
The Acts of the Apostles   153

9

Early Pauline Documents:
1 and 2 Thessalonians, Galatians, and Philippians   181

Philemon:
A Letter of Mediation 240

1 Corinthians:
A Catalogue of Questions and Opinions 245

2 Corinthians:
An Angry Paul and the Super Apostles 255

11

Documents Written in the Name of Paul: Colossians and Ephesians   259

Colossians: The Universal and Cosmic Messiah   259

Ephesians: A Predestined, Unified, and Orderly Church   267

12
Letters Written in the Name of Paul: 1 and 2 Timothy and Titus   275

1 Timothy: Implosion and the Gospel of Order   278

2 Timothy: A Suffering Apostle   286

Titus: A Dangerous and Stressful Assignment   289

13

Struggling with a New Religion: Hebrews and James   293

Hebrews:
A Sermon on Martyrdom   294

James:
An Egalitarian Philosophy of Life   304

14
Documents to Friends in Far-Away Places: 1 and 2 Peter and Jude 313

15
Conflict and Christianity:
1, 2, 3 John and Revelation   337

Preface

There must have been something in the coffee
we shared (Ted Bolen and I) that afternoon, because I agreed
to create a proposal (for a New Testament texbook).

In the previous volume, I set my standards high. I wanted to develop a text that would reflect the diversity of approaches and voices that have become part of an international dialogue about the New Testament. During the past thirty years of teaching the New Testament, I have changed, my students have changed, and so has the academy. But the amount of diverse material I added to the last volume proved to be too much for the average student to digest in one semester.

This volume continues my original goal of diversity. It incorporates not only historical and literary-critical research but also a host of feminist voices that are often ignored by other New Testament texts. New Testament introductions rarely discuss the effects of the New Testament on our culture and especially, how it has been used by people in both a negative and positive way. As professors, I think we have to recognize that many students in our classrooms have never read the New Testament, yet it influences them in myriad ways every day of their lives. We should address the New Testament honestly, without leaving an impression with students that the contents are neutral. While it is literature, the effect on world cultures has been and is profound. This volume does not leave the text timebound. It reaches out to whomever wants to read it with, hopefully, relevant words that continue to make the New Testament a timeless document.

Many people have contributed to the creation of this text. Without their encouragement and enthusiasm, this book would not exist. Many thanks to Anne Connole for reading the manuscript with a proofreader's eye. Thanks also must go to Ella Connole,

Julie Kendall, and C.J. Peacock for all of the office support during the preparation of the second edition. The library at St. Paul School of Theology became my entry way to the world of scholarship. Thanks to Logan Wright for his help and kindness in loaning rare books to me. Thanks also to Terry McNeeley and Jeremy Burt for assistance in production.

Many reviewers suggested helpful remarks that have strengthened this volume. I appreciate all the thoughtful energy that went into their criticisms. Hopefully, they have helped to make this text more useful in the classroom. I am grateful to: Ira J. Jolivet, Jr., Pepperdine University; Mark D. Given, Southwest Missouri State University; and Susan Calef, Creighton University.

Once again I must thank my anchor, companion world traveler, and golf buddy, Thomas C. Hemling, Ph.D., whose confidence and love have made this task possible. We are all a product of those around us who have touched our lives. The revision of this textbook is dedicated to many of my beloved friends and relatives who shared their lives with me in an unselfish way, and who, sadly, have departed this life since the printing of the first edition.

Marla J. Selvidge, Ph.D.
Central Missouri State University
mjs8674@cmsu2.cmsu.edu

Introduction

A Timeless Book
for ALL Peoples

This textbook is designed for entry-level college students who are taking a class in general studies or the humanities and have had little, if any, formal training in the academic study of the Bible. It presupposes that students will not understand theological jargon and so attempts, in a conversational style, to translate it into common language whenever possible. A glossary is provided to help students with words, geography, and selective names distinctive to the discipline.

This text is not encyclopedic. It does not attempt to cover all of the theories of any given book. It seeks to survey what is determined to be the most diverse and compelling research in order to lead the student through the maze of New Testament scholarship. It attempts to describe rather than define in a non-technical language, keeping biblical references to a minimum. When possible, it uses summaries and illustrations to clarify architecture and geography or to enhance understanding of the topic. The bibliography at the end of the book represents works consulted.

This introductory textbook is based on the assumption that the New Testament belongs to the peoples of the world. Its focus is pluralistic and interdisciplinary, hoping to bring the experiences of the student, and the best and most varied scholarship in the Bible, art, history, theology, ethics, and more, together in a readable format that will enhance classroom teaching and learning. It surveys each book, considering the best historical-critical and literary-critical suggestions available. When dealing with individual books, each chapter attempts to ask the historical questions of date, location, and author, but it also features sections on genre, prominent characters, and special emphases of the book.

The purpose of this textbook is to introduce the New Testament and its contents, not necessarily to teach a theological or historical point of view. A major goal of the text is to write inclusively. This edition contains additional maps and photographs which may help to make the contents live for the student.

Chapter 1 recognizes that students will greet the New Testament having come from a variety of backgrounds and skills. The New Testament is beloved by many because of its ability to reach across so many cultural and geographical lines. It is a popular document that is used by many as a good luck charm. And there is the occasional anecdotal story about how someone was carrying a bible in his back pocket and it saved his life by stopping the bullet. Yet on a more serious note, it also may provide liberating words that eventually help people overcome the oppression of poverty and subjugation by an elitist regime. The Bible has been used and abused by powerful governments and individuals. The word "heretic" was certainly born admid the religious struggle for power to dictate canon, interpretations, and applications of the Bible. Finally, this chapter ends with a discussion of definitions and origins of the New Testament with a brief survey of some of the myriad ways of interpretation.

Chapter 2 situates the New Testament within the cultural landscape of the Roman Empire with influences from Greek and Roman philosophies and religions. Most of the chapter is devoted to explaining the religion of the ancient Iraelites/Jews and their immense influence on the writing of the New Testament and founding of Christianity. The chapter ends with a survey of the geography of Palestine.

Chapter 3 tackles the synoptic problem while attempting to define the form of "gospel." It sets the stage for the upcoming chapter on the gospels. An explanation of the quest for the historical Jesus finishes the discussion.

Chapters 4 through 7 survey the gospels, Mark, Matthew, Luke, and John in that order. Each chapter, and all those that follow, considers date, audience, authorship, reasons for writing the works, sources, content and characters. The topics of the "secret messiah" and "geography" are highlighted in the Gospel of Mark. Both Matthew and Luke are compared briefly with Mark while their own distinctive stories/traditions are considered. The Gospel of Matthew is interested in the community/church and the Kingdom of God. There are hints that the writer employs a somewhat "violent" vocabulary. The Gospel of Luke gives substantial space to exploring relationships while creating an androgynous view of early Christianity. The writer is particularly interested in political operatives and their titles. The Gospel of John features long discussions on literary sources and a comparison of the characters of Nicodemus and the Woman from Samaria. Special attention is paid to John's anti-Jewish tendencies with the many dualistic references to love and hate.

Acts of the Apostles is featured in chapter 8. Created by the writer of Luke, he/she argues that Christianity belongs to the world. While the book is written in a quasi-historical-narrative style, it represents a particular theological view of how Christianity progressed throughout the Roman world. The church is portrayed in an idealistic manner, perhaps in order to unite disparate Christian groups, defend the ailing Paul, or to prove that Romans should not worry about a political assault by the Christians. Several prominent characters are discussed including Peter, Paul, Tabitha, and Lydia. The Jerusalem Council makes way for a discussion of the missionary expansion throughout the Mediterranean world. Topics of note include an analysis of the many speeches in Acts and a survey of "speaking in tongues."

Chapters 9 through 11 feature Pauline works. They are organized according to relative dates of composition and suspected authorhip. Chapter 9 introduces the person and writings attributed to Paul as well as the form and sources for many of the letters. Next, the letters of 1 and 2 Thessalonians, Galatians, and Philippians are considered. All of the letters are situated geographically and culturally while summarizing their basic teachings or themes and characters. First Thessalonians is very concerned with the parousia and struggles with demonic myths about Jews. Second Thessalonians is compared extensively with the first letter. Galatians considers the topics of circumcision, baptism, and justification. Peter's waffling on the issue of kosher foods is discussed in light of the stories found in Acts of the Apostles. Philippians is studied against the backdrop of a congregation who "loved" Paul and supported him when very few others did. Time is spent on exploring the relationship of Paul to females within the congregation.

Chapter 10 takes up the study of Romans, Philemon, and 1 and 2 Corinthians. After geographical, historical, and literary considerations, Romans is compared with Acts of the Apostles. Several characters are investigated including a list of important theological issues. Paul was interested in issues such as equality, sin, same-sex relationships, civil disobedience, and health. Philemon raises the topic of slavery which is also considered in other Pauline documents. 1 Corinthians contains myriad problems that were tackled by Paul. Among those discussed in this section are political parties, immorality, sexual relationships, celibacy, spiritual marriage, women and the meetings, the agape feast, the credentials of Paul, and health. 2 Corinthians explores the personal problems Paul had with opponents labeled "super-apostles" and the rumors floating around about Paul himself.

Chapters 11 and 12 explore the works and letters that are attributed to Paul. Ephesians and Colossians are linked together in Chapter 11 because of their obvious similarities. Both letters create metaphorical languages to help them deal with the intrusion of other religions. They are threatened with change and are attempting to foster unity in spite of forces that seem to be causing their disintegration. Some of the distinctive topics in Colossians include "cosmic mythology," "female saints," and the hierarchical "household codes." Questions of "who copied from whom" are also explored. Central themes within the book of Ephesians are "one new humanity" and the preoccupation with the control of God in the universe.

1 and 2 Timothy and Titus are letters attributed to Paul. Chapter 12 discusses the problem of placing these works within the life span of Paul and the very different ecclesiastical and sometimes narrow tones of the writers. The recipients of these letters were under fire and the writers attempted to help the readers to endure by setting rigid guidelines. Some of the problems addressed are "the political power of the widows," and "job descriptions and qualifications" of the leadership. The second letter to Timothy has no major theme. It is a personal letter that comes from a person who may have been incarcerated because of his or her faith. The writer reprimands many who have maligned him or her. The letter to Titus once again sets up a male-dominated hierarchical

structure to govern the church. Problems facing Titus included a "breakdown in the organization," " people who were taking advantage of other members financially," and a possible" civil insurrection."

Chapters 13 and 14 include disparate documents that deal with many different topics. They include the study of Hebrews and James in Chapter 13 and I and 2 Peter and Jude in 14. Hebrews and James are considered together because they are seemingly addressed to Jewish audiences. We know little about who created these works and when they were penned. Hebrews appears to be a sermon on martyrdom. The community had experienced violence and had possibly lost lives. Jesus is compared with the ancient Israelite religion and is demonstrated to be the perfect sacrifice. That sacrifice might be a precursor to their own. James is a mysterious letter of unknown origin that seems to be influenced by a host of Greek and Jewish literatures. It has no single plan but hopes that the social stratification taking place in the community will change. It argues for social and economic equality.

Chapter 14 contains analyses of 1 and 2 Peter and Jude. They were written to people who were under fire. Peter, the apostle found in the gospels and Acts, probably did not write I Peter because it depends upon a variety of written sources. As in the letters to Timothy and Titus, the writer advocates a strict hierarchical structure and urges people to submit to the authorities in order to avoid possible abuse. 2 Peter and Jude are remarkably similar in structure and language. 2 Peter argues with people who are teaching values and a theology that the author finds to be incorrect. The writer argues against teachers who believe that there is no parousia; that God is not in charge of the universe; that anyone can interpret scripture; and that people should have unlimited personal freedoms. Jude features many of the same problems. The community is changing and the writer hopes to direct the readers to a more traditional understanding of their faith.

The final chapter in this text explores 1, 2, 3, John and the Book of Revelation which have many common elements and themes that are discussed in the introduction. 1 John tackles the problem of dissenting groups that are forming in the community. They are at odds over the identity and person of Jesus, the concept of sin, their responsibility toward each other, and the end of time. 2 John is a personal letter to a "female" who is a leader of a church that is facing issues regarding the "real" humanity of Jesus. 3 John is another personal letter written to Gaius regarding administrative and financial problems of the church. They have neglected to pay itinerate preachers. As an aside, Demetrius is introduced.

The textbook ends by exploring the themes found within the Book of Revelation. Preliminary to that discussion are definitions and descriptions of apocalyptic literature. Several examples of ways of interpreting Revelation are explored. Whoever wrote Revelation had experienced extreme stress and the loss of power over his own life and possibly those around him. Revelation takes aim at supposed opponents with the hope of destroying them in a fiery mythological battle. A special feature of this chapter is a comparison of the portraits of Jezebel and the Woman Clothed with the Sun.

Figures and Tables

Tables

Suggested Web Sites

General Sites

Basic Vocabulary of Biblical Studies for Beginners
   http://www.wfu.edu/~horton/r102/ho1.html.

Bibles on Line
   http://ww2.mcgill.ca/religion/link-bib.htm

Database of Images Related to the Bible
   http: eikon.divinity.yale.edu/

Library.yale.edu/ div/divhome.HTM

Ecole Index of Images Related to Biblical Studies
   http://cedar.evensville.edu/~ecoleweb/images.html

From Jesus to the Christ. The First Christians
   http://www.pbs.org/wgbh/pages/frontline/shows/religion/

New Testament Visuals
   http://www.nd.edu:80/~kcoblent/newtesta.html

A Glossary for Judaism, Christianity, and Islam
   http://ccat.sas.upenn.edu/~rs2/glossopt.html

Biblical Studies E-Journals
   http://www.bsw.org/

The New Testament Gateway
   http://www.bham.ac.uk/theology/goodacre/links.htm

NTgateway.com

NTgateway.com

xxx   *Suggested Web Sites*

Society of Biblical Literature
> http://sbl-site.org
> This is the site for the national organization for Society for Biblical Literature. It supports more than 8,000 academics in the field of biblical studies and religion and contains a variety of public sites.

Wabash Center Guide to Internet Resources for Teaching and Learning in Theology and Religion
> http://www.wabashcenter.wabash.edu/Internet/front.htm

Selected Topical Sites

Development of the Canon of the New Testament
> http://shell5.ba.best.com/~gdavis/ntcanon/

Diotima. Study of Women and Gender in the Ancient World
> http://www.stoa.org/diotima/

Guide to Early Church Documents
> http://www.iclnet.org/pub/resources/christian-history.html

How to Interpret Ancient Manuscripts
> http://www.earlham.edu/~seidti/iam/interp mss.html

Mary Magdalene. A Gallery of Images
> http://www.haverford.edu/relg/mcguire/marymimages.htm

Missionary Journeys of Paul
> http://unbound.biola.edu/acts/index.cfm?fuseaction=frames&lang=English

Multiculturalism and Political Correctness and the Bible
> http://www.geocities.com/christianwitnesses/MCPC.html

Pauline Studies (select entries are useful)
> http://www.textweek.com/pauline/paul.htm

Sources for the Study of the Book of Revelation
> http://sunsite.dk/Revelation/

Viewing a Harmony of the Gospels: Parallel (Pages are placed side by side for study.)
> http://www.surfplaza.com/harmony/

(Web Sites change addresses regularly. We apologize if these sites have moved since printing of this book.)

Abbreviations

Acts	Acts of the Apostles
AV	Authorized Version
Col.	Colossians
Cor.	Corinthians
Eph.	Ephesians
Gal.	Galatians
Heb.	Hebrews
Jm.	James
Jn.	John
KJV	King James Version
Lk.	Luke
LXX	Septuagint
Mk.	Mark
Mt. or Matt.	Matthew
MT	Hebrew Bible or Massoretic Text
NEB	New English Bible
NRSV	New Revised Standard Version
Pet.	Peter
Phil.	Philippians
Rom.	Romans
Thess.	Thessalonians
Tim.	Timothy
Rev.	Revelation

1

A Stranger
in a Strange Land

Dear friends, ... as foreigners and strangers in the world...
—1 Peter 2:11, NRSV

A TIMELESS BOOK FOR ALL PEOPLES

The New Testament is more than a dusty relic unearthed occasionally to be admired by friends and family. It is more than the sum total of academicians', ecclesiastical professionals', and theologians' theories or landscapes. It is a thriving document that has fostered both living and lost religious traditions all over the world.

The New Testament has been a living document for almost 2,000 years, and its meaningfulness changes with each people and culture it touches, almost with each moment or each person in time. It has influenced people from Ethiopia to Russia, from China to Australia, from Melanesia to Great Britain. Some people have given their lives for the sake of beliefs based on this text. Others have burned its pages, hoping to destroy its messages. In friendly conversation, it is almost impossible to discuss the New Testament objectively because it means so many different things to so many people.

Academics and religious leaders have created a myriad of approaches to unlocking its pages. People view it as a code of laws or an object of worship and even consult it to determine future decisions. It has catapulted politicians into power and destroyed monarchs. It has been used and abused by powerful people throughout history. It is a book that should be read and discussed because it has had so much influence on all of us.

READING THE NEW TESTAMENT: WHO IS THE STRANGER?

The New Testament is everywhere! It is found on billboards, bumper stickers, and greeting cards. We hear it on the radio in commercials and in popular songs. We watch stories about it on television and at the movies. If it is all around us, then why do we feel as though we are strangers when we begin to open its pages? Do we really know anything about the origins and writers of this book?

Most students who take classes in the New Testament fall somewhere between the person who views the Bible as the inspired Words of God and the person who has never opened its pages. The study of the Bible can be complicated, but it can also be a challenge, a game, or an attempt to solve a puzzle. And some of those puzzles may never be solved.

Some may view the **New Testament** as an old favorite, having studied it at home or in religious classes. For others, reading the New Testament may be an alienating experience. It may be similar to the student who took an introductory course in the New Testament. The student's first assignment was to read the Gospel of Matthew. After finding the book in the Bible (with a little difficulty), he began to read in the **King James Version (Authorized Version)**,

> The book of the generation of Jesus Christ, the son of David, the son of Abraham. Abraham begat Isaac; and Isaac begat Jacob; and Jacob begat Judas and his brethren; And Judas begat Phares and Zara of Thamar; and Phares begat Esrom; and Esrom begat Aram; And Aram begat Aminadab; and Aminadab begat Naasson and Naasson begat Salmon. (Matthew 1:1–5 KJV)

He was overwhelmed by the vocabulary and could not begin to pronounce the names of the people, *if they were names of people,* in the verses. Words such as Jesus, David, and Abraham were recognizable, but what did the term *generation* mean? And if this was a genealogy, were these male or female names? And why were they included at the beginning of the first book of the New Testament? Frustrated, he nearly dropped the course. He was a stranger in an unfamiliar land. The New Testament appeared to be an impenetrable and a mysterious book.

Some may not be as inexperienced as the aforementioned student. Some students may be able to recite the books of the Bible from Genesis to Revelation, perhaps even in a song. These students have had years of training from their parents, the religious officials of their local congregations, and even through music and videos. They think they already know the contents of each book of the New Testament, who wrote it, and why it was written. It is a faith document. Their views of life and of themselves are intertwined with the stories and narratives as well as the myths of the New Testament.

The definition of "myth" is debated by almost every scholar of the bible. Some do not like the idea of attributing the term "myth" to the writings of the New Testament. A myth is a story that cannot be verified by objective, historical evidence. It is a story that has great and significant meaning which often unites people. We live in a world full of myths. Did Washington really throw the coin across the Potomac? Was Columbus the first settler of what we now call the United States? The term "myth" may at first seem to denigrate the New Testament but in reality it describes how important it has been in uniting people for almost 2,000 years. Yet in the same way that myth can unite people it can also encase those same people in an ideological prison. Barbara Sproul, in *Primal Myths: Creating the World,* captures this dilemma.

> Thus, the way in which … *myths* are transmitted, people often never learn that they are myths; people become submerged in their viewpoints, prisoners of their own traditions. They readily confuse attitudes toward reality with reality itself. Failing to see their own myths as myths, they consider all other myths false. (Sproul, 1979)

Many students have studied their own denominational stories and myths and come to class thinking that they understand the Bible completely. They declare that they have all of the answers. Many of these students are strangers to the critical or **analytical** study of the New Testament. They may have never studied the Bible from another person's or religion's point of view. These students may not, at first, find studying the New Testament difficult, but they soon discover that it is almost impossible for them to look at the Bible with a different set of eyes. The strange land of interpretation may present problems to them. If they continue reading with an open mind, they may discover that they are capable of seeing a variety of possible interpretations for any one verse in the New Testament, without experiencing a collapse in their own universe.

No matter how long we have studied the New Testament, we will always be strangers in a strange land. Consider how difficult it is to understand someone who speaks English and lives in another region of the country. Do we stop to consider that this book is read or heard by more people than any other book on earth? Can we fathom how someone in Turkey or Belize understands this ancient book? Now multiply all of that by time and language, and you may decide that we are lucky if we can understand anything at all about these ancient documents. We are strangers, not only because of who we are, but also because the books or documents in the New Testament were written by people who lived halfway around the world, probably somewhere in countries surrounding the Mediterranean ocean, spoke another language, **Koine**, or "common" Greek, and recorded their thoughts almost 2,000 years ago.

These early writers wrote about their experiences, beliefs, dilemmas, and rituals, which helped them sustain their lives, families, and friends. The answers to their dilemmas over 2,000 years ago may not be the answers for those who have entered the twenty-first century. As we read the New Testament, we will also discover that many of the books we read contain only the answers to questions. We still have to theorize about the nature of the problems, issues, or questions! Yet the Bible remains a best-selling book. It is a foundational block of the culture of the United States, as well as many other countries throughout the world.

POPULAR VIEWS OF THE NEW TESTAMENT

For many, the Bible holds the answers to all of their ethical dilemmas. It governs their actions in the now and hereafter. These people often claim that the Bible is a transcript from God, containing exact instructions from God. The Bible, more than anything else within the Christian religion, becomes an object of worship. People want to know the exact meaning or interpretation of a story, parable, or letter. They want concrete answers that time will not erode. Scholars themselves are not immune to this quest.

Becoming proficient in the exact interpretation and wording of a certain translation of the Bible becomes a lifelong pursuit. Reciting certain passages of Scripture becomes a healthy way of repeating the words of God for the benefit of other people. Games such as "Bible Trivia," help players memorize the Bible.

All sorts of Christians, **sects**, denominations, and political organizations claim that the New Testament is a record of sacred history. Each would see themselves as chosen by God to perform a special mission on earth. They use the Bible to define their communities in terms of theology, rituals, sexual relations, morals, and even clothing standards. In seeking personal guidance from its pages, they even detect appropriate political and ecclesiastical structures.

Crystal Ball   The Bible is a very important part of our cultural heritage. People respect it so much that they often do not know what to do with it. For some, its passages are filled with **enigmatic** words that hold keys to the solutions of personal dilemmas or future events. Speculations about the end of the world, as portrayed in the Book of Revelation, surface every time there is a major political power struggle in the Middle East.

Others have a more direct approach to divining the future. To discover an answer to a personal question, they open the Bible at random and point to a verse on the page. As the theory goes, God should direct the finger to the perfect verse that will answer a person's question.

Good Luck Charm   Many people adhere to superstitions about carrying a certain Bible verse in their wallets or purses as insurance. Many of these people never study their Bibles. They keep them around for comfort, protection, and to ward off evil from their front doors.

Ownership of the Bible   Does the New Testament belong only to those who worship or use it as a foundation for their religious traditions? Do only Christians have a right to determine the meaning of the Bible for everyone? Much of the contents of the New Testament may have been grounded, collected, and edited by people within these religious traditions, but should they be the only legitimate interpreters? The Bible's influence has always gone beyond the sanctuary. It has influenced family law, literature, architecture, art, political structures, availability of food stuffs, clothing styles, and more. Thus, those people who have felt its touch upon their lives or heard its doctrines have a right and responsibility to investigate it for themselves.

Many within Christian traditions would challenge the right of others to interpret faithfully their Word or Words of God. Some maintain that interpreters must study ancient, dead, and **esoteric** languages to **decipher** the meaning of the texts. Entrance into a particular society of interpreters (**denomination**, or order) is usually based on gaining mastery of the interpretation tools as well as assenting to dogmatic beliefs of a particular church or synagogue. The theory is that without linguistic tools and historical awareness, the texts can be misinterpreted. For many who are unfamiliar with Greek, Hebrew, or Aramaic, an interpretation using these foreign-sounding words seems like magic. And magic can be very powerful!

   Hope for the Poor   Not everyone in the world has two DVD players and a cellphone in every room. Some people live day to day, moment to moment, not knowing if they will survive. They have little food and no real property. For them, the New Testament becomes a tool that may help them overcome their circumstances. It contains within it the words that will enable them to find liberation. Some of these determined people claim that liberation is worth any price, even the death of the oppressors.

A POLITICAL TOOL OF THE FAITHFUL AND NOT SO FAITHFUL

Congress shall make no law respecting an establishment of religion, or prohibiting the free exercise thereof.

—First Amendment to the Constitution of the United States

Throughout the history of Christianity, the New Testament has been central to constructing the identities, rituals, ethics, and beliefs of its readers. Centuries of peoples have searched its pages to find meaning for their lives, their families, and their countries. It has spawned rituals for birth, death, and marriage. Many place the Bible at the center of their family activities, trying to adapt their lives to its moral guidelines. They use interpretations of the New Testament to enlighten difficult ethical dilemmas, but there are others who use the Bible as a tool to enhance their own power over others.

   The New Testament has legitimated kings and queens and cultural family norms and has offered a view of the future that, for some, made the here and now more bearable. The sword of truth has often become "The Only Truth." Many hoping to fulfill **apocalyptic** (doomsday) prophecies in the Bible have come preaching peace in the name of a God and have left their listeners in a pine box. Monarchs, popes, and ecclesiastical authorities, as well as unlikely political alliances, have governed people in the name of the God of the Bible. Early Protestant settlers from the Massachusetts Bay Colony to South Carolina thought that the best way to govern people was to enforce their interpretation of biblical mandates. So they created **theocracies** that reflected their own beliefs and forced everyone in their territories to obey the laws.

   Most Americans advocate the separation of religion and state (i.e., the separation of religion and government, or religious liberty); otherwise people who disagree with the religion advocated by the government would lose their freedom to worship. Yet there is no such thing as a complete separation of religion and state. The predominant faith of those elected to Congress in the United States is Protestant. A Christian opens each congressional session with prayer. To date, John F. Kennedy is the only Roman Catholic elected to serve as president.

Each year the Supreme Court hears cases dealing with the separation of religion and state. Some of those cases have included issues such as whether or not reading the Bible or prayer should be allowed in public schools, plural marriages, conscientious objectors, the use of public transportation for private religious schools, and so on.

Issues dealing with the influence of religion on government can be traced back to the founding pioneers in this country. The United States became a haven for people who wanted freedom from the religious intolerance they found in Europe. They did not want to worship as their country or king dictated. Protesters found their way to the new country with hopes of creating their own **utopia**. Instead, they actually patterned their governmental structures after those in Europe.

For example, the Puritans fled England because they did not appreciate Anglican worship. Anglicanism was born amidst a struggle between King Henry VIII and the Roman Papacy over whether or not the king should obtain an annulment. Henry won by confiscating most of the land, buildings, and financial holdings of the Roman Catholic Church in England. He began his own brand of Protestantism under the name of the Church of England. Yet the Puritans who sought to purify what they believed to be corrupt churches and clergy actually began their own form of theocracy in Massachusetts. They based their constitution on the teachings they found in the Bible.

The Bible was even used as a basis to execute people who were labeled **witches** during the founding years of the United States, and in Europe during the sixteenth and seventeenth centuries. Modern **feminists** contend that it has been used to subjugate women and entire nations, as well as to provide a rationale for the destruction of the earth's natural resources. Some suggest that it has kept women in a place of servitude for too long, doing little to advance causes of equality. Others would argue that the teachings in the Bible have raised the status of women throughout history, even helping women obtain the right to vote in the United States.

Thus, the Bible has been employed as a political tool by the "religious" and the not so religious to bring about positive social change and also to incite and prolong disastrous, debilitating wars such as the Bosnian conflict or the **Crusades** during the Middle Ages, which hoped to capture the Holy Land. It has been used to create state laws governing sexual relationships as well as to justify the subjugation of groups of people such as African Americans and women.

Dissenters, Martyrs, Heretics

Throughout the history of the world, there have always been dissenters who sought to **promulgate** or discover their own interpretations of the Bible, such as the **Cathars**, the **Waldensians**, the **Beguines**, and the **Gnostics**. George and Margaret Askew Fell Fox were dissenters in England during the founding days of Puritanism early in the seventeenth century. They appreciated neither the state religion nor the pious Puritans who they believed lived their own kind of hypocrisy. They looked to the New Testament for answers and found something termed the "inner light," which gave individuals the ability to interpret the Bible. The Foxes taught that all people who believe in the Bible gain this inner light, which makes them equal before God. This egalitarian concept revolutionized Christianity.

George Fox created Women's Meetings and gave women complete authority over their organization. This meant that women could pray, manage finances, and worship without the presence of men. Today, most people in the United States accept these ideals as normal, but 400 years ago they were virtually unknown in Great Britain. Fox's point of view was not shared by the majority of Christians, nor by his government. He was jailed and sentenced to prison many times throughout his life for breaking laws and preaching that women should have the right of free speech.

Martyrs.   Some, such as described in the letter written from the Church of Smyrna to the Church of Philomelium, the *Martyrdom of Polycarp*, willingly gave their lives for their New Testament faith. These people were labeled **martyrs** or witnesses. During the early years of Christianity, many thought if a person was executed for his or her faith in the Jesus of the New Testament, that person would then be transported immediately into heaven. Owning a mansion in glory was preferable to living a wretched, poor existence on earth or denying one's faith in Jesus the Christ. Countless people's lives ended by being burned at the stake, devoured by animals, or by the sword of a gladiator.

Heretics. Many dissenting voices, sometimes labeled **heretics,** were once lost and now are beginning to find their way into the mainstream of biblical study. Gnostic Christians during the first three centuries of Christianity inhabited Northern Egypt and produced gospels and Christian works known as the collection at **Nag Hammadi**. These manuscripts reflect beliefs and worship far different than the institutionalized form legitimated by state government or popular forms of Christianity that have survived until the twentieth century.

Gnosticism is a general term signifying many types of popular religions in the Near East. Throughout history, it has often been termed a *heresy.* Some contend that it originated within Judaism before the birth of Jesus. Others suggest a connection with Iranian religions. Gnosticism, which taught that "**gnosis**," or knowledge, was the key to understanding and experiencing the divine, came in many forms. It rivaled early institutional Christianity, perhaps because it offered a freer, or more emotionally intense way of worshipping. Women seemed to gravitate toward its worship practices and were reportedly ordained into its mysteries.

According to its mythology, Sophia was part of the spiritual world. For some reason, she failed. In the process of her restoration, the earth was created. Jesus' mission was to help restore her to her former glory. Jesus thus awakens a gnosis in all humans that can lead them to God. Part of this journey to the divine may involve conversations with angels as one climbs the stairway into the heavens. Many hoped to escape the earth, which they considered "evil," to a better, purer place. Consider the following quotes taken from *The Gnostic Gospels.*

From the Gospel of Thomas

Simon Peter said to them [the disciples]: "Let Mary leave us, for women are not worthy of Life." Jesus said, "I myself shall lead her, in order to make her male, so that she too may become a living spirit, resembling you males. For every woman who will make herself male will enter the Kingdom of Heaven."

From the Gospel of Philip

…the companion of the [Savior is] Mary Magdalene. [But Christ loved] her more than [all] the disciples and used to kiss her [often] on her [mouth]. The rest of [the disciples were offended by it…]. They said to him, "Why do you love her more than all of us?" The Savior answered and said to them, "Why do I not love you as [I love] her?" (Pagels 1981, 58 and 77)

In both of the excerpts, females are the topic of discussion. The Gospel of Thomas claims that women must deny their own natural biology to become equal to men who are the obvious inheritors of heaven. During the early years within Christianity, many female celibates cut off their breasts. The Gospel of Philip suggests that Jesus or the Savior loved Mary more than the disciples. Within the New Testament gospels, as we shall soon discover, there appears to be jealousy between the disciples and women. Both of these gospels represented points of view that were not accepted by the powerful institutional Church.

Other heretics became leaders within Christianity. Two heretics who are now heroes within the history books of Christianity are **John Calvin** (Calvinism) and **Martin Luther** (Lutheranism), who laid the foundation for Protestantism today. Martin Luther is often credited by historians with launching what we now know as the Reformation of the Roman Catholic Church, although his criticism of the bureaucracy and greed within the Church had been voiced by hundreds of others for centuries. As an Augustinian monk, doctor of theology, and vicar over eleven monasteries in Germany, Luther began the break with the Church when he placed the Ninety-five Theses on the door in Wittenberg in 1517. He questioned the use of **indulgences**, which were sold to parishioners. Monies obtained through the sale of indulgences were used to build the new St. Peter's Cathedral in Rome. His views on the priesthood and on faith as a basis of salvation rather than upon human endeavors paled when placed against the formidable attacks he made on the papacy and the Church in the book the *Babylonish Captivity of the Church*. In 1518, he was officially labeled a heretic by the Pope and would have been martyred if Frederick the Wise, a German prince, had not protected him.

John Calvin wrote the *Institutes of the Christian Religion* in 1536, a work that defended a Protestant position against any state-mandated religion. He taught that humans are incapable of good, that there are only two sacraments, baptism and the Lord's Supper, and that God had **foreordained** the future of all believers. He began an experiment in Geneva, Switzerland, which attempted to place into practice all of his ideals about how the Church should function as both a religious and governmental authority. It failed. Yet his ideas were accepted and patterned all over Europe. His influence reached France, Scotland, the Netherlands, the English Puritans, Hungary, Poland, and Ger-

FIGURE 1.1 John Huss was executed in 1415 by the King of Bohemia for attempting to reform the Roman Catholic Church. From Charles F. Horne, *Great Men and Famous Women* (New York: Selmar Hess, 1894).

many, and spawned a host of denominational churches, including Baptist, Puritan, and Reform Presbyterianism.

Social Reform   The writings of the New Testament have fostered unparalleled social reform through the founding of such institutions as hospitals, schools, universities, orphanages, and social action groups that feed, clothe, and sustain the forgotten, neglected, or abused. Modern **liberation theologians** claim equality for the poor, based on the Bible. Their words have ignited flames of passion that have resulted in violence and, at times, even revolt. For instance in Guatemala during the 1970s and 1980s, priests such as Father Conrado de la Cruz and Herlindo Cifuentes were killed for their work among the poor. They taught people that poverty was not inevitable. Christ could liberate anyone, not only spiritually but also economically and politically. In addition, Archbishop Oscar Arnulfo Romero lost his life in the same type of struggle in El Salvador that killed American female missionaries.

Today, a "green" movement that asserts that the earth must be preserved by any means necessary is sweeping the world. This movement is based on a belief in the Bible. Other laws have protected the rights of the religious to own property without paying taxes, the right to share textbooks and resources from public schools, and the right to educate children at home.

World Religion   It is impossible to list all of the churches, beliefs, and associations that the New Testament has generated. Many utopian communities such as the celibate Shakers and Oneida Perfectionists, who believed in multiple sexual relationships, no longer exist. Their radical views diminished when their founders were buried. But the Seventh Day Adventists and Jehovah's Witnesses still hold fast to their views about the end of time. **Hierarchical** organizations such as the Roman Catholic Church, the Methodist Church, Anglicanism, and Episcopalianism based their internal structures on readings found in 1 and 2 Timothy. Yet the Quakers, the Mennonites, and the Amish believe that the power of the church should be given to the average person, not necessarily to trained clergy. New religions such as the Reorganized Church of the Latter Day Saints, Christian Science, Christian Theosophy, and the Unification Church base most, if not all, of their **theology** on their interpretation of the New Testament.

THE NEW TESTAMENT: WHAT IS IT?

The New Testament is a collection of writings that includes gospels, letters, treatises, narratives, and an apocalypse. Produced by people living in various parts of the Middle East during the first and second centuries C.E., it amounts to only a small part of the literature produced by Christians during this time period and later. The discovery of the Nag Hammadi manuscripts in Egypt in 1945 provided additional evidence that Christian communities used a variety of literature in their rituals and for personal reflection. The New Testament contains a selected group of books that were declared acceptable by a variety of Christian councils and committees during a period of almost 1,600 years.

Books in the New Testament and Their Abbreviations

Matthew	Matt	1 Timothy	1 Tm
Mark	Mark	2 Timothy	2 Tim
Luke	Luke	Titus	Titus
John	John	Philemon	Phlm
Acts of the Apostles	Acts	Hebrews	Heb
Romans	Rom	James	Jas
1 Corinthians	1 Cor	1 Peter	1 Peter
2 Corinthians	2 Cor	2 Peter	2 Pt
Galatians	Gal	1 John	1 Jn
Ephesians	Eph	2 John	2 Jn
Philippians	Phil	3 John	3 Jn
Colossians	Col	Jude	Jude
1 Thessalonians	1 Thess	Revelation	Rev
2 Thessalonians	2 Thess		

The New Testament is part of the Bible, βίβλος or "Book," which also contains the Hebrew Bible/Old Testament and the Jewish **Apocrypha**. The name "New Testament" was given to the Christian collection of books, ironically, by one who never

TABLE 1.1 Relative Chronology of the Books
in the New Testament in Relation to Jesus' Life

Approximate	
4 B.C.E.	Jesus born
28 C.E.	Jesus dies
30–50 C.E.	Oral traditions, collections, Jesus' life, death, and sayings
50–64 C.E.	Paul writes letters to churches (1 Thessalonians, Galatians, Philippians, 1 and 2 Corinthians, Romans, Colossians, Philemon)
66–70 C.E.	Jewish Wars
70 C.E.	Gospel of Mark
70–90 C.E.	Gospel of Matthew and Gospel of Luke, Acts of the Apostles, Ephesians, 1 Peter, Revelation
90–100 C.E.	Gospel of John
90–125 C.E.+	1, 2, 3 John, James, Jude, 1, 2 Timothy, Titus, 2 Peter

served on an official church council or committee. **Marcion**, a wealthy businessman from Pontus, in the second century C.E. rejected the Jewish writings, now termed the "Old Testament," as being uninspired. This division between the Jewish Scriptures and the new Christian writings was eventually termed the "old" and "new" testaments. Marcion also divided the newer Christian books that were being read in the churches into "gospel" and "apostle."

The word "**Testament**" means "covenant," "agreement, " or "promise." Implicit in the naming of the Christian writings is the theological premise that the Jewish writings in what is termed the Old Testament were outdated. God had made an agreement with the Israelites exemplified by the law, which was the "old" literature. And while this literature was valuable, it was not the most important literature for Christians. God has now made a new agreement, or New Testament, with people who follow Jesus. The promises made in the "old" book have come true or have been fulfilled in the "new" book. The Old Testament and the New Testament are contained in one book today, yet this has not been the case throughout history.

In fact, Christian congregations throughout the world in those early years rarely had possession or access to all of the books contained in what was later to be called the New Testament. If they were lucky, they might have had one copy of a gospel or letter, and may then have borrowed other Christian writings from neighboring congregations. The Mar Thoma Church in India today uses the Gospel of Thomas, a gospel that was not included in the New Testament.

Abbreviated List of Christian Gospels Not Contained in the New Testament, sometimes labeled "The New Testament Apocrypha"

The Gospel of Thomas	The Gospel of Hebrews
The Dialogue of the Savior	The Gospel of the Nazoreans
The Gospel of the Egyptians	The Gospel of the Ebionites
Papyrus Oxyrhynchus 840	The Protevangelium of James
The Secret Gospel of Mark	The Infancy Gospel of Thomas
The Gospel of Mary	The Epistula Apostolorum
Papyrus Egerton 2	The Acts of Pilate
The Gospel of Peter	

The Canon in Time

Historians have attempted to chart the collection, edition, and organization of the books found in the New Testament, but their findings are not complete. No one knows exactly which Christians read which books. Neither do historians know if Christian communities actually followed recommendations about using certain books. This attempt at re-creating the history of the selection and use of New Testament texts is called the study of the **canon**. The word "canon" has come to mean "rule or measure." Presumably, ancient Christians had a standard by which they judged which books should be included in the New Testament. If there was such a standard, it has not been discovered.

The history of the development, copying, and editing of the New Testament texts is a fascinating story of political intrigue. The following is a very brief outline.

- First century C.E.—Collection of Paul's letters after his death
- Second century C.E.
    Lists of Paul's Letters and other books in the **Muratorian Canon** (an ancient fragment of this document exists today). Marcion's division of the Bible into the Old and New Testament Gospels accepted as Scripture/Canon and circulated anonymously.
- Third century C.E.
    Tertullian, a Latin scholar, from Carthage, North Africa, makes a list of acceptable books and uses the name the "New Testament."
    Origen, a Greek scholar living in Alexandria, mentions the book of James.
- Fourth century C.E.
    Various lists of books were accepted within the Latin-speaking churches, which at times included 1 and 2 Clement. Eusebius of Caesarea and Athanasius of Alexandria created lists which were eventually accepted by the Emperor of Rome.
- Fifth century C.E.
    Jerome creates the Latin Vulgate.

And while there was a general agreement within Roman Catholicism about the number of books that should be contained in the New Testament, it was never officially ratified until the sixteenth century, when Martin Luther and several other protesters challenged the rationale for including books such as James and the Book of Revelation in the New Testament. Students and factions within Christianity still argue over whether the Apocrypha, "hidden or secret books," should be studied and appreciated on the same level as books included in the New Testament.

Translations

The New Testament, as we have it today, has taken a long and circuitous journey. Most of us use a fax machine to send messages and cannot even imagine a time before computers. In fact, the printing press was not in wide use until the sixteenth century. The majority of manuscripts upon which the Western English New Testament translations are based is koine Greek, although there are very early editions in Latin, Syriac, Coptic, Armenian, Ethiopic, and Georgian.

The process of copying manuscripts before the invention of the printing press was greatly flawed. One popular method was to produce several manuscipts at a time. A monk would read a manuscript and several other monks would copy down the words as he read. Great errors of omission, transposition, and addition occurred as monks fell asleep, or misunderstood, misspelled, or transposed words or whole sections of a manuscript. Sometimes they even changed the story to fit their own beliefs. On occasion, the monks did not understand the language that was being read. For instance, ***The Book of Kells,*** a masterpiece of art, is riddled with errors.

One of the earliest printed versions of the New Testament was the **Gutenberg Bible**. A facsimile of this early printed Bible can be bought today for several thousand dollars. The first popular English translation of the New Testament was the King James Version (Authorized Version), published early in the seventeenth century, although John Wyclif is reported to have circulated his own English translation hundreds of years earlier. In the twentieth century, scholars are still attempting to find the oldest and best manuscripts. The originals have never been discovered. Consequently, year after year, all over the world, societies publish updated and newly translated versions of the New Testament. In the box on 1 Corinthians 7:1 that follows, you will gain a small perspective of the differences in translations, although scholars are using the same basic Greek text.

FIGURE 1.2
Gutenberg Bible. Photo by Marla J. Selvidge

CHART OF THE ENGLISH BIBLE

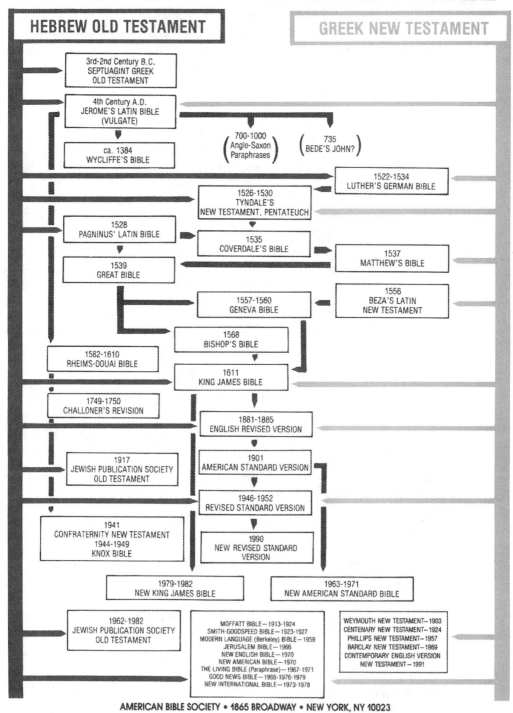

FIGURE 1.3 Chart of the English Bible. ©American Bible Society. Used with permission.

---

1 CORINTHIANS 7:1
COMPARISON OF TRANSLATIONS

Περὶ δὲ ὧν ἐγράψατε,
καλὸν ᾿ανθρώπῳ γυναικὸς μὴ ῾άπτεσθαι.   GREEK

"Now concerning the things whereof ye wrote unto me: KING JAMES
It is good for a man not to touch a woman."   VERSION

"Now concerning the matters about which you wrote.   REVISED STANDARD
It is well for a man not to touch a woman."   VERSION

"Now for the questions about which you wrote.   THE NEW
Yes, it is a good thing for a man not to touch a woman."   JERUSALEM BIBLE

"And now for the matters you wrote about.   NEW ENGLISH
It is a good thing for a man to have nothing to do with women."   BIBLE

"Now for the matters you wrote about: THE NEW
It is good for a man not to marry."   INTERNATIONAL VERSION

Compare the translations. Can you detect the bias of the translators? Or can you detect a different emphasis in the verses when you compare the different translators? Do the translations make the verses say something different?

INTERPRETING THE TEXT: HERMENEUTICS

Richard Simon, a Roman Catholic cleric, recognized very early in the seventeenth century that to understand the Bible, one should understand the languages in which it was written. But language ability is not the total answer to the questions surrounding the meaning of the text. How does one interpret the Bible? Or perhaps a better question is, what is interpretation? What is hermeneutics? Generally speaking, it is an attempt by a reader to have a conversation with a text. The goal is to find some type of meaning or understanding of the text. The *Interpreter's Dictionary of the Bible* explains that an interpreter is "one who unfolds the meaning of what is said, seen, or dreamed by another." According to *The Encyclopedia of Religion,* the study and practice of hermeneutics is much more complicated. It "refers to the intellectual discipline concerned with the nature and presuppositions of the interpretation of human expressions." This process of interpretation raises the issues of the "nature of the text, what it means to understand a text," and "how understanding and interpretation are determined by the presuppositions and beliefs (the horizon) of the audience to which the text is being interpreted." Historically, interpreters of the Bible have attempted to differentiate between **exegesis** and

hermeneutics. Hermeneutics was the task of the theologian, and exegesis was left to a biblical specialist.

For every passage of Scripture, readers can find numerous interpretations during the past 2,000 years. Yet, at the very basis of every interpretation is the relationship between the reader and the text. The text or the Bible can only supply answers to the questions posed to it by its readers. Sometimes the Bible does not appear to answer the questions; it is at this point that readers decide to look elsewhere for answers or to create an interpretative system that will help answer their questions.

For instance, the Bible was written long before the invention of computers. Does Matthew or Mark have anything to say about the use of computers or pirated software? No, not directly. But the writers may have something to say about the concepts of honesty and community. Matthew 7:12, in the sermon on the Mount, reads, "Always treat others as you would like them to treat you…" (NEB). From this verse, people can extrapolate an ethical value of community. They could create an application of this verse, which might sound like, "Treat no one differently than you treat yourself. If you love yourself, you will love others. If you love others then you would not misuse their equipment or copy files or software that did not belong to you. This would injure someone."

Exploring Interpretative Methodologies

Attempting to find uniform definitions of the major interpretative strategies used inside and outside of religious circles over the past 2,000 years is next to impossible. Scholars generally describe (not define) the methodology and its results. Neither can this chapter survey all of the major methodologies.

The following list summarizes the questions one might ask when using a particular type of modern methodology while studying the New Testament. A criticism is only a tool, a question. If you want a dialogue with the text, you will ask it questions. It would be impossible to consider all of these criticisms in depth and still complete a survey of the New Testament. The criticisms are listed and described to facilitate a broader understanding of biblical interpretations. There are no easy answers to questions posed to the texts. Critical approaches to the text are vast and complicated.

Translation   At best, every English version of the New Testament was translated by people wearing a myriad of glasses. Those spectacles do not always produce clear and precise translations. Although the students translate the Greek, they must still decide which groups or editions of manuscripts will be used in a translation to be included in the Bible (textual criticism). While we recognize that our interpretations of the Bible are conditioned by numerous cultural experiences, we must also realize that the translator is no different or less influenced than we are.

Literal Interpretation   Many readers claim that they have discovered the **literal** meaning of verses in the New Testament. What does the term *literal* mean? Does it mean "physical, plain, textual, grammatical or philological?" **Raymond Brown**, in the *Jerome Biblical Commentary*, suggests that, "It is the sense which the human author directly intended and which his words convey." But how do you know what the author intended? And how do you develop a methodology that will uncover this meaning?

Ethical-Theological Interpretation The New Testament has often become a source of ethical theory and practice for its readers. Many would ask the Book, how should I live my life? Throughout history, theologians looked to the New Testament for a basis in **dogmatic** theology, in practical psychology and devotion. Ancient interpreters labeled this approach "tropological."

Many people looked to the future to inform and interpret the present. **Rubem Alves** terms this a hope for the "presence of the absent." People hope for a perfect world and perfect life, which has been won by the death and resurrection of Jesus. They interpret many passages of Scripture as applying to this distant future home and life. This approach has many names: teleological, anagogical, mystical, eschatological, heavenly, and metaphysical theological speculation.

Symbolical Interpretation Symbolical interpretation is discussed more widely than any other by those who have researched the history of interpretation. Perhaps it is because so many passages within the Bible remain **opaque**, and interpreters want to penetrate the dark window to understanding. If they do not know what the text originally meant to the writer, then it must have some meaning or it would not be included in the Sacred Scripture. This type of approach to the Bible has many categories: typology, allegory, spiritual exegesis, figurative, analogy, Christological, and intellectual.

To rescue the Old Testament/Hebrew Bible, many taught that everything in the Old Testament corresponded to elements or activities found in the New Testament. (After all, most of the writers of the books of the New Testament used the Old Testament/Hebrew Bible as a source.) They found Jesus and the cross in every book. A death, a flower, a stream, everything had meaning because it pointed to the Jesus event. This typological approach totally divorces the passage from its literal and historical context, but it is very effective because, in essence, the reader or interpreter can make the text say anything he or she wants it to say.

An old quotation used by many attempts to explain typology or allegory by interpreting the use of Jerusalem in the New Testament. It reads,

> Thus Jerusalem signifies the city, the Church, a settled and moral order, and the everlasting life.

Raymond Brown enlarges the meaning of the aforementioned quotation by explaining the different types of interpretative approaches that have been employed.

> When Jerusalem is mentioned in the Bible, in its literal sense it is a Jewish city: allegorically, however, it refers to the Church of Christ, tropologically Jerusalem stands for the soul of man; anagogically it stands for the heavenly city. (Brown, Fitzmyer, Murphy, 1968, 612)

Feminist Criticism Feminism has produced many theories of interpretation and analysis during this century. **Feminist** literary criticism "includes gender as a funda-

SELECTED CRITICISMS
AND EXAMPLE QUESTIONS

Textual

What is the oldest and best reading of the text?

Is there evidence of changes in the text, based upon theology or politics?

Who copied these manuscripts and why?

Historical

Who wrote it? When was it written? Why?

What was life like when the book was written?

What is the setting of the writer and the readers?

What is the political, economic, religious, and cultural setting of the work?

Literary

What is the genre of the work?

Does the writer use other forms of genre?

Who are the characters?

How do the characters relate to one another?

Do you detect ascending and descending action in the work?

What about the grammar, language capabilities, and style of the writer?

Source

(A division of literary criticism.)

Can you detect sources the writer may be using?

What are those sources?

Why does the writer use those sources?

Redaction

(Some may want to classify this under historical criticism.)

Can you detect editing within the text?

Are there obvious omissions or changes in the narrative?

By studying the text, can you detect a writer's point of view?

Feminist

How are female characters portrayed in the narrative?

What point of view is taken by the writer of a narrative?

Can the interpreter detect a certain bias toward women that limits their abilities or place in society? Is there a patriarchal or an androcentric bias present in the text?

Sociological

Can social structures be detected within the narrative?

What types of social relationships, groups, rituals, worldviews, support structures, conflicts, and social stratifications are found within the books?

Reader-oriented

Who are the readers?

How has the writer configured the literature in order to appeal to the reader? What does the reader bring to the text that will influence the interpretation of the text? What does the New Testament have to say to people of different cultures, ethnic backgrounds, and class? Several different approaches are used here.

mental basis for literary analysis." **Elisabeth Schüssler Fiorenza** attempts to describe the process of feminist biblical interpretation in her book *Bread not Stone*.

> In our struggle for self-identity, survival, and liberation in a patriarchal society and church, Christian women have found that the Bible has been used as a weapon against us but at the same time it has been a resource for courage, hope, and commitment in this struggle. (Fiorenza 1984)

Mary Ann Tolbert recognizes two approaches to feminist interpretation: those that would argue for the equality of people and those that would argue for female ascendancy. She struggles to define what she terms *feminist hermeneutics* and concludes that it is "a reading of a text (or the writing of an analysis, or the reconstructing of history) in light of the oppressive structures of **patriarchal** society. Such a reading can have either a predominately negative or predominately positive orientation."

Feminists who interpret the Bible today have taken a wide variety of approaches to rereading the text. Some have isolated stories and found positive life-giving examples in the text. Others have pointed to **androcentric** origins and androcentric models of leadership in the Bible that do not fit modern living. Some study words; others attempt to reconstruct history. Some compare the biblical stories with ancient "feminist" literature and draw conclusions about the origins of Scripture.

Within the topic of feminist interpretation is an offshoot called **womanist** interpretation. This approach recognizes the androcentric nature of the text and its interpreters yet also asserts that people who have interpreted the New Testament from a feminist perspective have been primarily "white," not black or African American. Womanist hermeneutics attempts to relate the Bible to black women and men who are not the creators of culture in America but the recipients of a culture that ignores their distinctive experiences, dreams, and talents. Black women in America have had a very different experience living their Christianity compared to Caucasian women.

Methodologies are often as individualized as the people who use them. Usually, intepreters of the New Testament employ a variety of approaches when researching the texts. All of the aforementioned methodologies overlap in one way or another. During the past fifty years, the field of biblical studies has exploded. Within that field, people have established subspecialties that focus on one particular type of methodology.

K. H. Ting, a Chinese interpreter, reminds us in *Voices from the Margin,* that there is more to the Bible than the words we are reading. We must look between the lines.

> We must listen to what the Bible says to us; we must also pay attention to what the Bible does not say to us. There are some things which the Bible does not say and there are good reasons for this.

Summary   Everyone is a stranger to the New Testament. Anyone who studies the New Testament, even if he or she has traversed its pages often, is a stranger to the text because no one can go back in time and understand exactly what it meant to the people who first heard or read its words. There is always hope that a new archaeological or literary find will increase our knowledge of the Book.

Throughout history, in an attempt to re-create that original time, people have imposed or projected their own views on the Bible. Some have used it as a rule book, a good luck charm, named it a transcript from God, and venerated its pages. Many would want to restrict official interpretations of the Bible to their own denomination or group, but the Bible has been the foundation of cultures for 2,000 years. It belongs to everyone.

While some may want to claim that only one person wrote the New Testament, it is in fact a collection of various writings by many different people over a period of 200 years or less. Thousands of works were written during the early years of Christianity, but only a few books were considered worthy enough to be collected and placed in the New Testament. The process of the collection and translation of the New Testament began with the collection of Paul's letters. Newer translations, such as the New Revised Standard Version and the New International Version, emerge periodically.

The New Testament is a historic literature that reveals a new religious movement that has succeeded in multiplying itself into the most populous religion on earth. It also is a document that belongs to the world, and we respect the countless opinions about its relevance to the lives of people in the past and present.

The New Testament is a living document that belongs to no particular group. It provides a foundation for personal beliefs and family customs supporting governments, wars, and even racist and sexist attitudes. People have given their lives for the sake of their beliefs experienced in this book. Others found answers to ethical questions while claiming freedom from the constraints of culture, which had narrowly defined their roles in life. Some who claimed freedom were labeled "heretics" by an institutionalized Christianity, such as the Gnostics and the early protesters within the Roman Catholic Church. The call for freedom has also been extended to the environment and reflected in thousands of Christian groups and denominations throughout the world.

In the name of God, misguided founders of America who fled harassment in Europe created their own theocratic tyrannies. They used the Bible to force others into assenting to their demands of a uniform lifestyle and interpretation of the divine message.

Interpreting verses and sections of the New Testament is a controversial enterprise. Hundreds of methodologies and approaches have been developed over the years. Yet agreement on the meaning of the New Testament is still a future hope. Keep the door open (and an open mind) as you begin to walk through the pages of this text.

2

Cultural Heritage of the New Testament

In those days a decree went out from Caesar Augustus
that all the world should be enrolled.
—Luke 2:1 NRSV

LIVING IN THE ROMAN EMPIRE

From the moment Turner Broadcasting Company inaugurated the Cable News Network (CNN), the world has been a different place. CNN has changed the way we perceive the world and how fast we obtain international news. In much the same way, Roman roads, shipping, and daily courier service throughout the Roman Empire changed the lives of everyone in the first century C.E.

Roman power and might touched every person who lived within its boundaries. The Roman government appeared invincible. It boasted gigantic military machines, the use of insect and chemical warfare, and a huge standing army. Soldiering was one of the top occupations in the Empire.

Years before the wars of 66–70 C.E., people of Jewish and possibly Christian faith experienced terror and discrimination at the hands of Roman officials. Rumors surfaced periodically about those who worshiped the head of an ass, devoured children during services, or performed lewd sexual rites on initiates. People feared the new religion. Its adherents,

FIGURE 2.1 Caesar Augustus (63 B.C.E.–14 C.E.). From Charles F. Horne, *Great Men and Famous Women* (New York: Selmar Hess, 1984).

21

FIGURE 2.2 The Roman Forum. Photo by Marla J. Selvidge

similar to Jewish **Zealots** or **Sicarii**, respected neither the emperor nor his ancient pantheon of gods. They preached hope and change. The Roman government and policy makers could tolerate no loss of their power and so enacted laws and punishments for the insurrectionists.

Claudius, the Roman emperor in 50 C.E., deported Jews from Rome, making them homeless. **Nero**, a Roman emperor in 64 C.E., charged the Christians with burning his city and made a spectacle of burning them. Jews were massacred for an unknown reason by the people of **Caesarea** in 66 C.E. And **Pilate**, the **Roman Procurator**, during the time of Jesus (4 B.C.E.–28 C.E.) harassed the Jews for almost all of his term.

While little is known of the Jewish and Christian situations during the reigns of the Emperors Galba, Otho, and Vitellius (68–69 C.E.), there are many accounts about Christians who experienced intrigue, insatiable greed, terror, and rebellion within the Empire. Galba was murdered by his own soldiers. Otho committed suicide. And Vitellius, the mad man, was killed by a mob. **Tacitus**, a Roman historian, tells stories of soldiers going mad and pillaging their own home towns. German recruits took Rome like a fast moving storm. More than once the capitol buildings were burned to the ground.

The Romans were in control of the seas and the roads leading to the farthest points of the Empire. With a single order, the emperor could close all of the ports in the Mediterranean. This action would create an economic situation resulting in the starvation of people within a certain region of the Empire. That power brought fear, but it also brought peace between very diverse ethnic groups.

FIGURE 2.3 The Appian Way leading travelers to Rome, Italy. Photo by Marla J. Selvidge.

The Romans built roads that are still in use. They stretched from Egypt to the United Kingdom. Today, people walking through ancient groves in Europe discover Roman roads cutting a wide opening through the middle of the forest. No tree could penetrate its foundation, which included several feet of slag or molten rock. The old King's Highway leading from Israel to Egypt is still the main route used by busy truckers and travelers on their way to Cairo.

News crisscrossed the Empire daily. State-of-the-art aqueduct systems created cities in strategic locations throughout the Empire. Romans or their appointed officials built ports, amphitheaters, and sanctuaries all over the Mediterranean world. While Latin was the language of the conquerors, Greek became the language of the traveler and business person and was used in polite conversation. A standard currency facilitated trade and banking. People were changing, and so were their clothing styles, homes, and foods. There was interest in the Olympic games, and people began to learn the meaning of recreation. Teachers, philosophers, and artists had time to reflect on ethics, culture, and the ways of the gods. There was a great interest in tourism, creating museums, sanctuaries for unusual animals, and trade with such faraway places as China, India, and Southern Africa.

People with very different languages, nationalities, cultures, and religions began to talk in ways that were never possible in the past. They were thrust out of their secure towns into a global environment. This multicultural experience changed traditional ways of viewing life and religion. Religious ideas and philosophies began to merge and create more meaningful **ideologies** for the new world culture. All of these changes influenced and nourished the birth of Christianity and the subsequent writing of the New Testament.

AUGUSTUS
27 B.C.E.

NERO
54 C.E.

VESPASIAN
69 C.E.

TITUS
79 C.E.

DOMITIAN
81 C.E.

TRAJAN
98 C.E.

FIGURE 2.4 The Roman Emperors. From Camden Cobern, *The New Archaeological Discoveries Bearing Upon the New Testament* (New York: Funk and Wagnals, 1917).

GREEK AND ROMAN PHILOSOPHIES

While most people today do not consciously discuss **philosophical** theories, every conversation about politics, ethics, law, and religion reflects multiple philosophies. Everyone is influenced by the news, their neighbors, magazines, books, their religious leaders, elected officials, and the people for whom they work. And all of the aforementioned have a point of view or philosophy they are trying to communicate.

No one has all of the answers to all of the dilemmas faced in life. Consider the bombing of the Federal Building in Oklahoma, the September 11th World Trade Center demise in New York, or the gas incident in Japan by the **Aum Shinrikyo** sect that injured and killed hundreds. People wonder why anyone would want to kill innocent human beings. Did the killers think they were preventing a greater injustice from happening? Did they believe that their actions would make life better for everyone. Or perhaps they saw it as a way to gain power over others. Their actions were based on their philosophy.

Questions arise about what to do with the people who commit such terrorist activities. Should they be executed? Should they reimburse victims for their losses? Should

TABLE 2.1 Roman Emperors and the New Testament

Roman Emperors	Dates	References and Relation to New Testament
Caesar Augustus	27 B.C.E.–14 C.E.	Luke 2:1 Appointed Herod the Great, Archelaus, Herod Antipas, and Philip
Tiberius	14–37 C.E.	Luke 3:1
Caligula	37–41 C.E.	Appointed Herod Agrippa I
Claudius	41–45 C.E.	Acts 11:28 Appointed Felix and Festus
Nero	54–68 C.E.	Acts 25:11ff Appointed Herod Agrippa II
Otho, Vitellius, Galba	68–69 C.E.	
Vespasian	69–79 C.E.	Jewish War Titus destroys Jerusalem
Titus	79–81 C.E.	
Domitian	81–96 C.E.	
Trajan	98–117 C.E.	

Source: *Harper's Bible Dictionary* (New York: Harper and Row, 1961), "Roman Empire," p. 621.

they be offered an opportunity at rehabilitation? How you answer such an ethical dilemma reflects your philosophical approach to life.

The New Testament was created by people who were influenced by many philosophies. Scholars have written hundreds of books demonstrating how the ideas of Greek and Roman philosophers influenced Christianity and the writing of the New Testament. One of the most important ideas to influence Christian thinking was **Platonism**. **Plato**, a Greek (428–348 B.C.E.), taught that what we think is real is only a reflection of reality that exists in another realm. What does this mean?

Almost everyone dreams. Rubem Alves, a Latin American Protestant theologian, suggests that dreams and hopes are the presence of the absent. For instance, people plan vacations. In their minds, they can visualize the trip and the experiences they are going to have. But this visualization is not real. It is only a hope of what will occur on the trip. Plato suggested that life itself was only a dream and that the real existed within the realm of the divine. This idea of different levels or kinds of existence is also taught by the apostle **Paul** and the writer of the Gospel of John. Some might label the "real" world "heaven," the earth becomes only a distorted reflection of it. Paul says,

> For we know that if the earthly tent we live in is destroyed, we have a building from God, a house not made with hands, eternal in the heavens. (2 Cor. 5:1 NRSV)

FIGURE 2.5   Coin minted in C.E. 72 during the reign of Titus. From George C. Brauer, Jr. *Judaea Weeping: The Jewish Struggle Against Rome from Pompey to Masada, 63 B.C.–A.D. 73* (New York: Thomas T. Crowell Company, 1970).

Another important philosophical idea found in the Gospel of John is the concept of "logos" (word). The writer of John begins the gospel in the following way:

> In the beginning was the Word, and the Word was with God, and the Word was God. He was in the beginning with God. All things came into being through him, and without him not one thing came into being. (John 1:1 NRSV)

Today, readers of the New Testament understand that the Gospel of John was describing Jesus. But hundreds of years before John used the term *logos,* the Greek philosopher Zeno (335–263 B.C.E.) had created a school that was based on a belief in the "Logos."

Zeno founded what is today known as **Stoicism**. People who practice the Stoic philosophy were disciplined, rationale, and unemotional about traumas or good luck. (The character of "Spock" or "Data" in the Star Trek series epitomized this way of thinking.) Zeno taught that true living was the sum total of all the things one can see, taste, or touch. There is nothing outside the experiences we have on earth. The Logos was the Divinity that infused all of nature with itself. In a sense, all people are part of the divine. Therefore, people have complete control over their lives. The key to living a happy and successful life is for one to become whatever is natural for oneself. Yet when one discovers the route one will take in life, it is one's duty to fulfill the obligations of that role. This approach to life, taught Zeno, will make life better for everyone. In fact, it could produce the beginning of a new age, a new world order, or time in history.

Christianity, especially many of the stories of Jesus and the Twelve **Apostles**, may have been influenced by Cynicism, a philiosophy taught by a **Diogenes**. Diogenes taught people to abandon all responsibility in life and to seek the divine. Disciples or students lived like beggars and tried to persuade people that to indulge in material things was the wrong path in life. Diogenes' philosophies are mirrored in instructions given to the Twelve by Jesus, in Matthew.

> These twelve Jesus sent out with the following instructions: … Take no gold, or silver, or copper in your belts, no bag for your journey, or tunics, or sandals, or a staff; for laborers deserve their food. Whatever town or village you enter, find out who in it is worthy, and stay there until you leave. As you enter the house, greet it. If the house is worthy, let your peace come upon it; but if it is not worthy, let your peace return to you. If anyone will not welcome you or listen to your words, shake the dust from your feet as you leave that house or town. (Matthew 10:5–14 NRSV)

Countless other philosophies and literary works influenced the writers of the New Testament. Paul betrays a knowledge of the **rhetoric** used by the Cynics, an acquaintance with Gnosticism, **Epicureanism**, and classical Greek literatures. Cynics were itinerant street preachers who challenged accepted cultural values and behaviors by arguing at length in plain language with average citizens who had little education. Their method of instruction was described as a **diatribe**, which Paul employed in his works. In most of Paul's letters, he argues about the ethical standards he considers inappropriate for Christians. For example, in Romans, Paul describes at length how he believes that people have sinned.

> And since they did not see fit to acknowledge God, God gave them up to a debased mind and to things that should not be done. They were filled with every kind of wickedness, evil, covetousness, malice. Full of envy, murder, strife, deceit, craftiness, they are gossips, slanderers, God-haters, insolent, haughty, boastful, inventors of evil, rebellious toward parents, foolish, faithless, heartless, ruthless. They know God's decree that those who practice such things deserve to die—yet they not only do them but even applaud others who practice them. (Romans 1:28–32 NRSV)

Epicureanism taught that the highest good in life was the absence of pain. Its goal was to achieve absolute tranquility of mind, body, and spirit. Paul argued against living this kind of life in a letter to the Corinthians. The phrase in 1 Corinthians 15:32, "Let us eat and drink, for tomorrow we die," sounds very similar to a popular Epicurean epitaph of, "Eat, drink, play, and come hither."

The writer of Acts of the Apostles may have patterned that work after ancient Greek romances. Greek romances featured main characters on quests and adventures similar to those found in the story about Paul in Acts.

Passages that deal with a fiery end of time, such as those found in the Book of Revelation, may reflect ancient **Zoroastrian** views. Zoroaster was a prophet who followed Ahura-Mazda during the sixth century B.C.E. He taught that there would be three thousand-year periods before the world would end. One age would be when his god, Ahura-Mazda, would rule, a second would be a time of world war, and the third would renovate the earth. Zoroaster also taught a belief in an evil power by the name of Satan and the angels. These images of a dualistic world, angels, and time periods that culminate in the death and then the rebirth of the earth are central to the narrative in the Book of Revelation.

> Then I saw an angel coming down from heaven, holding in his hand the key to the bottomless pit and a great chain. He seized the dragon, that ancient serpent, who is the Devil and Satan, and bound him for a thousand years, and threw him into the pit, and locked and sealed it over him, so that he would deceive the nations no more, until the thousand years were ended.... I also saw the souls of those who had been beheaded for their testimony to Jesus and for the word of God.... They came to life and reigned with Christ a thousand years. (Rev. 20:1–5 NRSV)

STATE RELIGIONS

One facet of the Roman plan of controlling the Empire involved religion. The Emperor Augustine, with an enthusiasm for the past, began a revival of the ancient religions. He restored over eighty temples and began attending rituals to his favorite God, **Apollo**. While **emperor worship** was required occasionally by the state, most emperors declined to be labeled "divine." Worshiping the emperor was as common as the festivities of the Fourth of July in the United States. It was expected of all the populace and became an indicator of a person's loyalty to the state, but it was often not taken seriously by the average Roman citizen. Other religions were occasionally tolerated if they did not involve violence or murder.

Cicero, a Roman poet, wrote, "We must persuade our citizens, that there are gods who govern all things, benefactors of mankind, who observe the character, acts, and intentions of individuals and their **piety** or **impiety**." People in the Roman Empire were involved in a host of religious and superstitious activities, which included magic, black magic, astrology, conjuring up the dead, interpreting dreams, birds, lightning and thunder, and consulting all sorts of **oracles**. The slaves, common people, and citizens of the Roman Empire did not have to be convinced to be religious. Citizens were skeptical of a state that would attempt to revive worship of forgotten gods and goddesses. The **pantheon** was a relic, and so were its gods.

Earlier in the first century, the **Vestal Virgins** were held with high honor, later, their social activities were thwarted with accusations of corruption and sexual exploits. The Vestals were virgins who served Rome for most of their lives. (**Celibacy** became a way of creating an independent life for both females and males during the history of Christianity.) Some say that they were married to a phallic deity or the spirit of Rome. It was an honor to be chosen to their ranks. Vestals were charged with keeping the sacred fire of Rome burning. Their responsibilities included presiding over or being present at official functions of the state. They often were used as couriers of secret documents that were housed in their sanctuaries.

POPULAR RELIGIONS IN THE ROMAN EMPIRE

Social scientists suggest that religions are created or born in the midst of peoples who are searching for something to make their lives better. The beliefs within a religion answer questions relative to origins of humanity, purpose in life or postlife, identity, ethnic background, and personal relationships. Rituals give people a sense of community and common identity. In a rigid culture, such as the one produced by the Roman government, people who found no identity or meaning within the accepted state religions looked elsewhere for answers and friendship. Many local religions began to flourish outside of Rome. Their membership grew like a raging fire sweeping across the seas and mountains. Everyone was changed in some way by the enthusiasm of these new, yet ancient, religions. Some of those popular religions are classified as **mystery** religions.

A mystery religion is generally defined as a religion that has secret initiation rites (often performed at night), and secret membership, holy writings written in a code language, and other rituals (often oriented toward an agrarian culture). Only the **initiates** could participate in the secret ceremonies. Secret religions or societies are not only found in the past. Modern secret societies thrive in most cities and schools of higher education. They include, among many others, the **Masons**, **Wicca**, **Rosicrucians**, and most fraternities and sororities on college and university campuses. These normally include a secret written language or body language, a set of goals or guidelines for living, and a solidarity of community life. Some universities have been sanctioned because of "hazing," which has resulted in the death or maiming of college students during initiation ceremonies.

Some common elements found within the mystery religions and Christianity include the following:

1. A belief in a dying and rising **redeemer** god, who may offer resurrection to its adherents.
2. A wine/water and bread remembrance of a god, which is similar to a **Mass** or **Eucharist**, or the **Lord's Supper**.
3. Special holidays celebrating the birth and death of a god. (**Mithraism** claimed December 25 as the birthday of their god **Mithra**.)
4. Cleansing or baptism as an initiation ceremony.
5. A belief in a miracle-working god.
6. A belief in the virgin birth of a god.
7. A belief in angels who function as helpers within a system of cosmic layers, which leads to a heavenly place.
8. A belief that gods will be reborn into another life or ascend some type of stairway into a heavenly realm.
9. Fasting.
10. A belief in abstaining from certain foods or sex.

It is difficult to ascertain who influenced whom when comparisons are made between ancient popular religions within the Roman Empire and Christianity. The records are incomplete. The mystery religions had much in common with Christianity. Initiates within the mystery religions took vows of silence and believed that they could become divine. Certainly, most of the religions that predated the formation of Christianity helped set the stage for its emergence as a world religion. But many religions, such as the worship of **Isis** and Mithras, also coexisted alongside Christianity for many years, perhaps hundreds of years. Some contend that Christianity took much of its liturgy and basic beliefs from Mithraism and the worship of Isis.

TABLE 2.2 Mystery Religions
Abbreviated Summary

Religion/God	Date of Origin	Beliefs	Rituals	Geography
Mithraism	88–63 B.C.E.	Solar God Dying and Rising Birth Dec. 25	Bread/wine supper Mass Baptism	Origins in Asia Minor. Found throughout the Roman Empire as far north as Germany.
Cybele/ Attis	4th century B.C.E.	Great Mother and Son-Lover Protects women in childbirth and at home	Taurobolium Day of Blood March 15 Festival	Asia Minor and throughout the Empire.
Isis Osiris	4th century B.C.E.	Virgin Goddess Resurrected Osiris	Sacrifices of milk, honey, herbs Priestesses/ Priests	From Egypt throughout Empire.
Dionysus	400 B.C.E.	Child of Zeus and human A disguised god Temporary death	Orgies, intoxication Sexual initiation Eating of raw flesh	Eleusis outside Athens and throughout Empire.

Mithraism   Mithras, the solar warrior, is crystallized in sculptures and frescoes as slaying the bull. He was the god who gave soldiers their strength and courage to go into battle. He had even been the god worshipped by **Alexander the Great**. He promised a life after death or a progression into the heavens, and offered his male-only worshipers rituals and traditions that paralleled early Christianity. Similar to the Eucharist, the death of the slaying of the bull was celebrated by eating its blood and body with a wine/water and bread ceremony. As in the story about the birth of Jesus, Mithra's birth on December 25 was attested to by shepherds.

This secret male religion came into existence some time during the first century before the birth of Jesus, although some would trace its origins back to Zoroastrianism, 400 years earlier. Archaeological evidence of Mithraic worship can be found from Caesarea, Israel, all the way to Germany and Scotland. It rivaled and grew with Christianity until the Roman Emperor Theodosius I in 380 C.E. declared Christianity the only legitimate religion of the Empire. The following is an excerpt from a Greek magical writing that claims to be a Mithraic liturgy:

**Mithras Liturgy
taken from
a Greek Magical Papyri of Paris**

*This is the invocation of the ceremony:
First origin of my origin,
first beginning of my beginning,
spirit of spirit, the first of the spirit in me,
fire given by God to my mixture of the mixtures in me, the first of the fire in me,
water of water, the first of the water in me,
earthy substance, the first of the earthy substance in me
my complete body ...
now if it be your will, in another place,
give me over to immortal birth, and, following that, to my underlying nature,
so that, after the present need which is pressing me exceedingly, I may gaze upon
the immortal spirit....
that I may be born again in thought,
and the sacred spirit may breathe in me,
so that I may wonder at the sacred fire....
For I am the son
I am!*

(Meyer 1976 [The magical letters have been omitted at the end of each sentence.])

Parallels with Christianity are obvious. One particularly provocative verse from the Gospel of John reads in the following way:

> So Jesus said to them, "Very truly, I tell you, unless you eat the flesh of the Son of Man and drink his blood, you have no life in you. Those who eat my flesh and drink my blood have eternal life, and I will raise them up on the last day; for my flesh is true food and my blood is true drink. Those who eat my flesh and drink my blood abide in me, and I in them. Just as the Living Father sent me, and I live because of the Father, so whoever eats me will live because of me." (John 6:52–58 NRSV)

WORSHIP OF GODDESSES

The worship of mother goddesses, according to many **anthropologists** and **archaeologists**, was one of the first religions. In every **Paleolithic** site throughout the world, small figurines of pregnant women are found among the ritual objects at places of worship. This consistent find has led many to conclude that pregnant women may have been among the first objects worshiped by ancient Stone Age people. The worship of female goddesses was present in most cultures within the Ancient Near East during the first century C.E.

Goddess worship was outlawed by the ancient Israelites and never found a comfortable home within early institutional Christianity. But there is evidence that the influence of the goddess **Sophia** crept into the wisdom literature of the ancient Israelites and Hebrews within such books as Ecclesiasticus, hymns within Psalms, and Proverbs. It may even have influenced the stories about Jesus, in the Gospels of Matthew and

FIGURE 2.6   Frieze at the Temple of Aphrodite in Aphrodisias, Turkey. Photo by Marla J. Selvidge

John, as well as in the writings of Paul. The following excerpt is from Proverbs, which is found in the **Hebrew Bible/Old Testament**.

> Get Wisdom (Sophia); get insight; do not forget, nor turn away from the words of my mouth. Do not forsake Her, and She will guard you. The beginning of Wisdom is this: Get Wisdom and whatever else you get, get insight. Prize Her highly, and She will exalt you; She will honor you if you embrace Her. She will place on your head a fair garland; and She will bestow on you a beautiful crown. (Proverbs 4:5–9 NRSV [Caps added])

The mystery religions embraced many goddesses. Goddesses may have offered worshipers a relief from the rigid, male-dominated emperor worship, or boring worship of the ancient gods of the pantheon. It may also have given them an opportunity to experience religion personally on an emotional level, rather than on a politically correct social level. Females could excel in the religious realm when they had little direct power in the Roman Senate, in everyday social life, or in the Emperor's office.

Cybele   Cybele was also known as Juno, the wife of Jupiter. Many scholars contend that her name changed to Luna, Astarte, or Hecate, depending on where she was worshiped in the Empire. She was a goddess who protected women in childbirth, while ruling home and marriage. She was known as the great mother and son lover. Myths suggest that **Attis** (a younger male god) loved Cybele, but she denied his advances. In retribution, he castrated himself and was eventually reborn into a realm where he could be with Cybele forever.

Her rituals, similar to Mithraism, included the **Taurobolium**, a blood baptismal ritual that involved standing under a bull that was sacrificed. This act washed away the guilt of the old life and symbolized the birth of a new one. Both males and females followed her, but the male priests were often emasculated on the Day of Blood in the same manner as Attis. Her great festival was during the vernal equinox on March 15. The following is a somewhat critical description of an ordination of a Cybelen priest, which replicates the Taurobolium. The parallels with Christian baptism should be obvious.

The Taurobolium

The animal destined for sacrifice is at the appointed place. They consecrate a spear and with it pierce his breast. A gaping wound disgorges its stream of blood, still hot, and pours a steaming flood on the lattice of the bridge below, flowing copiously. . . . The priest in the pit below catches the drops, puts his head underneath each one till it is stained, till his clothes and all his body are soaked in corruption. Yes, and he lays his head back, puts his cheeks in the stream, sets his ears underneath, gets lips and nose in the way, bathes his very eyes in the drops, does not spare his mouth, wets his tongue til he drains deep the dark blood with every pore.... [E]veryone stands to one side, welcomes him, honours him, just because he has been buried in a beastly pit and washed with the wretched blood of a dead ox. (Prudentius 1970, 1011–1050)

Isis   Isis, the Egyptian goddess, had the power to resurrect her own brother, Osiris, and then to impregnate herself. She bore Horus and became known as the Virgin Goddess, the Moon Goddess, and the Goddess who could resurrect. Her sacrifices never involved the loss of life. Adherents brought milk, herbs, and honey to both priests and priestesses. Some contend that the worship of Isis was the most popular mystery religion in the Middle East during the first century C.E. Although her origins were Egyptian, her religion spread throughout most of the Roman Empire. She was worshiped at temples, in street festivals, and by individuals from every class of society, who looked to consecrated, often celibate clergy. Artistic representations of her breast-feeding Horus were later used as a model by Christians attempting to capture Mary and Jesus. Some suggest that the stories of Jesus going down into Egypt after his birth may have indicated some relationship or knowledge of the worship of Isis: "Out of Egypt have I called my son" (Matthew 2:15).

The Hymn of Praise for Isis, from a Stele in Memphis, Egypt, at the Temple of Hephaestus

I am Isis, the mistress of every land, and I was taught by Hermes and with Hermes I devised letters, both the sacred (hieroglyphs) and the demotic, that all things might not be written with the same (letters).

I gave and ordained laws for men, which no one is able to change ...
I am she who findeth fruit for men ...
I brought together woman and man.
I appointed women to bring their infants to birth in the tenth month ...
I ordered that parents should be loved by children ...
I made with my brother Osiris an end to the eating of men.
I revealed mysteries to men ...
I broke down the governments of tyrants.

I made an end to murders.
I compelled women to be loved by men ...
I am Lord.

(Kraemer 1988, 369. Used with permission of Scholars Press, The Society of Biblical Literature. Also found in Meyer 1987, 173–74 and Engelsman 1979, 64–65.)

The Bacchae   Dionysus was the god of revelry. His fame still flourishes during the festivities on Fat Tuesday during Mardi Gras in New Orleans. There were at least two stories circulating about his birth. The most popular placed him within the arms of Semele, his mother, who was a human, and his father-god, Zeus. He encouraged intoxication and was thought to be the god who taught humans how to make wine. Worshipers believed that the intoxication made Dionysus present to them. They entered into divine space and became divine themselves. The story in the second chapter of the Gospel of John about Jesus changing water into wine may have been written with Dionysus in mind. The following excerpt from *The Bacchae* was written by Euripides around 405 B.C.E. It portrays Dionysus as a god in human form, who was born to a virgin mother whose lover was a god.

The Bacchae

I am Dionysus, the son of Zeus, come back to Thebes, the land where I was born. My mother was Cadmus' daughter, Semele by name, midwived by fire, delivered by the lightning's blast.

And here I stand, a god incognito, disguised as man, beside the stream of Dirce and the waters of Ismenus.... [A]nd so along all Asia's swarming littoral of towering cities where Greeks and foreign nations, mingling, live, my progress made. There I taught my dances to the feet of living men, establishing my mysteries and rites that I might be revealed on earth for what I am: a god. (*The Bacchae,* Grene and Lattimore 1959)

The rites of Dionysus were secret and involved some type of sexual initiation. Critics of the **Bacchanal Mysteries** claimed that initiates ate raw flesh and danced to music until they exhausted themselves. Most of the worshippers were **maenads**, or mad women, who reportedly tore the flesh off of a victim (usually male) during rituals. Some suggested that Dionysus' mysteries included opium. His symbol, similar to the Hindu god Shiva, was an erect phallus.

Livy, a Roman historian during the first century, describes an investigation into crimes committed by worshipers of Dionysus. He summarizes the testimony of Hispala, who explained that "to consider nothing wrong was the highest form of religious devotion among them."

JUDAISM AND THE ROMAN EMPIRE

No one could ever quantify the influence Judaism had on the founding peoples of Christianity. Jewish political parties are mentioned often within the New Testament. Jesus argues with the Pharisees, Sadducees, Priests, Scribes, Elders, and several other political groups according to the gospel writers. Two main religious parties, Sadducees and Pharisees, dominated the Jewish legal body known as the Sanhedrin.

Pharisees, perhaps meaning "separate ones," are generally thought to have functioned in a manner similar to Rabbis today within Judaism. They were local teachers, healers, and counselors who helped people understand and live within the guidelines of the Hebrew Bible, more specifically, the Torah. They believed in life after death and angels and attempted to use a variety of interpretative methods when studying the Hebrew Bible. They hoped for a messiah and argued for the inclusion of more literature in the Hebrew canon.

The Sadducees, "righteous ones," or priests, ran the temple. They collected taxes, offered sacrifices, planned festivals, and kept to the strict order of the law found in the Torah. Their affluent heritage came from the time of Hasmoneans or Maccabees and continued while they kept close ties with Rome. Some have suggested that they procured taxes for the Roman government. They kept strict kosher guidelines and did not believe in anything that could not be found in the **Torah**.

Scholars know very little about the scribes or zealots. Scribes may have been members of either the Pharisees or Sadducees, functioning in some type of writing capacity. In the gospels and Acts of the Apostles, they are portrayed as anti-Jesus and anti-Christian. Zealots or Sicarii were revolutionary Jews whose main purpose was to regain governmental power. They planned violent attacks against the Roman military and personnel, which eventually lead to the retaliation attack from Rome in 66 C.E.

Another militaristic party, known as the Zadokites (Essenes, Dead Sea people, or the people of Qumran), was recently discovered during the twentieth century. Josephus describes a Jewish party by the name of the Essenes, which many thought was "pure fantasy." Today, most scholars link the **Essenes** with **Qumran**, or the people who wrote the Dead Sea Scrolls. While the Zealots planned to personally war with Rome, the **Zadokites** believed that the coming messiah would do battle with the forces of evil for them.

Fleeing Jerusalem, which they believed was desecrated by foreign hands, they established a desert retreat near the northwest edge of the Dead Sea, some time in the second century B.C.E. They believed in the old ways, the keeping of rigid kosher laws, and did not appreciate the hellenizing influence that took place under their own brothers and sisters, the Maccabees, who ruled Palestine during the second century B.C.E. There is some discussion about the gender of the community. Because females are rarely mentioned in the Scrolls, many have suggested that Qumran was celibate and male. Yet others, based on evidence from a local cemetery, conclude that women must have been part of the community.

The Qumran Scrolls envisioned a climactic battle between a mighty god of the clouds with the Sons of Darkness. In the end, the Sons of Light would prevail, and the Essenes would begin ruling the entire world. They even created a constitution that would be used when they assumed power. During the time that they were waiting for this intergalactic battle, they copied almost all of the books of the Hebrew Bible, some **pseudepigrapha**, and established rules for their community. The following excerpt is taken from "The War Scroll" (The Cave 1 Copy) from Qumran.

FIGURE 2.7 The Caves at Qumran. Photo by Marla J. Selvidge.

And [the sons of justice] shall shine in all the edges of the earth, they shall go on illuminating, up to the end of all the periods of darkness; and in the time of God, his exalted greatness will shine for all the [eternal] times, for peace and blessing, glory and joy, and long days for all the sons of light. And on the day on which the Kittim fall, there will be a battle, and a savage destruction before the God of Israel, for this will be the day determined by him since ancient times for the war of extermination against the sons of darkness. On this (day), the assembly of the gods and the congregation of men shall confront each other for great destruction. (Martinez, 1996, 95)

When the Scrolls were found in the caves near the Dead Sea, many scholars theorized that they were evidence of the first Christian community. There are many literary similarities with the New Testament, especially the Gospel of John. John the Baptist was thought to have been an Essene, or to have lived in a similar community. Today, almost everyone agrees that Qumran was Jewish, and the documents predate Jesus. A list of some of the documents discovered at the Dead Sea follows:

The Manual of Discipline
The Book of Hymns
The Litany of the Angels
Memoirs of the Patriarchs
The War of the Sons of Light and the Sons of Darkness
The New Covenant
Manual of Discipline for the Future Congregation of Israel
The Wiles of the Harlot

The Epochs of Time

The Copper Scroll and the Prayer of Nabonidus

Most of the New Testament was written by Greek-speaking Jews. They quoted the Old Testament/Hebrew Bible/**Septuagint**, interpreted the life of Jesus against the history of the Israelites, and cast him as a **Messiah**. Many of their festivals became special days for Christians. Jews set aside one day each week to rest and worship, that is, Sabbath on Friday and Saturday, but Christians worship on the first day of the week, or Sunday. Jews celebrate Passover in the spring, at about the same time Christians celebrate Easter. Jews remember the Maccabean victory over the Seleucids with the festival of lights, Hannukah, during the same time of year that Christians celebrate Christmas.

Jews and Christians are **monotheists** who place the study of literature at the core of their belief systems. Early Christian organizations maintained the hierarchical organization they found within the priesthood of the Jews. Archaeological remains reveal that many Christians worshiped side by side with Jews in buildings that were known as synagogues. The Christians created churches that resembled synagogues, with an altar at the front and divided galleries for seating. Indeed, Paul, who brought the message of the resurrection of Jesus to Asia Minor and Greece, reportedly began preaching in local synagogues. Many first- and second-century Christian writers urged Christians to follow and pattern their lives after both the Old Testament (Hebrew Bible) and the New Testament.

The ancient Israelites, and later Jews, also provided the **metaphorical** foundation for many Christian beliefs, such as sin and salvation. These beliefs were explained by using the Israelite stories of the Exodus, the giving of the laws on Mt. Sinai/Horeb, the offering of animals, and more. Table 2.3 on page 38 is a chart of some of the ancient Israelite and modern Jewish holidays observed today.

While Christianity's roots lay firmly within Judaism, it eventually broke away and became a new religion, or sect. Robin Scroggs suggests that Christianity began as a sectarian movement because it met the following criteria:

1. The sect begins as a protest.
2. The sect rejects the view of reality taken for granted by the establishment.
3. The sect is egalitarian.
4. The sect offers love and acceptance within the community.
5. The sect is a voluntary association.
6. The sect commands a total commitment from its members.
7. Some sects are **Adventist**.

As we begin the study of the New Testament, we will learn that Jesus and his followers protested the injustices of what they perceived as rigid **social stratification** and separation dictated by the Pharisees and Sadducees. They challenged Sabbath guidelines and purity systems regarding women, the diseased, and personal relationships. Membership within the early Jesus movement was open to all classes of people, including **publicans**, street people, and political outsiders. Demanding that new members walk the same self-sacrificial road of Jesus, some early Christians looked toward the reappearance of Jesus as a sign of a new kingdom and an opportunity to fulfill their dreams.

TABLE 2.3 Religious Days*
of the Israelites and Jews

Day	Hebrew Name	Purpose	Time of Year	Reference
Sabbath	Shabat	To rest and worship	From sundown on Friday to sundown on Saturday every week	Ex. 16; 20; Deut. 5

Israelite Festivals

Passover (Unleavened Bread)	Pesach	To remember the Exodus from Egypt	Spring	Ex. 12; 13; Lev. 23
Weeks Pentecost	Shavuoth	To celebrate the fruits of harvest	Fifty days after Passover	Ex. 23; 34, etc.
Booths Tabernacles	Succoth	To remember being lost in the desert before the entrance into the promised land	Usually the fall	Ex. 23; Deut. 16

Later Jewish Festivals

New Year	Rosh Hashanah	To begin a new year	Usually in the fall	
Day of Atonement	Yom Kippur	To remember and forgive	Usually in the fall	Lev. 16
Dedication	Hannukah	To celebrate the restoration of temple	Usually at end of year	I Mac. 4
Lots	Purim	To remember how Jews were delivered from Haman	Usually late winter, early spring	Esther 9

*"Three times a year all your males shall appear before the Lord your God at the place that he will choose: at the festival of unleavened bread, at the festival of weeks, and at the festival of booths" (Deuteronomy 16:16 NRSV).

A Closer Look at Jewish Heritage

Daughters of Jerusalem, do not weep for me:
but weep for yourselves and your children.
For the days are surely coming when they will say,
'Blessed are the barren, the wombs that never bore,
the breasts that never nursed.' (Luke 23:28–30 NRSV)

By the time the gospel writers had penned their remembrances of Jesus, Rome had devastated Jerusalem during the Jewish Wars of 66–74, C.E. According to **Josephus**, a Jew who worked for the Romans, **Titus** turned the shining city into a pile of rubble and took thousands of prisoners. A brief survey of the Roman Empire during and before these years reveals that the majority of cities and provinces experienced outbreaks of civil disorder and violence. The people of Palestine and her neighbors learned firsthand about the Roman lust for power. The despair these people experienced still cries out through the stories preserved in the gospels. Their mourning, pain, and social outrage is the backdrop of much of the New Testament.

Before the Wars The history of the ancient Israelite and Jewish traditions dates back to as early as 1800 B.C.E. Some would place their origins in ancient Sumer around 3,000 B.C.E. These people had a long history of domination by other cultures. Only for a brief period during the United Monarchy under Saul, David, and Solomon, and perhaps under the Maccabees, did Israel/the Jews exercise great control over their lives. According to stories told in the Hebrew Bible, they faced hundreds of years of civil disorder and finally were deported from their own country to Babylon. (See the chart that follows for a shorthand outline of the history of the Israelites/Jews up until the first century C.E.) They returned in the sixth century B.C.E. but never managed to conquer and administer all of the land. Alexander took over the peaceful administration of Palestine in the fourth century, until his death. The cruel Seleucids (and Ptolemies) ruled until the Maccabean Revolution, which finally placed Palestine back into the hands of the Jews. They lost the land again to the Romans in 63 B.C.E.

History of the Ancient Israelites and Jews

1800 B.C.E	Abraham?
1000	Saul, David, Solomon—the United Monarchy
921	End of United Monarchy: Two States, Israel and Judah
722	Israel conquered by Assyria
587	Judah conquered by Babylon and eventually Persia
537?	Return of the Exiles to Palestine
320	Alexander the Great conquers Palestine
175	Seleucid Rule
167	Maccabean Revolt
63	Pompey with Roman Army conquers Palestine
27	Herod the Great becomes King
4	Jesus is born
28 C.E.	Death of Jesus
40–65	Paul and Letters
66–70	Jewish Wars
65–98	Gospels are created

FIGURE 2.8 A model of Herod the Great's Temple at the Holy Land Hotel in Israel. Photo by Marla J. Selvidge.

FIGURE 2.9 A model of Herod the Great's Temple in a cave underneath the city of Jerusalem. Photo by Melissa A. Luppens.

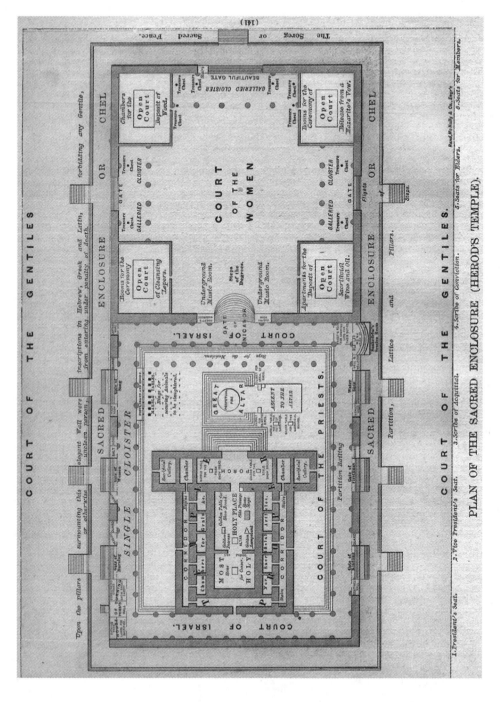

FIGURE 2.10 Plan of Herod's Temple. From J.L. Hurlbut, *Manual of Biblical Geography* (Chicago: Rand, McNally & Co., 1884).

The Jewish Rebellion **Judea**'s story is remembered by Josephus, a Jewish general who was captured by the Romans. He tells a brutal tale of destroyed cities in Palestine, all the way from **Galilee** in the north to **Perea** in the south. Some question his motives for writing the history of Jews and wonder if the war was as violent as he claims. He could have been writing propaganda designed to intimidate the Jews into submission to Roman rule.

At the southernmost part of the Sea of Galilee was Tarichaeae. The following is Josephus' account of that horrible capture by Titus, a Roman general:

> As they streamed forth from them many were speared in the water; many sprang on land, where they were slain by the Romans. One could see the whole lake red with blood and covered with corpses, for not a man escaped. During the following days the district reeked with a dreadful stench and presented a spectacle equally horrible. The beaches were strewn with wrecks and swollen carcasses: these corpses, scorched and clammy in decay so polluted the atmosphere that the catastrophe which plunged the Jews in mourning inspired even its authors with disgust. Such was the issue of this naval engagement. (Josephus, *Jewish Wars*, III, 525–31)

This scene was not uncommon for the Romans who systematically starved and pillaged every city that did not surrender to their authority. Hardly anyone won against the Romans during these horrible years.

During the siege of Jerusalem by Titus in 70 C.E., the city rocked with its own civil war as militant Jewish factions fought for control. They beat and imprisoned people, used the Temple as an outpost, hid food and water for themselves, and finally, burned a huge storage of food in defiance of the Romans. They were ready for anything. They thought God was on their side. God would return and vindicate them, protect them, and elevate them to positions of power over the entire world.

Josephus estimated that over 115,000 dead bodies were carried out of the city in a two-week period after Titus had claimed victory. Ninety-seven thousand people were taken as prisoners, and 600,000 people lay dead in the streets. The Temple was burned to the ground. The war cry of the Romans could be heard throughout the city. Priests were executed. The remaining Temple treasures were plundered, and 11,000 prisoners starved to death while being detained by the Romans. To commemorate this victory, Vespasian minted a coin picturing a Jewish woman weeping while sitting under a palm tree.

FIGURE 2.11 Brass coin of Vespasian. From Frederic W. Madden, *History of Jewish Coinage, and of Money in the Old and New Testament* (New York: KTAV Publishing House, Inc.), p. 185.

FIGURE 2.12 Josephus in the Cave. From William Whiston, *The Works of Flavius Josephus* (Cincinnati, OH: E. Morgan and Co., 1840).

After the long siege at Jerusalem, Titus and the armies headed south to the last outpost of a militant Jewish revolutionary group known as the Sicarii, who with blinding force, overtook **Herod the Great's** southern palace, known today as **Masada**, after plundering nearby towns in the area of Ein Gedi. Herod had cleared the top of a mountain in order to build the southern getaway as a safeguard against Cleopatra, whom he feared. The Sicarii dared the Romans to conquer them. They lost the dare. Jews on top of Masada, rather than face imprisonment, slaughter, or slavery by the Romans, committed suicide. (Many scholars doubt the authenticity of this story today.) Some of Rabbi Eleazar's last words, according to Josephus who supposedly hid in a cave and witnessed the slaughter, are the following:

> Long since, my brave men, we determined neither to serve the Roman nor any other save God, for He alone is man's true and righteous Lord, and now the time has come which bids us verify that resolution by our actions. At this crisis let us not disgrace ourselves, we who in the past refused to submit even to slavery involving no peril, let us not now, along with slavery, deliberately accept the irreparable penalties awaiting us if we are to fall alive into the Roman hands.

Let our wives thus die undishonored, our children unacquainted with slavery; and, when they are gone, let us render a generous service to each other, preserving our liberty as a noble windingsheet. But first let us destroy our chattels and the fortress by fire; for the Romans, well I know, will be grieved to lose at once our persons and their lucre. Our provisions only let us spare; for they will testify, when we are dead, that it was not want which subdued us, but that, in keeping with our initial resolve, we preferred death to slavery. (Josephus, *Jewish Wars*, VII, 249–401, and 577–617. For Eleazar's speech, see VII, 331–88, or 598–99)

After the War Little information is available concerning the postwar years in Palestine. Evidently thousands of people died in the military campaigns throughout Palestine. What did this slaughter of humanity mean to the countryside? Modern scholars of twentieth-century wars point out that war causes chaos. It also destroys the economic system. In Jerusalem, all of the shops and businesses were obliterated. Money is useless if there are no goods to buy.

What happened to the people who survived the wars? Where did they go? How did they survive the wars of 66–74 C.E.? Many did not survive, as the staggering losses are counted. Some Christians are reported to have migrated to the city of **Pella** to escape the Romans. Other Christian communities were scattered down the coast as far as **Joppa** to the south and **Samaria** to the north. The racial or religious lines between Jews and Christians were not so clearly drawn then as they are today. The poor, no matter what their faith or cultural background, seemed to be in a class of their own.

Aristocratic Jews managed to escape to a city that had surrendered to the Romans. **Jamnia** was protected; thus Judaism, led by the Pharisees, began to flourish for a while in this southern town. Later they moved north to a town called Usha.

Rome confiscated much of the land in the **Palestine** and then decided to lease it. A staggering tax was levied against every Jew in the Empire for the Jewish revolt against Rome. Previous to this enactment, only males between the ages of twenty and fifty (including slaves and freed proselytes) were taxed by the Temple, which later forwarded some of this tax to Rome. Now the tax was payable by both sexes, from the age of three. Although no records tally the total amount that this revenue brought to the Romans, there are traces of the tax found in receipts in **Alexandria**, Egypt. It appears that the tax was so large that the people were allowed to make it in installments. To further humiliate the Jews, the Romans took the funds collected by this tax and began to build a temple to Jupiter on the ruins of their holy Temple in Jerusalem.

Some survivors became traitors or lost their lives later as sport for the gladiator games. Jewish revolutionaries made their way to both Alexandria and Cyrene, where revolts were later reported. In Leontopolis, Egypt, the **Temple of Onias** was burned to the ground, largely because of the threat of a Jewish rebellion. Despair over the confiscation of their land, the loss of their children, their riches, and their comfortable lives led many Jews to become **ascetics**.

Many years after the wars, the harassment of Jews and Christians continued. In the Roman province of Bithynia, which lies in the northern part of Asia Minor (Turkey today), letters of Pliny to the Emperor Trajan (111 C.E.) reveal continued oppression.

Oppression in Bithynia

Having never been present at any trials of the Christians, I am unacquainted with the limits and methods to be observed in examining and punishing them....

In the meanwhile, the method, I have observed towards those who have been denounced to me as Christians is this: I interrogate them whether they were Christian; if they confessed I repeated the question twice again, adding the threat of capital punishment; if they still persevered, I ordered them to be executed. (Kee 1973, 51)

This war spawned not only the gospels in the New Testament but also Jewish writings such as the **Talmud**. People had been devastated by the conflict and needed to remember the past. The gospels attempted to capture a Jesus who had been dead for over thirty-five years. Much of the social upheaval preserved in the gospels dates from after the destruction of Jerusalem.

GUIDE TO PALESTINE: THE LANDSCAPE

All of the gospels refer to geographical areas visited by Jesus. While some prefer one area over another, all suggest that Jesus traversed north to south in Palestine. Palestine is the name given by Herodotus, a Greek historian during the fifth century B.C.E., to the area between Asia Minor and Egypt. It is based on the word for Philistia, or the **Philistines**, who were enemies of the Israelites. The name came into official use sometime during the second century C.E. It also is known as Canaan, Judea, or the promised land of the Hebrew Bible.

Anyone studying the gospels should familiarize themselves with the towns and regions discussed by the writers. On the map of Palestine (Figure 2.13 on page 46), locate the following places: the Mediterranean, the Jordan, the Dead Sea, the Sea of Galilee, Samaria, Galilee, Peraea, Decapolis, Caesarea, Jerusalem, Nazareth, Capernaum, Judea, Bethlehem, Cana, Bethsaida, Tyre, Caesarea Philippi, Phoenicia, Judaea.

Notice that there are specific political regions that encompass all of Palestine. To the north are the provinces of Syria, Galilee, and Decapolis. To the south one will find Judea and Perea. These regions often experienced political and governmental change.

The Jordan River, originating in the north runs almost the entire length of Palestine. It was a much-needed source of water because most of the region on either side of it, traveling southward, is desert. Small mountain ranges run north and southwest of the Jordan.

As the study of the gospels begins, keep in mind the sources and resources used by the writers and the geographical locations mentioned in the text. Paying attention to these details will help keep the story interesting by associating activities and people with different locales. Each time a place is mentioned in the gospels, try to find it on the map. See Figure 2.13

Summary   In spite of all we know about the wars and collection of the documents that are included in the New Testament, the writers and earliest copies of its contents remain a mystery. We know that from the very beginning of Christianity its adherents

FIGURE 2.13 The Palestine of Josephus. From Tessa Rajak, *Josephus: The Historian and His Society* (Philadelphia: Fortress Press).

claimed that their religion was designed for the world. It began within an ethnically diverse culture, continuing its march forward until it met its goal of reaching to the ends of the earth. It is a marvel that these ancient documents have survived for so long and influenced so many millions of people over the past 2,000 years.

The diverse roots of the New Testament may be untraceable. It blossomed during the Roman expansion in the Mediterranean during the first century C.E. Greek, Roman, and even Zoroastrian (Persian) philosophies and religions influenced the worldviews of the writers of the New Testament. As a breakaway group from Judaism, Christianity has retained much of the cultural heritage of the ancient Israelite traditions, rituals, and culture.

3

The Unexpected News of Jesus

The disciples went and did as Jesus had directed them;
they brought the donkey and the colt, and put
their cloaks on them, and he sat on them....
The crowds that went ahead of him and that followed
were shouting, "Hosanna to the Son of David."

—Matt. 21: 6–9 NRSV

INTRODUCTION

Every four years during presidential campaigns, we hold our breath hoping to elect an honest person, sometimes a military leader, who can foster economic prosperity and perhaps world peace. We hope the new president will find or possess the money, knowledge, and political genius to feed, educate, clothe, employ, and protect everyone in the United States. First-century citizens in Palestine had many of the same hopes or dreams. They wished for a strong military leader who could sustain peace and prosperity, especially in Jerusalem where tempers flared over governmental controls and taxes. Many thought that Jesus from the northern town of Nazareth would be the next emperor or king. He would protect them and lead them into a prosperous and secure life.

Jesus was called the "Messiah," the "anointed one," or "king" by all four gospel writers. If he was a king, it was a kingship without land, money, soldiers, or servants. When he rode into Jerusalem, shortly before he was murdered, he was not carried like

FIGURE 3.1   An icon of one of the gospel writers portrayed in the Lorsch gospels around 810 C.E. Photo by Marla J. Selvidge.

a dignitary, nor did he flank himself with war machines and a powerful army of ferocious killers. His friends would probably have been thrilled to see him gallop into town on a tall Arabian horse, yet he entered the city riding a common donkey.

While violence and violent acts permeate the gospels, Jesus generally taught a message of thoughtful accommodation and peaceful coexistence. The epitome of his career would not be realized during the lives of those who heard him teach, according to the gospel writers. His kingdom was to be found on another plane of life or in the distant future. His kingdom would be won with compassion, not destruction. His message and the kind of kingdom he advocated were unexpected. He "shocked" his followers.

Robert McAfee Brown writes about news that shocks readers or hearers. In his book *Unexpected News: Reading the Bible with Third World Eyes,* he suggests that even today when people read about Jesus the stories shock them.

> The title *Unexpected News* suggests that when we turn to the Bible, the "news" we find is always "unexpected": religious people are often put down (scribes, Pharisees, and church folk); worship is attacked … pagans are described as doing God's will.… It is certainly not the way we would have written the script. (Brown 1984, 12)

James Karman, a professor of English and humanities, wrote about his own frustration in the classroom in an article, "If We Try to Blunt the Edge of a Great Idea to 'Protect' Our Students, Education Suffers," in the *Chronicle of Higher Education.* He wishes students would cherish new thoughts rather than attempt to protect themselves

FIGURE 3.2   Christ as Judge. From the ceiling of the Baptistry of Saint John in Florence, Italy. Photo by Marla J. Selvidge.

from learning. The following is a summary of one experience with a student who complained that the educational process had destroyed his identity.

> But I felt sorry for him, sorry that in his four years of college he had missed out on the excitement of the life of the mind. . . . He represented countless other students I have encountered recently who have been so threatened by new ideas that they either resist them altogether or are crushed by them, students for whom there seems to be no middle ground.
>
>   To be true to our calling we do not have to "destroy the drawers of the brain and spread demoralization" wherever we go.... But we do have to help students understand that new ideas (even old ideas; if they are new to the person who hears them) are by nature revolutionary: they overturn what was there before. New ideas are iconoclastic; they break through old ways of seeing. (Karman 1981, 64)

The gospels are and were by their very nature **iconoclastic**. They eventually changed the way the Romans thought of Jesus and his message, and they have changed minds for hundreds of years. As we study each gospel individually, remember that the content of each may differ with popular portrayals of Jesus. Most Americans are accustomed to hearing a story about Jesus that **harmonizes** all four gospels. The idea that there were at least four separate gospel writers in the Bible may be new for some. This textbook will look at each gospel writer to discover the individual points of view of the writers. These differences and distinctive messages within the gospels may shock a person who has never compared them. Consider how such stories must have been experienced by people who first read or heard them.

THE GOSPEL GENRE

The compilers of the New Testament chose four gospels, Matthew, Mark, Luke, and John, to showcase the myriad of **traditions** about Jesus and the growth of the early Christian community. Their choices may have come from among hundreds of gospels. Many of these **extracanonical** works are now labeled the Christian Apocrypha or pseudepigrapha. (See list on page 12). Gnostic writings would also be included in this list.

Most people who read the Bible assume that they understand the literary form of **gospel**. But what does the term *gospel* mean, and is it really a legitimate **literary form**? To determine the content or definition of the term, students must search outside of the Bible, or consider **external evidence**, then within the Bible itself or, **internal evidence**.

External Evidence

The English word "gospel" is a translation of the Greek word εὐαγγέλιον "euaggelion," (sounds like "uangelion"), which means "good news," or "good message." The word is a combination of two Greek words meaning "well" and "angel." A gospel is therefore literature that announces something healthy and good.

Students of the Bible question the use of "gospel" as a genre that is used to describe the first four books of the New Testament. Was this a legitimate literary form used by ancient Greeks or Romans? Some would affirm this theory and others would suggest that it was a new form of literature created by Christians. Long before Christianity began to flourish in the first century C.E., people had written stories about gods and goddesses, such as Dionysus, Isis, and **Asklepios**. Yet the question remains, did Christians use a literary form that was known to people throughout the Roman Empire?

Some students of the gospels of the New Testament suggest that they were based upon what is now termed "Divine Man" stories, or "**aretalogies**," popularized among Egyptians, Greeks, and Romans. These stories of humans included claims of divine power, proved by their miracle-working abilities. Aretalogies often told of a physical union between a deity and a mortal, producing a god that claimed both human and supernatural qualities. The deity could be a great healer, warrior, protector, or savior. More recently, some have argued that the gospels were created as popular biographies.

Many stories were told of a miracle-working god named Asklepios, whose father reportedly was Apollo. Asklepios was often portrayed in paintings wearing a white robe and sandals, carrying a staff, and with a lamb at his feet. The following inscriptions were taken from a temple at Epidauros dating from the fourth century B.C.E.:

Asklepios

Cleo was pregnant five years. She, already five years pregnant, was brought prostrate in bed to the God [Asklepios] as a supplicant. Immediately as she came from him and from the temple, she bore a boy; as soon as he was born, he washed himself in the spring and walked around with the mother. After she had accomplished this, she wrote about it on the votive offering. One should be amazed not at the greatness of the tablet, but at the

God. Five years Cleo bore the burden in her womb until she slept in the temple and she became healthy.

Ambrosia from Athens had one good eye. She came, a supplicant, to the God. But, as she walked around the temple of healings, she mocked some things as incredible and impossible, that the lame and blind could be healed at only seeing a dream. While lying there, she saw a vision. It seemed that God [Asklepios] stood over her and said to her that he would make her healthy, but it was necessary that she set in the temple a silver pig as a reward, that is, a remembrance of her stupidity. While saying these things, he cut into the place where her other eye was diseased and poured in some medicine. When it was day, she went out healthy. (Cartlidge and Dungan 1980, 151–52. Used with permission of Augsburg Fortress.)

Internal Evidence

How do the gospel writers describe their own works? Below is a list that summarizes the words used to describe each gospel.

Gospel	Translation	Greek Word
Matthew 1:1	An Account	The Greek word is βίβλος, or book
Mark 1:1	Good News	The Greek word is εὐαγγέλιον, or gospel
Luke 1:1–4	Orderly Account	The Greek word is διήγησιν, or narrative
John 20:30–31	Book	The Greek word is βιβλίῳ, or book, scroll (Translation from NRSV)

A student could conclude that what we now know as the gospels were viewed quite differently by their writers and first readers. Perhaps there was a great variety of literary forms used to relay traditions about Jesus and the beginnings of early Christianity.

THE SYNOPTIC PROBLEM

When comparing the gospels, students soon discover that not only do the writers describe their works differently but also that the contents of each differ. Matthew, Mark, and Luke are known as the synoptic gospels, because while the basic outline of the story of Jesus is similar, the details in their accounts are quite different. This dilemma is known as the **synoptic problem**.

How could writings be so similar, that is, it almost appears that they copied from each other line by line, and yet also be so different? When similar stories are written, details which will affect the entire meaning of the story are changed. Scholars have compared the synoptics for centuries in order to ascertain the reasons why they are different yet much the same. The Gospel of John has a very different outline of the life of Jesus but appears generally to follow the death of Jesus found in the synoptics. Table 3.1 attempts to demonstrate the broad similarities and differences within the synoptics.

If Table 3.1 is analyzed, it quickly becomes clear that the Gospel of Mark does not include a story about the birth or **resurrection appearance** of Jesus. Neither does the

TABLE 3.1 Broad Structural Differences in the Gospels

Mark			Ministry of Jesus	Death of Jesus	
Luke	Birth Story	Genealogy	Ministry of Jesus	Death of Jesus	Resurrection appearance story
Matthew	Genealogy	Birth Story	Ministry of Jesus	Death of Jesus	Resurrection appearance story
John	Prologue	Signs Source	Farewell stories	Death of Jesus	Resurrection appearance story

writer include an extended genealogy. Mark merely claims that Jesus was the "son of Mary" (6:3). These differences are obvious, but on a more complicated level that studies Greek words and verses within stories, the differences among the synoptics are profound.

Some students would like to explain away these differences by claiming that the gospel writers were companions and friends of Jesus. They wrote stories about events they witnessed. One can compare their stories about the life and death of Jesus to witnesses of an automobile accident. If a reporter asks for accounts about "what happened," the witnesses will generally disagree because they saw the accident from a different vantage point. This argument sounds plausible, but in reality it ignores the careful attention to detail found in the Greek manuscripts. It also ignores the evidence that all of the gospels are anonymous and that the earliest gospel was written by someone at least three decades after the death of Jesus. Authorship of each gospel will be considered in future chapters.

Priority of the Gospel of Mark

Most biblical experts today subscribe to a theory known as the **Marcan Priority**, or the **Priority of Mark**. After a careful study of the synoptics, they have determined that Matthew and Luke copied from the Gospel of Mark. Matthew and Luke use Mark as a source and then rewrite the material taken from Mark in order to fit into their own points of view regarding the life and death of Jesus and the early Christian community.

This theory may appear highly unlikely to a casual reader of the gospels. For example, most teachers can detect when students are quoting sources or composing their own papers. This involves recognizing grammatical style, literary competence, and the varying content of the written materials. Students also can detect the composition of literature. Choose any article from a newspaper. Now read it casually. Go back and pick out quotations from interviews or definitions of words taken from resource books. Do you detect different points of view? The more you read the article, the more you can detect the sources used in its composition or creation.

Editing by Matthew and Luke is noticeable in what is known as the temptation of Jesus. The boxed text that follows contains all three stories of the temptation found in the gospels. Do you notice any similarities or differences between Mark and Matthew, Mark and Luke, and Luke and Matthew?

THE TEMPTATION OF JESUS
THREE POINTS OF VIEW

Mt. 4:1–11

1 Then Jesus was led up by the Spirit into the wilderness to be tempted by the devil. 2 He fasted forty days and forty nights, and afterwards he was famished. 3 The tempter came and said to him, "If you are the Son of God, command these stones to become loaves of bread." 4 But he answered, "It is written, 'One does not live by bread alone, but by every word that comes from the mouth of God.'" 5 Then the devil took him to the holy city and placed him on the pinnacle of the temple, 6 saying to him, "If you are the Son of God, throw yourself down; for it is written, 'He will command his angels concerning you,' and 'On their hands they will bear you up, so that you will not dash your foot against a stone.'" 7 Jesus said to him, "Again it is written, 'Do not put the Lord your God to the test.'" 8 Again, the devil took him to a very high mountain and showed him all the kingdoms of the world and their splendor; 9 and he said to him, "All these I will give you, if you will fall down and worship me." 10 Jesus said to him, "Away with you, Satan! for it is written, 'Worship the Lord your God, and serve only him.'" 11 Then the devil left him, and suddenly angels came and waited on him.

Mark 1:12

And the Spirit immediately drove him out into the wilderness. 13 He was in the wilderness forty days, tempted by Satan; and he was with the wild beasts; and the angels waited on him.

Luke 4:1–13

Jesus, full of the Holy Spirit, returned from the Jordan and was led by the Spirit in the wilderness, 2 where for forty days he was tempted by the devil. He ate nothing at all during those days, and when they were over, he was famished. 3 The devil said to him, "If you are the Son of God, command this stone to become a loaf of bread." Jesus answered him, "It is written, 'One does not live by bread alone.'" 5 Then the devil led him up and showed him in an instant all the Kingdoms of the world. 6 And the devil said to him, "To you I will give their glory and all this authority; for it has been given over to me, and I give it to anyone I please. 7 If you, then, will worship me, it will all be yours." 8 Jesus answered him, "It is written, 'Worship the Lord your God and serve only him.'" 9 Then the devil took him to Jerusalem, and placed him on the pinnacle of the temple; saying to him, "If you are the Son of God, throw yourself down from here, 10 for it is written, 'He will command his angels concerning you, to protect you,' 11 and 'On their hands they will bear you up, so that you will not dash your foot against a stone.'" 12 Jesus answered him, "It is said, 'Do not put the Lord your God to the test.'" When the devil had finished every test, he departed from him until an opportune time. (NRSV)

After a comparison of the three gospels, did you discover the following similarities?

the number 40

the use of angels

a wilderness

The differences among all three accounts are enormous. These differences raise many questions. Is the "tempter" the same character as "Satan" and the "Devil"? Is the "Spirit" the same character as "the Holy Spirit"? Is Matthew making a different point about the temptation than the writer of Luke? Why are Matthew's long extensions so different? Luke seems to suggest that the Devil will be waiting for Jesus in the bushes. Why is this point of view not found in the other gospels? Matthew and Mark suggest that angels took care of him. Who or what are the angels? Where were they when all the action was occurring?

A student could draw a variety of additional conclusions about the composition of the texts. Mark could have abbreviated either Matthew or Luke. If Mark did abbreviate Luke then why are there so many similarities between Matthew and Luke, or are there? Most scholars suggest that Mark's story was written first, and then the two independent writers, Matthew and Luke, amplified the original.

Other changes and additions in the synoptics are not so obvious to the modern reader of English. Sometimes the gospel writer will add a sentence, or a paragraph, or omit significant sections of stories. Subtle changes in Greek nouns, verbs, and modifiers are sometimes glossed over by well-intentioned translators who refuse to acknowledge the striking differences in the gospels.

Unlike English, Greek has several cases for each noun and many verb tenses. Endings of nouns signify how the word is to be interpreted in a sentence, that is, if it is to be the subject, object, or is to be used as an adjective. This is true of verbs as well. Both the beginning and end of every verb can change, depending on the tense used by the writer. The combinations and changes made by the gospel writers can be overwhelming. In one sentence, there might be twenty different changes made to verbs and nouns. Factor in changes of grammar, substitution of similar words, changes in pronouns and other connectives and one is faced with analyzing a very complicated puzzle. If you have any detective blood in your veins these differences and similarities could haunt you.

FIGURE 3.3 The cover of the Golden gospels of Echternach, eleventh century. Photo by Marla J. Selvidge.

Oral Traditions

The differences and similarities in the synoptics may also be attributed to problems with the **oral transmission** of the texts. People met Jesus, heard his stories, and watched him apply healing techniques to people who were very sick. They talked about him. Some of those stories were passed on to relatives or friends. Those stories may have been collected in oral or written lists. Some of the lists could have been wise sayings attributed to Jesus, or places he had visited, or stories about his death, often referred to as the **passion** story. Every time a person retells a story it changes, because people hear, understand, and speak differently. What was the original language of the people who remembered Jesus? Was Aramaic, Greek, Latin, or some other language spoken in the Empire? While we may theorize, we really do not know, because their conversations were never recorded. Neither have scholars found any lists of Jesus' words or activities.

The stories and activities of Jesus were never captured on video. If this type of technology had been available, then perhaps modern investigators would not have as many questions, or would they? The gospel writers used material about Jesus that had been circulating for at least thirty years. Consider the deaths of John F. Kennedy, Marilyn Monroe, or Elvis Presley, who have been dead for at least twenty years. Some people claim that Elvis is still alive. Their evidence consists of personal meetings and photos. Most of us have viewed clips of the shooting of Kennedy. But do we really have hard evidence to substantiate how he died and who was involved in the murder? Do we know the real reason for the apparent suicide of Marilyn Monroe? The answer is obviously, "no." Video and film clips of all three of these people have survived their deaths, but the questions concerning their deaths and personal lives still remain a mystery. Technology may provide a visual portrait of a person, but it does not provide all the answers regarding motives and activities during someone's life.

While the writers of the gospels did not use modern technology, they did use a variety of sources while composing their stories about Jesus. Although it has been suggested that the writers of Matthew and Luke used the Gospel of Mark as a source, the writer of Mark probably used sources as well. Some scholars have suggested that there may have been a "**Proto-Mark**" and an independent passion narrative that circulated together or independently.

There are many names for theories that attempt to explain the composition of the gospels. Figure 3.4 (Creation of the gospels, on page 58) represents the Two-Document theory that is accepted by most biblical scholars today. While Matthew and Luke use Mark as a source, they also use something termed "**Q**," a designation for "Quelle" or source. Q is a hypothetical document that contained (primarily) the sayings of Jesus. Both Luke and Matthew contain similar, almost identical, sermonic material that is not found in the Gospel of Mark. Q is the name given to this material. In addition to Q both Matthew and Luke used material that is found only in their gospels. This material is designated "**M**" for Matthean material and "**L**" for Lucan material.

For instance, "M" contains stories about the death of babies at the birth of Jesus, an extended Sermon on the Mount, Peter walking on water, Judas and the thirty pieces

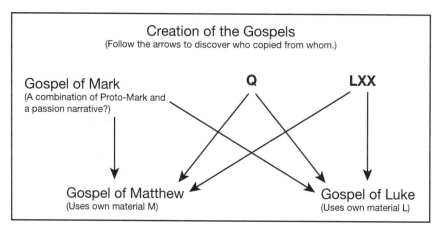

FIGURE 3.4   Creation of the Gospels.

of silver, and a distinctive genealogy. "L" adds stories about the two on the road to Emmaus, Mary, Anna, and Elizabeth at the beginning of the gospel, and the conversion of a man named Zacchaeus. An abbreviated list of material found only in Matthew or only in the Gospel of Luke follows:

Material Found Only in Matthew (Abbreviated List)*

Healing of Two Blind Men, Matt. 9   Laborers in the Vineyard, Matt. 20
Deliverance of a Demon-possessed Man, Matt. 9   Wise and Foolish Virgins, Matt. 25
Pearl of Great Price, Matt. 13   The Great Judgment, Matt. 25
The Fish Net, Matt. 13

Material Found Only in Luke (Abbreviated List)*

Miracle of the Fishes, Luke 5   The Good Samaritan, Luke 10
Resurrection of the Widow's Son, Luke 7   The Friend at Midnight, Luke 11
Healing of a Woman, Luke 13   The Rich Fool, Luke 12
Healing of a Man, Luke 14   The Barren Fig Tree, Luke 13
The Ten Lepers, Luke 17   The Lost Coin, Luke 15
Healing of the Ear, Luke 22   The Prodigal Son, Luke 15
The Two Debtors, Luke 7   The Unrighteous Judge, Luke 18

The beatitudes, part of Q, are found only in Luke and Matthew. While the sayings are similar, if one compares them, one will note quite a different emphasis. In the Scripture passages in the box on page 59, what are the differences and similarities?

* Lists are excerpted from W. Graham Scroggie, *A Guide to the Gospels* (Michigan: Kregel Publishing, 1967).

THE SERMON ON THE MOUNT: THE BEATITUDES

Matthew 5:1–12

When Jesus saw the crowds, he went up the mountain; and after he sat down, his disciples came to him. 2 Then he began to speak, and taught them, saying: 3 "Blessed are the poor in spirit, for theirs is the kingdom of heaven. 4 "Blessed are those who mourn, for they will be comforted. 5 "Blessed are the meek, for they will inherit the earth. 6 "Blessed are those who hunger and thirst for righteousness, for they will be filled. 7 "Blessed are the merciful, for they will receive mercy. 8 "Blessed are the pure in heart, for they will see God. 9 "Blessed are the peacemakers for they will be called children of God. 10 "Blessed are those who are persecuted for righteousness' sake, for theirs is the kingdom of heaven. 11 "Blessed are you when people revile you and persecute you and utter all kinds of evil against you falsely on my account. 12 "Rejoice and be glad, for your reward is great in heaven, for in the same way they persecuted the prophets who were before you."

Luke 6:12, 20–23

Now during those days he went out to the mountain to pray; and he spent the night in prayer to God. 20 Then he looked up at his disciples and said: "Blessed are you who are poor, for yours is the kingdom of God. 21 "Blessed are you who are hungry now for you will be filled. Blessed are you who weep now, for you will laugh. 22 "Blessed are you when people hate you, and when they exclude you, revile you, and defame you on account of the Son of Man. Rejoice in that day and leap for joy, for surely your reward is great in heaven; for that is what their ancestors did to the prophets." (NRSV)

A long discussion about the differences and similarities is not important at this point in the text. An observant student will notice that the sayings are quite similar but their emphasis is totally different. Luke is concerned about the social conditions that are happening in his lifetime. The hungry will be fed, and the poor have something greater in the kingdom. Matthew is concerned about personal and political righteousness (pureness/moral uprightness) and believes that peace makers and sons of God are very important.

The LXX as a Source

In addition, Matthew and Luke both use the Old Testament/Hebrew Bible as a source. Many of the Old Testament verses were taken from the Septuagint, or the **LXX**, a Greek translation of the Hebrew Bible (the **MT**). Sometimes gospel writers refer to Israelite prophecies that they believe have come to pass, or have been fulfilled in Jesus. For example, the following is a story about Jesus in the Gospel of Luke:

And he rolled up the scroll, gave it back to the attendant, and sat down. The eyes of all in the synagogue were fixed on him. Then be began to say to them, 'Today this scripture has been fulfilled in your hearing.' (Luke 4:20–21, NRSV)

At other points in the narrative, stories challenge the present religious system by claiming that Jesus is changing accepted Jewish laws.

Again, you have heard that it was said to those of ancient times, 'You shall not swear false-ly, but carry the vows you have made to the Lord.' But I say unto you, Do not swear at all, either by heaven, for it is the throne of God, or by the earth, for it is his footstool, or by Jerusalem, for it is the city of the great King. (Mt. 5:33–35, NRSV)

Both writers of Luke and Matthew use the Old Testament/Hebrew Bible in a variety of other ways. Sometimes their own special stories are based on traditions of the Israelites, or Jews. For instance, compare the story of Jesus' escape to Egypt in Matthew 2 with the story about Moses escaping from Egypt in Exodus 1. Gospel writers also quote the Hebrew Bible without acknowledging that they are citing it. A casual reader who did not know the contents of the Old Testament would not recognize that the gospel writers were using it as a source.

In summary, the gospel writers used a variety of sources when composing their gospels, including oral traditions and collections of sayings, acts, and perhaps places Jesus visited. Mark may have employed sources such as Proto-Mark and the passion narrative. The Gospel of Matthew was created by someone who used most of the entire Gospel of Mark, Q, the LXX, and M. The writer of Luke used similar sources in creating the Gospel of Luke. Most of Mark, Q, various references to the LXX, and L are the foundation of the Gospel of Luke.

THE HISTORICAL JESUS

For at least two hundred years and perhaps longer people have been interested in discovering the actual historical life of a person by the name of Jesus. After studying the gospels, the student soon discovers that there are multiple images or interpretations of the meaning of the life of Jesus.

Thousands of documents and discussions about the historical Jesus have been held all over the world. In the United States, scholars met for decades, in the Jesus Seminar, attempting to discern which words in the gospels were (beyond a doubt) from the lips of Jesus. Others have attempted to re-create the travels and events of Jesus' ministry. Some are interested in discovering the Jewish background of Jesus' life. Many have attempted, like a detective, to determine the historical sequence of the ancient sources which tell the story of Jesus. They have uncovered layers of traditions. To date no major group of people has reached a consensus about the historical Jesus.

Yet what is most obvious in this search for a historical Jesus is the bias of the researchers. Scholars have begun to write books about the "myth" of the historical Jesus.

In attempting to determine criteria to be used in designating something as historical, scholars have discovered that they are often dominated by their own point of view or their faith perspective. Underlying many quests to find the historical Jesus is a hope to prove one's faith, or put in another way, to find that the things that mean most to you were also the things that meant most to Jesus.

Below is an outline of the life of Jesus that is generally accepted by most scholars in the fields of Biblical Studies. It does not address the self-conception of Jesus, nor does it attempt to force all of the stories about Jesus into one theory about the true meaning of his life and death.

The Life of Jesus

6-4 B.C.E.	Jesus was born a Jew.	
	Mother was named Mary.	
	Possible Levitical Descent	Luke 1:5, 36
	A lay person; not ordained	
	Had brothers and sisters	Matt. 15:55; Mark 6:33
	Unmarried	
	Had a job as a carpenter.	Mark 6:3
	No formal education	John 7:15
	He associated with lower classes	
	He did not practice asceticism	
	He was a healer	
27-29 C.E.	Baptized by John	Luke 3:1ff
	Students of John began a relationship with Jesus	Matt 4:14ff; John 1:35ff
14-33 C.E.	Jesus' public career	
30-33 C.E.	Death of Jesus	Lk 24:39; John 20: 20ff
	Betrayed by a student, Judas	
	Trials before Sanhedrin	
	Trial before Roman officials	
	Death ordered by Pontius Pilate Some witnesses may include: Simon of Cyrene, Alexander, and Rufus	Mark 15:21

Summary   The stories found in the gospels unexpectedly portray a variety of points of view about Jesus. Many people presume that they know the story of Jesus and the contents of the gospels. In reality, the stories that have been told through the media harmonize all four gospels.

Scholars have attempted to classify and define the term *gospel.* Many similar works were published before and after the death of Jesus. An exact literary form is unknown among the Greeks. Stories about divinities known as "aretologies" and "ancient biographies" come very close to the form labeled "gospel."

One of the problems that arises early when studying Matthew, Mark, and Luke is that the phrases within the stories are similar, yet different. (John's selection of stories does not follow the synoptic pattern.) How could this occur if all three writers were eyewitnesses? If this were true, they would not need to copy from one another. To account for these questions, scholars have theorized that none of the writers were eyewitnesses, because all of them used sources. Matthew and Luke used the Gospel of Mark as a source when creating their gospels. They also used the LXX, a hypothetical document "Q," and their own special material "L" and "M." The gospels also have similar geographical emphases centered in Palestine. A knowledge of the geography of Judea, Samaria, Decapolis, and Galilee will help facilitate the reading of the gospels. In spite of all of these differences or because of them, thousands of people have embarked on the journey to find the historical Jesus.

4

A Humble Community Anticipating a Hopeful Future

The Gospel of Mark

But go, tell his disciples and Peter that he is going ahead of you
to Galilee; there you will see him, just as he told you. So they went
out and fled from the tomb, for terror and amazement had seized
them; and they said nothing to anyone, for they were afraid.

—Mark 16: 7–8 NRSV

INTRODUCTION

Within the history of Christianity, the Gospel of Mark has never been very popular, although it presents a fast-paced and readable story of Jesus' life and death. It is only within the last fifty years that scholars have paid special attention to its contents. Luke and Matthew were preferred to Mark because of their extensive sermons, parables, and personal stories about Jesus' life and resurrection. Many readers of the gospels reasoned that if Matthew contained about 96 percent of Mark's work, then it was not necessary to read Mark. In fact, the earliest surviving **commentary** on Mark written by **Victor of Antioch** dates from the fifth century C.E. In contrast, commentaries or major references to the other gospels begin as early as the second century.

Part of Mark's obscurity or unpopularity may also be because it contains no stories about Jesus' birth, his early childhood, or appearances after his death. It neglects stories about Joseph, has no extended genealogy, and is quite critical of **the Twelve**. For many, the ending of Mark is unsatisfactory. Women discover the empty tomb but out of fear they keep their discovery to themselves. Over the centuries, people who read the

63

other gospels wished that Mark's ended with a life after death appearance by Jesus. Some even attempted to create endings for Mark.

LOCATION AND AUDIENCE

Scholars suggest that all of the gospels were written to readers (an audience) who lived in the Roman Empire during the first century C.E. No one lived in a major city or near a village road without being influenced by several cultures. Most businesspeople and travelers were at least bilingual, speaking Greek and one other language.

Traditional scholarship suggests that the Gospel of Mark was written to Roman Christians, the Gospel of Matthew to people of Jewish heritage, the Gospel of Luke and the Gospel of John to a global audience. Irenaeus, who wrote during the later part of the second century C.E., suggests that the message found in the gospels was intended to reach people living all over the earth.

> As there are four quarters of the world in which we live, as there are four universal winds, and as the Church is scattered all over the earth, and the gospel is the pillar and base of the Church and the breath of life, it is likely that it should have four pillars breathing immortality on every side and kindling afresh the life of men. (*Against Heresies*, 3.11.8)

Yet it is difficult, if not practically impossible, to assign each gospel a specific location and time in the first century. Some scholars have argued that the creation of the gospels should be dated during the second century or later.

In what part of the Empire or for what particular audience/readership was the Gospel of Mark composed? Many students of Mark place the origin of the gospel in Galilee or in another Roman province. They base their conclusions on special language and geographical descriptions employed by the writer. Mark supposedly understood at least three languages, Aramaic, Latin, and Greek. For instance, in Mark 5:9, the Roman word "**legion**" is explained as meaning "many." In 12:42 and 15:16, the writer uses Latin terms to explain currency and the name of the governor's headquarters. And in 5:41 the Aramaic words "Talitha cum" are translated into Greek. Most of Mark's quotations of or allusions to the Old Testament/Hebrew Bible are taken from the Septuagint.

While the writer of Mark mentions geography, some contend that those references are inaccurate. This suggests the writer did not have firsthand experience in Palestine, especially in Galilee. Therefore, the writer was probably not a resident of Galilee when the gospel was written. For example, in 7:31, Jesus seems to be going north and east at the same time.

> Then he returned from the region of Tyre, and went by way of Sidon towards the Sea of Galilee, in the region of Decapolis. (NRSV)

Jesus is supposedly traveling west to "the way of Sidon" in order to reach people in the far east, "Decapolis."

AUTHORSHIP

Who wrote the gospel? There is no hard evidence to support any particular person. Most scholars assume the book to be anonymous, yet there are many stories and traditions about the author of this book that people accept as fact. If someone named Mark did write the gospel, then who was he or she? Most people assume that Mark was a disciple of Jesus, even though the name Mark is never mentioned in any list of disciples. Compare the lists in Table 4.1.

The writer leaves no personal insights in the gospel either. The name of Mark is not found anywhere in the narrative, although there is a curious verse about a naked young man who was following Jesus during his arrest. Could this be a reference to the author of Mark? No one knows.

> A certain young man was following him, wearing nothing but a linen cloth. They caught hold of him, but he left the linen cloth and ran off naked. (Mark 14:51 NRSV)

Who was Mark, and why do some scholars think that a person named Mark wrote this gospel? The earliest evidence of authorship comes from **Papias**, bishop of Hierapolis during the second century. According to **Eusebius**, who writes in the fourth century C.E., Papias knew John, presumably the author of the gospel of John, and **Polycarp**, an early Christian martyr. The following words were written by Eusebius, claiming to quote Papias.

> This also the elder [John] used to say. When Mark became Peter's interpreter, he wrote down accurately though by no means in order, as much as he remembered of the words

TABLE 4.1 Lists of Disciples/Apostles

Matthew 10:2–4	Mark 3:16–19	Luke 6:13–16	Acts 1:13
Simon Peter	Simon Peter	Simon Peter	Peter
Andrew	Andrew	Andrew	John
James Zebedee	James	James	James
John	John	John	Andrew
Philip	Philip	Philip	Philip
Bartholomew	Bartholomew	Bartholomew	Thomas
Thomas	Thomas	Thomas	Bartholomew
Matthew	Matthew	Matthew	Matthew
James Alphaeus	James	James	James
Thaddaeus	Thaddaeus	Simon, Zealot	Simon, Zealot
Simon, Canaanite	Simon, Canaanite	Judas of James	Judas of James
Judas Iscariot	Judas Iscariot	Judas Iscariot	

and deeds of the Lord; for he had neither heard the Lord nor been in his company, but subsequently joined Peter as I said. Now Peter did not intend to give complete exposition of the Lord's ministry but delivered his instructions to meet the needs of the moment. It follows, then, that Mark was guilty of no *blunder* he wrote, simply to the best of his recollections, an incomplete account. (Eusebius, *History,* 3. 39.15)

Both Eusebius and Papias acknowledged that popular opinion thought there was something wrong with Mark's story. What was Mark's *"blunder"?*

Even if we assume someone named Mark wrote the gospel, what else do we know about this person? There are several references to a John Mark and a Mark in the Acts of the Apostles and letters within the New Testament. How do we know if the Mark mentioned in these works is the same person Papias claims wrote the Gospel of Mark? The answer is obvious. How many Marks or Marys do you know? The same was true within the Roman Empire. Mark was a common name.

Many scholars attempt to re-create a personality profile of the person who wrote Mark by analyzing the references to Mark in the New Testament. According to Acts 12:12, John Mark was the son of a wealthy woman, Mary, who lived in Jerusalem. Christians gathered at their home. Paul, who will be introduced later, visited many countries telling people about his new found faith in the resurrected Jesus. Mark went with him on the first round of travel, but for some reason, Mark, who reportedly was the cousin of Barnabas (Col. 4: 10), left Paul in Perga in Pamphylia (Acts 13). Later when Paul and Barnabas planned another trip, they argued over whether or not Mark should be included.

> After some days Paul said to Barnabas, "Come, let us return and visit the believers in every city where we proclaimed the word of the Lord and see how they are doing." Barnabas wanted to take with them John called Mark. But Paul decided not to take with them one who had deserted them in Pamphylia and had not accompanied them in the work. This disagreement became so sharp that they parted company: Barnabas took Mark with him and sailed away to Cyprus. (Acts 15: 36–39 NRSV)

The name of Mark also is mentioned in 1 Peter, Colossians, Philemon, and 2 Timothy.

After studying the passages in the Bible that refer to someone named Mark, the student is no closer to discovering the identity of the writer of the Gospel of Mark. At best, the fanciful reconstruction of Mark 's life is only guesswork.

REASONS FOR CREATING MARK

If the writer's identity were known, perhaps students of the Bible could discover the exact reasons for writing the gospel. One reason for creating the gospel may be found in the social upheaval in which the book was written. Wars ravaged Palestine from 66 C.E. until the mid-seventies. Jerusalem as well as many other cities had been devastated by Titus, who was ordered by Vespasian to control the Jews. Earlier in the century, zealots, during a surprise attack, had killed many young recruits who were practicing war games in a Palestinian desert. Vespasian, who was in charge of the men, vowed to retaliate against the terrorists. When he was crowned Emperor in 69 C.E., he ordered the capture of Jerusalem. Both Jews and Christians found themselves without homes, occupations, and communities. It was during these times that the gospels were written.

Another reason for writing the gospel may have been to give people hope that a messiah would come. This messiah would not be a literal king but would have the power to rescue people from their present circumstances. Thus Mark may have written a gospel for the oppressed, the poor, or the outsider, who had little hope for reasonable success in their lifetimes.

Those who were oppressed may have identified with Jesus. The Marcan Jesus is characterized as a servant who suffers and is hanged on a cross designed for criminals. He is an innocent victim. People who read the gospel are encouraged to follow the pattern or the way of Jesus in their lives.

> For the Son of Man came not to be served but to serve, and to give his life as a ransom for many. (Mark 10:45 NRSV)

> If any want to become my followers, let them deny themselves and take up their cross and follow me. For those who want to save their life will lose it, and those who lose their life for my sake, and for the sake of the gospel, will save it. (Mark 8:35 NRSV)

Mark's Jesus is exploited by the government as well as by others. Shortly before his arrest, he prayed for a rescue from imminent death.

> "Abba," Father, for you all things are possible; remove this cup from me; yet not what I want, but you want. (Mark 14:36 NRSV)

Still other scholars attempt to divorce the Gospel of Mark from its war-torn historical situation and the people to whom it was written during the first century. Philip Carrington suggests that the book was a **lectionary**. The first ten chapters of Mark were used on special holy days throughout the year during worship services. Some hold to something called the Dictation Theory. They believe that the divine dictated the words of the gospel to Mark and that he wrote down the words exactly as he was told. They conclude that Mark needed no reason to write the gospel, because his pen was controlled by the hand of the divine.

DATING THE GOSPEL

While it is impossible to know the exact time the Gospel of Mark was created, scholars have determined that it must have been written during or after the wars of 66–73 C.E. They base their conclusions on verses that describe the destruction of the Temple in Je-

FIGURE 4.1   The Wailing Wall or Western Wall in Jerusalem. Photo by Marla J. Selvidge.

rusalem. Herod's Temple was under construction during Jesus' entire life. It was a massive structure, employing as many as 10,000 construction workers. The following words about the temple are written in a predictive or prophetic style, although they were probably composed after the demise of the Temple, around 70 C.E.

> As he came out of the temple, one of his disciples said to him, "Look, Teacher, what large stones and what large buildings!" Then Jesus asked him, "Do you see these great buildings? Not one stone will be left here upon another; all will be thrown down. (Mark 13:1–2 NRSV)

Josephus remembers the violent sight of the Temple being destroyed in his book *Wars of the Jews.*

> And now the Romans, judging that it was in vain to spare what was round about the holy house, burnt all those places, as also the remains of the cloisters and the gates....(Whiston 1972, 6:2, 582)

Today, the Dome of the Rock, a Muslim mosque, sets upon the very soil and foundation of this ancient Temple. Jews consider the foundation holy and have popularly named it "the Wailing Wall" or "the Western Wall."

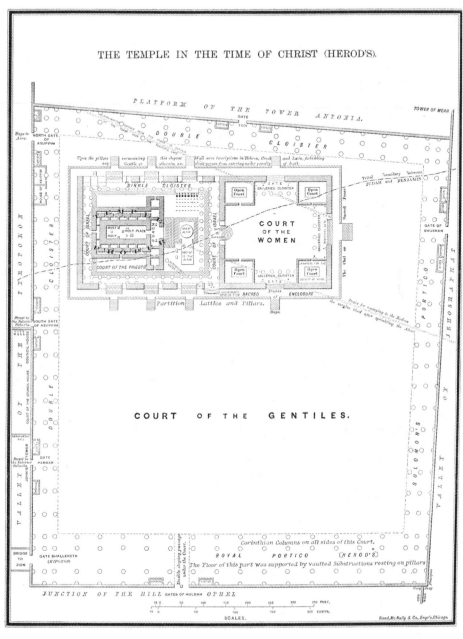

FIGURE 4.2 Plan of Herod's Temple in Jerusalem. From J.L. Hurlbut, *Manual of Biblical Geography*, Chicago: Rand McNally and Co., 1884.

CONTENT AND CHARACTERS

Reading the Gospel of Mark for the first time can be an exhilarating experience. Its fast-paced narration draws the reader into the action with Jesus, moving quickly from one location to another. There are many ways to summarize or study the contents of Mark. This section will concentrate on Mark's most important characters, themes, geography, and questions.

It is easy to outline the contents of Mark. The first part of the book deals with the activities of Jesus' public life or service, and the last part summarizes his arrest, death, and burial stories. The list that follows is a basic outline.

Outline of the Gospel of Mark

Introduction of Jesus	1:1–13
Jesus' Public Life in Galilee	1:14–9:50
Journey to Jerusalem	10
Arrest, Trial, Death	11–15
The Women at the Tomb	16:1–8
Later Appendix	16:9–20

Mark, unconcerned about the birth and early life of Jesus, differs from the gospels of Matthew and Luke. Yet it is helpful for the student to consider a few approximate dates in Jesus' life and the beginnings of early Christianity, before considering the contents of Mark.

The Time Frame of Jesus' Life and Death (Approximate Dates)

4 B.C.E.	Jesus is born, death of Herod the Great
4–39 C.E.	Herod Antipas becomes ruler of Galilee and Perea
4–6 C.E.	Herod Archelaus rules Judea, Samaria, and Idumea
26 C.E.	Pontius Pilate as Procurator of Judea
28–33?	Death of Jesus
50–60	Paul writes letters to churches
66–73	Jewish wars
70	Creation of Gospel of Mark
80–85	Creation of Gospels of Matthew and Luke
90s	Creation of Gospel of John

Characters

Many people who read the Gospel of Mark would not classify it as "literature." To them it is more; it is a holy writing. Yet the people who wrote the holy works employed standard writing practices. Those practices can be analyzed to determine the meanings within the gospel. To understand the dynamics of any work, the reader must scrutinize the characters, as the characters often lead the reader to the most important messages in the literature. This approach to studying the gospel employs literary criticism.

The Gospel of Mark has only a few named characters including Herod Antipas, Caiaphas, Mary of Magdala, Mary the Mother of Joseph and James, Simon of Cyrene, and a few more. There also are a host of unnamed characters that include the Twelve, a rich young man, unclean spirits, Peter's mother-in-law, the women at the tomb, and angels. The most important character is Jesus.

The Character: Jesus   Mark begins the gospel with the verse, "The beginning of the good news of Jesus Christ, the Son of God" (1:1 NRSV). Note that the word "Christ" is a **transliteration** and *not* a **translation** of the Greek word "christos." As we have noted earlier, "christos" means "anointed one" or "king." It is not Jesus' last name. It is a descriptive title. Mark is declaring that Jesus is king, and then the writer adds, "Son of God." The phrase "Son of God" may have been added later. The addition of "Son of God" defines and amplifies the content of what it means to be a king. The reader makes an association and concludes that Jesus, who is king, is really from God. The original writer of Mark may not have had this association in mind.

If we omit the phrase "Son of God," the gospel takes on a more political tone. A better translation might read, "The beginning of the good news of Jesus the King (or Messiah)." This translation fits better with the content of the gospel, because we will learn that Jesus was a rejected Messiah and that many did not understand what kind of kingdom he was offering to people.

Son of God   What is a Son of God? Throughout Middle Eastern history, there are many stories about gods who had relations with humans and then bore children. These unions produced superhumans. This phrase could identify Jesus as a "Divine Man," born of a union between human and divine, who has extraordinary powers and abilities. It certainly links him to divinity. It may also declare Jesus to be part of a priesthood. In Genesis 6:4, an odd phrase, "sons of God," is used.

> When people began to multiply on the face of the ground, and daughters were born to them, the sons of God saw that they were fair; and they took wives for themselves of all that they chose. (Gen. 6:1–2 NRSV)

No one really knows to whom this phrase refers, but many speculate that it was a synonym for people who officiated at religious services for the ancient Israelites. Perhaps the writer is signaling that the office Jesus will hold is highly religious in nature. Yet Mark or a later editor of Mark uses the singular Son of God. Could the phrase single out Jesus as the only legitimate offspring of "God"? The gospel also ends with the centurion crying out at the moment Jesus died, "Truly this man was God's Son" (15:39). These two instances at the beginning and end of the gospel frame the Marcan story of Jesus.

There are several other instances when Jesus is characterized as a "Son of God" in the Marcan story. A voice out of a cloud cries out, "This is my Son, the Beloved, listen to him" (9:7). Unclean spirits recognize Jesus as the son of God (3:11), Jesus refers to himself as "son" (13:32), and the high priest asks Jesus, "Are you the Messiah, the Son of the Blessed one?" (14:62).

Certainly Jesus performs extraordinary feats in the gospel that seem to support his status as Son of God. He heals a man with a withered hand (3:3); a man who could not hear or speak (7:31–37); a blind man (8:22–26); the daughter of the woman from Syrophenicia (7:24), and many more. He seems to be in control of nature as he feeds 4,000 and 5,000 people, respectively (8:1–9; 6:35–44), stops a storm in its tracks (4:35–41), walks on water (6:45–52), and raises a little girl from the dead (5:22–24). But he is not in control of everything. The Twelve do not follow his guidelines, and he cannot control the politicians and government officials who arrest and sentence him to death.

Rabbi   Jesus is portrayed as a teacher or rabbi. He had many followers, including the crowds, women, his mother and brothers, John the Baptist, Simon and Andrew, James and John, Simon's mother-in-law, a leper, tax collectors, "sinners," and many more. Mark suggests that Jesus had a dynamic personality, with an authoritative voice. People listened to him. There were so many people who followed him that he chose only the Twelve, who also were called the "apostles" (3:16). Notice that Mark uses *the Twelve* instead of *disciple* to refer to those who are chosen as personal students of Jesus. And while Jesus taught this select group, Mark also hints that many others listened to the discussions (4:1). The content of his message involved the kingdom of God, which he explained in parables. According to Mark, not everyone understood the parables. (Similar to when someone tells a joke today, some people understand the thrust of it and some do not (4:33).)

Jesus' message to the Twelve was personal discipline and an extremely austere lifestyle. Jesus gave the following orders to the Twelve as he sent them traveling two by two:

> He gave them authority over the unclean spirits. He ordered them to take nothing for their journey except a staff; no bread, no bag, no money in their belts, but to wear sandals and not to put on two tunics. (6:8–9)

Today we would call the Twelve "**sannyasins**," or holy people who are similar to the people who agreed to become disciples or students of an important philosopher in ancient times. Sannyasins are renouncers within Hinduism. They give up everything they own, including clothing, to search for the divine. The Twelve found the divine, but they also were told to cast out demons and heal the sick (6:13) as they journeyed from town to town.

Jesus' message to the religious bureaucratic elite within Judaism was freedom. He taught freedom from laws that inhibited people and freedom to follow a personal conscience (chapter 7). He encouraged people to take care of those who were less fortunate (8:41–42) and to appreciate equality between men and women (chapter 10). He loved children and taught respect of parents (10:13–19). He recognized that people depended on material things and demanded a renunciation of the good life (10:21–22). Power over others was never a goal (10:41–45). Self-denial was expected of every follower.

In his role as teacher, Jesus portrayed himself as a servant who suffered for those he loved. He declared for all to hear that he was not a user or manipulator of people. That service involved giving up his own desires, career ambitions, and life (10:45).

Son of Man: A Human Being   Another title or description of Jesus is "Son of Man." It seems logical that Jesus was a son of someone, although Mark does not discuss his father. The term *Son of Man* has many different meanings. It may be defined as a "human being" or a "member (son) of humanity." Mark may be stressing the human vulnerability and strength of Jesus.

Mark's portrait of Jesus is more human than any of the other gospels. Jesus is hungry and tired (4:38; 6:31). He shows love and remorse as well as agitated anger (10:14; 3:5). Jesus spits, sighs, and embraces the sick (7:33–34; 8:33; 9:36). Notice how often he touches other human beings. He seems to reach out to people.

Like any human being who senses imminent death, Jesus was afraid. Immediately prior to his arrest, he said, "I am deeply grieved, even to death; remain here, and keep awake" (14:34 NRSV). "And going a little farther, he threw himself on the ground and prayed that, if it were possible, the hour might pass from him." And when he was about to die, he cried and said, "My God, my God, why have you forsaken me?" (14:35 NRSV).

Son of Man: An Apocalyptic Messiah   The phrase "Son of Man" is also an apocalyptic title. The word "apocalyptic" describes a certain type of literature that is born out of frustration. People are oppressed (real or imagined) and create literature that portrays God rescuing them and destroying their enemies. Usually there is a fiery battle and the creation of a new life that vindicates those who are oppressed.

Long before Jesus was born, ancient Israelites and Jews believed a Messiah would come to rescue and protect them. This Messiah was called the Son of Man. The book of Daniel in the Old Testament/Hebrew Bible predicts the coming of a king whose reign would last forever.

> As I watched in the night visions, I saw one like a human being coming with the clouds of heaven. And he came to the Ancient One and was presented before him. To him was given dominion and glory and kingship, that all peoples, nations, and languages should serve him. His dominion is an everlasting dominion that shall not pass away, and his kingship is one that shall never be destroyed. (Daniel 7:13–14 NRSV)

This hope for an everlasting king who would rescue people was a popularly held dream.

The *Book of Enoch* preserves this myth or dream. *Enoch* was translated into many languages in the Middle East and was perhaps as popular in the first century C.E. as the *Star Wars* or *Star Trek* legends are today. Enoch was a character in the Old Testament/Hebrew Bible. Genesis says the following about him: "Enoch walked with God; then he was no more, because God took him" (Genesis 5:21 NRSV). The real question is, What happened to Enoch? The *Book of Enoch* attempts to answer this question. It says Enoch was taken to be with God in heaven, where he was shown all of the wonders of time and life. He also discovered a Son of Man was coming. The following excerpt is from one of his visions:

> And I asked the angel who went with me and showed me all the hidden things, concerning that Son of Man, who he was, and whence he was, (and) why he went with the Head of Days. And he answered and said unto me: This is the Son of Man who hath righteousness, With whom dwelleth righteousness, and who revealeth all the treasures of that which is hidden.… And this Son of Man whom thou has seen shall raise up the kings and the mighty from their seats, [And the strong from their thrones,] And shall loosen the reins of the strong, And break the teeth of the sinners. [And he shall put down the kings from their thrones and kingdoms]. (Charles 1982, 64)

Enoch was not the only literature that preserved the hope of a messiah or a god who would rescue people from abusive tyrants, governments, or organizations. The *Dead Sea Scrolls,* discovered in the desert in 1947, unearthed the archaeological and literary remains of a community who had separated themselves from the rest of the world in a desert retreat called Qumran. They believed a messiah would rescue them, that there would be a battle in the skies between the sons of darkness against the sons of light, and that the sons of light, with the help of God, would win.

The Zadokites (Essenes, Qumran) prepared for the day of victory by composing a legal code that would govern the entire world. They believed they would rule, with God, and waited patiently in the desert for history to reach its end or climax. Meanwhile, they polished their swords, copied books of the Hebrew traditions, and created books of their own that regulated their behavior.

Many people have compared the *Dead Sea Scrolls* to the New Testament. In the early stages of research, some thought the Teacher of Righteousness was Jesus, and thus, this community was Christian. Today most scholars agree that the Qumran community grew out of Judaism and was a reaction to the oppressive foreign governments dominating Jerusalem, plus the tendency under the Maccabees to shy away from ancient Jewish customs and practices.

There are many apocalyptic references to the Son of Man in Mark. Two follow:

> Then they will see 'the Son of Man coming in the clouds' with great power and glory. Then he will send out the angels, and gather his elect from the four winds, from the ends of the earth to the ends of heaven. (13:26–27 NRSV)

> Jesus said, "I am; and 'you will see the Son of Man seated at the right hand of the Power,' and 'coming with the clouds.' " (14:62 NRSV)

While Mark neglects to include a story about Jesus appearing after his death, the writer does include a compelling story about Jesus being changed or transformed into some type of divine essence. In the presence of Peter, James, and John, Jesus' clothing goes through a metamorphosis into a brilliant light. He informs them that the Son of Man will rise from the dead (9:2–10).

Then they asked him, "Why do the scribes say that Elijah must come first?" He said to them, "Elijah is indeed coming first to restore all things." (9:11–12 NRSV)

Elijah and Enoch were characters in the Old Testament who did not die a natural death. Elijah could be a **synonym** or another metaphor for the Son of Man.

The concept of a messiah appearing as the Son of Man would be particularly appealing to people who have recently experienced and survived the ravages of war. While the writer of Mark does not offer a Resurrection appearance story for the readers, there is hope that Jesus will return. This return is given a name, the **parousia**, or the "coming." This message of a hope for the return of Jesus is also inextricably interwoven into two other themes that will be considered shortly, the messianic secret and the geographical bias of Mark.

John the Baptist   John the Baptist is thought to have belonged to an ascetic community in the desert. Mark begins his story, "John the baptizer appeared in the wilderness...." (Mark 1:4). He came out of the desert wearing camel's hair and ate honey and bugs (locusts) (1:6). Scholars suggest that people followed John thinking that he was the messiah to come. He was very popular, and many compared Jesus to him. When Jesus asked Peter and the Twelve, "Who do people say that I am?" his disciples replied, "Some say that you are John the Baptist" (Mark 8:28).

FIGURE 4.3   John the Baptist painted by Hubert Van Eyck in 1432 in Saint Bavo's Cathedral in Ghent, Belgium. Photo by Marla J. Selvidge.

John the Baptist is a curious peripheral character who briefly enters the story in Mark. Evidence suggests that he was the founder and leader of a messianic movement whose headquarters could have originated in the desert east of Jerusalem. John was a lonely, odd preacher whose appearance shocked onlookers. People listened because he was different. He spoke with authority. His voice commanded attention. While Matthew and Luke broaden the picture of John's life by linking him to Jesus personally, Mark does not know these stories. According to Mark, those who listened to John were encouraged to look elsewhere for the coming messiah. His sermons pointed to Jesus. That person coming after him would be more powerful and would be linked to the Holy Spirit (1:8).

Jesus' itinerant ministry begins after John's arrest. Ironically, John's story parallels Jesus' life and death. John was arrested, imprisoned unfairly, and killed by the Roman establishment. People also hoped for his return and equated him with Elijah or a prophet. After his death, people continued to baptize and follow his ethical guidelines (2:18). We find remnants of his religious group throughout the Acts of the Apostles and the letters of Paul.

The Twelve   If we read the gospel of Mark with a sensitive eye, we find something startling. Although the Twelve are selected as personal assistants of Jesus, they never actually carry out his teachings. They do not risk their lives. They do not deny themselves, nor do they give up all of their possessions. They follow, but their journey does not take them down the same road walked by Jesus.

Mark includes only a summary statement about the activities of the Twelve. Having left home, they briefly engage in an itinerant healing campaign, which includes **anointing**, healing the sick, and casting out demons (6:13). They are featured in only one healing story where they fail to cure a boy possessed by a demonic spirit (9:18).

Many scholars today conclude that Mark is portraying the Twelve as failures. Who turned Jesus over to the authorities? Who abandoned Jesus at the moment of his arrest? "All of them deserted him and fled" (14:50 NRSV). Who stayed with Jesus until his last breath? Who understood the meaning of self-denial and service? Certainly it would appear that James and John are portrayed as being more interested in their own careers than in helping others when they discussed the bureaucracy in Jesus' future administration.

> James and John, the sons of Zebedee, came forward to him and said to him, "Teacher, we want you to do for us whatever we ask of you." And he said to them, "What is it you want me to do for you?" And they said to him, "Grant us to sit one at your right hand and one at your left, in your glory." (10:35 NRSV)

> When the ten heard this, they became angry with James and John. (10:41 NRSV)

The Twelve, who so quickly left their family business and responsibilities, appear to follow Jesus for all the wrong reasons. They continually fail. Peter complains about leaving too much behind (10:28) and is unable to accept Jesus' imminent death

(8:31). He alone recognizes Jesus' identity as the Messiah, but he also misinterprets the term. Jesus reprimands Peter by claiming that he thinks like men and not like God (8:33). In the end, Peter totally denies Jesus (14:71) by cursing him. The Twelve are cast as poor examples of leadership for the readers of Mark. They cannot follow Jesus completely.

The Women in Mark   This total abandonment of Jesus by the Twelve is placed next to stories about other people who do not abandon Jesus. Uppermost on the list of people who remain loyal to Jesus are the women, according to many scholars. Although women do not have large verbal roles in the narratives, they are always present in the crowds and on the sidelines; they are among the "little people." These characters are successful followers and may have been a source of inspiration for people during the troubled times of the first century.

Stories/Parables about Women

Simon's Mother-in-Law	1:31
The Hemorrhaging Woman	5:25–34
The Healing of a Daughter	5:24–34
The Syro-Phoenician Woman	7:24–30
Woman Who Marries Seven Brothers	12:18–24
Widow Who Gave All	12:38–44
A Remembered Woman	14:4–9
Persistent Women Followers	15:40–41
Fearful Women	16:8

What makes these women so successful in the narrative? The key is found in Jesus' mandate "to serve." People generally do not aspire to be servants. Western culture thinks of service in menial terms, and throughout history, society has often relegated women to occupations of service. Valerie Saiving summarizes the problem by assuming " service" to be the most appropriate role for women.

> A mother who rejoices in her maternal role ... knows the profound experience of self-transcending love. But she knows, too, that it is not the whole meaning of life.... The moments, hours, and days of self-giving must be balanced by moments, hours, and days of withdrawal into, and enrichment of, her individual selfhood if she is to remain a whole person. She learns, too, that woman can give too much of herself, so that nothing remains of her own uniqueness; she can become merely an emptiness, almost a zero, without value to herself, to her fellowmen, or, perhaps even to God. (Saiving 1960, 100–12)

But for the writer of Mark, service is at the center of what it means to follow Jesus (10:45). Explained another way, service defines following. Jesus teaches that it is the highest level anyone can achieve. Peter's mother-in-law serves after she is healed by Jesus (1:31). Women from Galilee follow and serve Jesus. They are present at his death and at his tomb (15:40–41). A destitute religious widow gives up her last penny to the temple. Jesus remembers no other like the woman who anointed him with expensive oil. He promised that all would remember her for her self-sacrificial giving (14:4–9).

The Hemorrhaging Woman takes the initiative to touch Jesus, and for her courage she is healed of a debilitating disease (5:24–34). According to Jewish law, women had to be cloistered or separated from the rest of the family during their menstrual periods. Leviticus 12–15 details many ancient Israelite laws governing a woman's biological processes. Leviticus reads,

> When a woman has a discharge of blood that is her regular discharge from her body, she shall be in her impurity for seven days, and whoever touches her shall be unclean until the evening. Everything upon which she lies during her impurity shall be unclean; everything also upon which she sits shall be unclean. Whoever touches her bed shall wash his clothes, and bathe in water, and be unclean until evening. (Lev. 15: 19–21 NRSV)

> If a woman conceives and bears a male child, she shall be ceremonially unclean seven days; as at the time of her menstruation, she shall be unclean.... Her time of blood purification shall be thirty-three days; she shall not touch any holy thing, or come into the sanctuary, until the days of her purification are completed. If she bears a female child, she shall be unclean two weeks, as in her menstruation; her time of blood purification shall be sixty-six days. (Lev. 12: 1–5 NRSV)

In a society that followed the laws of the ancient Torah, the Hemorrhaging Woman would be considered "unclean" during her entire illness. This attitude could potentially separate her from all normal daily functions with other people. The miracle story about her healing emphasizes her actions in achieving her own cure. She is a model for others who would seek healthy lives. She speaks the truth, and Jesus wishes her well, "Go in Peace."

In the midst of this story is another miracle called a **doublet**, which involves the healing of a little girl. There is some evidence to suggest that after the Jewish wars, female children were abandoned to die because there was not enough food for everyone. Mark makes a strong point about the importance of women in this story and in the story about the healing of the daughter of the Syro-Phoenician Woman (7:24–30). Mark thinks women's lives are important and worth preserving. They are models of living for the followers of Jesus. Women's assertiveness, endurance, persistence, and self-sacrificial lifestyles mimic the goals set by Jesus himself.

Unclean Spirits   Some people today claim they have witnessed demon possession and believe invisible demons inhabit the entire earth. The Gospel of Mark is full of invisible beings who understand the mission of Jesus and cause people all sorts of problems. While we use the English word "demon," the Gospel of Mark does not use that term, but prefers "unclean spirits." These spirits obey Jesus (1:26–27), cause illness (3:30), have names such as Legion (5:8), can control a human being (9:25; 7:25), and proclaim that Jesus is the Son of God (3:11). Who are the unclean spirits?

We know Mark places unclean spirits in the narrative in a way that enhances and attempts to prove the divine identity of Jesus. Jesus is in control of forces that are unseen to most. There are many levels of conflict in the Marcan Gospel, and this conflict between the unclean spirits and Jesus suggests that there is much that people do not experience or know. Jesus exercises complete control over this invisible existence.

THE SECRET MESSIAH

The Messianic Secret is the name of a literary theme created by the writer of Mark. In explaining this theme, the topic of political geography and the abrupt ending of Mark must be considered. Throughout Mark, as Jesus travels from one place to another, He often attempts to keep his abilities a secret. Some of the enigmatic and puzzling statements follow:

> After healing a leper Jesus said, "After sternly warning him he sent him away at once, saying to him, "See that you say nothing to anyone; but go, show yourself to the priest,…" (1:44 NRSV)

> In a mysterious parable Jesus talks about himself as a bridegroom. "The days will come when the bridegroom is taken away from them, and then they will fast on that day." (2:19 NRSV)

> In a story about escaping from the crowd in a boat after he had cured many people, he said this, "Whenever the unclean spirits saw him, they fell down before him and shouted, 'You are the Son of God!' But he sternly ordered them not to make him known." (3:11 NRSV)

> After raising the little girl, Mark writes, "He strictly ordered them that no one should know this, and told them to give her something to eat." (5:43 NRSV)

> After healing a man who could not hear or speak, Mark says, "Then Jesus ordered them to tell no one; but the more he ordered them, the more zealously they proclaimed it." (7:36 NRSV)

> Peter recognizes Jesus as the Messiah but cannot tell anyone about the discovery, "And he sternly ordered them not to tell anyone about him." (8:30 NRSV)

> Peter, James, and John have an experience of a transformed or changed Jesus. But again, they cannot share their information. "As they were coming down the mountain, he ordered them to tell no one about what they had seen, until after the Son of Man had risen from the dead." (9:9 NRSV)

> And finally, when Jesus is confronted by the religious authorities, he refuses to reveal his identity. "Neither will I tell you by what authority I am doing these things." (11:35 NRSV)

Why does Mark include so many instances where Jesus attempts to suppress a story about a miracle? At other times in the narrative, Jesus does nothing to prevent the person from relaying exciting news to friends and family. Why is the Marcan story so inconsistent? And why does Mark allow the Twelve to view special events while Jesus teaches them secret material?

There are many theories and analyses of this problem. The best solution suggests that when Jesus was alive neither his disciples nor the crowd understood that he was going to die. After his death they remembered his words and realized that the kind of Messiah they wanted was not the kind Jesus would be. Mark's literary theme leaves the reader perplexed. Perhaps the ancient original readers felt a real loss of their Messiah and wondered about their own personal future. Mark answers the question about their future and the future of the Messiah by pointing toward Galilee.

GEOGRAPHY AS POLITICAL STATEMENT

In future chapters of this text, we will learn that there were many different political groups within early Christianity. As it is today, it was difficult for people to agree on Christian theology and religious practices. Splinter groups within early Christianity emerged along ethnic, language, and geographical lines. This political stratification can be detected in the proposed geographical location of Jesus' promised return or appearance after his death. In the Gospel of Matthew, Jesus makes an appearance after his death in Galilee (28:16). Luke tells a different story. Jesus appears to two people outside of Jerusalem (24:13). And in Acts of the Apostles, Luke places Jesus in Jerusalem (1:11). The writer of the Gospel of John tells an extended story about Jesus' appearance in Jerusalem, which includes the touching by Thomas and Jesus walking through walls (20:24–29).

Casual readers of the gospels have a tendency to read all of these stories as one story with different variations. They do not detect geographical differences. Scholars suggest that there was tension and even hostility between the Christians in northern Palestine and those in the Jerusalem area. Jerusalem housed the traditional Christians who had long histories within Judaism, while Galilean converts may have had a Greek or other ethnic background. The return of Jesus to one place or the other would suggest that the person composing the gospel was writing for a particular audience or viewpoint. The Gospel of Mark emphasizes Galilee and does not include a resurrection appearance story. It closes with an empty tomb and an abrupt ending, which can be interpreted in a variety of ways.

Mark ends the gospel with the following phrase in 16:8: "and they said nothing to anyone, they were afraid for." It almost seems as if someone erased the end of the verse. The sentence ends with the preposition "gar," which is rarely used at the end of a sentence. It is a Greek grammatical error, much like in English, when we end a sentence with a preposition. As you will note from the footnotes in your Bible, there are several endings that were attached to Mark. People who studied the Gospel of Mark felt uncomfortable with the women finding out about the empty tomb and then keeping the information to themselves. The women must have told someone because we have their story in Mark. What is really happening in this narrative?

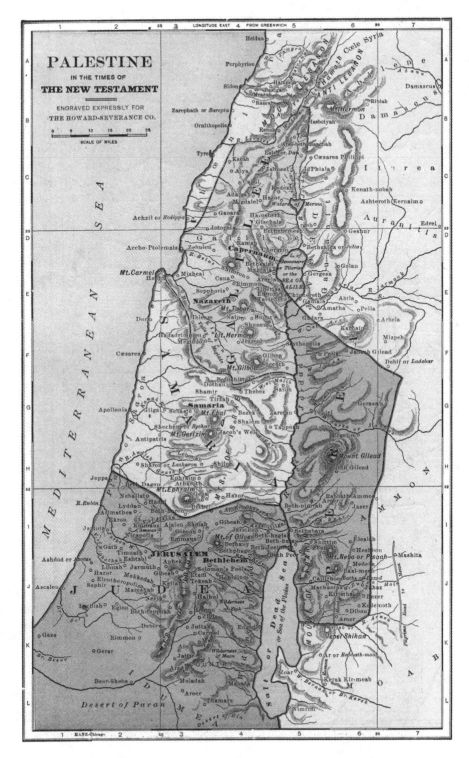

FIGURE 4.4 Map of Palestine in the Times of the New Testament. From Samuel Fallows, *The Popular and Critical Bible Encyclopedia*, Vol. 2 (Chicago: Howard Severance, 1903).

While it seems as though the words on the pages in the Gospel of Mark are now hard and fast and immovable, this was not the case throughout history. People felt free to add to Scripture which they thought needed changing. Someone probably edited Mark in 16:8 and added two other striking phrases at the end of Mark. Look at Mark 16:7, "But go, tell his disciples and Peter that he is going ahead of you to Galilee; there you will see him, just as he told you" (NRSV). If we study the other gospels, we will find that Peter is a very important character in stories about the resurrection of Jesus. Here in Mark, Peter is nowhere to be found. The phrase in Mark 16 recognizes the importance of Peter. Oddly, if we look earlier in 14:28, another verse mentions Galilee in a context with Peter, "But after I am raised up, I will go before you into Galilee" (NRSV).

What is Mark attempting to communicate about Peter, the fearful women, Galilee, and the abrupt ending? Scholars have suggested that all of these themes fit into the notion that Jesus would return as the Messiah. He has not returned in the Gospel of Mark, but there is a prediction that he will appear to the people in Galilee, not Jerusalem. An early editor probably added the phrases about Peter because he was well known and important in early Christianity. The scribe may have thought he was correcting Mark. In any case, the first readers of Mark were given hope for the future. The appearance of Jesus was coming soon! He was coming back to lead the little people, the crowd, the dispossessed, the alienated, sick, poor, and lonely. He was coming back to Galilee, not to the expected place, holy Jerusalem.

FIGURE 4.5   Sea of Galilee. Photo by Marla J. Selvidge.

Summary of the Gospel of Mark   Mark wrote a gospel for people who had lost their leader, Jesus, about the time of the Jewish rebellion. He was not the kind of messiah for which they had hoped. The stories found in Mark portray a people who were dispossessed and searching for Jesus to return. His human portrait of Jesus is supplemented by stories about people who demonstrate what it means to become a follower of Jesus. Mark knows only of Jesus' public ministry and death. His genealogy includes only a mother. There are no official Resurrection appearance stories, but Mark leaves the readers with hope that Jesus will return to Galilee.

Mark's gospel has always been questioned because of its omissions of the birth of Jesus, the father of Jesus, the sermons of Jesus, and the Resurrection of Jesus. Only recently has it become an important gospel to study.

While there are many possibilities about the identity of the Mark who wrote the gospel, his or her name remains elusive. Its date of creation is somewhere between 66–73 C.E. It may have been written to preserve traditions about Jesus which could have been lost because of the wars. It offers hope to its readers that the Messiah will soon appear. Some suggest that it was a lectionary, while others want to place its origins in the hands of a god.

Mark's gospel is easily outlined into (1) the career of Jesus and (2) the death of Jesus. The writer includes numerous unnamed characters whom scholars have termed "the little people." These people play a vital part in unfolding the tragic story of Jesus.

Jesus is viewed from several viewpoints, which include Christ, the Son of God, the Rabbi, and the Son of Man. Other important characters include John the Baptist, the faithful women followers, the Twelve, and unclean spirits.

The writer of Mark betrays several biases in the quest to tell the story of Jesus. There is an uncertainty about the identity of Jesus; thus Mark employs the "messianic secret" motif. It appears that Mark is decidedly in favor of a Galilean home and a return for Jesus, which suggests that readers are from northern Palestine or that they are not Jews from Jerusalem.

5

A Traditional Community Facing Change

The Gospel of Matthew

Go therefore and make disciples of all nations, baptizing them in the
name of the Father and of the Son and of the Holy Spirit, and teaching
them to obey everything that I have commanded you. And remember,
I am with you always, to the end of the age.

—Mt. 28: 19–20 NRSV

Go nowhere among the Gentiles, and enter no town of the Samaritans,
but go rather to the lost sheep of the house of Israel.

—Mt. 10: 5–6 NRSV

INTRODUCTION

Matthew wrote to people who were in transition taking readers beyond the public career
of Jesus. We learn about Jesus' Jewish heritage, his birth to an unmarried woman, his
sermons, and his return from the dead. The writer argues that Jesus' life and work were
not accidents in history. He is a continuation or fulfillment of dreams from a cherished
Jewish past.

But the past Matthew remembers does not focus on historical events or traditional interpretations of the Hebrew Bible. The writer's goal is to point to a future that embraces a different kind of religion. This newer religion is open to people of all races, both

FIGURE 5.1 Icon of Matthew from the
Book of Kells. Photo by Marla J. Selvidge.

sexes, and many ethnic and socioeconomic backgrounds. Its view is global, with an
emphasis on authentic religion and peaceful community relationships. For Matthew,
there is something very real and comforting about the remarkable promise that Jesus
would never leave them.

Matthew enlarges the story of Mark to explain the heritage and vocation of Jesus
and his followers. The two quotations at the beginning of this chapter illustrate the tension that pervades the book. While the writer seeks to reach the world with the messages
of Jesus, there are many, many statements that could be considered ethnocentric. For instance, while criticizing inauthentic religion, Jesus points to the Pharisees.

> And whenever you fast, do not look dismal, like the hypocrites, for they disfigure their
> faces so as to show others that they are fasting. Truly I tell you, they have received their
> reward. (Mt. 6:16)

For another example, a woman from Canaan who is a non-Jew pleads with Jesus to
heal her daughter. His reply to her is, "I was sent to the lost sheep of the house of Israel" (Mt. 15:24).

When this gospel was created, the writer/editor stood at the gateway to a very different religious experience. The immediate community understood the ancient traditions of the Israelites and Jews, but it was evolving into something different. The writer

of Matthew seeks to open people's minds to the possibility of an inclusive and ethnically diverse community. At the same time, the writer preserves stories that seem to suggest that early followers of Jesus had difficulty integrating new ideas with the old. The writer loves ancient Jewish traditions, but they must be reinterpreted and reapplied. If they are left in their ancient time frame, they can become devices that limit, surround, and oppress people.

Matthew probably used Mark as a source and therefore should be placed second or third in the gospel sequence within the Bible. No one knows the exact reason the Gospel of Matthew is placed first in the New Testament. It may be its size, or that it is so closely linked with Judaism. Early Christians may have used this book more often because it contains additional sermonic material and details about the life of Jesus.

Matthew's Major Additions to Mark

Tradition	Chapter
Genealogy	1
Birth of Jesus	1
Visit of the Magi	2
Escape to Egypt	2
Massacre of Children	2
Death of Herod	2
Sermon on the Mount	5–7
Parable of the Wedding Banquet	22
Criticism of Scribes and Pharisees	23
Parable of the Ten Bridesmaids	25
Parable of Talents	25
Suicide of Judas	27
Resurrection Appearance of Jesus	28

LOCATION, AUDIENCE, DATE, AND AUTHORSHIP

Who received the first copy of this gospel? Various places throughout the Roman Empire have been suggested, including **Antioch in Syria** and Caesarea Maritima. Traditions handed down from Papias, who lived during the second century C.E., seem to suggest that the original work may have been written in Hebrew or Aramaic. No evidence has been produced to verify his conclusion.

Who wrote the Gospel of Matthew? Some time in history the title of Matthew was given to this gospel, but no one knows if a person by the name of **Matthew** created it. Matthew 9:9 mentions a tax collector.

> As Jesus was walking along, he saw a man called Matthew sitting at the tax booth; and he said to him, "Follow me." And he got up and followed him. (NRSV)

Mark's version names the character **Levi**.

> As he was walking along, he saw Levi, son of Alphaeus, sitting at the tax booth, and he said to him, "Follow me." And he got up and followed him. (Mark 2:14, NRSV)

Could these quotations refer to the writer? If we consult the lists of the disciples of Jesus found in the gospels and Acts, the name of Matthew in one form or another is listed, but Levi is not (see Lists of Disciples, Table 4:1). The aforementioned verse could refer to a disciple who wrote a gospel, but the Gospel of Matthew could not have been written by someone who knew Jesus personally. Why would an eyewitness need to use someone else's work in order to write the story of Jesus? Most people conclude that the Gospel of Matthew was written in Greek by someone who lived at least ten or fifteen years after the writing of the Gospel of Mark. They date it to about 85 C.E. because of references to the fall of Jerusalem (Mt. 24), which suggests that it was written after 70 C.E.

Why Did Matthew Write Another Gospel?

No one knows if a male or female wrote the Gospel of Matthew. We do know that the author studied the Gospel of Mark, the Septuagint, or the LXX of the Hebrew Bible and was familiar with the social and religious problems within the Christian community. Some have suggested that the author was a scribe because the Gospel of Matthew is so well organized. As will be discussed shortly, it is organized into five different sections that may have been used as a teaching tool for new converts entering the early Christian community. See Table 5.1.

Matthew portrays Jesus as the culmination of Jewish religious writings, which date back to the time of the Israelites. Pharisees, Sadducees, and scribes are represented as failing in their tasks to help people live out their lives in an authentic, meaningful, religious way. Matthew attempts to set a new standard of ethical conduct and community living based on additional traditions (stories) of Jesus. Jesus has returned from the grave, in spite of all the rumors to the contrary, and has given promises and a message that can include and propel the Matthean readers out among the peoples of the earth. Implicit in this version of the Jesus story is the correcting of Mark's point of view.

SPECIAL LITERARY FEATURES

The gospel can be outlined in many ways. The following schematic is based on recurring transition verses that appear at the end of the five sections within Matthew. Many would suggest that these sections contained in Matthew mirror the five books of the

TABLE 5.1
"[A]nd when Jesus had finished saying these things...."

Chapter		General Summary of Contents	Transition Verse
1–2		Introduction	
3–7	Book 1	John the Baptist and the Sermon on the Mount	7:28
8–10	Book 2	Miracles, The Mission of the Twelve, Discipleship	11:1
11–13	Book 3	John the Baptist, Sabbath Lesson, Parables, and Signs	13:53
14–18	Book 4	John the Baptist, Miracles, Parables, Criticism of Pharisees and Sadducees, Message of Self-Denial, The Transfiguration	19:1
19–25	Book 5	Sermonic Material: Prophecy of Jesus' Death, Miracles, Jesus Enters Jerusalem, Parables, Tax Questions, Criticism of Scribes and Pharisees, Prediction of Destruction of Jerusalem	26:1
26–28		Parables: Jesus Anointed, Jesus Betrayed and Arrested, The Last Meal, Peter Denies Jesus, Judas Commits Suicide, Jesus Is Tried and Killed and Buried, Jesus Is Raised from the Dead, Jesus Returns to the Eleven	

Old Testament, or the Torah. These teaching sections, theoretically, held as much authority for Christians as the Torah did for Jews.

Another popular outline of Matthew is based on the "fulfillment" phrases that are positioned in at least nine different places throughout the gospel. At the end of each section, the writer claims that prophecies have been realized in the life of Jesus.

Matthew consulted and copied from a wide range of sources in the creation of the gospel. Over 90 percent of Mark is used as a basis to which is added sayings from "Q," quotations from the Greek translation of the Hebrew Bible (LXX), and another source that has not been identified. Most scholars call this unknown source Matthew's own material, or "M."

Throughout the gospel, Matthew quotes or alludes to the Old Testament/Hebrew Bible, ignoring the original meaning and context of these verses in favor of a more relevant or contemporary interpretation and application. The writer argues that verses found in these ancient literatures are completed or find their rightful place in history (or are "fulfilled") in the times and life of Jesus. The box on page 90 identifies some of Matthew's quotations from the Hebrew Scriptures. Matthew quotes and also alludes to hundreds of passages in the Old Testament. Some of the stories in Matthew may even mimic or model ancient Israelite traditions.

SAMPLING OF QUOTATIONS

Matthew	Old Testament/Hebrew Bible/LXX
4:7 Jesus said to him, "Again it is written, 'Do not put the Lord your God to the test.' "	Deut 6:16 Do not put the Lord your God to the test as you tested him at Massah.
8:17 This was to fulfill what had been spoken through the prophet Isaiah, "He took our infirmities and bore our diseases."	Isa. 53:4 Surely he has borne our infirmities and carried our diseases; yet we accounted him stricken, struck down by God, and afflicted.
12:7 But if you had known what this means, 'I desire mercy and not sacrifice,' you would not have condemned the guiltless.	Hos. 6:6 For I desire steadfast love and not sacrifice, the knowledge of God rather than burnt offerings.
21:9 The crowds that went ahead of him and that followed were shouting, "Hosanna to the Son of David! Blessed is the one who comes in the name of the Lord! Hosanna in the highest heaven!"	Ps. 118:26 Blessed is the one who comes in the name of the Lord. We bless you from the house of the Lord.
27:46 And about three o'clock Jesus cried with a loud voice, "Eli, Eli, lema sabachthani?" that is, "My God, my God, why have you forsaken me?"	Ps. 22:1 My God, my God, why have you forsaken me? Why are you so far from helping me, from the words of my groaning?

While Matthew uses Mark as a source, the writer edits the Marcan material to fit into personal goals. Sometimes miracle stories and discourses are abbreviated; other times they are enlarged or amplified. For example, Mark has only two verses that pronounce woes (criticisms) or indictments of the Pharisees (Mk. 6:7–11; Mt. 10:1–42). Matthew expands those verses into an entire chapter. The story of John the Baptist also takes a different turn in Matthew. Consider the following story about John's attack of the religious elites of Jerusalem.

The Baptism of John

Mark 1:7–8

He proclaimed, "The one who is more powerful than I is coming after me; I am not worthy to stoop down and untie the thong of his sandal. I have baptized you with water; but he will baptize you with the Holy Spirit."

Matthew 3:7–12

But when he saw many Pharisees and Sadducees coming for baptism, he said to them, "You brood of vipers! Who warned you to flee from the wrath to come? Bear fruit worthy of repentance. Do not presume to say to yourselves, 'We have Abraham as our ancestor'; for I tell you, God is able from these stones to raise up children to Abraham. Even now the ax is lying at the root of the trees; every tree therefore that does not bear good fruit is cut down and thrown into the fire. "I baptize you with water for repentance, but one who is more powerful than I is coming after me; I am not worthy to carry his sandals. He will baptize you with the Holy Spirit and fire. His winnowing fork is in his hand, and he will clear his threshing floor and will gather his wheat into the granary; but the chaff he will burn with unquenchable fire." (NRSV)

Matthew often abbreviates Mark with the express purpose of heightening the supernormal or divine character of Jesus. This often results in the omission of details about minor characters in Mark who display extraordinary powers or talents. In the story of the Hemorrhaging Woman, for example, Matthew omits all of the details of her struggle with the gynecological disease, as well as her assertive touch of Jesus which brings her health. In Mark, Jesus recognizes her health, but in Matthew, Jesus pronounces or heals her himself (Mk. 5:24–34; Mt. 9:18–26). The box below surveys some of Matthew's abbreviations of Mark's work.

MATTHEW ABBREVIATES MARK

Mark	Matthew
1:13 He was in the wilderness forty days, tempted by Satan; and was with wild beasts; and the angels waited on him.	4:2 He fasted forty days and forty nights, afterward he was famished.
1:29 As soon as they left the synagogue they entered the house of Simon and Andrew, with James and John.	8:14 When Jesus entered Peter's house,...
3:7–12 Jesus departed with his disciples to the sea, and a great multitude from Galilee followed him; hearing all that they came to him in great numbers from Judea, Jerusalem, Idumea, beyond the Jordan, and the region around Tyre and Sidon. He told his disciples to have a boat ready for him because of the crowd, so that they would not crush him. Whenever the unclean spirits saw him, they fell down before him and shouted, "You are the Son of God!" But he sternly ordered them not to make him known.	12:15–16 When Jesus became of this, he departed. Many crowds followed him, and he cured all of them, and he ordered them not to make him known.

The human or vulnerable side of Jesus is not important to Matthew. The phrases describing Jesus' faults or emotions seem to be offensive because they portray Jesus as being one who has human failings and negative emotions. Consider the following omissions by Matthew.

Matthew Ignores the Vulnerable Jesus

Mark 3:5 (Mt. 12:13)
"He looked around at them with anger;
he was grieved at their hardness of heart...."

Mark 8:12 (Mt. 16:4)
"And he sighed deeply in his spirit and said...."

Mark 10:14 (Mt. 19:14)
"He was indignant and said to them...."

Mark 10:21 (Mt. 19:21)
"Jesus, looking at him, loved him and said,..." (NRSV)

In summary, Matthew relies heavily on the Gospel of Mark and the Old Testament/Hebrew Bible in formulating a story about Jesus. Both sources in various ways are manipulated into portraying Jesus as the divine prophesied Messiah who has supernatural powers over disease and even ancient divine law.

CHARACTERS

Matthew adds very few new characters to the gospel story featuring Jesus. Some of the additions include Joseph, the Magi, and the mother of James and John, with added twists to the story of the Twelve and Peter.

The Character: Jesus

Matthew's view of Jesus is diverse and multifaceted. Drawing on many of the stories from Mark, Matthew affirms that Jesus is the Son of Man, the Son of God, and a healer. One of the most important characterizations of Jesus comes from the lips of Peter. Jesus asked his disciples,

> "Who do people say that the Son of Man is?" And they said, "Some say John the Baptist, but others Elijah, and still others Jeremiah or one of the prophets." He said to them, "But who do you say that I am?" Simon Peter answered, "You are the Messiah, the Son of the living God." (Mt. 16:13–16 NRSV)

To Mark's recognition of Messiah, Matthew adds the profound insight that Jesus is "living" and is "from God." In Mark's version, Peter could have been hinting that Jesus was thought of as a military king, such as the Emperor of Rome. There is no mistaking Jesus' identity in Matthew. Jesus is from God, and although Matthew's story ends with the death of Jesus, there is a promise that the Messiah will continue to live on. People do not have to wonder about whether Jesus will return or not; he did return. He is present in their lives now and into the future.

FIGURE 5.2 "The Pantocratore" (Jesus as King). Christ at Monreale in Palermo, Sicily. Photo by Marla J. Selvidge.

Messiah or King The Gospel of Matthew begins with an atypical genealogy that refuses to continue the androcentic emphasis found in similiar family lists in the Old Testament. Jesus' ancestry is traced back to David, one of the greatest but most human and vulnerable Israelite kings, and then secondarily to Abraham (1:1). Some conclude that David's reign was the most significant of all Israelite kings, because it was under his rule that Israel became a solid, united state, with its capitol in Jerusalem. Jewish hopes for a future free of Roman domination lay in the traditions about a Davidic Messiah.

The New Moses (Teacher) Jesus is presented as an authoritative and a knowledgeable teacher using a commanding style of speech. Throughout the Sermon on the Mount (Mt. 5–7), Jesus may be contradicting laws and lessons learned from the Hebrew Bible by reinterpreting them for his audience. Consider the following verses in Matthew:

5:17 Do not think that I have to abolish the law or the prophets; I have come not to abolish but to fulfill.

5:21–22 You have heard that it was said to those of ancient times, ... But I say to you....

5:27 [Y]ou have heard that it was said, ... But I say to you....

5:31 It was also said, ... But I say...

5:33 Again, you have heard that it was said to those of ancient times, ... But I say to you,...

continued

5:38, 43 You have heard that it was said, ... But I say to you, ...

6:5 And whenever you pray, do not be like the hypocrites....

6:1 Beware of practicing your piety before others in order to be seen by them; for there is no reward in heaven.

6:16 And whenever you fast, do not look dismal, like the hypocrites....

Jesus teaches a new standard of living that goes beyond following rigid and legalistic rules. His emphasis is authentic living for the individual. No longer should religion be an external standard by which people judge themselves. Merely going through the rituals of fasting or praying (the motions of religion) is not enough to satisfy Jesus' new standards. Individuals should make decisions based on their own consciences. People should recognize that the ancient Israelite-Jewish purity system had nothing to do with the integrity or worth of a person. The Matthean Jesus boldly asserts, "Listen and understand: it is not what goes into the mouth that defiles a person, but it is what comes out of the mouth that defiles" (Mt. 15:10 NRSV).

Son of God   Jesus is a product of a union with the divine. According to Matthew, Mary was impregnated by the Holy Spirit. Jesus performs miracles of healing, and, most especially in Matthew, Jesus is portrayed as being in control of nature. In two important miracles, Jesus walks on water and calms a threatening storm (Mt. 14:2). He also destroys a fig tree (16:18ff) and finds a coin in a fish (17:24–27). As in Mark, he has the supernatural ability to cure all types of diseases, and more.

Most importantly in Matthew, Jesus is raised from the dead after being crucified. During the crucifixion, the earth shook, rocks split, tombs were opened, saints were raised from the dead, and darkness "covered the earth" (Mt. 27:45ff). The resurrection is authenticated by a conversation Jesus had with Mary Magdalene, the other Mary, and later, the Eleven (Mt. 28).

Unlike other gospel narratives, the writer of Matthew thinks rumors about someone stealing the body of Jesus from the grave should be refuted.

While they were going, some of the guards went into the city and told the chief priests everything that had happened. After the priests had assembled with the elders, they devised a plan to give a large sum of money to the soldiers, telling them, "You must say, 'His disciples came by night and stole him away while we were asleep.' If this comes to the governor's ears, we will satisfy him and keep you out of trouble." So they took the money and did as they were directed. And this story is still told among the Jews to this day. (Mt. 28:11–15 NRSV)

The Twelve

For the writer of Mark, the Twelve are less than successful. Matthew does not totally agree with those traditions. In several stories, Matthew omits negative references about the Twelve as the following box illustrates.

MATTHEW AND THE TWELVE

Mark

4:13 And he said to them, "Do you not understand this parable? Then how will you understand all the parables?"

6:51f For they did not understand about the loaves, but their hearts were hardened.

9:6 (Peter) He did not know what to say, for they were terrified.

9:9 He ordered them to tell no one about what they had seen, until after the Son of Man had risen from the dead. So they kept the matter to themselves, questioning what this rising from the dead could mean.

Matthew

13:16f But blessed are your eyes, for they see, and your ears, for they hear. Truly I tell you, many prophets and righteous people longed to see what you see, but did not see it, and to hear what you hear, but did not hear it. ***Omits Ignorance***

14:32f Not found in Matthew. ***Omits a bad attitude.***

17:4f Then Peter said to Jesus, "Lord, it is good to be here; if you wish, I will make three dwellings here, one for you, one for Moses, and one for Elijah. ***Omits fear.***

17:9 Matthew ***omits their ignorance.***

Matthew also omits fear (Mk. 9:32, Mt. 17:23) and arguing (Mk. 9:34; Mt. 18:1) among the Twelve.

The Twelve are sent on an itinerate journey, but Matthew's Jesus bids the Twelve to "proclaim the good news" (Mt. 10:7), whereas Mark says that they were "given authority over unclean spirits" (Mk. 6:7). Thus Mark claims they had cast out demons and healed the sick (6:12), while Matthew omits that tradition in favor of extended teaching sessions with the Twelve on topics that include predictions of violence in their lives and family disruption (Mt. 9:16–42).

FIGURE 5.3 Icon of the Twelve from an illuminated manuscript. Photo by Marla J. Selvidge.

The Character: Peter

> And I tell you, you are Peter, and on this rock I will build my church, and the gates of Hades will not prevail against it. I will give you the keys of the kingdom of heaven. ... (Mt. 16:18–19 NRSV)

Peter (Simon), a bittersweet character, was one of the Twelve. If Matthew had not revealed that Peter made his living through fishing (4:18), one could have concluded that he was in public relations (18:21; 26:40). Whenever Jesus speaks to the Twelve, Peter's name seems to appear. Peter does not understand parables (15:15), yet recognizes that Jesus is from the living God (16:16). He walks on water with the help of Jesus, is given the keys to the Kingdom of God, but denies Jesus three times and nearly drowns (14:28). He is the one who complains that, "We have left everything and followed you" (19:27) and wonders when and how often one should forgive (18:21). Matthew says that after Jesus was arrested, Peter followed at a distance (26:58). Peter is privileged to see Jesus transfigured with James but, as in the Gospel of Mark, not included in the stories of Jesus' death and resurrection. In summary, the character of Peter is stronger in Matthew because of the prediction of building the church upon the rock, but Peter's honor is not completely vindicated. His close relationship with Jesus does not hinder his criticism and betrayal of him.

The Female Characters

Matthew understands the Jewish exclusive and restrictive heritage which prohibited women from becoming voting members of a local Jewish synagogue. Yet he ignores Jewish prohibitions in favor of a more egalitarian point of view. Within Judaism, women could not be circumcised. Moreover, their biology prevented them from participating in most cultic festivities. These traditions inform the developing Matthean community, but they do not restrain or hinder it. As Matthew tells the story of Jesus, women are not neglected. Rather, they are strategically included within Marcan stories that featured only men. For example, women characters are included in the genealogy, as well as in the story of feeding the 4,000 and the 5,000 (Mt. 14:21; 15:38). In addition, a mother is featured in the dialogue about the quest for power in Jesus' future administration by the sons of Zebedee (Mt. 20:20).

Women in the Genealogy   Unlike the Gospel of Mark, women characters in Matthew are not an alternative to soured leadership. They are and have been an integral part of the history of Israel and life of Jesus. Unfamiliar women of foreign extraction serve as foundational models of the past and future.

The first example of Matthew's inclusion of women in the narrative is unexpectedly found within the genealogy. These characters mirror Matthew's own philosophy about the ideals of **pluralism** within an early Christian Community.

> An account of the genealogy of Jesus the Messiah, the son of David, the son of Abraham. Abraham was the father of Isaac, and Isaac the father of Jacob, and Jacob the father

of Judah and his brothers, and Judah the father of Perez and Zerah by ***Tamar,*** and Perez the father of Hezron, and Herzon the father of Aram, and Aram the father of Aminadab, and Aminadab the father of Nahshon, and Nahshon the father of Salmon, and Salmon the father of Boaz by ***Rahab,*** and Boaz the father of Obed by ***Ruth,*** and Obed the father of Jesse, and Jesse the father of King David.

And David was the father of Solomon by the *wife of Uriah [**Bathsheba**],* and Solomon the father of Rehoboam, and Rehoboam the father of Abijah, and Abijah the father of Asaph, and Asaph the father of Jehoshaphat, and Jehoshaphat the father of Joram, and Joram the father of Uzziah, and Uzziah the father of Jotham, and Jotham the father of Ahaz, and Ahaz the father of Hezekiah, and Hezekiah the father of Manasseh, and Manasseh the father of Amos, and Amos the father of Josiah, and Josiah the father of Jechoniah and his brothers, at the time of the deportation to Babylon. (Mt. 1:1–11 NRSV)

Tamar, Rahab, Ruth, and Bathsheba are not typical Jewish women who live their lives according to the Torah. Yet these women are responsible for producing Jesus. Matthew includes their names because they fit into the nontraditional and perhaps disreputable family pattern of Jesus' birth, life, and death.

Ruth, a **Moabite** (a non-Jew) was a single woman who, after the death of her husband, chose to live in a foreign land with her Israelite mother-in-law Naomi. Eventually she managed to attract Boaz, a wealthy Israelite, to be her husband. (See the Book of Ruth.) Rahab was a Canaanite who lived in the city walls of Jericho. She helped two spies aligned with the Israelites who were waiting in the desert (Josh. 2:1; 6:17). Bathsheba, probably a Hittite, was David's lover and then wife. She eventually bore Solomon, who became the next king of Israel. David won her through planning the assassination of her husband (2 Sam. 11:2–5; 12:24; 1 Kings 1:1–2:25). Several Tamars are mentioned in the Old Testament. In Genesis, Tamar tricks her father-in-law into sleeping with her. She gives birth to children who were illegally denied to her (Gen. 38:6–30). (This probably is the story to which the author was referring, because her ancestors appear to be in the line of David.) In 2 Samuel, Tamar is the daughter of David. Amnon, her brother, rapes her. For this deed, Absalom murders him (2 Sam. 13:1–32). (See also, Ruth 4:12.)

Matthew's inclusion of these women in the genealogy raises scores of questions. But the basis for all of these debates rests in the ideals of a community described in the opening sentences of Matthew's story. While Jesus is rooted in the best of ancient Hebrew traditions, Matthew reminds everyone that Jesus could never have been born without the help of these unusual women. Their presence signals the honest declaration that the Matthean community is open to all people no matter what their race, ethnicity, religious heritage, or sex.

JESUS AND WOMEN

Matthew cautiously presents women not only in intimate family relationships but also with Jesus. While appreciating the ancient Hebrew past, Jesus is not afraid to break Jewish social laws. Neither is he afraid to be alone with unfamiliar women. Many of the women Jesus meets need help. He is alone with Peter's Mother-in-Law (Mt. 8:14–15), the ruler's daughter (Mt. 9:25), and the Canaanite woman (Mt. 15:27–28). No intimate friends are integrated into the dialogue that Jesus has with the Hemorrhaging Woman (Mt. 9:20–22). Jesus chooses to "touch" (Mt. 8:15), "grasp" (Mt. 9:25), "converse with" (Mt. 9:22), and "heal" women (Mt. 8:16; 9:21, 25–26). Matthew preserves only one story in which Jesus initially denies help to a woman, Mark's story about the Syro-Phoenician mother.

The New Family: Mary and Joseph   Matthew affirms the traditional legal family unit of man and woman but also preserves traditions that redefine family living and structure. Matthew includes a genealogy (Mt. 1:1–16), an infancy story (Mt. 1:16–2), and changes the story about the brothers and sisters of Jesus found in Mark so that it includes a father and disciples (Mt. 12:46–50; Mark 3:31–35). All of these reflect a more inclusive approach to family roles and living. Matthew prevents no one from becoming a member of the new community.

Although Joseph assumes a father's role in the escape story about Jesus, Matthew highlights Mary in both the genealogy and the flight from Herod. The genealogy says that Joseph was "the husband of Mary" (Mt. 1:16). The great Israelite line ends with Mary. Joseph's lineage is not important. His heritage is grounded in Mary's line. This genealogical statement is highly unusual for a patriarchal Jewish religion that permitted only the man to acquire a spouse. In the narrative, Matthew portrays Joseph as Mary's husband before Joseph married her (Mt. 1:24, 25).

Although Joseph is mentioned six times in the birth narrative, the mother of Jesus—Mary—is mentioned seven times (Mt. 1:18, 20; 2:11, 13, 14, 20, 21). She is an essential character. Similar to Joseph, she received a message from the angel. Together, they leave Bethlehem (Mt. 1:12).

Matthew wants the readers to understand that Jesus had both a father and a mother. In Mark's story, people begin to wonder about the miraculous powers of Jesus. They begin to discuss his background. Mark narrates a story about only one parent. Matthew traces Jesus' lineage to both a woman and a man.

Mark 6:3

Is not this the carpenter, the son of Mary and brother of . . . ?

Matthew 13:55

Is not this the carpenter's son? Is not his mother called Mary? And are not his brothers James and Joseph and Simon and Judas? (NRSV)

Matthew has set the tone for the gospel by telling a story about a person who has an ancient historical heritage that includes a diversity of people. Jesus' present and future will be like his past. He will welcome all into the new community.

A Loving Father   Matthew uses the term *father* over fifty-nine times in many different ways. It is clear that Jesus understands that God is a father to him. Moments before his death, he prayed, "My Father, if it is possible, let this cup pass from me…" (26:39). He taught his disciples that they should pray, "Our Father in heaven,… (6:9), yet praying is not something one should do to gain public acclaim (6:6, 14, 15, 16). Jesus asserts that on earth no person should be called "father" (23:9), reserving this title for the divine. And when disciples reach out to their neighbors, their baptism should include the name of the father (28:19).

Fathers are integrated into all of the main stories in Matthew, from Joseph to the sons of Zebedee. One potential disciple pleaded with Jesus to allow him to go home to bury his father (8:21). But waiting for a father to die might have taken forty years. Jesus was not willing to wait. On the other hand, this is a story about a man who treasured life with his father. Children are told at least twice to continue to treasure or honor both their father and their mother (15:4; 19:19).

A Redefined Family Nearly all of the Marcan stories about family find their way into Matthew's gospel. Mothers and fathers are honored in Matthew (see, for instance, Matthew 10:37, 38; 11:11; 19:18), and a daughter is brought back to life (Mt. 9:25). Matthew understands a woman's grief and anxiety about her children during war (Mt. 9:18–26; 24:19). Yet the writer also agrees that anxiety and grief can be produced by a mother, such as Herodias (Mt. 14:3–12).

Although Matthew appreciates the traditional family, it appears that the family is threatened by both external and internal divisiveness. The effects of the wars linger on in the ruined family structures. The following quotation speaks of this alienation, fear, and dissolution:

> Do not think that I have come to bring peace to the earth; I have not come to bring peace, but a sword. For I have come to set a man against his father, and a daughter against her mother, and a daughter-in-law against her mother-in-law; and one's foes will be members of one's own household. (Mt. 10:34–36 NRSV)

Family must be reconsidered and redefined if it is to survive.

Traditional marriage gives way to celibacy (whatever the exact nature), and virginity seems to be a timely topic. Traditional Jewish practices allowed a man to divorce his wife for almost any reason, even bad breath! And Matthew's hard-line stand on divorce (19:19) may have been a protective device for women who could easily find themselves without family or home.

The following **allegory** about virgins speaks of the fragility of the times, the waiting and the inability to know the future or to control it, and the hope that is rewarded to some and not to others:

> Then the kingdom of heaven will be like this. Ten bridesmaids took their lamps and went to meet the bridegroom. Five of them were foolish, and five were wise. When the foolish took their lamps, they took no oil with them; but the wise took flasks of oil with their lamps. As the bridegroom was delayed, all of them became drowsy and slept. But at midnight there was a shout, "Look! Here is the bridegroom! Come out to meet him." Then all those bridesmaids got up and trimmed their lamps. The foolish said to the wise, "Give

us some of your oil, for our lamps are going out." But the wise replied, "No! There will not be enough for you and for us; you had better to the dealers and buy some for yourselves." And while they went to buy it, the bridegroom came, and those who were ready went with him into the wedding banquet; and the door was shut. Later the other bridesmaids came also saying, "Lord, lord, open to us." But he replied, "Truly I tell you, I do not know you." Keep awake therefore, for you know neither the day nor the hour. (Mt. 25:1–13 NRSV)

This allegory about ten virgins seems absurd. Ten female virgins are waiting for one bridegroom. Five make it and five do not. Are they viable candidates for the marriage, or are they part of the wedding party? How many men could have afforded to feed and clothe five women even before the Jewish wars? People are waiting. Choices must be made. Some are chosen, and some are left behind.

How and why those choices are made is not clear in Matthew. Perhaps the allegory is a recollection of the wars when some survived and others did not. Matthew's readers understand the fickleness of war (Mt. 22:23–33). These stories and others speak of a dismal time in history. Matthew attempts to rebuild his world by reiterating the traditions of the past, coupled with an openness to build something new for future generations.

SPECIAL EMPHASES OF MATTHEW

A Community in Transition: The Church

For the Matthean community, life has been challenged by the effects of a violent war and the intrusion of people who come from a variety of backgrounds. New faces seem to be a fact of life. The "now" of this new community is not in the ruins of Judea and its social structures, but neither is it in the ancient traditions preserved by the Jews. Their heritage of an exclusive past must give way to a more inclusive and open-ended community.

No one will ever know if Matthew consciously chose to preserve violent traditions. Perhaps the language of war and destruction was normal for the writer. The environment may have been permeated with violent language. Death, disease, and hostile relations may have been everyday events in the life of the evangelist who attempted to bring some kind of organization and hope into an unstable world.

Readers of the gospel are not normally aware of (much less outraged by) the violent traditions preserved in Matthew. The cross is a symbol of both suffering and new life. Jesus' death is foretold and anticipated before the actual death scene (Mt. 12:14; 16:21; and possibly, 10:17). The murder of Jesus is a focal point in this gospel, yet the reader is only partially prepared for the account of the resurrection and appearance stories (Mt. 17: 1–8). Though the good news brings life, it also brings news of a terrible and an undeserving death.

The Gospel of Matthew is framed by stories of violence. At the beginning of the narrative of the life of Jesus, we find a story about a holocaust of children and a hasty flight into Egypt by Jesus' family. The scene turns to Rachel weeping for her children (Mt. 2:18), yet tears will not wash away the pain, blood, and personal grief found here. The tone is an indication of the troubled times. The wars have left Rachel alone. Her husband and children are not there to comfort and help her. This same tone is found in the story of the pregnant women at the end of the gospel: "How dreadful it will be in those days for pregnant and nursing mothers" (Mt. 24:19–22). These two stories set the tone for the entire gospel.

Matthew has an extensive vocabulary on the subject of violence. Consider the words in the following list.

Violent Words in Matthew*

People can be:

flogged (21:35; 23:34; 27:26)
drowned (18:6)
murdered (5:21; 15:19)
cast out (7:19)
stoned (21:35; 23:37)
crucified (23:34; 26:1)
killed (2:13, 16; 10:28, 39; 12:14; 14:5; 16:21, 25; 17:23)
choked (13:22; 18:28)
beaten (5:39; 27:30)
hit (26:67)
bullied (24:49)
plundered (12:29)
persecuted (5:10, 11, 44; 10:23; 13:21; 24:9)
maimed (15:30)
beheaded (14:10)
tortured (8:29)
insulted (5:11)
tormented (4:24)
trampled upon (5:13; 7:6)

People become angry (3:7; 5:22) and have all types of problems (8:6; 16:21; 17:12). If certain listeners do not obey or follow some of the mandates spoken by Jesus in the parables, the consequences are often violent. They could be "torn or cut into pieces" (7:6; 24:50), or end up weeping and grinding their teeth (8:12; 13:42; 24:51; 25:30). Houses are destroyed (12:29), servants are beaten (21:35; 22:6), and cities are burned (22:7). While the context of each tradition and its intended meaning for the reader may differ, it appears that a common thread of violent traditions and the experience of abuse runs through most of the Matthean writings.

*From Marla J. Selvidge, *Woman, Violence, and the Bible* (New York: Edwin Mellen Press, 1996), 37–59.

Against this hostile backdrop, Matthew inaugurates something new, the "church." The word "church" comes from two Greek words meaning "to call out." Family, community, and church may be synonyms for Matthew. Facing the organizational needs of the future, Matthew begins to lay the foundation of an ecclesiastical structure. Peter is important, for he receives the keys to heaven and is primary to the founding of this new structure. The new church does not need an excessive administrative bureaucracy, for Jesus promises that even when two or three worship, he will be there (18:20). Yet members within the church can have a certain type of power over others in resolving disputes between members: "If the member refuses to listen to them, tell it to the church...." (18:17).

Kingdom of God: Parables

Matthew employs at least forty different parables or parabolic sayings. For centuries, scholars have debated the meaning of the term *parable* and the closely aligned term the *Kingdom of God.* A parable is a metaphor. Metaphors may be found in stories, proverbs, dialogues, discourses, and more. Any short story with a double meaning may be a parable. The real question about parables written by Matthew and other gospel writers is how to interpret them. Since parables are in essence signs or symbols of something else, it may be impossible to recover the meaning of the parable for the original audience or writer. Sometimes the context will offer solutions to the problem. We know that parables were designed to shock an audience into listening, thinking, or acting differently.

The term or concept of the "Kingdom of God," or, as is found in Matthew, the "Kingdom of the Heavens," is closely aligned with the parabolic sayings of Jesus in the gospels. In its most basic definition, the Kingdom of God is the "rule or reign of God." An obvious question is, 'When is God going to rule?' There are a host of explanations on the meaning of the Kingdom of God for the synoptic gospel writers. Some suggest that the kingdom was present during the life of Jesus and is present in the life of anyone who becomes a Christian. This is termed *realized* **eschatology**. Others suggest that the kingdom will emerge at the end of time, when Jesus returns as the Messiah. This is termed *future eschatology.* And third, some scholars suggest that both of these explanations are correct. The kingdom was present with Jesus and will be present in the kingdom to come (termed *tensive eschatology*).

Parables are timeless and have been interpreted by millions of people in at least a thousand different ways. The important message about parables is that their meaning can still ring true for people who live in the twenty-first century.

Summary of the Gospel of Matthew   Matthew wrote at least fifteen years after the creation of the Gospel of Mark to a group of people living somewhere in the Roman Empire who had survived physical violence, possibly a war. The writer and perhaps the people to whom he wrote had ties to the ancient Israelites and Jewish religions. Matthew believed that a man named Jesus was the person for whom they waited. He was the coming Messiah, the Son of God, and even more, he made a promise that he would never leave them.

Matthew urges readers to open their minds to change. Change comes in unfamiliar packages. No longer could people afford to live in an ethnically or a religiously pure community. From the beginning to the end of the gospel, Matthew urges readers to reinterpret their sacred beliefs, thoughts, and rituals. Opening the doors would bring pluralism, a redefined family, and possibly a new religious alliance—the church. With high hopes, Matthew sprinkles the traditions of Mark and the familiar Old Testament/Hebrew Bible with parables and miracle stories to give evidence or warning that the Kingdom of God is very near.

6

A Diverse Community Engaged in Social Reform

The Gospel of Luke

He has ... lifted up the lowly; he has filled the
hungry with good things, and sent the rich away empty.

—Luke 1:52–53 NRSV

The twelve were with him, as well as some women who had been
cured ... Mary, called Magdalene, ... and Joanna, the wife of
Herod's steward Chuza, and Susanna, and many other women,
who provided for him out of their own resources.

—Luke 8:1–3

INTRODUCTION

Mark's gospel thrusts readers into the future, hoping for the quick return of Jesus to Galilee. Matthew links Jesus' story to a Jewish past, assuring the audience of a confident and lasting divine presence. Luke's work is more concerned about the present socio-economic problems. The writer argues for the creation of an equitable community that will support all of its members. Social injustice must be replaced with tolerance and love.

Many Lucan stories feature Jesus championing the diverse poor while ridiculing the rich and politically powerful. There are poverty and disease. There are people who need help and are not finding it. The rich are not sharing with their neighbors. The underclasses are ignored and used by the politically astute. Religious leaders are no longer religious models or ethical examples to the people but are corrupt and should be ignored. People must stop worrying about the future and begin to love and trust each other now.

AUTHORSHIP, DATE, LOCATION, AND RECIPIENTS

Authorship   Identifying and locating the person who wrote the Gospel of Luke has alluded students for centuries. Who was Luke? According to the opening verses of the gospel, the writer was a researcher who compiled two or three volumes of work on early Christianity.

> Since many have undertaken to set down an orderly account of the events that have been fulfilled among us, just as they were handed on to us by witnesses and servants of the word, I too decided, after investigating everything carefully from the very first, to write an orderly account for you, most excellent Theophilus, so that you may know the truth concerning the things about which you have been instructed. (Luke 1:1–4 NRSV)

If we also turn to the opening verses of the Acts of the Apostles, we find a similar notation, "In the first book, **Theophilus**...." (Acts 1:1). Most students of the Bible suggest that whoever wrote the Gospel of Luke must also have written Acts. The literary style, vocabulary, and points of view are exactly the same. Some contend that the word "first," or **"protos"** in Greek, meant the first of a trilogy; thus Luke and Acts are only two volumes of a three-volume set. Book One (Luke) was about the life of Jesus. Book Two (Acts) told the stories of Peter and Paul as founders of Christianity. Book Three was lost or never written. Many reason that the writer intended to continue the story of Paul in Acts because Luke leaves the reader "hanging on the edge." The narrative abruptly ends with Paul under house arrest in Rome. No one really knows what happened to Paul.

While the author's name is not mentioned in either Luke or Acts, there is a curious change in the use of pronouns during the recounting of Paul's travels. About midway in Paul's traveling adventures in Acts, the narrator's point of view changes. A passage from Acts follows. Pay special attention to the italicized words.

> *They* went through the region of **Phrygia** and **Galatia**,... When *they* had come opposite **Mysia**, *they* attempted to go into Bithynia ... *they* went down to **Troas**. During the night Paul had a vision: there stood a man of Macedonia pleading with him and saying, "Come over to **Macedonia** and help us." When he had seen the vision, *we* immediately tried to cross over to Macedonia, being convinced that God had called *us* to proclaim the good news to them. (Acts 16:6–10 NRSV)

The change from "they" to "we" may indicate that the writer is including himself or herself in the story. The **"we" passages** found in Acts could have been penned by the author of Luke-Acts, but they could also have been copied from a ship's log or someone's diary (See: 20:5–15; 21:1–18; 27:1–28:16). Researchers and writers in ancient times often used sources "word for word" without citing any documentation.

From the second century on, traditions based on conclusions drawn from the "we" passages suggested that Luke was a traveler-companion of Paul. Some scholars from the turn of the century suggested that Luke had training in medicine and that the gospel contains words normally employed by a physician. Today, most students disagree with this theory. There also is evidence that someone named Luke was well known to the writers of **Pauline** and **Pseudo-Pauline** letters because he or she is mentioned in the Letters of Philemon, Colossians, and 2 Timothy.

> **Epaphras**, my fellow prisoner in Christ Jesus, sends greetings to you, and so do Mark, **Aristarchus**, **Demas**, and Luke, my fellow workers. (Philemon 25)
>
> Luke, the beloved physician, and Demas greet you. (Col. 4:14)
>
> Only Luke is with me. (2 Tim. 4:11)

But is there any evidence to link the Luke in Paul's works with the writer of the Gospel of Luke? Probably not. Even if we compare the **theology** or beliefs, stories, and literary speeches found in Luke-Acts with Paul's letters, the vocabulary and points of view are quite different. Luke seems to be unaware of Paul's works. What we know about the writer of Luke is best discovered within the gospel itself.

We know that Luke wrote in excellent Greek, was aware of stories in the Septuagint and Hebrew Bible, and used a varied literary style and complicated vocabulary in order to rehearse the deeds of Jesus and Paul. According to **Frederick Danker**, Luke's introduction follows similar Greek inscriptions during the reigns of the Emperor Augustus to Nero, which suggests that the writer was well educated in the literary forms of the day.

Date, Location, Recipients   No one really knows when the Gospel of Luke was written. It was included in a list in the Muratorian Canon late in the second century and appears to have used the Gospel of Mark as a source, which we have dated around 65–70 C.E. Most people suggest that it was written after the Jewish war, around 73 C.E. and before the Muratorian Canon. Luke seems to have witnessed the fall of Jerusalem, "When you see Jerusalem surrounded by armies" (Luke 21:20 NRSV). Titus surrounded Jerusalem before it fell. The date of the creation of the gospel is usually placed around 80–85 C.E.

The letter could have been written to a person or an entire community. Theophilus, the recipient of Luke and Acts, could have been a wealthy Roman political operative. The name means "lover of God," but the name could also be a general word appealing to all people who were interested in Christianity who loved God.

Speculations about where the gospel was written and about who received it are numerous, but there is no external evidence linking the book with any city in the Roman Empire. Most agree that the recipients were Greek-speaking Christians. Many could have been converted God fearers. Some have suggested likely places of composition to be Asia Minor, Caesarea Maritima, Rome, and even Achaia.

Reasons for Writing the Gospel

Why would anyone want to write another gospel? There may have been hundreds floating around the Roman Empire. The writer of Luke had several personal, political, theological, and practical reasons for writing a newer, edited version of the old standby Mark.

1. ***Political. Christians were friends of Rome.*** Having survived a terrible civil war, Luke appears to be wary of governmental conflict and perhaps wanted Rome to know that Christians were friends of the Empire. We know from historical accounts during the reigns of Nero and Domitian that Christians were singled out for torture and even martyrdom.

2. ***Practical. Protect Christians from Roman harassment.*** Luke places the death of Jesus on the shoulders of the Jews who forced Pilate to have Jesus executed. Pilate is portrayed as finding Jesus innocent. "I find no basis for an accusation against this man" (Luke 23:4 NRSV). And Herod exclaims that Jesus "has done nothing to deserve death" (Luke 23:15). Even a **centurion** is commended because "he loves our people …" (Luke 7:5). The author continues this theme throughout the Acts of the Apostles, where the Jews are portrayed as killers and instigators of riots. (Today, many scholars are analyzing what is called **antisemitism** in Luke's works.) Romans remain competent administrators who often rescue Paul from threatening circumstances. These themes will be expanded upon when we consider Acts in its own chapter.

3. ***Practical. Create a peaceful environment.*** Luke uses the word "peace" more often than any other gospel. **Zechariah**'s poem or hymn, known as the "Benedictus" at the beginning of the gospel, expresses thankfulness for the Lord God who protected him from his enemies and from those who hate him. He also wishes that that same God would "guide our feet into the way of peace" (1:68–79) The host of heaven, at the birth of Jesus, wishes for peace on earth (2:14), and the seventy who are appointed by Jesus are told to say at every house they enter, "Peace to this house" (10:5). Jesus approaches Jerusalem riding a colt, and people exclaim, "Peace in Heaven" (19:38). Peter is greeted with a word of peace after the Resurrection of Jesus (24:36).

4. ***Practical. Avoidance of tax.*** After the Jewish wars, Jews were levied a tax payable for many years to Rome in order to replenish all of the funds used to fight the war (see Chapter 1). Perhaps Christians wanted to differentiate themselves from the Jews so they would not have to pay the money. Hostility between Jews and Romans continued, and another revolution could erupt soon. Luke may have wanted to make it clear that Christians were not revolutionaries and did not want to bring down the government but wanted to live in peace.

5. ***Theological. De-emphasis of the Parousia.*** We know from studying Paul's letters that there was an early belief within Christianity that Jesus would return very soon. The Gospel of Mark ends with a hope that Jesus would return to Galilee shortly. But Jesus did not return, and many scholars have theorized that Luke wrote this gospel as a sort of transition document. According to Hans Conzelmann, Luke envisioned Jesus' life at the center of time and those who worshiped him (the Church) must understand that Jesus would not return for a long, long time. Meanwhile, people must begin preparing for a future

that earlier Christians did not believe would happen. They must learn to live in the present instead of placing all of their hopes in the future.

6. ***Theological. Universalism.*** Christianity may also have been viewed as a narrow, **sectarian** offshoot of Judaism. Luke makes it plain that the teachings of Jesus were meant for the entire world. Universalism and a hope for all peoples to join their community is a foundational theme for Luke (2:10–14; 3:4–5; 14:23; 17:15–19; 24:47). Luke traces Jesus' heritage back to Adam, neither a Jew nor a Greek or Roman, but one who, in theory, was the first human (Luke 3:23–28) and the father of all humanity. Luke's gospel opens its doors to anyone regardless of nationality, occupation, health, sex, political stance, or religious orientation. All are welcome in Luke's international community.

SOURCES

The writer attempts to be more thorough and "objective" in considering the past (Luke 1:1–4) and thus may have consulted numerous sources. Some argue that Luke was a historian, yet others find factual errors in the gospel. For instance, in chapter 2, Mary and Joseph are traveling in order to be enrolled. According to historians, there is no record of an order for enrollment during the time Jesus was born, and Roman officials did not rule concurrently (Luke 2). Other scholars have criticized the writer of Luke for inaccurate geographical notations, descriptions of persons and events, and illogical stories. **Anna**, a prophetess in Luke, is portrayed as having lived in the temple. According to all of the evidence collected about the Temple, women were not allowed to enter it. They stood outside the gates with the **Gentiles**, or non-Jews.

It is known that Jewish and Roman historians wrote about Jesus. While there is no evidence to suggest that Luke read the writings of Josephus, a Jewish historian during the first century, it is interesting to read his words about Jesus (although some would suggest that his words were created by Christians).

> Now, there was about this time, Jesus, a wise man, if it be lawful to call him a man, for he was a doer of wonderful works,—a teacher of such men as receive the truth with pleasure. He drew over to him both many of the Jews, and many of the Gentiles. He was [the] Christ; and when Pilate, at the suggestion of the principal men amongst us, had condemned him to the cross, those that loved him at the first did not forsake him, for he appeared to them alive again the third day, as the divine prophets had foretold these and ten thousand other wonderful things concerning him; and the tribe of Christians, so named from him, are not extinct at this time. (Works of Flavius Josephus, 379)

Josephus' account is very short and probably was written after the Gospel of Luke.

Luke chose to use the Gospel of Mark and a collection of Jesus' sayings, called "**Q**," as primary sources. The writer seems to have a knowledge of both the Septuagint and Hebrew Bible, while adding traditions that are contained in no other gospel. This material is usually labeled "L," indicating Luke's special material. "L" includes such stories as the infancy narrative, the genealogy, stories of the Good Samaritan, the Prodigal Son, the Widow of Nain, Mary and Martha, Sending out of the Seventy, the Two on the Road to **Emmaus**, and more.

FIGURE 6.1 Josephus. From William Whiston, *The Works of Flavius Josephus* (Cincinnati: E. Morgan and Co., 1840).

ORGANIZATIONAL STRUCTURE

Building on the Marcan story of the death of Jesus and his healing and miracle ministry in Galilee, Luke adds several traditions. The births of John and Jesus are placed at the beginning of the gospel, and the story about "Two on the Road to Emmaus" is a postscript. In the middle of the work, he employs the following stories, parables, and miracles:

Examples of New Traditions in the Gospel of Luke

Jesus as a Boy	Anointing by a Woman
The Seventy	Mary and Martha
Conversion of Zaccheus	Two Robbers
Two on the Road to Emmaus	Jesus Weeps over Jerusalem
Jesus before Herod	Words to the Women before the Cross
Resurrection of the Widow's Son	Ten Lepers
Ear of the Slave	

While employing about 70 percent of Mark, Luke chose to ignore a substantial amount of material.

Examples of Traditions Found in Mark But Not in the Gospel of Luke

The Story of Herodias	Syro-Phoenician's Daughter
Mark 6:45—8:26: The Great Omission	Feeding of the Four Thousand
Jesus Walking on the Water	Blind Man at Bethsaida
Ceremonial Washing	

Luke often simplified and shortened the Gospel of Mark by reorganizing material and correcting grammar, while adding diverse connectives and **synonyms**. Compare the "Parables of the Mustard Seed," which follows. Notice how Luke shortens and rearranges the material.

Parables of the Mustard Seed

Mark 4:26–29	He also said, "With what can we compare the kingdom of God, or what parable will we use for it? It is like a mustard seed, which, when sown upon the ground, is the smallest of all the seeds on earth; yet when it is sown it grows and becomes the greatest of all shrubs, and puts forth large branches, so that the birds of the air can make nests in its shade."
Luke 13:18–19	He said therefore, "What is the kingdom of God like? And to what should I compare it? It is like a mustard seed that someone took and sowed in the garden; it grew and became a tree, and the birds of the air made nests in its branches." (NRSV)

There are several ways of outlining the Gospel of Luke. A basic approach looks like the following:

Basic Outline of the Gospel of Luke

Introduction	1:1–4
I. Jesus and John	1:5–4:13
II. Career of Jesus	4:14–19:27
III. Trial and Execution of Jesus	19:28–23
Epilogue: The Resurrected Jesus	24

CHARACTERS

Jesus

The main character in Luke, as in all of the other gospels, is Jesus. How does Luke portray Jesus? From the first chapter of Luke until the end, Jesus is the champion of the underclasses. His origins can be traced to a union between the **Holy Spirit** and a young, unmarried woman, Mary (Luke 1). He is the Son of God. In the ***Magnificat,*** a poem or song about Jesus, Mary understands that her child is or will be special. "He has brought down the powerful from their thrones, and lifted up the lowly; he has filled the hungry with good things, and sent the rich away empty…" (Luke 1:52–53 NRSV).

Most of us can retell the story of Jesus' birth. We have heard it time after time on the radio and on television during the Christmas holidays. Yet the story we all hear is a combination of the stories found in Luke and Matthew. While there are a few similarities between them, that is, the characters of Mary, Joseph, Angel of the Lord, Bethlehem, and Jesus, the stories are entirely different. The following summarizes some of those differences and similarities.

Comparison of the Birth Narratives

Matthew 1:18–2:21	**Luke 1:26–2:28**
Travel to Egypt	Travel: Nazareth to Judea
Magi	Shepherds
Jesus in a house	Jesus in a manger/barn
Bethlehem	Bethlehem
Dreams to Joseph	Gabriel speaks to Mary
Herod	Caesar Augustus
	Quirinius, Governor of Syria
Angel of the Lord	Angel of the Lord
Jesus is King of the Jews	Jesus is Savior, Christ the Lord
Joseph, husband of Mary	Joseph, betrothed to Mary
	Anna and Simeon

Jesus' entrance into life is in modest, if not poor and unsanitary, surroundings. The birth appears to be an accident that happened during a journey from Nazareth to Bethlehem. Mary and Jesus spent their first few days together in a manger or a stall in a barn. She kept him warm with "rags" or "bands of cloth."

He is the cousin of John, the miraculous child of Elizabeth and Zechariah, a "Savior, who is Messiah, the Lord" (Luke 2:11). Many scholars suggest that the followers of John the Baptist and Jesus intermingled toward the end of the first century. In the Gospel of Mark, John and Jesus do not seem to know each other; in Matthew they seem to develop a speaking relationship; and in Luke they become relatives. People have speculated that John may have been viewed by many as the promised Messiah, but when he was abruptly killed, his followers turned to Jesus. Others suggest that followers of the baptism of John kept themselves separate from the followers of Jesus. Luke wrote the Gospel of Luke and Acts as a way of uniting these divergent groups of early Christians.

Throughout the gospel, Luke proves how Jesus is indeed a **savior**, messiah, and **lord**. The word "savior" means "one who rescues." **Simeon** and Anna recognize his greatness and so do his parents, who found him discussing questions with the teachers

FIGURE 6.2   Jesus at the Chora Church. Found in Istanbul, Turkey. Photo by Marla J. Selvidge.

in the Temple when he was a boy (Luke 2). After John's arrest, Jesus is baptized by the Holy Spirit, who stays with him throughout the rest of his life. A heavenly voice proclaims that Jesus is a son (Luke 3:20–22), and Jesus asserts that his career will be centered in service (Luke 22:23).

Jesus, according to Luke, was the champion of the oppressed and spent his entire career helping to alleviate the suffering of the diseased and seemingly helpless segment of society. The writer of Luke is very concerned with poverty and the resulting problems of disease, homelessness, starvation, and possibly political unrest by the disenfranchised. According to **Walter E. Pilgrim**, people who lived during the time of Jesus did not eat on days that they could find no gainful employment. The poor consisted of day laborers, slaves, small landowners, the handicapped, tenant farmers, beggars (blind, lame, lepers, destitute, diseased people), widows, and orphans. Many of Jesus' own disciples came from the poor. Jesus regularly associated with the lowest segments of society, which included tax collectors, publicans, and anyone who did not live according to Temple regulations—sinners.

Many of Luke's parables address the needs of people who were abused by the wealthy and religious elite. The parable about the Good Samaritan beginning at Luke 10:25 criticizes the powerful while favoring the weak and generous. Remember that the ancient Jews despised the **Samaritans** because they did not keep kosher guidelines. Neither did they worship at the same temple nor recognize the religious hierarchy.

FIGURE 6.3 "The Good Samaritan" by Kim Ki-Chang.

In Jesus' first public appearance, he is rejected by his friends in the synagogue who attempt to murder him, but he survives (Luke 4: 29–20). Their rage was a result of Jesus preaching his first sermon in **Nazareth**. He had criticized them for their hypocritical lives, insulted them by telling stories which indicated that God loved those who were despised by the Jews, and claimed that the divine was present in his life. In fact, Jesus indirectly claimed that he was the long-awaited Messiah. This is something no Jew would do, for it was sacrilegious.

While Jesus is just as active in the Gospel of Luke as in the other gospels, he is also portrayed as taking time to pray. Prayer is a significant activity and theme for Luke. Zechariah, Anna, the Pharisees, the Tax Collectors, and the followers of John pray (Luke 1:13; 2:37; 18:10; 5:33). Jesus often challenges his listeners to solve problems through praying (Luke 10:2; 6:28; 11:1; 21:36; 22:40, 45). Jesus exclaimed to those buying and selling in the temple, "My house shall be a house of prayer..." (Luke 19:45).

Mark portrays a Jesus who does not understand why he must die. Matthew begins to suggest that Jesus is in control of not only the natural elements but also perhaps the future. Luke's Jesus knows where he is going and sets his sights on Jerusalem. He appears to be in control of his own death. Several verses throughout the Gospel of Luke mention that Jesus has a destiny in the holy city Jerusalem. The following box shows a sampling of those verses:

JESUS AND JERUSALEM

9:31   During the Transfiguration.
"They appeared in glory and were speaking of his departure, which he was about to accomplish at Jerusalem."

9:51   Near a Samaritan Village.
"When the days drew near for him to be taken up, he set his face to go to Jerusalem."

9:53   "...but they did not receive him because his face was set toward Jerusalem."

13:33   The Pharisees warn Jesus that Herod wants to kill him.
" 'Yet today, tomorrow, and the next day I must be on my way, because it is impossible for a prophet to be killed outside of Jerusalem.' "

18:31   While teaching the Twelve.
" 'See, we are going up to Jerusalem, and everything that is written about the Son of Man by the prophets will be accomplished.' " (All quotations are taken from the NRSV.)

Luke has not forgotten Jesus' heritage and often suggests that he is fulfilling Old Testament/Hebrew beliefs about the future. Jesus even intimates that there is merit in the laws of Moses and the prophets (Luke 16:29–31). The writer cites verses directly from the Old Testament/Hebrew Bible at least twenty-five times and uses direct references over forty times. The following box shows a sampling of the citations and references.

CITATIONS AND REFERENCES OF THE OLD TESTAMENT/HEBREW BIBLE

Gospel of Luke	Old Testament/Hebrew Bible
1:17 "With the spirit and power of Elijah he will go before him, to turn the hearts of parents to their children, and the disobedient to the wisdom of the righteousness, to make ready a people prepared for the Lord."	Malachi 4:6 He will turn the hearts of parents to their children and the hearts of children to their parents, so that I will not come and strike the land with a curse.
4:4 Jesus answered him, "It is written, 'One does not live by bread alone.' "	Deuteronomy 8:3 He humbled you by letting you hunger, then by feeding you with manna, with which neither you nor your ancestors were acquainted, in order to make you understand that one does not live by bread alone, but by every word that comes from the mouth of the Lord.
23:46 Then Jesus, crying with a loud voice said, "Father, into your hands I commend my spirit."	Psalms 31:5 Into your hand I commit my spirit; you have redeemed me, O Lord, faithful God.

Luke's multidimensional view of Jesus has been explored by thousands of researchers who have attempted to capture the writer's point of view. Frederick Danker describes Luke's multifaceted Jesus in his book *Luke: Proclamation Commentaries*. Danker thinks that Luke's Jesus challenged the tyranny of tradition. Today he would have spoken out against the powerful corporate giants. Jesus would have been outraged by the exploitation of the weak. He would have encouraged people to seek their own individuality yet not at the expense of others.

The Holy Spirit and Satan

The writer of Luke believed in the power of unseen beings to intersect and even control human life (Luke 22:3, 31). Lurking at every step in Jesus' career were negative forces embodied in the character of Satan, the Devil, and demons. Jesus seems to be the center of a battle of good and evil forces. Sometimes the evil forces step forward, and at other times the good forces from God or the Holy Spirit dominate the story. Jesus uses the negative influences to produce good, even during his temptation (Luke 4) and throughout healing narratives or miracle stories (Luke 11, 13). He also appears to have some type of relationship with both forces, for he says to Peter, "Simon, Simon, listen! Satan has demanded to sift all of you like wheat, but I have prayed for you that your faith may not fail…" (Luke 22:31).

The positive forces are from God and are embodied in the presence of the Holy Spirit. Jesus and those who were close to him were led and protected by the Holy Spirit. Zechariah and Elizabeth are filled with the Holy Spirit (Luke 1), Mary is impregnated by the Holy Spirit (Luke 1), and Simeon was guided by the Spirit (Luke 2). Jesus was filled, rejoiced in (Luke 10), and led by the Spirit into the wilderness (Luke 4). In his first and last major public appearance, he claimed that the "Spirit is upon me" (Luke 4:18), and he gave over the Spirit to the Father (Luke 23:46). This mysterious Holy Spirit strongly influences Jesus, and we will discover later in the Acts of the Apostles that this same Spirit planned and controlled the journeys made by Paul and his friends.

Female Characters

Luke assumes that women are independent and resourceful. The writer presents the inspiring stories of Mary and Elizabeth. They were mothers, but their child-rearing responsibilities did not prohibit them from adding distinctive thoughts and gifts to their communities. The writer tells more stories about widows than any other gospel writer.

For Luke, widows seem to be able to take care of themselves. They are astute in their perceptions of religious traditions and ideals. They overcome, at times, with the touch of Jesus. At other times, they overcome by their own endurance and persistent determination. Luke recognizes that some widows can be abused by the religious elite, but the writer does not weep for the widow, nor are widows encouraged to marry in order to make their lives economically or socially secure.

FIGURE 6.4 An icon of Mary from Saint Catherine's Monastery. Photo by Marla J. Selvidge.

Luke admires single women. Mary and Martha support themselves and seem to have the right, obligation, and responsibility to choose their own careers. Other women who are in charge of their own private resources support Jesus during his itinerate journeying (Luke 8:2–3). Many demonstrate love greater than any other character in the Lucan story. The traditions about females are powerful stories of successful people. While Luke's editorial nuances are important, the discussion that follows will center on the traditions about women unique to Luke's gospel.

Mary—the Lucan Mary   The story of the birth of Jesus provides an excellent opportunity for Luke to use personal material to highlight major characters. The writer features Elizabeth and Mary, Elizabeth and Zechariah, Zechariah and Mary, Joseph and Mary, and Anna and Simeon. Many writers have found traces of Hebrew poetry behind the songs and narratives. Together, these characters become storytellers as Luke unfolds the early life of Jesus. Their heritage is wound together as the births of two charismatic leaders—John and Jesus—are told. While all of the characters are important, Mary is accentuated by Luke. She is the one who courageously chooses, gives, and steps forward out of the background of Jesus' life to become the most important figure in his childhood.

Who is she? She is a virgin/young woman. She is living in Nazareth of Galilee. She is betrothed without an occupation or a trade. According to Luke, she has no known background, although she owns her own home (Luke. 1:57). Throughout the birth accounts, Mary is featured for her strength of character. She is called "favored" (Luke 1:28), "The Lord is with you" (Luke 1:28). No other secondary character receives such special praise. She is a servant, and she is blessed (Luke 1:42; 1:38). Elisabeth Schüssler Fiorenza says that Mary becomes the hope of the poor. Mary views herself as a very

FIGURE 6.5 Vie de Jesus Mafa, "African Virgin." All Rights Reserved. Vie de Jesus MAFA. 24 rue du Marechal Joffre. F-78000, Versailles, France.

humble person (Luke 1:48) who is not caught up with her own importance. She often ponders or thinks (Luke 2:19) of her role as mother (Luke 1:43) and leader of the family.

Mary and Joseph   In Matthew's version of the gospel, the story of Jesus' birth centers on the experience and decision making of the father, Joseph (Mt. 1–3). The audience meets Mary and knows about her relationship to Joseph but never has an opportunity to hear her side of the story. Luke's story offers the audience Mary's point of view.

From the beginning of the narrative until the story about Jesus' temptation, Mary is the main character. Her decisions are hers alone. She makes the choice to conceive and bear the child (Luke 1:38; 2:7). Joseph's opinion is never registered, although he does bring Mary to Bethlehem in order to register to pay their tax (Luke 2:4).

Mary's name is mentioned first when the shepherds come to visit (Luke 2:16). Often the story breaks away to reveal a concerned and reflective woman. "But Mary treasured all these words and pondered them in her heart" (Luke 2:19 NRSV). Joseph is Jesus' father and is from the house of David (Luke 2:3; 4:23; 6:42). They are a couple. They are together at the birth of Jesus, his circumcision, and at his presentation at the Temple (Luke 2:21). They travel together to Jerusalem, but Mary is always featured.

Mary, although neglected in the rest of the gospel, is portrayed as an insightful and self-directed person who is in charge of her life and family. Her positive responses as a couple and parent set the tone for the rest of the gospel. She is a mother, wife, kinswoman, and friend. Luke never allows the audience to lose sight of this woman's contribution. She is the center of the story of Jesus' early life.

Women of Independence: Singles   None of the synoptic writers advocates one particular lifestyle for anyone, especially women. More than any other synoptic writer, Luke writes stories about women who choose alternate lifestyles and seem to be independent and financially astute. Their stories are intermingled among the many adventures of Jesus.

Luke presents a balanced view on woman and childbearing and child rearing. Mothers and singles are important to the community. Two verses or stories illustrate this. Elizabeth declares at the conception of John, "This is what the Lord has done for me when he looked favorably on me and took away the disgrace I have endured among the people" (Luke 1:25 NRSV). And several different types of women seem to be constant companions of Jesus.

> The twelve were with him, as well as some women who had been cured ... Mary, called Magdalene,... and Joanna, the wife of Herod's steward Chuza, and Susanna, and many other women, who provided for him out of their own resources." (Lk. 8:1–3)

Their personal identities and names are lost forever. Yet Luke identifies them as being essential ingredients in Jesus' itinerant ministry. They are part of the group "with him" (Luke 8:1–3). **J. Massyngberde-Ford** concludes that they were disciples. Luke may be hinting that they were affluent women. There is ample evidence throughout the history of the Church to support such an idea, although **E. Moltmann-Wendel** thinks that Joanna had a political background and questions whether women would fit into the ideal of Lucan discipleship and poverty.

Independent women are part of the heart of the gospel. Luke continues this theme by telling stories about single women who are single-mindedly dedicated to their religious beliefs. Mary and Martha are single women (Luke 10:38–42) living at home. They entertain Jesus. Therefore it has been assumed that the central teaching of this story is domestic, yet there is ample evidence during the first century to suggest that Christianity began and flourished in houses similar to Martha's.

If the setting for the story about Mary and Martha is a house church, then very different conclusions can be drawn. Luke may be reflecting issues within the early house church communities. Most commentators want to interpret the issue of choosing to do "the dishes" or staying in the front room with the men while they talk. Some recent scholars have even suggested that Mary is a role model for women to be passive and submissive. Yet Luke may be suggesting something much more revolutionary.

If this is a house church, then the main quarrel may be between women who want to work in different types of positions. Martha may be acting as an administrator of a house church, and Mary may be arguing that she does not want to participate in that type of role. Both may serve in at least two key positions, as an administrator of a house church or an itinerate preacher (following the life of Jesus). Both women have a choice of vocations, neither of which revolve around a married home life. These women are women of independent means who have futures within the community that meets in the name of Jesus.

ANDROGYNY: PARTNERSHIP AND FRIENDSHIP

Luke includes more stories and references to women than any other gospel. While this is generally interpreted as being noteworthy and a positive sign of the author's confident attitude toward women, several scholars take issue with the writer of Luke and argue that the writer has an insidious view of women. And while Luke may or may not have a negative agenda toward women, the writer includes many stories about both male and female characters who can be young and old, single and married, rich and poor, commoner or politician, sick or healthy. This selection of material, which results in a "communal" vocabulary, seeks to unite rather than separate people. It allows the audience to see both sexes participating in the story about Jesus. People are sent out two by two (Luke 10). Luke is not concerned with their names or sex. In reading the story about the two on the road to Emmaus (Luke 24), Luke never clearly reveals their identity. One is called **Cleopas**, and we have no name for the other. Are they a couple going home? Or are they two men or two women heading back to their lodging?

Pairing Traditions

Luke often matches traditions. If the writer tells a story about a man, a story about a woman will immediately follow, or vice versa. The following is a select list of the pairs.

Pairing Traditions

Women	Men
Widow of Nain 7:11–17	The Centurion's Slave 7:2–10
Mary and Martha 10:38–42	Good Samaritan 10:29–37
Woman and the Lost Coin 15:8–10	Man with the Lost Sheep 15:3–7
Crippled Woman 13:10–16	Man with Dropsy 14:2–6

Male-female pairing is not the only partnership device used by Luke. Women and women, men and men, and women and men become friends and companions in the Lucan drama. Note the following pairs:

Mary and Martha (Luke 10:38–42)
Herod and Herodias (Luke 3:18–20)
James and John (Luke 5:10)
Mary and Joseph (Luke 1–3)
Simeon and Anna (Luke 2:22–38)
Elizabeth and Zechariah (Luke 1)

In these stories, Luke emphasizes individuality plus companionship—the sharing of life with another person. This sharing of life is most noticeable in the "communal" vocabulary employed by Luke. Of all the synoptic writers, Luke has the most diverse vocabulary when describing personal relationships.

Friends and Acquaintances

Luke is fond of using the word "friend." Matthew uses the term only once, and Mark omits it. According to *The Random House Dictionary*, a friend is "a person attached to another person by feelings of affection or personal regard; a patron or a supporter; a person who is not hostile (acquaintance, companion, comrade)."

Indeed, even in ancient times, the term *friend* was a special word for a close association with a loved one, a favorite, or even an ally. It often had political ramifications.

For Luke, the word friend is almost magical. All types of people become friends and share joys and intimacies together in the Lucan story. Luke is the only writer to include a parable about a friend (Luke 11:5–8) and to tell the audience that Herod and Pilate became friends (Luke 23:12). Celebrations with friends occur after a lost sheep and a coin are found (Luke 15:6–9). The woman who finds her lost coin calls her woman friends to celebrate with her. The brother of the prodigal son laments to his father, "[Y]et you have never given me even a young goat so I might celebrate with my friends" (Luke 15:29 NRSV). Not only is family invited to huge parties, so also are friends (Luke 16:9).

Like the closest family, friends can become traitors (Luke 21:16), yet Luke believes friends are an asset and certainly worth pursuing. Jesus calls the disciples his friends (Luke 12:1–4) and claims that he was a friend to tax collectors and sinners (Luke 7:34).

The idea of friendship as close companionship is supported by other Lucan words, suggesting that a close bond can be made between people. This bond does not have to be based on a family bloodline. Luke seems to be aware of the "other" and "one another" more than any other gospel. "Other" is used thirty-three times by Luke and "one another" is used twice as often when compared with the other synoptics. This underscores Luke's major concern for universalism.

Along with this emphasis on friendship, Luke adds words that imply a closeness. There are people with Jesus. Some of these people are called "partners" (Luke 5:7, 10), "sharers" (Luke 5:10), "acquaintances" (Luke 2:44), and "company" (Luke 2:44).

This emphasis by Luke on friendship is not at the expense of a family tradition. The stories of the births of John and Jesus are strong evidence of the importance of relatives. In addition to regular family members, Luke adds the word "kinsperson" (Luke 1:36, 58, 61; 14:12; 21:16), denoting a special family member. Not only are members of the family special, so also are the neighbors (Luke 1:58; 4:14; 10:27, 29, 36).

POLITICAL OPERATIVES

Luke is tuned in to local, regional, and national politics. Throughout the gospel, Luke mentions powerful political officials and includes them as characters in the stories and subjects in the parables. It would be time consuming to study each of the politicians and political groups but the following will summarize their involvement in the story of Jesus.

A string of rulers is mentioned at the beginning of the story about the birth of Jesus (Luke 2), the inauguration of John the Baptist's career (Luke 3), and the miraculous conception of John by Elizabeth and Zechariah (Luke 1). Most of these officials have nothing to do with the progress of the narrative.

The reader has few glimpses into the activities and personal lives of these characters. Caesar or the Emperor (Luke 2, 3) is the subject of questions and accusations about paying taxes (Luke 20, 23). Herod Antipas arrested, imprisoned, and killed John the Baptist because he did not enjoy being publicly humiliated by the prophet (Luke 3:19–20; 9:7–9). This same monarch allowed soldiers to humiliate Jesus before his death sentence (Luke 23).

Jewish political operatives seem to have constantly dogged Jesus. Many were interested in his provocative thoughts, and others laid traps for him by asking leading questions. Some warned him of impending doom, while others pushed him toward inevitable disaster. The Sadducees, the party of priests, are rarely mentioned (Luke 20:27), but the Pharisees, the intellectual religious, conspire with the scribes (Luke 6:7), lawyers (Luke 7:30), and others to lure Jesus into arguments about religion. Their questions on the topics include sin (Luke 5:21), breaking the sabbath by healing or fasting (Luke 5:30), and the Kingdom of God (Luke 17:20).

Luke directs many harsh words toward the Pharisees. In spite of Jesus' highly critical condemnations of the Pharisees, he accepts invitations to dinner at least three

THE ROMAN AND JEWISH POLITICAL ESTABLISHMENT

Roman	Luke	Jewish	Luke
Caesar Augustus	2	Anna, High Priest	3
Quirinius, Governor of Syria	2	Caiaphas, High Priest	3
Tiberius Caesar	3	Priests	6
Pontius Pilate	3	Chief Priests	9
Herod Antipas, the Tetrarch, King	3	Elders	9
Philip the Tetrarch	3	Scribes	19
Lysanias. Tetrarch of Abilene	3	Teachers of the Law	5
Herod's Servant	8	Disciples of the Pharisees	5
		Pharisees	7
		Sadducees	20
		Chief of the Pharisees	14
		Lawyers	14
		Rulers	23
		Officers of the Temple	22
		Publicans	7

Only one reference is given for each entry. While studying the Gospel of Luke, you will find other entries too numerous to list here.

A Genealogical Chart
of the Herodian Dynasty

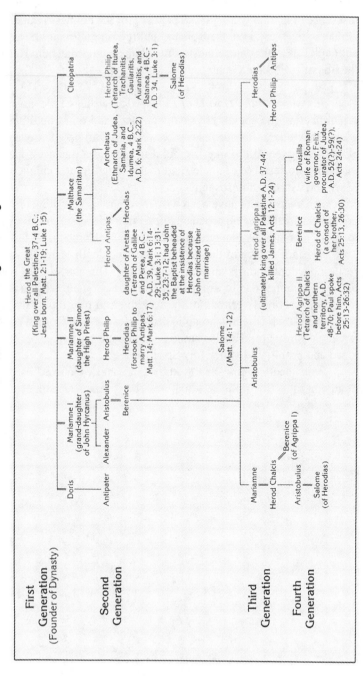

FIGURE 6.6 A genealogical chart of the Herodian dynasty. From *Chronological and Background Charts of the New Testament* by H. Wayne House. Copyright © 1981, by the Zondervan Corporation. Used with permission of Zondervan Publishing House.

times (Luke 7:39; 11:37; 14:1), suggesting that Jesus' worst enemies posed as his friends. Their main faults are founded in their highbrow attitude, their love of money, and their lost sense of justice, fairness, and concern for the helpless (Luke 11:37ff; 16:14). At the climax of the story, both the Romans and Jewish politicians have a hand in Jesus' death, although Luke takes away most of the blame from Pilate and Herod. See Figure 6.6 for the line of Herod the Great.

Summary of the Gospel of Luke   The writer of the Gospel of Luke is interested in meeting the social, physical, spiritual, and emotional needs of humans. It is a gospel that tells a story of Jesus who welcomed all people, regardless of their status or ethnic locality in life. Luke is careful to present a balanced view of Jesus' career by including stories about females and males. Highlighted characters include Zechariah, Mary and Martha, and Joseph.

The gospel may have been written to protect Christians from Roman hostility. A high priority is placed on producing peaceful situations. Luke may have been attempting to help Christians avoid paying the tax levied by Rome on all Jews after the Jewish war.

To Mark's story of the public career and death of Jesus, Luke adds stories about Jesus' conception, birth, and early childhood. The gospel ends with the romantic story of the two on the road to Emmaus sharing a light meal with Jesus.

Luke is highly critical of the wealthy and religious who take advantage of the poor. Jesus' own career is complicated by Jewish and Roman political operatives who hope to destroy him. He also battles with the unseen forces of Satan, while being energized and prompted by the Holy Spirit.

Jesus' death is foreshadowed by Luke and welcomed by the Jews, who seem to be in control of the political situation. The Romans remain seemingly guiltless at the Crucifixion.

7

A Troubled Community
in Search of the Truth

The Gospel of John

If the world hates you, be aware that it hated me before it hated you.

—John 15:18 NRSV

'I tell you the truth,' Jesus answered, 'Before Abraham was born, I am!'
At this, they picked up stones to stone him, but Jesus hid himself
slipping away from the temple grounds.

—John 8:58–59 NIV

Many Samaritans from that city believed in him because
of the woman's testimony.

—John 4:39 NRSV

INTRODUCTION

At the very instant our eyes touch the words of the first chapter of the Gospel of John, we know we have stumbled into unknown territory. After reading the Synoptics, we are unexpectedly propelled into a profound mystical time warp that describes the Word. Who or what was the Word? John attempts to describe how Ultimate Reality (the divine) in past time entered present time. In spite of this unprecedented act, the world did not recognize, understand, or appreciate the light or the divine coming its way. It even tried to suppress it.

The remainder of the gospel describes the Word or activities of Jesus and his speeches. Jesus heals the sick and challenges both the religious elite and foreigners, while preparing his followers for the time he will leave. Throughout the story, Jesus faces controversy, misunderstanding, and hostility, which results in his rejection and death.

This unique gospel was no doubt created during the birth of a new breed of Christians who argued for inclusion into a major religious body but who were probably excluded because they held different beliefs about the divinity of Jesus. John offers no long-term solutions to the hostility produced by this religious bias. His emphasis on love cannot stop opponents from threatening or killing members of his community. John also believes that they have the Holy Spirit, who will comfort and continue to lead them after the death of Jesus.

AUTHORSHIP, DATE, AND AUDIENCE

The Gospel of John is anonymous. The name of the author, if there was a single writer, was omitted from the gospel. But a curious person by the name of the "disciple whom Jesus loved" and the "other" disciple is mentioned (13:23; 18:15; 19:26; 21:7; 21:20–24; 18:15). This person is present at the last meal with Jesus, when Peter denies Jesus, at the cross, and at the appearance of Jesus after his death.

> When Jesus saw his mother and the disciple whom he loved standing beside her, he said to his mother, "Woman, here is your son." Then he said to the disciple, "Here is your mother." And from that hour the disciple took her into his own home. (John 19:26 NRSV)

Who was this person and why does the writer use the word "love" to describe the feelings of Jesus? Perhaps the "other" disciple is a symbol of the ideal Christian. Whom did Jesus love? Earlier in the gospel, Mary, Martha, and Lazarus are said to have been loved by Jesus. Could it be Lazarus or Judas? Could it be one of the sisters? Was it a mysterious person who has gone nameless throughout the centuries? Is it a reference to the writer of the Gospel of John?

Many scholars have speculated and early church writers have affirmed that the mysterious person was John, the son of Zebedee, a disciple of Jesus. For centuries, people hypothesized that late in life the son of Zebedee wrote the Gospel, the letters of 1, 2, 3 John, and possibly the Book of Revelation.

W. Graham Scroggie wrote a commentary over fifty years ago, *Guide to the Gospels,* which continued ancient speculations about John. An excerpt from his commentary follows:

> His home was Bethsaida, and there was a family of four, the father and mother, Zebedee and Salome, and two sons, James and John. The father and sons were fishermen. Salome, the mother, was ambitious for her boys. There is clear evidence that the family was prosperous, for they had hired servants, they ministered of their substance, and they were influential in official quarters....

Tradition tells us that John left Jerusalem and went to Asia. That, perhaps on account of the deaths of Paul, Peter, Timothy, and Titus, which would leave Asian Churches without a leader, John settled in Ephesus, and afterwards became bishop there. That at Ephesus he spent a great part of his life, died, and was buried there, tradition affirms. (Scroggie 1967, 398–99)

Most scholars today would agree that whoever wrote the Gospel of John did not fish for a living. This person was a superb writer and scholar but probably not an eyewitness or a close associate of Jesus. Some might conclude because of the narrator's powerful suggestions that John understood the mind of Jesus, that is, that the author knew Jesus personally. Yet students of the Bible should be aware that the writer is purposely choosing an all-knowing or omniscient narrator in order to sound more convincing to the audience.

The earliest evidence of the Gospel of John is found in the second century C.E. In fact, many early Christians complained that the gospel should not have been included in the canon because there were so many contradictions in the text. For instance, in John 6:1, Jesus is in Galilee yet only a few verses before, in 5:1, the scene is in Jerusalem. This inconsistent pattern continues throughout the gospel. There are also displacements of texts, as if the pages were arranged incorrectly. For instance, chapters 15 and 16, which are sermons to the disciples, are placed after 14:31, which says that they had already left, "Come let us go." Most of the written traditions we have about the author of the gospel date from the fourth-century writings of Eusebius, a church historian. Eusebius, who is quoting Irenaeus (around 180 C.E.), claims that John (the same John who leaned on the chest of Jesus) lived in Ephesus and published the gospel.

There is some evidence that the author of John used the Synoptics and Luke-Acts as sources for the gospel. If this is correct, then the writer could not have been an eyewitness. In fact, John, the son of Zebedee, is not mentioned in the gospel until the last chapter. Some have argued that another John, living in Ephesus, could have written the gospel—John the Presbyter. Others have suggested possible other authors to be the John Mark, whom we will meet in the Acts of the Apostles, John the Baptist, or the John found in John 1:42.

We know the author wrote in simple but readable Greek that was influenced by Gnostic or **dualistic** thought. This person understood Jewish literature and culture, while enjoying different types of argumentation. He or she was compelled to defend the divinity of Jesus in spite of many people who could cause the readers harm because of their beliefs.

Students of John today theorize that there was more than one person who edited and wrote the gospel. It is possible that the first version of the gospel contained notes from John, the son of Zebedee, although no one has proven this thesis. The original version could have been edited by what some call the "Johannine School," a religious group within an early Christian community or a place of study for Christians where John's writings were studied. The final version that we have today of the gospel of John has been pieced together from many different sources and by many people over several decades.

The Gospel of John was probably written very late in the first century or early in the second century. It is highly unlikely that any of the disciples would have been living sixty to ninety years after the death of Jesus. The life expectancy in the first century was in the forties. A date of 98–125 C.E. is generally assigned to the gospel. Scholars have reached these conclusions based on the following reasons: The gospel is not mentioned in any writing until the second century, although a copy of some of the verses from John 18 has been found in a papyrus fragment from Egypt, which is dated to around 100 C.E. The Gospel of John reveals knowledge of the other gospels, and the writer appears to have witnessed the destruction of Jerusalem (John 11:48). This means that it must have been written after 70 C.E. (the war) and after Matthew and Luke were composed (85 C.E.). And finally, the readers of the gospel seem to be an established community whose beliefs about the divinity of Jesus are more advanced than those found in the Synoptics.

No one knows where the gospel was composed. Ephesus, Antioch in Syria, and Alexandria are popular suggestions. The people who received the gospel could have been living anywhere in the Empire. They were no doubt Christians who had close ties with Judaism.

The readers seem to be struggling with the questions of social status (3:1), education (3:2, 10), tradition (3:2; 4:9), traditional authority (4:12), perhaps morality (4:16), and ethnic heritage (4:20). They are looking for answers to their everyday questions about food and water (4:13–15) and life and death (4:16–21). The writer points them to something beyond their normal everyday life (3:3; 4:13). He challenges the people to a new awareness and an appreciation of the differences among themselves. Change is a necessary element if problems are going to be solved.

At the moment of composition, the people of the Johannine community are facing a crisis because they appear to have been excommunicated from a local synagogue. (Some early Christian meeting places were also termed *synagogues*.) The difference of opinion may have its origin in a theological controversy involving a belief in the divinity of Jesus. It may also have erupted because of the tax (two **drachma**) placed on all male Jews who were twenty-one years or older, after the Jewish wars of 66–70 C.E. by the Roman authorities.

Richard Cassidy, in *John's Gospel in New Perspective: Christology and the Realities of Roman Power,* theorizes about the problems associated with taxing people based on their religious or ethnic background. How did the Romans define "Jew"? Was a Jew a person who converted to Judaism? What about the people who were born Jewish and rejected the religion? Were Christians or **God fearers** considered Jews? Some evidence suggests that the Romans used circumcision as one evidence of Jewishness. But this physical indication could not solve all of the problems associated with identifying Jews and collecting the taxes. In the Johannine community, Christians may have viewed themselves as something different than their Jewish brothers and sisters, and they were therefore untaxable. This would certainly have caused great tensions within a community.

LITERARY INFLUENCES

John's sources are illusive and varied. Ninety percent of John is original to the New Testament. No consensus of opinion has been achieved about where John obtained the material for the gospel. A few scholars have argued that Luke's writings form the basis of John (the story of 7:53–8:11 is not Johannine; many claim a Lucan authorship for the story about Jesus responding to a woman who was allegedly committing adultery). But most would agree that there are some quotations of and allusions to the Synoptics and to other literature that may have been lost to time.

The Synoptics

John assumes that those who read the gospel are already familiar with the stories and characters of the Synoptics. The list that follows surveys some of the similarities between the Synoptics and John.

Selected Similarities Between the Synoptics and the Gospel of John

Choosing Personal Disciples	1
Temple Incident	2
Healing of Official's Son	4
Miracle of the Loaves and Fish	6
Walking on the Sea	6
Peter's Confession	6
Last Days in Jerusalem	12
Anointing of Jesus	12
Meal and Prophecies	13
The Passion	

There appears to be some literary dependence upon the Gospel of Mark, but scholars also have theorized that Mark and John could have been using the same source.

Stories Found in the Synoptics But Not in the Gospel of John

Birth
Baptism of Jesus
Exorcising Demons
Temptation Story
Farming Parables
Last Supper
Agony in Gethsemane
Predictions of the Fall of Jerusalem
Transfiguration
Acension

SELECTED VERSES FOUND IN BOTH THE GOSPEL OF JOHN AND THE GOSPEL OF MARK

Gospel of John

5:8 Jesus said to him, "Stand up, take your mat and walk."

4:44 . . . (for Jesus himself had testified that a prophet has no honor in the prophet's own country).

6:20 But he said to them, "It is I; do not be afraid."

12:3 Mary took a pound of costly perfume made of pure nard, anointed Jesus' feet, and wiped them with her hair.

12:7 Jesus said, "Leave her alone. She bought it so that she might keep it for the day of my burial."

19:17 . . . and carrying the cross by himself, he went out to what is called The Place of the Skull, which in Hebrew is called Golgotha.

19:29 A jar full of sour wine was standing there. So they put a sponge full of the wine on a branch of hyssop and held it to his mouth.

Gospel of Mark

2:11 "I say to you, stand up, take your mat and go to your home."

6:4 Then Jesus said to them, "Prophets are not without honor, except in their home town . . .

6:50 But immediately he spoke to them and said, "Take heart, it is I; do not be afraid."

14:3 While he was at Bethany in the house of Simon the Leper, as he sat at the table, a woman came with an alabaster jar of very costly ointment of nard, and she broke open the jar and poured the ointment on his head.

14:8 She has done what she could; she has anointed my body beforehand for its burial.

15:22 Then they brought Jesus to the place called Golgotha (which means the place of the skull).

15:36 And someone ran, filled a sponge with sour wine, put it on a stick, and gave it to him to drink. (NRSV)

There appears to be some literary dependence upon the Gospel of Mark, but scholars also have theorized that Mark and John could have been using the same source (see box above).

While both the Synoptics and John ascribe a career in preaching and teaching to Jesus, John's order of events is much different than the Synoptics. In the Synoptics, Jesus has a public ministry in Galilee and then travels to Jerusalem, where he is executed. John appears to suggest that Jesus traveled back and forth from Jerusalem several times and attended as many as three Passovers. Many scholars theorize that John's gospel covers three years of Jesus' life. Jesus' harassment of people in the Temple occurs at the beginning of his public life in John and at the end in the Synoptics. John also suggests that both John's and Jesus' careers occurred during the same period. In the Synoptics, John is jailed before Jesus' public career is launched.

Gnostic Revelation Source

In Greek, the term *gnostic,* or *gnosis,* is translated as "knowledge." Gnosticism covers a wide range of diverse religious groups that generally taught that knowledge rather than faith was the key to understanding the divine, which would result in liberation from an "evil" world. A description found in *Harper's Bible Dictionary* follows:

> One element or "aeon" in that world, Sophia, fell and produced from her passion and repentance the psychic and material realms of existence. In a movement that typifies the whole soteriological process, Christ came to restore her to her original condition. Humanity is composed of the results of this process, having spiritual, psychic, and material components. The gnosis provided by Jesus, a being separate from Christ, awakens the awareness of the spiritual component of humanity about its essential identity with the Godhead and leads to ultimate restoration. (350)

Its exact origins are debated and may lay within Hellenistic Judaism during the time of Seleucids in the third to the second century B.C.E., or within Zoroastrianism around the sixth century B.C.E. Most agree that Gnosticism influenced and helped popularize early Christianity.

Scholars debate whether or not there was direct Gnostic influence on the Gospel of John. Gnostic ideas could have pervaded the culture, much like technological language and science fiction color or influence our own media today. Or the writer of John may have employed Gnostic language in the gospel to argue against Gnosticism or Gnostic practices. There are many writings, such as the **Nag Hammadi Library**, written slightly before or after the composition of John, that reflect similar foci on the topics of "Word," truth, mysterious knowledge, and a mystical orientation toward the divine.

A popular theory created by **Rudolph Bultmann** suggests that John used a **Gnostic** Signs (Revelation or Miracle Stories) Source, a Discourse Source, and a Passion Story in the creation of the gospel. Most outlines of the gospel are based on Bultmann's theories of these three basic sources. Chapters 1 and 21 were added later.

Structure of the Gospel of John

	Chapter
Prologue	1
Book of Signs	2–12
Discourses	13-16
Last Words of Jesus	18–20
Epilogue	21

John's gospel is structured around speeches and signs. First a sign or a miracle story is narrated, then a very long speech follows that interprets the sign.

What Are Signs?   Most of us are happy to see a road sign that points to a gas station, especially if we are hungry or the gas gauge is on empty. Signs help people find their way in unfamiliar places. Consider all the different types of signs we use in our culture. For the writer John, signs not only point the way to the Ultimate Reality but they also prove that Jesus is the divine. Signs become miracles. This differs considerably from the Synoptics, which tells a story about a Jesus declaring that he will not be tricked or pushed into performing a sign to prove his true identity.

> The Pharisees came and began to argue with him, asking him for a **sign** from heaven, to test him. And he sighed deeply in his spirit and said, "Why does this generation ask for a **sign**? Truly I tell you, no **sign** will be given to this generation." (Mk. 8:11–12; see also Mt. 16:1–4; 12:38–42 NRSV)

> Others, to test him, kept demanding from him a **sign** from heaven....This generation is an evil generation; it asks for a **sign**, but no **sign** will be given to it except the **sign** of Jonah. (Luke 11:16, 29–32 NRSV)

Compare the aforementioned verses with the following verses found in the Gospel of John:

6:30   So they said to him, "What **sign** are you going to give us then, so that we may see it and believe you?

2:11   Jesus did this, the first of his **signs,** in Cana of Galilee, and revealed his glory; and his disciples believed in him.

2:23   When he was in Jerusalem during the Passover festival, many believed in his name because they saw the **signs** that he was doing.

6:14   When the people saw the **sign** that he had done, they began to say, "This is indeed the prophet who is to come into the world"

20:30   Now Jesus did many other **signs** in the presence of his disciples, which are not written in this book. (NRSV)

Miracle, Wonder, and Sign   It is difficult to define the term sign for the writer of the Gospel of John. In ancient times, signs were used to predict future events. For instance some would attempt to read the lines on one's palm or chart the course of the stars. A falling star could be a good or bad omen or sign.

Most biblical scholars have generally understood "sign" to mean "miracle," but translators use the word "miracle" for several Greek nouns, that is, "wonder," "power", and "sign." The words "sign" and "wonder" are often used together (Mt. 24:24; Mark 13:22; John 4:48). Is a "sign" the same as a "power" or "wonder?" We do not really know. Some have suggested that "powers" refer to the activities associated with the "underworld" and that "wonders" have to do with supernatural events.

Other Judeo-Christian Writings

It cannot be proven that the writer of John copied data from Gnostic documents, but there are many similarities among the texts. Scholars have compared John with **Mandaean** texts, Philo, the Book of Enoch, Sophia traditions in the Old Testament/Septuagint, Greek philosophical literature such as Neo-Platonism, the Dead Sea Scrolls, and many others. Below is a sampling of other possible literary influences on the Gospel of John.

The Old Testament/Septuagint   We know that the writer of the Gospel of John used many quotations and images from the Old Testament/Septuagint. Some of the images include a lamb, a shepherd, water, manna, a tabernacle, a vine, and a pillar of fire. And Jesus' authority is attested by Jacob, Joseph, Moses, Abraham, and the King of Israel. On almost every page of the gospel, John makes allusions to Jewish traditions. What follows are a few of the quotations used by John.

Old Testament/Septuagint

John	Old Testament/Hebrew Bible
1:23 He said, " I am the voice of one crying out in the wilderness, Make straight the way of the Lord."	Isaiah 40:3 A voice cries out: "In the wilderness prepare the way of the Lord, make straight in the desert a highway for our God."
10:34 Jesus answered, "Is it not written in your law, I said, you are gods?"	Psalm 82:6 I say, "You are gods, children of the Most High, all of you...."
15:25 It was to fulfill the word that is written in their law, "They hated me without a cause."	Psalm 119:161 Princes persecute me without a cause....

Wisdom literature or philosophical writings pervade the Old Testament. For many years, the word "Sophia" was translated "wisdom" with a lowercase "w" because scholars thought that the writers were using a metaphor for Yahweh. Now, after the discovery of the Nag Hammadi Library, many believe that the "Sophia" or Wisdom within the Septuagint refers to the worship of an alternative goddess, Sophia.

No one knows exactly when she emerged, but many theorize that the roots of her worship go back to the times of the Seleucids, when Jews were required to abandon all of their religious practices and heritage on pain of death. Antiochus IV slaughtered many Jews. Some Jews abandoned the worship of a god, Yahweh, who could no longer protect them. During this time, the worship of an alternative goddess, Sophia, emerged. This may have been the beginnings of Jewish Gnostic faith. Remnants of that faith remain in the Hebrew Bible and Apocrypha. An excerpt from Proverbs follows.

Sophia, "Wisdom"

Does not wisdom call, and does not understanding raise her voice?

The Lord created me at the beginning of his work, the first of his acts long ago.
Ages ago I was set up at the first, before the beginning of the earth.
When there were no depths I was brought forth, when there were no springs abounding
    with water.
Before the mountains had been shaped, before the hills, I was brought forth—when he
    had not yet made earth and the fields, or the world's first bits of soil.

When he established the heavens I was there,
   when he drew a circle on the face of the deep,
   when he made firm the skies above,
   when he established the fountains of the deep,
   when he assigned to the sea its limit, so that the waters might not transgress his
     command,
   when he marked out the foundations of the earth,
   then I was beside him, like a master worker; and I was daily his delight, rejoicing
     before him always, rejoicing in his inhabited world and delighting in the
     human race.

And now, my children, listen to me: happy are those who keep my ways.
Hear instruction and be wise, and do not neglect it.
Happy is the one who listens to me, watching daily at my gates, waiting beside my doors.
For whoever finds me finds life and obtains favor from the Lord....
(Proverbs 8:1, 22–35 NRSV)

The Dead Sea Scrolls   John's writings mirror many contemporary types of literature during the second century C.E. For years, scholars attributed John's philosophical or mystical tone to the Greek philosophers. With the discovery of Qumran or the Dead Sea Scrolls, we now know that there were Jewish communities that produced literature that was similar to the Gospel of John. When the Dead Sea Scrolls were first discovered, many thought that they had found the beginnings of Christianity. Today we know that this self-exiled community was Jewish. Its hopes lay in the future, when the son of man would become the new ruler on earth, when the sons or children of light, with the help of the divine, win the battle over sons or children of darkness. The following excerpt is from the "Manual of Discipline" or the "Rule of the Community." Do these words remind you of the Gospel of John?

> He created man to rule the world and placed within him two spirits so that he would walk with them until the moment of his visitation: They are the spirits of truth and of deceit. In the hand of the Prince of Lights is dominion over all the sons of justice; they walk on paths of light. And in the hand of the Angel of Darkness is total dominion over the sons of deceit; they walk on paths of darkness. (1QS 3.17–21)

James H. Charlesworth and Raymond E. Brown note that there are many similarities between the Qumran community and those to whom the gospel of John was written. Both had a leader who was a teacher of righteousness and had similar beliefs:

Common Beliefs/Practices of the Johannine and Qumran Communities

Communities were exclusivistic
Believed that they were the Sons of Light
Set up barriers to outsiders
Love was reserved for the insiders in the community
Rejection of Jewish Temple religion
Cosmic dualism of two powerful forces

Messianic consciousness of the end of time
Creation by a monotheistic god
Spirit of truth and spirit of darkness/perversion
Believed they were chosen for a purpose
Hated evil and loved good
Kept festivals and sabbaths
Purified themselves with a water bath

Ancient texts are being discovered yearly. Perhaps someday we will find the sources for the Gospel of John, or perhaps it will remain a mystery.

REASONS FOR WRITING THE GOSPEL

Evangelization and Confirmation   The author of John ends the twentieth chapter with the following words:

> Now Jesus did many other signs in the presence of his disciples, which are not written in this book. But these are written so that you may come to believe that Jesus is the Messiah, the Son of God, and that through believing you may have life in his name. (20:21 NRSV)

Based on this text, many have concluded that John wrote in order to convert people to Christianity. The verse seems to suggest that some who might read or hear the gospel may not believe in the messiahship or divinity of Jesus (John 7–9; 12, 16, 18). The story

FIGURE 7.1   A painting on the wall at the Villa of Mysteries at Pompey of a beaten and naked worshipper of Dionysus.

of the miracle of wine at Cana could be an allusion to the Dionysiac mystery where Dionysus performed the same miracle. Indirectly, Jesus is being portrayed as a type of divine being with which people are already familiar. John also affirms that even though Jesus lived as a human, his origins were divine and eternal. Perhaps John also wants to prevent people from leaving the community by assuring them that they too will have some kind of eternal existence.

Theological Differences   People who followed Gnosticism, such as **Cerinthus,** a gnostic Christian, taught that Jesus could not have come into this life in the "flesh" as a human being. They adhered to something that is now termed "**Docetism**." For them, the flesh is corrupt or "evil," and so is all of the material, touchable world. Jesus, if Jesus was God, must have only appeared or seemed human because the divine is too perfect or pure to be soiled by being encased in a human body. John counters these claims by arguing in John 1 that Jesus was indeed born of flesh and blood. He was not a ghost or spirit or merely an image on the wall. "And the word became flesh and lived among us …" (1:14 NRSV). Thomas, at the end of the gospel, exclaims that he must touch the flesh of Jesus after his death, so John gives him that opportunity (20:27).

Community Politics   John also may be writing in order to encourage Christians not to abandon the struggle to keep their faith.

> They will put you out of the synagogues. Indeed the hour is coming when those who kill you will think that by doing so they are offering worship to God. (John 16:2 NRSV)

It appears that John's community has been rejected by a larger group of people who are oriented toward the traditional faith found in the Hebrew Bible, that is, the Jews. John's powerless community may be on the verge of extinction. It is fighting for its life and the existence of its religious beliefs in Jesus. This social conflict involves persecution, inquisition, expulsion, and possibly death. John believes that Jews or the sons of darkness were totally responsible for the death of Jesus. A list of the political players follows:

Groups

Disciples of John the Baptist
Disciples of Jesus
Samaritans
Brothers of Jesus
Masses
Pharisees
Jews
Chief Priests
Greeks

There are many anti-Jewish statements made by the writer. No one will ever know if these vitriolic statements were actually directed toward ethnic and religious Jews.

FIGURE 7.2   Jews in Jerusalem today. Photo taken by Melissa Luppens.

The names for the political parties could have been only symbolic names for people that could have been based on types of behavior or theological beliefs. A few of the anti-Jewish statements follow.

Anti-Jewish Statements

Gospel of John	Statement
5:18	For this reason the Jews were seeking all the more to kill him....
5:37ff	And the Father who sent me has himself testified on my behalf. You have never heard his voice or seen his form....
5:45	Do not think that I will accuse you before the Father; your accuser is Moses, on whom you have set your hope.
7:1	He did not wish to go about in Judea because the Jews were looking for an opportunity to kill him.
7:19	Did not Moses give you the Law? Yet none of you keeps the law. Why are you looking for an opportunity to kill me?
8:44ff	You are from your father the devil, and you choose to do your father's desires.
19:7	The Jews answered him, "We have a law, and according to that law he ought to die because he has claimed to be the Son of God." (NRSV)

Social and personal upheaval may also have been fostered by the long arm of the Roman government. John may be writing in order to support Christians who were facing physical harassment and possible martyrdom by the Empire for their faith. Many of the titles attributed to Jesus such as Lord, Savior, and King were also titles used by the emperors of Rome. Christians may have felt compelled to worship the emperor.

John's gospel affirms that no one has divine status but Jesus, and that, indirectly, no one should worship the emperors. His arguments about the divinity of Jesus are compelling, yet he does not attack Rome directly. Similar to the Gospel of Luke, he portrays the Jews as the villains and the Roman officials as pawns of the masses. Pilate attests that Jesus is innocent, "I find no case against him" (John 18:38 NRSV), and offers the masses (Jews) the opportunity to free him, which they decline.

Internal Political Struggles   Several scholars have studied the abusive statements made about Jews in John's gospel. In chapter 15:6, John appears to threaten those who differ with the Johannine community's or author's point of view. "Whoever does not abide in me is thrown away like a branch and withers; such branches are gathered, thrown into the fire, and burned" (NRSV). John is certainly sending a powerful message to those who do not agree with the Johannine theology. If they do not believe, they will then be destroyed. John may even be threatening the opponents with some type of retaliatory violence.

Other possible internal political problems surface in the gospel. Among them are the verses that seem to diminish the work of John the Baptist. "He himself was not the light, but he came to testify to the light" (1:8 NRSV). Scholars theorize that some people venerated John more than Jesus. (In our study of the Acts of the Apostles, we will meet some of these people.) The writer of John argued that Jesus was the true and only Messiah. "John performed no sign, but everything that John said about this man (Jesus) was true" (John 10:41 NRSV).

Still others suggest that John wrote to challenge the authority of Peter. Those who followed the ways of Peter may have represented a faction within the early church (see 1 Cor. 1), and John writes in order to argue that new leadership is needed for the present community. John portrays Peter as having to go through "the disciple whom Jesus loved" in order to speak with Jesus and suggests that Peter was kept on the outside of the courtyard when Jesus was tried, while the "other disciple" escorted Jesus (13:24; 18:15). If Peter was so important, then why did Jesus not speak with him as he did to "the other disciple" when he was on the cross? All of the aforementioned may suggest that there is a crisis in leadership and differences of theology within the Johannine community. The Jesus preached by those who followed the ways of Peter may not have sounded like the Word or God in the Gospel of John.

CHARACTERS AND ANALYSIS

John includes several new characters such as Philip, a blind man, Nicodemus, and the Woman of Samaria while increasing the roles for others we have already met in the Synoptics.

The Word: Jesus

As if beginning a play, song, or sonnet, the writer of John takes readers on a journey outside the realm of experience and time. The chorus sings, "In the beginning was the Word, and the Word was with God, and the Word was God" (1:1). The words are almost unforgettable and would have propelled Jewish readers back to the first words of the Torah, "In the beginning God … (Genesis 1:1), linking the discussion with **Yahweh**, **Adonai**, and **Elohim** and concluding that Jesus was preexistent and immortal.

For Greek readers, the use of "Word" (in Greek, "logos") would evoke images of Ultimate Reality whose knowledge reaches out to their lives with a divine spark, drawing them into eternity. It would denote rational, correct, and ordered reasoning and values. This divine entity created and ordered the universe and was synonymous with love.

For Gnostics, it brought to mind images of the power of speaking or an utterance. Logos was the name of a deity and with a thought could create whole galaxies. Words bring knowledge and foster wisdom. There is power in words.

I Am   The first words of the Gospel of John declare Jesus to be divine. This theme continues with the use of "I am" statements. In the Old Testament/Hebrew Bible, there is a story about Moses being called by a divine voice to lead the people of Abraham out of Egypt to freedom. Moses agrees to take the mission but asks a simple question.

> If I come to the Israelites and say to them, 'The God of your ancestors has sent me to you,' and they ask me, 'What is his name? What shall I say to them?' God said to Moses, 'I am Who I am.' He said further, Thus you shall say to the Israelites, 'I am has sent me to you.' (Exodus 3:13–14 NRSV)

While Jesus does not directly claim that he is the eternal, all-knowing, all-powerful God of Moses, he does indirectly link himself with that God, the Father. A list of some of the "I am" statements in John follows. All of these statements would have angered and offended a traditional Jewish audience that would not speak the holy name of God. For them, Jesus' attributions were blasphemy (8:56).

"I Am" Statements

I am the bread of life.	6:35
I am the light of the world.	8:12
I am the resurrection and life.	9:25

Not only does the writer of John compare Jesus to the "I Am" of the ancient Israelites, but his life and authority are also measured against that of Moses. "The law was given through Moses; grace and truth came through Jesus Christ" (1:17). And "If you believed Moses, you would believe me, for he wrote about me" (5:45 NRSV).

Jesus is also portrayed as an enemy of various Jewish groups that wanted to kill him. After a lecture or a healing, they often exclaimed that he was demon possessed and wondered if he was going to kill himself. His family (7:5) and many disciples (6:66) abandoned him. In spite of all of his sermons about the Father, people wonder how a man born as the son of Joseph could come from heaven (6:42). For the writer of John, Jesus is part of a master plan conceived in eternity past. Forces of evil are at odds with the divine, yet Jesus has the upper hand or holds the trump card.

While Jesus' claims of fulfilling prophecy, his miracle-working ability, and his speeches cause conflicts, the writer of John suggests that there is a greater eternal cosmic conflict behind the Jesus story. Jesus breaks the Sabbath (5:16; 39; 7:21–23; 9:16), rejects the people running the Temple (2:13–22), appears to be breaking the law of Moses, and intimidates the religious authorities.

From the beginning until the end of the gospel, Jesus is portrayed as being in control of everything (6:14) and everyone who is around him. A mysterious Jesus can read people's minds and often plans activities in secret (7:11; 8:59; 16:19). It is as if the life he was living was planned in eternity past. There are verses placed periodically in the narrative that suggest that the time had not arrived for Jesus to be killed (7:30). Jesus knows his fate and plans for it by preparing his disciples. Although he has the power to control natural forces and heal incurable diseases, he chooses to place himself on the cross and die. He is not afraid of his death; he welcomes it.

John's portrayal of Jesus is difficult to summarize in a single chapter. He fulfills many roles but acts primarily as a healer and teacher. A summary of some of the descriptive titles attributed to Jesus is listed below.

Titles Attributed to Jesus in the Gospel of John

The Word

Christ

Lamb

Shepherd

Vine

The Life

The Light

Savior of the World

Bread of Life/Living Bread

The Holy One of God

The True Vine

If a guest lectured in your class today and claimed that he or she was God, how would you react? What conclusions would you draw? Look at the bewildered faces of the people listening to the speaker in the cartoon (Figure 7.3).

FIGURE 7.3 From *The Bible. Now I Get It!* by Gerhard Lohfink. Copyright © 1979 by Doubleday, a division of Bantam, Doubleday, Dell Publishing Group, Inc. Used with permission of Doubleday, a division of Bantam Doubleday Dell Publishing Group, Inc.

The Speech of Jesus Understanding and summarizing Jesus' relationships with people, activities, and speech are even more complex than identifying his person. Norman R. Petersen, in *The Gospel of John and the Sociology of Light*, designates Jesus' speech as anti-language. Jesus rarely speaks to the point on any issue. While it appears that he is using commonly understood words, Jesus reinvents or gives new meanings for the terms. Peterson calls this an **inversion**.

Jesus takes control of the situation by changing the issues and using double and multiple meanings, irony, metaphors, symbols, contrasts, and numerous literary devices that negate or give an opposite or a different point of view. The words are simple, yet the meaning is profound. In an audience situation, Jesus' language would be heard as nonspeech, as riddles, except to those who understood the true or secret definition of his words. Many words have a double meaning, such as "born again," "lifting up," and "crucifixion" (3:16; 8:28; 12:32–34; 5:24). For instance, while Jesus was teaching in the temple courts he said,

> I am with you for only a short time, and then I go to the one who sent me. You will look for me, but you will not find me; and where I am, you cannot come." The Jews said to one another, "Where does this man intend to go that we cannot find him? Will he go where our people live scattered among the Greeks, and teach the Greeks? What did he mean when he said, "You will look for me, but you will not find me," and "Where I am, you cannot come?" (John 7:33–36 NRSV)

Regardless of the discussion or situation, the writer portrays Jesus turning the question or problem into something that is unflattering to those opposing him. Nicodemus, a Pharisee, is "ignorant" on the topic of the new birth (John 3). The disciples and the Woman from Samaria are foiled as Jesus speaks of living water and the essence of real food (John 4). The story of the man blind from birth is used as an opportunity to mirror the ignorance and utter blindness of the Pharisees (John 9). And the resurrection of Lazarus makes everyone, including the mourners, look silly, especially when he emerges from the tomb in his grave clothes (John 11).

For John, Jesus is the savior of the world who is like a lamb slaughtered for the sins of Israel. He is the messiah, the one who sends the comforter to them after his death. Yet while Jesus is divine, he is also very human. He weeps at the death of Lazarus and is emotionally upset about the prospect of Judas betraying him (11:35; 13:21).

Judas

Jesus Christ Superstar, a play and a movie about Jesus, portrays Judas as the only person who is not swept away with the personality and charisma of Jesus. He warns that the crowd may kill Jesus and questions his associations with women who make their living on the streets. According to the video, Judas never intended to betray Jesus. He may have wanted to protect himself or force Jesus' hand to claim his right as "king," but Judas never intentionally plans the death of Jesus—it is an accident! The following is an excerpt from the song "Heaven on Their Minds":

> My mind is clearer now. At last all too well I can see where we all soon will be. If you strip away the myth from the man, you will see where we all soon will be. Jesus! You've started to believe, The things they say of you. You really do believe This talk of God is true. And all the good you've done Will soon get swept away. You've begun to matter more than the things you say. All your followers are blind, too much heaven on their minds. It was beautiful but now its sour.

The writer of John seems to have the inside story on Judas Iscariot, who was one of Jesus' closest friends and students. There are hints that Judas was controlled by superhuman forces and therefore not responsible for his actions. Early in the narrative, John names Judas the antagonist by predicting that he will be the downfall of Jesus. He, as one of the Twelve, was "going to betray Jesus" (6:71), and later, the "devil had been put into the heart of Judas …" (13:2).

During the erotic scene, where Mary pours fragrant oil on Jesus' feet, brushing them with her hair, Judas accused Jesus and Mary of questionable behavior. The money should have been given to the poor. John allows the audience again to have a special view of Judas' character and personal motivations. "He said this not because he cared about the poor, but because he was a thief: he kept the common purse and used to steal what was put into it" (John 12:6). During the last meal of the Twelve, John says that Satan entered Judas (13:27). Finally, Judas brings the soldiers and police from the chief priests and Pharisees to arrest Jesus (18:5) and is never placed in the narrative again. The writer of the Acts of the Apostles claims that he committed suicide (Acts 1:15–20.)

WOMEN CHARACTERS

> Jesus loved Martha and her sister and Lazarus.
> —John 11:5 NIV

John places female characters in the most important stories in the gospel. The Mother of Jesus observes Jesus' first miracle at the wedding at Cana, travels with him to Capernaum (2:12), is known by the local townspeople (6:42), and is present at the death of Jesus (19:25–27). While she is not an integral part of the resurrection accounts, the writer assures the reader that she was well taken care of by the disciple whom Jesus loved. Mary and Martha are loved by Jesus, and it is their brother Lazarus whose life is returned by Jesus. Jesus demonstrates intense emotion when he sees them mourning for Lazarus. Mary, Clopas' wife, and Mary Magdalene accompanied Jesus' mother to the Crucifixion. Magdalene was the first to experience Jesus after his death. The story of the Woman from Samaria is essential to understanding John's emphasis on breaking down class and ethnic barriers. She will be considered momentarily with another important character, Nicodemus.

Almost all of the scholars who have studied the theme of women in the Gospel of John have high praise for the stories. There is mutuality, respect, and recognition of the importance of women. Robert J. Karris calls the woman stories heroines and models of early Christian living. Elisabeth Schüssler Fiorenza concludes that John is not typically patriarchal, thereby creating models of co-equality. Sandra M. Schneiders argues that the roles of women in John were unconventional, and the male disciples had difficulty adjusting to them.

The Woman from Samaria and Nicodemus

Two of the most thought-provoking stories in the Gospel of John involve a man and a woman. Nicodemus and the Woman from Samaria are central to John's narrative. Who are these people? Nicodemus is "out of the Pharisees" (3:1), and she is a woman "out of Samaria" (4:7). Her personal name is not given.

It would appear that their status and points of origin are quite different. He is a ruler or a person of authority among the Pharisees (3:1); she has no occupation. The meetings with Jesus occur at different times of the day. Nicodemus comes at night (3:2), whereas the Woman meets Jesus during the middle of the day (4:6). The Woman is unaware of Jesus' sign-working ability. Some suggest that the well was the best place for lovers and future partners to meet. The writer may be suggesting that the meeting may not have been accidental. Nicodemus comes to Jesus as a result of his signs (2:23–25), seeking enlightenment (3:10). He may have become a secret disciple of Jesus (7:50; 19:38). The Woman asks for water and becomes a spokesperson for her people.

The Woman from Samaria

You are right in saying, "I have no husband"; for you have
had five husbands, and the one you have now is not your husband.

—4:17 NRSV

Unlike Nicodemus, the Woman's status within the community is a mystery. No particular profession is listed. Her personal life and its effect on her community (4:17, 38) are of prime importance to the writer. She is honest, blunt, even antagonizing. Her response to Jesus' request for a drink seethes with hostility born out of racism. "How is it that you, a Jew, ask a drink of me, a Woman of Samaria?" (4:9). Jesus waits for a drink. She is a Samaritan; therefore she is ritually unclean according to Jewish purity laws. She is a woman. Why would any Jew break common custom by talking to a woman in public?

Jesus is neither master of the conversation nor of the Woman. She has the choice of whether or not to fulfill the request for water from Jesus. She chooses to continue the dialogue on racism. "For Jews have no dealings with the Samaritans" (4:9). Jesus ignores her question and his own physical thirst by thrusting the conversation into the future. He reveals himself. "If you knew the gift of God and who it is that is saying to you, 'Give me a drink,' you would have asked him ..." (4:10). The Woman ignores the source of his response and continues her own dialogue. She questions Jesus' claim to be the source of living water. He does not possess any jars of his own (4:11). She challenges him. "Are you greater than our father Jacob?..." (4:12), or rather, "Who do you think you are?"

In this episode, John depicts a sensitive, intelligent, and forceful woman who interrogates Jesus. Her antagonism explodes at his claim of knowledge and power. Jesus copes with the explosion by offering water to quench a thirst and a hope for an eternal existence (4:15). She virtually says, "Produce it then. Show me the sign." The sign Jesus provides for her is his intuition or omniscience. He knows of her private life (4:15–18). The knowledge Jesus exhibits is a device used to bring this woman to a position of belief in the person of Jesus. There is no evidence of repentance in her life.

John makes no judgment about this woman's sex life or patterns of marriage. While the New Revised Standard Version translates the word "men" as husbands, it is possible to interpret this verse differently. Perhaps she has lived with several men in her life and the man she is living with now could be an uncle, a nephew, or a brother. In fact, all of the men could have been relatives, not lovers.

Parenthetically, the writer inserts critical remarks about the disciples of Jesus. The disciples seem to be amazed that Jesus was talking with a woman—any woman. They do not understand. They cannot overcome their own backgrounds of sexism and racism to see the value of Jesus' conversation with the Woman. They are blind, and their blindness causes fear. They are unable to verbally question the motives of Jesus and this woman.

After Jesus' intuitive display, the Woman concedes to him, "You are a prophet" (4:19). "Seeing" brings understanding (4:19). Yet she continues to question him about the issue of sacred places (4:20). Jesus begins to reveal to her his own message, which is neither nationalistic, sexist, nor racist. All will worship God in spirit and truth (4:22–23); locale and person are incidental.

The Woman recognizes his words as a hope for the future, and she equates that with her personal belief in the Messiah. The primary sign or test of this Messiah is "he will show us all things" (4:25). He agrees, and in her presence reveals her personal life and asserts that he is the great "I am" (4:25).

Her response to this revelation demonstrates her thirst and zest for life. The knowledge and the revelatory experience of Jesus demands action. "So the Woman leaves her water jar," (4:28) very much like the disciples in the Synoptics who left their nets, and followed him. Her dynamic response to Jesus' self-disclosure and sign stirs an entire village.

Who was the Woman? Why did she and not those characterized as disciples have such an influence on a village in Samaria? The Samaritans call him "rabbi," similar to the aristocratic Nicodemus (3:2). The disciples are unaware of the tremendous reshaping of Judaism that John captures by portraying Jesus speaking with a woman (4:35–28).

The narrative implies that the disciples were in the same city, Sycar, and nothing happened because of their contact with the residents. "His disciples had gone into town to buy food" (4:8). Their view was linear; food and the Woman alone at the well in the middle of the day. After their return, they insisted on pressing the issue of eating. "Rabbi, eat" (4:31). Perhaps food would bring Jesus to his senses. His reply reveals their uninformed vision (4:35–38).

The Woman's influence on the city is unprecedented in the Book of John. She is the key to dissolving racism, sexism and the acceptance of a new theology; Jesus as messiah and savior. Here in a foreign village, Jesus is welcomed. He stays, and converts emerge (4:41). Jerusalem was no place for Jesus, "But Jesus on his part would not entrust himself to them," (2:24 NRSV). Jesus trusted the Woman, and the entire village, and went on to disclose additional information about himself. The people believe, hear, and understand that Jesus is the Savior (4:41).

The writer of John is concerned about the effect and influence of the Woman from Samaria. She sees, dialogues with Jesus, questions his authority and motives, challenges his theology, and is gradually convinced that he is a prophet, a messiah, a savior. She is a disciple. She learns, leaves her present tasks, and passes on the experience she had with Jesus. The response of the town to her words about Jesus is remarkable. She is portrayed as an example to the questioning disciples and the inhabitants of the city. In spite of her religious tradition, status, occupation or profession, and even her private life, she becomes a vehicle for revelation and transformation. The cleanliness or status of this woman is never questioned.

Nicodemus the Pharisee

"Now there was a Pharisee named Nicodemus, a leader of the Jews."

—John 3:1 NRSV

The Johannine Nicodemus is curious, a seeker of answers, and somewhat enigmatic. He is representative of a class of people within Judaism. He addresses Jesus in the first person plural "we know." For him, Jesus is a rabbi or a teacher that has come from God. God is somehow with him (3:2). Nicodemus is not concerned with Jesus' Jewishness or his prophetlike abilities (4:8).

The issue of the meeting between Jesus and Nicodemus is direct identity and discipleship. Jesus centers the conversation on rebirth (3:4–8). Nicodemus reports, "How can a man be born when he is old?" (3:4). His apparent lack of insight triggers, "Are you a teacher of Israel, and yet you do not understand this?" (3:9). This statement is similar to Jesus' response to the Woman, "You worship what you do not know" (4:22). Both characters have faulty perceptions of Ultimate Reality.

Jesus appears to reject Nicodemus. "But you do not receive our testimony" (3:11). Nicodemus exits at this point, and the discussion of the meaning of rebirth is continued (3:12–21). References are made to those who do not believe (3:12), and a pronouncement of doom follows all who love darkness (3:19).

What happens to Nicodemus? Does he become a follower of Jesus or does he choose to remain in his present status as a leader within Judaism in Jerusalem? The writer of John gives the reader two brief hints of Nicodemus' future relationship to Jesus in the remainder of the work.

In chapter 7, Nicodemus defends the person and work of Jesus by asking the question, "Does our law judge a man, before it first hears from him and knows what he is doing?" (7:51). The crowd, which must include the chief priests and Pharisees, answers, "Are you also from Galilee?" (7:52). The reader remains unconvinced about Nicodemus' loyalty to Jesus. By "being one of them" (7:50), is he one of the crowd that is cursed by the law or one of the rulers of the Pharisees who believe in Jesus? (7:48).

Nicodemus' special relationship with Jesus is seemingly divulged after the passion. He is listed with Joseph of Arimathaea, a secret disciple of Jesus (19:38–39). Both assume responsibility for Jesus' corpse. Thus ends the account of the character of Nicodemus. The reader is given no information regarding his influence within the community, or his effect on the leaders of Judaism.

The writer of John uses both of these characters with the dual purpose of identifying Jesus and reprimanding readers. Jesus is more than a rabbi, a teacher, a man sent from God, or a prophet. He is the messiah to all peoples and the savior of what John calls the "world." Jesus is knowledgeable. Jesus is a symbol of love that goes beyond class, education, sex, race, religion, and country.

The Woman and Nicodemus are examples of two very different followers. They are almost opposites, yet they are united in a common pursuit—Jesus. Although they should know Jesus (3:10; 4:10), they do not. They are still asking identity questions. Neither is an outcast because of social background. Neither knows all of the questions or answers regarding Jesus. Both question and both receive appropriate answers for who they are.

The obtuseness of the disciples and the indecisiveness of Nicodemus may signal paralyzed communities/readers who are unable to project their dreams into the future or to deal with the present situation (4:35). They are satisfied with the status quo. The writer of John attempts to rouse the readers by embarrassing them. The future, the present, and the immediate past are given to a strange woman from a despised locale and religion. She is an example of change, vitality, and growth from which the readers can learn.

SPECIAL FEATURES

Dualism

John's dualistic emphasis is present throughout the gospel. There is never a middle ground. Either one is an insider or an outsider. The dualism could be a result of a Gnostic influence, tensions within the community that have polarized people, or for John, a way of characterizing opponents. A list of selected dualisms follows:

Positive	Negative
Children of Light	Children of Darkness
Light	Dark
Love	Hate
Life	Death
Heaven	Hell
God	Satan

Two of the most important dualisms are "love" and "hate." Raymond Brown subtitles a commentary on John, "The Life, Loves, and Hates of an Individual Church in New Testament Times." This is an excellent title for a community that seemed to have such strong feelings toward both insiders and outsiders. What follows are some of the love and hate sayings:

Love

5:42	But I know that you do not have the Love of God in you.
8:42	If God were your Father, you would love me ....

10:17	For this reason the Father loves me …
13:34	… love one another. Just as I have loved you. …
13:35	By this everyone will know that you are my disciples, if you have love for one another.
14:15	If you love me, you will keep my commandments.
14:23	Those who love me will keep my word, and my Father will love them, and we will come to them and make our home with him.

(See also 14:21, 31.)

(Other verses include: 15:9,10,12,13,17,19; 17:26; 21: 15,16,17.)

Hate

3:20	For all who do evil hate the light …
7:7	The world cannot hate you, but it hates me because I testify against it that its works are evil.
12:25	Those who love their life lose it, and those who hate their life in this world will keep it for eternal life.
15:18	If the world hates you, be aware that it hated me before it hated you.
15:24	But now they have seen and hated both me and my Father.
15:25	It was to fulfill the word that is written in their law, 'They hated me without a cause.'
17:14	… and the world has hated them because they do not belong to the world, just as I do not belong to the world.

(Other verses include 15:19, 23.)

Love and hate are very strong emotions. Some psychologists have suggested that the two emotions are quite similar. According to *Webster's New World Dictionary,*

> hate "implies a feeling of great dislike or aversion, and, with persons as the object, connotes the bearing of malice." Love "implies intense fondness or deep devotion and may apply to various relationships or objects (sexual love, brotherly love, love of one's work, etc.")."

What does it mean to love and hate, and can we experience these emotions at the same time? Can you detect different types of love or hate in the Gospel of John? In the last chapter of John, the writer employs two different Greek words that are both translated "love" in English. He asks Peter, "Do you love me?.." (21:15). The word that is translated here is *"agapao,"* a strong form of love that can be equated with a self-sacrificial love of and from the divine. Peter answers, "I love you," but the word here is *"phileo"* or a brotherly type of love. Peter cannot say that he truly loves (*agapao*) Jesus.

Obviously the writer and reader of John are living under tense conditions that can produce feelings of hopelessnes and a need for protection. If lives and finances are at stake, one can understand the hostility toward others and the choices people must make between warring factions.

The Paraclete: The Comforter

John portrays Jesus as a loving and concerned teacher in the last speeches in chapters 14 through 16. Knowing that there was little time left on earth, Jesus takes the opportunity to warn his disciples of problems that lay ahead of them and to assure them that they will not be alone. Another entity, the "Comforter," in Greek the "paracletos" or the "one who comes along side," will teach and guide them. John describes the entity with the following:

14:16–17	Advocate
14:26	Holy Spirit
15:26	Spirit of Truth

Its mission is varied.

14:16–17	Will be with them forever.
15:26	Will testify on behalf of Jesus.
16:7–11	Will come to the disciples after the death of Jesus.
	Will prove the world wrong about sin, righteousness, judgment.
16:13–15	Will guide the disciples into all truth.
	Will glorify Jesus.
	Will prophesy about future events.
	Will serve as a mouthpiece for the divine.

The writer of John gives the readers hope that they are not alone and that the words and ethical ideals of Jesus will not be lost. Jesus, the Word, left them, but the entity will remain. While Jesus is gone, readers are still in contact with a source of divine power. The situation is not totally hopeless.

The Eucharist (Lord's Supper, Communion)

The Eucharist is a ritual that helped Christians for thousands of years to remember that Jesus or the Holy Spirit is present in their lives. It is odd that the Gospel of John did not describe and instruct people about how to perform the Eucharist. Yet its verses are foundational in interpreting the meaning of this ritual for Roman Catholics. Consider John 6:50–56.

> I am the living bread that came down from heaven. Whoever eats of this bread will live forever; and the bread that I will give for the life of the world is my flesh. The Jews then disputed among themselves saying, 'How can this man give us his flesh to eat?' So Jesus said to them, 'Very truly, I tell you, unless you eat the flesh of the Son of Man and drink his blood, you have no life in you. Those who eat my flesh and drink my blood have eternal life, and I will raise them up on the last day; for my flesh is true food and my blood is true drink. Those who eat my flesh and drink my blood abide in me, and I in them.' (John 6:50–56 NRSV)

The following **canon** (law) of the **Council of Trent** (1543–1563 C.E.), "Decree Concerning the Most Holy Sacrament of the Eucharist," describes the official **Roman Catholic** belief that the wine and bread served during communion became the actual blood and body of Jesus. It is considered a miracle. This canon drew a line between Roman Catholics and their sister **Protestants**, who believed that the bread and wine were symbols, or a way of remembering the death and Resurrection of Jesus.

Roman Catholics consider the Eucharist the high point in the Mass. What follows is an order of service for **catechumens**, taken from the Apostolic Constitutions in Syria around 380 C.E. It appears that the Gospel of John and the Synoptics are foundational to the ritual.

Let Him be Anathema

And because that Christ, our Redeemer, declared that which he offered under the species of bread to be truly his own body …

If any one saith, that in the sacred and holy sacrament of the Eucharist, the substance of the bread and wine remains conjointly with the body and blood of our Lord Jesus Christ, and denieth that wonderful and singular conversion of the whole substance of the bread into the body, and of the whole substance of the wine into the blood—the species only the bread and wine remaining—which conversion indeed the Catholic Church most aptly calls Transubstantiation: let him be anathema. (Thirteenth Session, October 11, 1551. Decree Concerning the Most Holy Sacrament of the Eucharist and On the Most Holy Sacrament of the Eucharist IV and Canon II.)

FIGURE 7.4   Vie de Jesus Mafa, "The Lord's Supper." All Rights Reserved. Vie de Jesus MAFA. 24 rue du Marechal Joffre. F-78000, Versailles, France.

Summary of the Gospel of John   The Gospel of John was probably written over a significant period of time by several different editors or authors. Its date of composition is somewhere between 98–120 C.E., and it was probably written to Christians who were influenced by Judaism and Gnosticism. Sources for the gospel may include the synoptics and the Old Testament/LXX. Literary influences may include the Odes of Solomon, the Dead Sea Scrolls, and Greek philosophical literature.

John was written in order to win new converts, while encouraging familiar faces not to leave. It reveals internal strife and possible physical violence over differences of opinion that include Gnostic ideals, Jewish traditions, the worship of John the Baptist, and the role of Peter in the future church.

John adds new characters to a wide cast first discovered in the Synoptics. In this chapter, we consider Jesus, the Women, Judas, Nicodemus, and the Samaritan Woman. John has many unique features, among which are the use of dualisms, a promise of a Paraclete, and a call for the disciples to ingest the blood and body of Jesus.

8

Christianity, a World Religion

The Acts of the Apostles

But you will receive power when the Holy Spirit has come upon you; and you will be my witnesses in Jerusalem, in all Judea and Samaria, and to the ends of the earth.

—Acts 1:8 NRSV

God did extraordinary miracles through Paul, so that when the handkerchiefs or aprons that had touched his skin were brought to the sick, their diseases left them, and the evil spirits came out of them.

—Acts 19:12 NRSV

Awe came upon everyone, because many wonders and signs were being done by the apostles. All who believed were together and had all things in common; they would sell their possessions and goods and distribute the proceeds to all as any had need.

—Acts 2:43–44 NRSV

INTRODUCTION

The Acts of the Apostles is a remarkable and an idealistic story about the origins of the early Christian communities throughout the Roman Empire during the first century C.E. More than in any other book we have studied in this text, the writer of Acts aims to include all ethnic groups, socio-economic classes, and peoples of the world. This goal may perplex the first-time reader, because lists of geographical names and locations can be overwhelming. The cast of characters seems to roll on infinitely. Behind this detail is

FIGURE 8.1 Photo of a sailing vessel set in a sidewalk in front of a shop in Ostia Antiqua, the ancient port of Rome where Paul would have disembarked. The mosaic on the sidewalk would have told travelers about the business inside. Photo taken by Marla J. Selvidge.

an honest attempt to defend and portray Christianity as a world religion, with adherents in every sector of the globe.

AUTHORSHIP AND SOURCES

No one left a name on the manuscript of the Acts of the Apostles, and therefore it is presumed anonymous. Many theories have surfaced, but most would agree that the writer of Acts and the Gospel of Luke is a person we call "Luke." Conclusions are based on a close study of vocabulary, literary style, composition, and the opening statements of both volumes. Acts begins,

> In the first book, Theophilus, I wrote about all that Jesus did and taught from the beginning until the day when he was taken up to heaven, after giving instructions through the Holy Spirit to the apostles whom he had chosen. (Acts 1:1 NRSV)

Some have suggested that the Greek word "protos," which means "first," denotes the first volume in a series of two or three volumes. Acts was the second volume of a possible set of three volumes. Charles Talbert finds many parallels between Luke and Acts (see the list below).

Parallels Between Luke and Acts

The Preface
The Spirit Descends
Sermons Begin with a Fulfillment of Prophecy
Lame Men Are Healed
Conflict with Religious Authorities
Centurion Invited Character to Home
Widows and a Resurrection
Missionary Journey to Gentiles
Journey to Jerusalem to Die
Hero Arrested on False Charges

Was the writer of Acts, commonly known as Luke, a companion and a friend of Paul's? Based on a study of all passages that contain the first-person plural "we," many contend that the writer had a personal association with Paul and wrote a history of those events (16:10–17; 20:5–15; 21:1–18; 27:1–28:16). Some theorize that Luke was a medical doctor and that the "we" passages appear when Paul was ill and needed care from a physician. The "we" passages then are from a doctor's journal. Others disagree and suggest that the "we" passages are a source, perhaps a ship's log or a diary, that was used in composing the story. Yet no evidence has been discovered to prove any of these theories.

The portrayal of Paul in Acts is not the Paul we will later discover in his letters. Many scholars insist that the writer of Acts did not know Paul. They have compared the letters of Paul with the events and speeches in Acts and have found many inconsistencies. For instance, in Acts, Paul is a great miracle worker; not so in the letters. In Acts, Paul makes speeches that stir great crowds; in the letters, he is sometimes feeble and defensive. In Acts, the Twelve who are later Apostles, are a select group of which Paul is not a member; in his letters, he claims to be a member of this apostolic group.

The writer of Acts portrays Paul's beliefs in sermons and speeches. It would seem logical that these beliefs would be the same in both the sermons in Acts and Paul's letters. But scholars have determined that many of the beliefs differ. For instance, on the question of whether people who are not Christian can also have a close relationship with God, in Acts, Paul claims that they are in the family of God. But in Romans (a letter of Paul's), they will experience the wrath of God because they are ignorant (Acts 17:22–31 and Romans 1:18–23), which means that they are not part of the family.

Another important question is "How do Christians view Jewish Law?" In Acts, Paul is portrayed as appreciating the law. He has Timothy circumcised and even agrees to go through purity rituals in Achaia and Jerusalem. In his letters he contends that the law cannot save a person from the wrath of God (Romans 10:4). And finally, in Paul's letters, there is an urgency about Jesus' return. It may be tomorrow. In Acts, Jesus' second coming is not as important (Acts 17:30–31). Paul even takes time to help organize and give directions to the elders from Ephesus. And oddly, in all of his travels and conversations in Acts of the Apostles, Paul is never portrayed as sending or writing a letter to anyone.

OLD TESTAMENT SOURCES FOR ACTS

Acts

3:13   The God of Abraham, the God of Isaac, and the God of Jacob, the God of our ancestors has glorified his servant Jesus....

4:24   ... "Sovereign Lord, who made the heaven, the earth, the sea, and everything in them...."

7:3   'Leave your country and your relatives and go to the land that I will show you.'

7:37   'God will raise up a prophet for you from your own people as he raised me up.'

Hebrew Literature

Exodus 3:6   He said further, "I am the God of your father, the God of Abraham, the God of Isaac, and the God of Jacob."

Psalms 146:6   "... who made heaven and earth the sea, and all that is in them...."

Gen. 12:1   "Go from your country and your kindred and your father's house to the land that I will show you."

Deut. 18:15   The Lord your God will raise up for you a prophet like me from among your own people; you shall heed such a prophet. (NRSV)

Sources   Debate continues about whether Acts of the Apostles was written entirely by one person. In addition to the "we" passages, which could have been anything from a ship's log, a diary, or an ancient way of telling a mariner story, there are other indications that Luke used sources, perhaps even a shipwreck narrative.

Several scholars detect seams or breaks in the narrative and suggest that the writer had many sources, or that the book went through stages of editing. Some suggest that Acts was first written in Aramaic because of its heavy emphasis on the stories of the Old Testament/Septuagint. For example, the box above shows a few of the quotations taken from the Old Testament/Hebrew Bible.

Others suggest that Luke used a source from Antioch, perhaps Stephen or Barnabas, who kept a log of activities and shared it with Luke. This may account for the many doublets throughout the book. There are two accounts of Peter reaching out to Cornelius, a God fearer (10:1–48; 11:1–18), and three accounts of Paul defending himself (9:19; 22:4–16; 26:9–18).

TITLE, DATE, AND CONTENTS

Most scholars agree that the title does not fit the contents of the work. Some have suggested that more accurate titles might be the "Acts of Peter and Paul," or "The Acts of the Holy Spirit." The book is the story about apostles. But who are apostles? Are disciples the same as apostles? The word "apostle" comes from a Greek word meaning "to send out"; therefore apostles are those who are sent out. Disciples can also be apostles. The word "disciple" in Greek means "learner or student." And there are a host of people who are called disciples or apostles, but they play very small parts in the narrative.

No one knows in what part of the Empire the book was written, or who received it. Suggestions include Rome, Ephesus, Macedonia, and Achaia. It seems logical that it would be written to Gentile Christians, but it could also have been written to the government in Rome, or to people whom the writer was trying to convert.

Acts was probably written after the Gospel of Luke and before the end of the first century, C.E., although some scholars place its creation around 130 C.E. Most would agree that it was written some time between 70 C.E. and 100 C.E., usually around 85 C.E.

Acts can be outlined in many ways. One popular approach is to consider Acts 1:8. Acts follows the broad outline of this verse. The gospel begins in Jerusalem, travels south into Judea with the Ethiopian Eunuch, to Samaria with Simon Magus and others, and then heads for parts unknown throughout the Empire. The book can also be divided into the Acts of Peter (chapters 1–7) and the Acts of Paul (14–28). Their activities overlap in chapters 8 through 13.

The geographical outline of Acts takes Peter and Paul to many cities throughout Judea and the Empire. Scholars debate whether or not the writer of Acts had firsthand knowledge of the landscape in Judea, because there appear to be mistakes. For instance, the term *Judea* is used in a variety of ways: to refer to a Roman province, to all of Palestine, and to only that part of Palestine inhabited by Jews. Some suggest that the writer did not know where the various locations were in the Temple, that is, Solomon's Portico and the Beautiful Gate. And Luke ignores Galilee, listing very few towns or areas in Judea outside of Jerusalem. Most agree that Luke knew the cities and geography of the coast and the Empire better than Palestine. A list follows of some of the places visited by Paul on his three missionary journeys, which can be located on the map (Figure 8.2) on page 158.

Major Places Paul Visited in Acts

Journey One	Journey Two	Journey Three	Journey Four
Antioch, Syria	Syria	Ephesus	Jerusalem
Seleucia	Cilicia	Troas	Caesarea
Salamis, Cyprus	Lystra	City in Greece	Sidon
Paphos, Cyprus	Iconium	Philippi	Sea Journey
Perga, Pamphylia	Troas	Sailing Islands:	Malta
Antioch, Pisidia	Philippi, Macedonia	Assos	Rome
Iconium	Thessalonia	Mitylene	
Lystra	Beroea	Samos	
Derbe	Athens	Miletus	
and return to	Corinth	Cos	
Antioch, Syria	Cenchreae	Rhodes	
	Ephesus	Tyre	
	Caesarea	Ptolemais	
		Caesarea	
		Jerusalem	

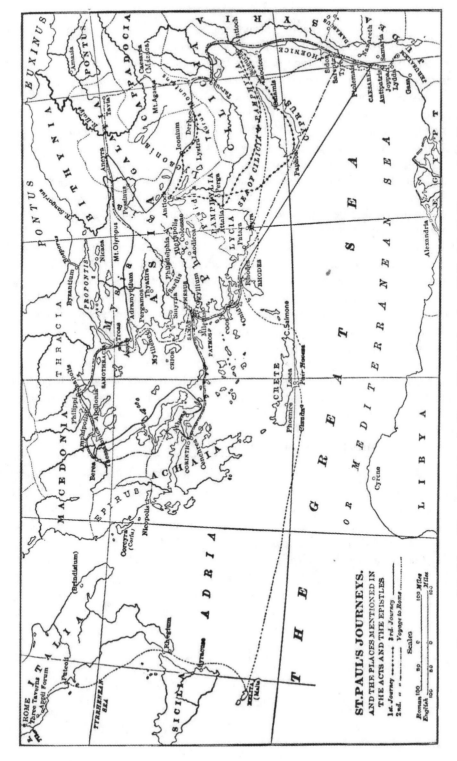

FIGURE 8.2 Map of Roman World at the Time of Paul. Taken from Philip Schaff, *History of the Christian Church* (William B. Eardman, 1890).

REASONS FOR CREATING THE ACTS OF THE APOSTLES

During a first reading of Acts, it seems logical to assume that Acts is "factual" history because it is written in a narrative style, noting many details in the story of early Christianity. Some scholars today hold to this view. Yet upon a closer reading of the stories, it may not be so easy to detail the reasons for writing the work. Some reasons for the creation of the Acts of the Apostles follow.

To Argue That Christianity Belongs to the World

Acts begins with several dramatic scenes. After the disciples watch Jesus ascend into the sky, they wait. Within days, a supernatural event changes their lives forever. Tongues of fire appear over their heads, they begin to speak in languages understood by many people, and an enthusiasm is ignited that fulfills the expectations of Acts 1:8 during the remainder of the book.

> But you will receive power when the Holy Spirit has come upon you; and you will be my witnesses in Jerusalem, in all Judea and Samaria, and to the ends of the earth. (NRSV)

With the help of the Holy Spirit and "power," or in Greek, "dunami," they would become witnesses "to the ends of the earth." Throughout Acts, the word "power" legitimates the ministry or activities of the person (2:22; 3:12; 4:7, 33; 6:8; 8:13; 19:11). It is a special term signifying that the people are connected with the divine. This power enabled them to do extraordinary things (6:8; 4:33).

Step by step the writer takes the reader from the narrow streets of Jerusalem, south to the sands of Joppa and Lydda, and north to the hills of Samaria. Eventually the mission to all peoples reaches Northern Palestine (Antioch in Syria) and then springs forward to Asia Minor, Macedonia, Achaia, and even to the steps of the Emperor's Imperial Palace in Rome.

Internationalism is a theme found in almost every chapter of Acts. Characters take journeys to distant lands. Most of those characters are linked with a specific geographical area of the world. For example, during the first speech made by Peter after the tongues of fire experience, the writer lists the following places of origin of people who were listening. Consult the map (Figure 8.2) to pinpoint these locations.

People	Location
Parthians	Northeast Iran
Medes	Persian
Elamites	East of Tigris in Mesopotamia
Mesopotamians	The land between the Tigris and Euphrates
Phrygians	Western Asia Minor, Galatia, and Asia
People of Pamphylia	Southern Asia Minor

People	Location	(continued)
Egyptians	Egypt	
Libya (Cyrene)	Northern Africa, west of Egypt	
Romans	Rome	
Judeans	Southern Palestine	
Cappadocians	Central Asia Minor	
People of Pontus	Northern Asia Minor	
Asians	Asia Minor?	
Cretans	Island of Crete, south of Athens	
Arabs	Possibly people from Saudi Arabia	

As you continue your study of Acts, make a note each time the writer describes a character by referring to his or her geographical location.

To Portray an Idealistic View of the Early Church

It is apparent from the early chapters of the work that the writer believes Christianity will inaugurate an utopian community where people share everything, so no one starves or sleeps on the streets. The writer portrays the early Judeo-Christian community as possessing the best of both religions. They worshiped together, accepted the apostles as

FIGURE 8.3   "Pentecost." All Rights Reserved. Vie de Jesus MAFA. 24 rue du Marechal Joffre. F-78000 Versailles, France.

authoritative, and sold all of their property (2:42–47). The proceeds were distributed to other needy believers. This harmonious story about the first few days of the Church characterizes an idyllic environment for the reader. Everyone agreed on everything.

> Now the whole group of those who believed were of one heart and soul, and no one claimed private ownership of any possessions, but everything they owned was held in common… there was not a needy person among them, for as many as owned lands or houses sold them and brought the proceeds of what was sold. They laid it at the apostle's feet, and it was distributed to each as any had need. (4:32, 34–35 NRSV)

Luke carries the theme of unquestioning agreement throughout most of the book. "With one mind" characterizes both those who are spreading the new religion and those who are resisting it. "With one mind" believers pray together (4:24), assemble in the same place together (5:12), and make decisions together (15:25). So also do the enemies of the Jesus movement. "With one mind" they killed Stephen (7:57), attacked Paul (18:12), and rushed the theater at Ephesus (19:29). Both sides seem to have abandoned individual thoughts or criticisms. Luke even characterizes these new converts as "simple of heart" (2:46). By using the word "all" 170 times in Acts, Luke generates a sense of unswerving unity among those who would follow "the way." This unity or solidarity may have given hope to people who had no real community life, or hope to a community that was torn apart by dissension.

Into this tranquil scene of a common cause and life comes the awful and terrifying story of Ananias and Sapphira, who are apparently killed for not telling the truth. And while it is wonderful to claim that thousands were converted and life for early Christians was perfect, it is unrealistic. It is also unrealistic to assume that the early Apostles, such as Peter, had the power to give or take life.

To Unite Divisions within Early Christianity

Political parties within Acts are numerous. There are scores of different types of Christians from multiple cultural, religious, and ethnic backgrounds. One by one, the writer of Acts links their histories and adventures together. Preeminent among the parties may have been those that followed Peter (Hebraists), Paul (Hellenists), or the late John the Baptist. Scholars have naturally argued about who belonged to which group, but as one can conclude from the list that follows, Luke attempts to portray an enormous diverse political situation. Traditional scholarship suggests that the Hebraists were converted Jews who held that Christians needed to keep all of the ancient Jewish laws and practices. Their primary language may have been Aramaic. Hellenists were Greek-speaking Christians who may or may not have lived in Palestine. Christianity was a new religion, and the old Jewish rules did not apply to them. By using all of the titles and names of political groups, Luke may be arguing that Christianity is now the religion of choice in the Empire.

To Defend Paul at His Trial in Rome

Many industrious legal scholars have actually taken the book of Acts and demonstrated that it would fit into a legal brief used during Roman times. It is possible that this document was used to defend Paul before Rome against his opponents (Acts 22–28). Paul rehearses his story several times before both Jewish and Roman officials, but Acts contains more than a defense of Paul. The first eight chapters include numerous characters and situations that would not fit into a legal brief about Paul. Paul's legal plea could also have been written in order to be used as a model defense for Christians who had been arrested or imprisoned for their faith.

To Suggest That Christianity Is Not a Threat to Rome

If there was a riot almost every time Paul visited a new town, then someone would have to be blamed. Paul is jailed or imprisoned often. The writer of Acts blames the Jews and local, narrow-minded people such as Demetrius, the silversmith at Ephesus. Agrippa the Governor claims that Paul had broken no Roman law, yet apparently he was kept under arrest for two years in Caesarea. Roman officials are often portrayed as treating Paul in a neutral fashion. They are not bare-teethed adversaries. His travels put him in touch with such notables as Gallio in Corinth, Festus, Felix, Agrippa in Caesarea, Publius on Malta, the Asiarchs in Ephesus, and his personal centurion Julius. The Romans or governmental officials may want to be bribed (Felix) and flattered, but they are not interested in killing innocent people (see Acts 18–28).

In the case of Peter and John, they are portrayed as following God rather than the rules of tradition. The hostilities that follow them are religious and have little to do with Roman laws. James is killed by King Herod Agrippa I, and Stephen is stoned by the Sanhedrin. Both the Sanhedrin and the Kingdom of Judea existed because the Romans needed it to preserve order among the volatile groups and to collect taxes. Herod the Great, the first King of Judea, came from an Idumean family and was appointed by Rome. The Sanhedrin was elected from the ranks of the Pharisees and Sadducees.

Luke argues that there are many divisions within Christianity, but it is a peaceful religion that has been abused by its sister religion Judaism and by local religions that consider these divisions a threat to the local economies or cultures. Christians are not revolutionaries. Their Christ died on the cross and will not return with an army to invade Rome and destroy it. Instead, their Christ offers forgiveness and a future hope of a new life.

To Answer Theological Questions

Many writers view Acts as an evangelistic document designed to convince people that Christianity was a religion in which they would be accepted. It may also have been written to assure early Christians that there is a future for those who believe in Jesus within a religious organization. Jesus may have ascended to another place, but the Holy Spirit is front and center and available for them.

Some also view Acts from a theological point of view, suggesting that it is "salvation history." The writer of Acts believes God has a plan, as revealed in the Scriptures, and that there is a period of the Jews, as evidenced in the Old Testament/Hebrew Bible, a period of Jesus, as in the gospels, and a period of the Church, as described by the writer of Acts. People who now live in the twenty-first century are in the period of the Church. There is one last time period to come, which will be when Jesus comes to rule on earth at the end of time. This "parousia," or coming of Jesus, for Acts, seems to be in the very distant future.

GENRE

Identifying the genre of Acts is not an easy task. Suggestions about its form are numerous. Some argue that it is a memoir, a myth, a monograph, a violent **aetiological legend**, and a story about divinities, or a **hagiography**. Others believe it is the first church history, and for them it is factual data, or provable history. For John Calvin, in 1552, it was a "sacred" history that shows

> that God has cared for His Church from the beginning, that always He stood by, a just vindicator, for those who turned to Him for support and protection, and that he was gracious to miserable sinners. (The Acts of the Apostles, 1:17)

An Ancient Romance or Historical Novel

Acts has been compared to ancient historians such as Josephus or **Thucydides**, Jewish Apocryphal books such as the Maccabees, and ancient romances or novels such as *Apollonius of Tyre* and *Daphnis and Chloe*. Other scholars look for traditional inspiration of Acts by claiming that it mimics the Hebrew stories of Elijah and Elisha. They point to the abundance of quotations from the Old Testament. Some conclude that the Acts of the Apostles is written in the classical tradition of important Greek and Latin writers. In comparing Acts with typical Greek romances, there are some surprising similarities. Both contain the following characteristics:

travel

heroes and heroines

fidelity to a person, idea, or even a god

heroes and heroines are mistaken for deities

performance of miracles or miraculous rescues

apparent deaths

suicides or suicidal tendencies

dreams and oracles

trials

storms at sea and shipwreck

numerous characters that include pirates, robbers, sorceresses, villains, witches

a happy ending

Perhaps the one great similarity that is missing in Acts is a lover of Paul's or Peter's. Some might argue that their great love was not a woman but God or Jesus. While Paul meets several women in his journeys in Acts, he never takes a female companion or travels with a female. Early Christians thought that this was odd. Surely there must have been one strong, vibrant woman, equal to the great stories about Paul. Out of this longing for a heroine, "The Acts of Paul and Thecla" was born. There is significant evidence to conclude that for the first two centuries early Christians considered this book genuine history. It was supposed to have been written by a man in Asia Minor around the end of the second century C.E. Consider the following heroine who baptized herself and others, who reportedly kissed the chains of Paul while he was in prison.

The Acts of Paul And Thecla*

And while Paul was thus speaking in the midst of the assembly in the house of Onesiphorus, a virgin named Thecla—her mother was Theocleia—who was betrothed to a man named Thamyris, sat at a nearby window and listened night and day to the word of the virgin life as it was spoken by Paul; and she did not turn away from the window, but pressed on in the faith rejoicing exceedingly. Moreover, when she saw many women and virgins going in to Paul she desired to be counted worthy herself to stand in Paul's presence and hear the word of Christ;

And taking her by the hand, Paul led her into the house of Hermias, and heard from her everything that had happened, so that Paul marveled greatly and the hearers were confirmed and prayed for Tryphaena. And Thecla arose and said to Paul: "I am going to Iconium." But Paul said: "Go and teach the word of God!"

Similar to the ancient story of Thecla, Acts was written in a popular style with the hope of creating an interesting story for the reader.

A Foundational Legend Steeped in Violence

We have already hinted that the writer of Acts presents a very negative view of Judaism. This polemic may be normal for the birth of a new sect or religion. As it seeks to identify itself as something different, it negates the group from which it is breaking away.

*From "The Acts of Paul and Thecla" in *The Other Bible,* ed. Willis Barnstone (San Francisco: Harper & Row, 1984), 448–53. Copyright © 1984 by Willis Barnstone. Used with permission of Bantam Books, a division of Bantam Doubleday Dell Publishing Group, Inc.

Stephen, Peter, and Paul used inflammatory language and accused the Jews of atrocities and of abandoning their own traditions. They rejected the Messiah, Jesus. The writer of Acts predicts judgment and destruction.

Paul's plan for taking the news of Jesus to people began with synagogues. When that failed, he approached people on the street. Throughout the empire, Jews are portrayed as instigators of riots and planners of murders. They make vows to take Paul's life in Jerusalem, and even attempted to stone him in Iconium. In Acts, Stephen was an official victim. Even Saul's earlier life was filled with violence against the Christians (Acts 8–9), although there are some Jews who believe and convert to Christianity, even Pharisees (Acts 23:9).

Could the Book of Acts be warning its readers to expect violence? Luke's idyllic recounting of idealistic situations of the beginning of Christianity are punctuated with words of revenge, accusation, and hostility against (primarily) the Jews. It may be a story of a religio-political struggle between those who believe in the suffering, dying, and rising of God and those who do not. With hopes of transforming the entire world, Luke fears that theological conflict will generate violence.

People are caught in the middle of a religious struggle (7:7; 2:4; 17:24, 31) where God battles the powers of the earth and heaven. This divine conflict is mirrored in the lives of the valiant missionaries who are called by God to change the world, to become warriors for the faith. The majority of the stories found in the Acts of the Apostles portray conflict and confrontation. Peaceful resolutions are rare.

In Jerusalem, after the experiences of Pentecost and before an international crowd, Peter accused his audience of murdering Jesus. "... [A]nd you with the help of wicked men, put him to death by nailing him to the cross" (2:23). For him, they were a "corrupt generation" (2:40). To a similar audience, "Men of Israel," after the healing of the crippled man, he says, "You handed him (Jesus) over to be killed, and you disowned him before Pilate.... You killed the Author of life..." (3:13–15 NIV).

Peter and John were arrested (4:2). When asked about their powers, Peter answered "...you crucified" (4:8). They were repeatedly arrested and finally flogged, but they would not stop their accusations. The Sanhedrin complained, "You have filled Jerusalem with your teaching and are determined to bring this man's blood on us" (5:28 NRSV).

Next, Stephen addressed a body of religious leaders who eventually murdered him. What provoked them into such frenzy? An answer lies in Stephen's own confrontational language. He tore into the traditions of the Jews and insulted their foundations of faith. After giving a rather short and negative account of the history of Israel Stephen exclaims,

> You stiff-necked people, uncircumcised in heart and ears, you are forever opposing the Holy Spirit, just as your ancestors used to do. Which of the prophets did your ancestors not persecute?... You are the ones that received the law as ordained by angels, and yet you have not kept it. (7:51–54 NRSV)

The group reacted furiously when Stephen claimed to see God (7:56). This was the final insult. For no Jew could speak the name of God nor look upon God's face. Is

FIGURE 8.4   Old city wall of Jerusalem. Photo by Marla J. Selvidge.

the writer of Acts warning that his insensitivity and accusations provoked a violent retribution?

Interwoven among the stories about the spreading of the new inclusive religion (2:17ff) are narratives about control. Independent inquiry, freedom of speech, and self-expression were not ideological goals of the beginnings of Christianity, according to the writer of Acts. Liberation came through conformity in action and word. To disagree could be fatal, as in the cases of Ananias and Sapphira (5:1-11).

Values Portrayed within the Acts of the Apostles

If Acts is a legend of violence, it also preserves religious values. Consider the following statements. Do you think they represent the writer's point of view? Why or why not?

1. You are a special people if you believe in the same God of Peter, Stephen, Paul, Dorcas, and Lydia.
2. You will receive special gifts that will have extraordinary manifestations.
3. You are entrusted with the responsibility of changing the world to your way of thinking.
4. Your religion is inclusive, but only on your terms.
5. Your happiness will come through singular, unquestioning devotion and obedience to the tenets of faith.

6. You will experience violence and hardship in your life because of your faith.
7. You may have to die for your faith.
8. You will have personality clashes with your fellow workers, others of different faiths, and even government officials. This is normal.
9. Violent and abusive language may be used to convey the good news. You may have to defend yourself physically.
10. You will have the power to decide who is Christian and who is not.
11. God will aid you in moments of danger. Your opponents will be supernaturally vanquished.

Acts of the Apostles may be a legend about a divinely commissioned religious revolution that aimed at the conversion and control of the entire world. Verbally armed, convinced of the proper interpretation of the truth, Luke set out to tell this story through the lives of well-known Christians. The writer exhibits little appreciation for the beliefs of Jews or worshipers of other Gods. When faced with the message of a suffering and dying God, there is only one choice. This belief may have been so radical that it necessitated suffering for the faith. The writer of Acts wanted to bring about change, and may have been willing to risk everything for that change.

CHARACTERS

Peter: A New Man

Do you remember the high points in the career of Peter? The Gospel of Mark places a hopeful Peter with the other disciples waiting for Jesus to return to Galilee (Mark 16:7). While Peter is not an eyewitness of the empty tomb, he is one of the three who glimpse a "transfigured" or changed Jesus on top of the mountain (Mark 9:2–8).

In Matthew, Peter is given the keys to the Kingdom of God. He identifies Jesus as "the Messiah, the son of the Living God" (Mt. 16:18–20). Again, although Peter was not an eyewitness of the empty tomb events, he was presumably with the Eleven who went to Galilee. Jesus gave them the directive to make disciples of all nations (Mt. 28:16–18). The Gospel of Luke disagrees with Mark and Matthew by placing Peter as a witness of the empty tomb (24:12).

John's view of Peter is decidedly more complicated. In the Gospel of John, Peter is mentioned more than any other disciple. He denies Jesus, as in the Synoptics, but the writer adds additional material such as the cutting off of the servant's ear (18:10–11) and Jesus washing Peter's feet (13:6–11). In John, Peter seems to be on a different level (or in a different relationship with Jesus) than the disciple Jesus loved (13:23–26; 18:15–16; 20:2–10). He is on the outside, although still a member of the inner circle. He uses the other disciple as an intermediary to ask Jesus questions, and he has very little to do with the scenes involving Jesus' death. Yet Peter does witness the empty tomb. In John's epilogue, Peter converses with Jesus and is never able to say, "I love you and would sacrifice my life for you" (John 21), although there is a hint that he will be or was martyred for his faith (13:36).

FIGURE 8.5   Peter, depicted in the knave at Monreale in Palermo, Sicily. Photo by Marla J. Selvidge.

The aforementioned ambivalent picture of Peter changes in Acts. Peter becomes the first hero of the early church. The writer of Acts places the founding of the early Christian Community in Jerusalem and in the hands of Peter and those who waited in the upper room. After Jesus left them, they waited. The spirit arrives, and Peter begins his speaking career. A miracle happens. Almost everyone who hears him understands his words in their original tongue, although some complained that they thought he and others had been drinking. Peter preaches, heals, and understands as he has never understood in the gospel narratives. Legends about his great powers over life and death grow to enormous proportions.

> Yet more than ever believers were added to the Lord, great numbers of both men and women, so that they even carried out the sick into the streets, and laid them on cots and mats, in order that Peter's shadow might fall on some of them as he came by. A great number of people would also gather from the towns around Jerusalem, bringing the sick and those tormented by unclean spirits, and they were all cured. (Acts 5:14–16 NRSV)

Peter raises Tabitha from the dead, cures Aeneas, a bedridden man for eight years, and cures a man who was lame from birth (Acts 9:32–43; 3:2).

For his newfound skills, he is arrested, threatened, beaten, and imprisoned. In spite of all the hardships, he remains loyal to his belief in Jesus. Not only does Peter overcome personality difficulties, he is able to transcend kosher regulations and eat with a God fearer, Cornelius, which he reports to all the believers in Judea (Acts 11:1f). A God fearer was probably a monotheist who chose to accept part of the Jewish faith. Normally he was not circumcised and did not keep kosher laws. He was not allowed to worship up front with male Jews, being required to sit in the back or behind a curtain with the females in a synagogue.

When Peter was in prison, "an angel of the Lord" opened the doors and released him (Acts 12:6). James, a good friend, was killed by the state, but Peter eluded prison and death. He became a leader of the Jerusalem Church, and with the help of Barnabas is portrayed introducing Paul to the elders of this group (Acts 15:7).

What happened to Peter? Why does his role stop in Acts 15? No one knows. Some contend that he traveled on his own missionary journeys and ended up in Rome, where he was eventually crucified upside down with Paul. Christian traditions claim that he was the first Pope.

Saul, or Rather, Paul

Paul is the most important character in the Acts of the Apostles, yet ironically, when the Eleven choose a person to fill the place of Judas, they elect Matthias (1:26). Paul is only called an "apostle" once in Acts, and that is in connection with Barnabas in 14:14. He may be the "ideal" apostle! His character is portrayed as embodying most of the important lessons or ideas that the writer wants to convey to the audience. His early life was divided between the narrow Jewish sect of the Pharisees and the obvious cultural benefits of living in a Roman free city, Tarsus, in Cilicia. His greatest achievement was his ability to step out of his sectarian past to shake hands with others throughout the Roman Empire. Paul's egalitarianism touched the lives of women from different classes, slaves, uncircumcised Jews, politicians, artisans, tent makers, followers of John the Baptist, sailors, Jewish-Christians, and even procurators and kings.

Paul's international character includes knowledge of several languages (Acts 21:37–22:2). Within the context of Acts, he speaks both Aramaic/Hebrew and Greek, and one could presuppose that he might have known some local dialects as he journeyed through the mountains of Asia Minor across the Aegean Sea to Macedonia.

It is interesting to compare the story of Jesus portrayed in the Gospel of Luke with the character Paul in Acts of the Apostles. Their activities are remarkably similar.

Both enter the temple.
Both have disciples who follow them.
Both have supernatural experiences of the divine.
Both heal people.
Both preach to great audiences.
Both have plots against their lives.
Both travel extensively.
Both are misunderstood.
Both appear to manipulate governmental systems.
Both have powerful women associates.

Both break bread and give thanks at a meal.

Both are seized by a mob.

Both are slapped.

Both are brought to trial four times and declared innocent three times.

Both are rejected by Jews.

We first meet Saul while he watches the Sanhedrin stone Stephen to death. He raises no questions or objections to the death. Some have speculated that he was a member of that religious body. Later, he himself is found imprisoning and possibly causing the death of female and male Christians. He was a proud, arrogant, and successful religious person. Change came into his life the day he saw a light in the sky while traveling north to Damascus. Now Saul becomes Paul, converting to Christianity and evolving into an equally zealous missionary for his new cause.

His adventures in Acts put him in touch with Christians in Antioch, such as Barnabas and Silas, and the more traditional arm of Christianity in Jerusalem, led by Peter and James, the brother of Jesus. Paul becomes, for Luke, the most important link in the dissemination of information about the new religion, "The Way." (One wonders what happened to the rest of the Apostles and why their lives and activities have not been remembered.)

After what we will call the "Jerusalem Council" in Acts 15, Paul begins a marvelous adventure throughout Asia Minor, Macedonia, and Achaia, which results in his ultimate arrest in Jerusalem and final journey to Rome in order to appeal to the Emperor. With divine fortitude and strength, Paul challenged religious powers from the synagogue to the sorcerer. In a concentric pattern, driven by a divine impulse, Paul began to win the world over to his view of God. His enthusiasm brought violence to his own life and to almost every city he visited (20:23). Many vowed to take his life (20:3; 21:31, 36; 23:12). Threats of suicide, stonings, a snake bite, a shipwreck, trials, being tortured, plots against Paul's life, mobs, and murder were all part of Paul's journey. In one of Paul's letters to Corinth, he seems to remember some of these challenges.

Are they descendants of Abraham? So am I. Are they ministers of Christ? I am talking like a madman—I am a better one: with far greater labors, far more imprisonments, with countless floggings, and often near death. Five times I have received from the Jews the forty lashes minus one. Three times I was beaten with rods. Once I received a stoning. Three times I was shipwrecked; for a night and a day I was adrift at sea; on frequent journeys, in danger from rivers, danger from bandits, danger from my own people, danger from Gentiles, danger in the city, danger in the wilderness, danger at sea, danger from false brothers and sisters, in toil and hardship, through many a sleepless night, hungry and thirsty, often without food, cold and naked. (2 Cor. 11:22–28 NRSV)

The Christian world has forgiven the deeds of Saul/Paul because of the great conversion in his own life. Paul was zealous for his faith, Judaism. Was he any less zealous for Christianity? Before a huge crowd in Jerusalem, Luke writes about the dark side of Paul.

I am a Jew, born in Tarsus in Cilicia, but brought up in this city at the feet of Gamaliel, educated strictly according to our ancestral law, being zealous for God, just as all of you are today. I persecuted this Way up to the point of death by binding both men and women and putting them in prison, as the high priest and the whole council of elders can testify about me. From them I also received letters to the brothers in Damascus, and I went there in order to bind those who were there and to bring them back to Jerusalem for punishment." (Acts 22:3–5 NRSV)

Because of Paul's violent nature he was promised a life of pain. "I will show him how much he must suffer for my name" (Acts 9:16).

Paul's speeches and activities are unusual by today's standards of evangelism. Paul used supernatural powers to blind a man (13:11, Elymas). Through magic, he conquered human ills (19:11–12). In cosmic duels, he always won (19:11–20). He baited the crowds by calling some of them perverse (20:30). He wished violence upon them: "Your blood be upon your head" (18:6).

According to Luke, Paul believed that his view of God, his view of being religious, was the only acceptable point of view. His religious ideology influenced everything he did in the Book of Acts. His own convictions were so strongly presented that it appears that he insulted and harassed people who did not accept his message. Consequently, Paul was accused of sedition and insanity by both Jews and Roman officials (24:5–7; 26:24–25).

In Thessalonica, political charges were leveled against Paul and his entourage.

These people who have been turning the world upside down have come here also, and Jason has entertained them as guests. They are all acting contrary to the decrees of the emperor, saying that there is another king named Jesus. (Acts 17:6–7 NRSV; see also 21:21)

Tertullus, in presenting his case against Paul before the Roman Procurator Felix in Caesarea, said, "We have, in fact, found this man a pestilent fellow, an agitator among all the Jews throughout the world, and a ringleader of the sect of the Nazarenes" (24:5–7 NRSV). Agrippa calls Paul "mad." This is the only instance where the term *mad* is used in the New Testament. "To rave or to become insane "mainomai" is used only one other time in Acts (12:15). Did the Roman authorities think Paul was mad? At times he certainly did not seem rational. In addition to preaching and teaching a new faith, Paul heard voices (9; 16:9; 18:9) and fostered controversies and riots all over the Empire.

One thing is clear about Saul/Paul. While he experienced a life-changing **theophany** (chapter 9), it did not change his personality. His voracious enthusiasm for his religion came with him when he converted to Christianity. He was on fire for God. His ideological stance gave him economic power in some communities such as Ephesus, where the silversmiths were losing money because they were no longer selling statues of Artemis. With each word about the good news, he also lived a life of conflict that followed him to almost every city he visited. The fire and enthusiasm for God consumed him until he no longer thought of himself (20:24; 21:13).

Luke's portrayal of Paul borders on idealism. He rarely, if ever, makes mistakes. He follows the whispers of the Holy Spirit. He even makes vows at Cenchreae and in Jerusalem to appease those who criticized him. While caught in the web of controversy, Paul always manages to escape. His story ends in Rome, under house arrest. What happened to him? Some say he was martyred in Rome under Nero, around 64 C.E. Others say he went on to Spain to an even greater missionary career throughout the Empire. We will never know the end of the story until perhaps the third volume of Luke's writings is discovered.

Women in the Acts of the Apostles

Many feminist scholars criticize Luke's portrait of women in the Acts of the Apostles because they are not given primary roles in the narrative. Ivoni Richter Reimer, a Brazilian scholar, concludes that Acts is androcentric and that it does not write a unified or connected story about the lives of women. It is true that women are not at the center of Luke's narrative, but it is also true that Luke portrays more women in the Acts of the Apostles than in any other book in the New Testament. Luke may not have given women the starring roles in Acts, but the writer portrays a variety of independent women who were actively engaged in commerce, politics, government, and religious activities. Men and women are mentioned together throughout the first nine chapters of Acts. They are present in every town Paul visits. It would take too long to summarize all of their stories. We will consider the narratives of Tabitha (9:36–42) and Lydia (16:1–40) and references to female politicians.

Tabitha, a Person of Charity   Tabitha, or Dorcas, "meaning gazelle," was a disciple who lived at Joppa near the sea. The term *disciple* is a most unusual construction. It is a feminine form of the Greek word for disciple and is used only here in the New Testament. Luke appears to be placing Tabitha in a special class or an office of "students" or "learners." Paul and Barnabas are also called "disciples" (13:52).

Tabitha was very active and perhaps a leader or an official among those called "holy ones and widows" (Acts 9:41). After her resurrection from the dead, Peter stayed a little while but then moved on to Caesarea. Tabitha's resurrection indicates that women were crucial to the advancement of Christianity. Her unique person and work could not be replaced.

Peter left the work of Joppa in the hands of a capable woman who was devoted "to good works and acts of charity." Luke points out quite discreetly that Peter did not stay with Dorcas but with Simon the tanner, unlike Paul, who roomed with Lydia, a merchant who sold fine linen.

Lydia, a Worshiper of God   Lydia lived in a Roman colony, Philippi, in Macedonia, at the center of East and West trade on the **Via Egnatia**. In a dream, Paul heard a man from Macedonia urging him to cross the waters, so he traveled by ship to this distant place. He met Lydia and the women waiting for him near the river outside of the city of Philippi. In those days, for Jews to have a quorum, or minyan, there had to be ten worshiping Jewish males in the community. Apparently there were not enough males, so the women met together to pray. All of Lydia's house was converted by Paul. It appears that Lydia was head of her own household and her own company, which traded and sold "fine purple cloth." Paul stayed with her in her house until he was arrested. One of Paul's most romantic and sensitive letters is written to the women living in this city, Philippians.

Women Politicians   One could argue that Bernice and Drusilla were not politicians, but they are portrayed as influencing affairs of state. Candace, queen of Ethiopia, is mentioned only in passing, but placing her name in the narrative recognizes her power and influence (Acts 8:27). Luke quietly inserts many women into the narratives of cities in Asia Minor and Macedonia. They were the "devout women of high standing" in Antioch of Pisidia (Acts 13:50). "Leading women" are mentioned in Thessalonica (17:4). The Greek word is literally translated "first ones," and this term is used for city officials in nonbiblical documents relating to the people who ran the city of Caesarea. In Beroea, honorable or high-standing women became converts (Acts 17:12). Many other women are present in the upper room, in the house of Mary the mother of John Mark, or living with Philip the Evangelist, who carried on the grassroots politics that helped ignite the wildfire of the new religion.

God as a Character in the Story

How can God be a character? For the writer of Acts, God is very important and is involved in the growth of early Christianity as much as the Holy Spirit. God's activities pervade all of the stories in Acts. Luke believes that God controls and intervenes in human history (2:32; 7:6, 25; 17:24). God chooses people (7:25, 37; 13:23; 16:10) or sends angels (10:3; 8:26; 12:8–9; 14:27; 15:4, 7, 8; 27:23), or speaks through the Holy Spirit (1;2, 5; 2:4, 33; 8:39; 15:8; 16:6, etc.). God is both creator and liberator (2:24; 7:35; 17:24). This ancient judge of the world (17:31) was first worshiped by the people of Israel (2:13; 7:32; 13:17; 22:14), who witnessed God's active involvement in their history (7:6, 45).

Luke does not label God a "warrior," but all the same he fulfills that role in Acts. Implied in many of the narratives is a belief in a God that battles the Devil, Satan, other deities, and people who call themselves "God" (12:22; 14:11; 17:23; 19:26; 23:4) for the domination of the universe. In this struggle, God does not hesitate to use supernatural powers that maim (chapter 9, Paul). God chooses recruits to do battle for the new faith. One of God's most important choices was a person who would take the new religious movement outside of Palestine. God chose Saul, an impassioned and a zealous man, to do battle.

Holy Spirit as a Character

The spirit, Holy Spirit, or Spirit of God is mentioned over seventy times in Acts, compared with Peter who is mentioned at least forty-five times and Paul who is mentioned over 100 times. Both the Spirit and the Angel (of the Lord) work mysteriously behind the scenes to support, rescue, and direct the missionaries. While it is impossible to know whether the writer equated the two characters, it is safe to conclude that they had similar missions. The importance of these characters in Acts cannot be underestimated.

SPECIAL FEATURES

The Jerusalem Council (Acts 15)

This council among the apostles, elders, Pharisaic Christians, Peter, James, Paul, and Barnabas is an effort by the author of Acts to portray how early Christians solved ethnic, political, and theological problems. Apparently there was a lot of resistance among the Jewish Christians or Hebraists in Jerusalem to recognize other people as Christians who did not also follow Jewish law. Throughout the remainder of the New Testament, this struggle and discussion continues among believers about how to live a proper Christian life.

After some deliberations, and an introduction by Peter, James, the brother of Jesus, decides,

> Therefore I have reached the decision that we should not trouble those Gentiles who are turning to God, but we should write to them to abstain only from things polluted by idols and from fornication and from whatever has been strangled and from blood. (Acts 15:19–20)

This message was also included in a letter that missionaries were to take with them on their journeys throughout the Empire (15:29). No one knows exactly what James meant by the aforementioned quote. It was certainly a concession to accepting Christians who were neither circumcised nor practiced kosher laws. James may be saying that Gentiles do not have to be circumcised, but they should keep the kosher regulations of not eating bloody meat or improperly slaughtered animals. They should also stop visiting other religious shrines (idols) where cultic prostitution is prevalent (fornication). The term *blood* could mean a variety of things. It could have to do with diet (not drinking blood), but it also could refer to murder, or the practice of **niddah**.

It is odd that Luke takes so much effort in Acts to portray the two disparate groups agreeing on rules and regulations of the new church, yet Paul in his speeches and throughout his journeys never mentions the decision of James. In fact, it is never mentioned in Paul's letters either. And when Paul arrives in Jerusalem with Asian (Gentile) friends, in spite of his relationship with James and the elders, the Jews from Asia were

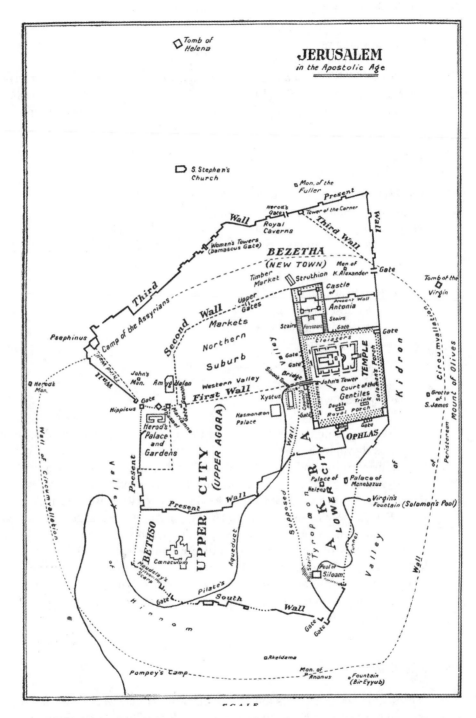

FIGURE 8.6 Plan of Ancient Jerusalem. Taken from James Hastings, *Dictionary of the Apostolic Church*, Vol. 2 (T & T Clark, 1915).

allowed to start a riot and accuse him of defiling or making common the Temple (Acts 21). No one from the party of James defended Paul.

Today, both Jews and Christians continue to discuss how a religious person should live. Some Jews look for Jesus' return as the Messiah, while some Christians have maintained many of the purity laws found in the Torah, such as **holiness** groups.

The Speeches

Many scholars have assumed that the speeches given by Peter, Stephen, and Paul were the literal accounts. After a closer comparison of the speeches that comprise at least one-third of Acts, it appears that they were created by the writer of Acts. Researchers have discovered a common vocabulary and grammatical structure. A list of some of the elements follows:

- request for a hearing
- the present situation is mirrored
- usually begins with Scripture
- preaching about Jesus
- Scripture to prove points made about Jesus
- appeal to accept ideas and repent
- disciples are witnesses

Ben Witherington has outlined the three speeches made by Paul about his conversion as shown in the box on page 177. Compare and contrast all three versions. Are they similar or different? Why does the writer change the stories? Theorize!

While the speeches have a common vocabulary, many of them seem to have different goals. For instance, Paul's speeches in Caesarea were usually an apology or a defense. Peter's speeches in the first few chapters of Acts were evangelistic, geared toward winning converts to the new faith. Stephen's speech was an indictment, and James' gave a summary of deliberations regarding religious laws. To the Ephesian elders at Miletus, Paul gave his last will and testament. The Athenians received a curious speech that involved the use of Hellenistic philosophical arguments regarding an unknown God. Some suggest that the key to understanding the mind of the writer of Acts is to study the speeches.

Speaking in Tongues

"Glossolalia," or speaking in tongues—what is it? The answers are as varied as the persons who have experienced this phenomena. It appears that speaking in tongues for Peter had to do more with translation than with a personal prayer experience (Acts 2).

Acts 9.1ff	Acts 22.1ff	Acts 26.1ff
"Rise, enter city. You will be told what to do." (verse 6)	"What shall I do, sir?" "Rise, go into Damascus. You'll be told all that is appointed for you to do." (verse 10)	"Rise, stand on your feet. I have appeared to you for this purpose, to appoint you to serve and bear witness to the things in which you have seen me and to those in which I'll appear to you. Delivering you from the people and from Gentiles to whom I send you, to open their eyes, for they might turn from darkness to light."
Men stood speechless, hearing voice, seeing no one (verse 7)	Men saw light, did not hear voice of one speaking to me. (verse 9) (verses 16–18)	
Saul arises. Can see nothing. Three days without sight and food. Led by hand into Damascus. (verses 8–9)	Paul cannot see because of brightness of light. Led by hand of companions into Damascus. (verse 11)	
Vision of Ananias (verses 10–16)	Ananias (no vision) mentioned "Brother Saul, receive your sight." (verse 13)	
Third person	First person in Hebrew/Aramaic Paul's Greek	First person spoken by Paul to Festus
Saul to high priest letters to synagogues bring Christians back to Jerusalem (verse 2)	Letters from high priest and council bring back Christians to Jerusalem for punishment	Authorization from chief priests (verse 10)
Light from heaven flashed about him (verse 3)	At noon, great light from heaven shone about me (verse 6)	Midday, light from heaven shining around me and with me (verse 13)
Fell to ground, heard a voice saying (verse 4)	Fell to ground, heard a voice (verse 7)	We all fell to ground, I heard voice in Hebrew (verse 14)
"Saul, Saul, why do you persecute me?"	Same as Acts 9	Same as Acts 9
"Who are you, sir?" "I am Jesus, whom you are persecuting." (verses 4, 5)	Same as Acts 9 "I am Jesus of Nazareth, whom...." (verses 7–8)	"It hurts you to kick against the goads." The Lord said: "I am Jesus whom you are persecuting." (verse 15)

From "Editing the Good News," by Ben Witherington III, in *The Book of Acts*, ed. Ben Witherington III. (Cambridge: Cambridge University Press, 1996). Reprinted with permission of Cambridge University Press.

But in other verses in Acts, speaking in tongues seems to be a result of a conversion or an experience of the Holy Spirit.

Some Christian denominations today would suggest that a person is not a Christian until an experience of speaking in tongues has penetrated his or her life. Others claim that it is a gift to be used only in personal prayer. Paul, in his letter to the Corinthians (chapters 12–14), gave guidelines on how speaking in tongues should be used in a gathering. Someone had to translate. People should not go on babbling and causing confusion.

Speaking in tongues may sound like babbling to the uninitiated. For a Roman Catholic, it may sound like chanting; for a Pentecostal, it may sound like a high-powered Evangelist; for a Muslim, it may sound like Arabic. A negative description by Eusebius, an ancient Christian historian, about an early group of people called Montanists, who spoke in tongues, follows:

> … He was one of the recent converts, and he became possessed of a spirit, and suddenly began to rave in a kind of ecstatic trance, and to babble in a jargon, prophesying in a manner contrary to the custom of the Church which had been handed down by tradition from the earliest times.
> … And he also stirred up two women and filled them with the bastard spirit so that they uttered demented, absurd and irresponsible sayings…. And these people blasphemed the whole Catholic Church under heaven, under the influence of their presumptuous spirit, because the Church granted to the spirit of false prophecy neither honor nor admission. (Bettenson, 1963, 77)

Contrary to Eusebius, the writer of Acts portrays speaking in tongues as something positive. Several verses tell stories about people receiving the Holy Spirit and speaking in tongues after being touched by an apostle (4; 11; 10; 19:2–13). Tongues appears to be an indicator, but not the only sign, of converting to Christianity.

Today there are many theories about the nature and content of speaking in tongues. Psychologists suggest that it is an emotional phenomenon similar to a **catharsis**. It is a release of emotional pressure. Stress can be released in many ways and speaking in tongues may be a healthy way to do it. It may be a form of self-hypnotism which provides a rest and an escape. And many today continue to claim that it is the miracle of the presence of the Holy Spirit, as in the book of Acts, which gives them the ability to speak in another language.

Summary of the Acts of the Apostles   The Acts of the Apostles is a remarkable and an idealistic story about the diverse origins of early Christian groups. It is a journey related by a person who believed that the message of Jesus should be taken to the boundaries of the Empire. It was written by, some say, a friend of Paul's late in the first century C.E. Evidence suggests that the writer did not know Paul personally, because Paul's life and beliefs portrayed in Acts differ considerably with those discovered in Paul's letters.

Some of the sources used in creating Acts include the Old Testament/Hebrew Bible, Hellenistic philosophical texts, a personal account labeled the "we" passages, and possible eyewitness accounts from people in Antioch in Syria. Discussion continues about the reasons for creating Acts. It could have been written to persuade Romans and others that Christianity was not a mere breakaway sect but a full-fledged world religion. In spite of hostility and violence within the earliest Christian communities, Luke may have created a work that projected idealistic and unrealistic models of community living. This may have helped people endure their emotional, physical, or economic hardships.

There are always differences of opinion within new movements or organizations, and Luke may have written a story to demonstrate that everyone was "family." All of the Christian factions were united in the same cause and had the same roots within Judaism. Acts may also have been originally written as a defense for Paul, which may have been used by other Christians facing similar circumstances.

After the Jewish wars, hostile relations continued between the Jews and the Romans, partly because of the war tax. Luke may have written Acts to argue that Christians were not a threat to Rome. Reports of riots may have followed them, but those brawls were created by Jews and others who were against the new religion. Their King was not a revolutionary, and his kingdom was not a threat to the Emperor. Acts may also have been written to convince people of all classes and ethnic backgrounds to convert to Christianity. Some think Luke believed in a time of Israel, a time of Jesus, and a time of the Church. The Church was in the center of God's plan for saving the universe.

While the genre of Acts of Apostles may mimic ancient novels, historical narratives, or monographs, scholars are unsure about how to classify it. It may also have been a foundation legend that excluded and condemned others who were different.

The writer of Acts involves a cast of hundreds. In this text we have considered the following characters: Peter, Paul, Political Women, Tabitha, Lydia, God, the Holy Spirit, and the Angel of the Lord. The Paul we have met in Acts continues into the next chapter, as we begin to discuss his career, his relationship to the converts and the established church, and his letters. There are many interesting themes that could be explored. We chose to summarize the first ecumenical Jerusalem Council, to discuss the speeches created by Luke, and to define the practice of speaking in tongues, which seemed so essential to the founding of the early communities.

9

Early Pauline Documents

1 and 2 Thessalonians, Galatians, and Philippians

The Life and Works of Paul

If anyone has reason to be confident in the flesh, I have more:
circumcised on the eighth day, a member of the people of Israel,
of the tribe of Benjamin, a Hebrew born of Hebrews; as to the law,
a Pharisee; as to zeal, a persecutor of the church;
as to righteousness under the law, blameless.

—Phil. 3:4–6 NRSV

A ZEALOUS MISSIONARY

Nothing has influenced the development of Christianity more than the writings attributed to Paul. These letters take up more than one-third of the New Testament, and the Acts of the Apostles spends at least one-half of its twenty-eight chapters on Paul. Many people point to Paul as the creator of Christianity. But do we really know the identity of Paul? Could we recognize him in a mall? What did he look like? According to the "Acts of Paul and Thecla," he was, "…a little man, bald headed, bowlegged, healthy, with meeting eyebrows, a slightly long nose, and full of grace." Artists have interpreted Paul in various ways throughout history. Consider the perceptions of Paul on the following pages.

181

FIGURE 9.1 Picture of Paul from the catacomb of Domitilla. Taken from Camden Cobern, *The New Archaeological Discoveries Bearing Upon the New Testament* (New York: Funk & Wagnalls, 1917).

Calvin Roetzel, in *The Letters of Paul,* summarizes modern attitudes toward Paul. Students view Paul's writings as abstract, complex, and obtuse. Paul is seen as a bully who forces his point of view on others. Some think he is a chauvinist, while others see him as daring and imaginative, as well as a genius, a source of inspiration, and counsel for their lives.

Many textbooks on the New Testament begin with the letters of Paul because most scholars think that they are the oldest documents contained in the New Testament. But studying Paul can be a difficult journey if a student does not have a background in the history of Christianity, especially theology or the beliefs of Christians. We have begun our study of Paul after considering the gospels and Acts because those books provide a foundation or a framework within which to view Paul.

PAUL IN THE ACTS OF THE APOSTLES

In Acts we learned that Saul was an obsessed Pharisee whose life changed. He was also known as Paul, a Christian missionary. The writer of Acts claims that he was highly educated. His home was the city of Tarsus in the area of Cilicia in Asia Minor. While it is suggested that he had a sister and nephew, nothing is known about his early or personal life. Most people assume that he was not married at the time he wrote the letters, although he may previously have been married and widowed or divorced. He must have had access to some finances because there is very little emphasis on earning income in either Acts or the letters of Paul. Acts says he was a tent maker or a weaver. (Many scholars suggest that Paul made tents of animal skins, but skins are impractical because they are heavy and expensive. Most tents throughout history have been woven out of some type of cloth.) According to both Acts and the letters, Paul's career consisted of traveling throughout the Empire. Some of the stops included time in prison or house arrest.

Paul's greatest ambition was to convince the world of the valid claims of Christianity. He believed that the end of time was approaching and that every moment should be spent fostering the growth of Christianity. He never denied his violent past. To the Galatians, he wrote, "You have heard no doubt, of my earlier life in Judaism. I was violently persecuting the church of God and was trying to destroy it" (1:13–14). We know Paul was a man of strong emotions. He used threats and insults to make important points. He was not beyond expressing wild affection, anger, or personal boasting. He quarreled often with friends, associates, and people within Christian communities. Some have suggested that Paul was ill later in life, or developed an illness that hindered communication with people. He may have had some type of facial or physical deformity. To the Galatians, he writes, "From now on, let no one make trouble for me; for I carry the marks of Jesus branded on my body" (Gal. 6:17), and

> You know that it was because of a physical infirmity that I first announced the gospel to you; though my condition put you to the test, you did not scorn or despise me, but welcomed me as an angel of God, as Christ Jesus. (4:14)

CULTURAL INFLUENCES

Paul's foundations lay within Judaism, with Pharisaic leanings. He studied with Gamaliel, one of the most famous Jewish rabbis in the first century (Acts 22:3). Gamaliel was known for his generally liberal approach to the Torah. It is said that he advised some people to walk longer distances on the Sabbath, thus breaking the law, and that he demanded wives to be present when husbands attempted to annul divorce proceedings.

It is difficult to characterize how the Jewish background and education influenced Paul. His career changed drastically, and with that change he attempted to abandon his former life. In his letters, he recognizes his debt to Moses (1 Cor. 10:1–5) and the traditions of his ancestors, but he challenges their exclusive claims to knowledge, faith, and rituals leading people to **redemption** or **salvation** by a monotheistic god. While he accepts the Hebrew notion that people are estranged from God and need to be rescued, he appears to reject the Jewish ritual system of sacrificial offerings and purity legislation. A quick comparison of Judaism and Christianity today demonstrates that even while Paul spoke harshly of his heritage, Judaism was the foundation for Christianity. A few similarities follow:

Comparison of Judaism and Christianity

Judaism	Christianity
Monotheistic	Monotheistic (Trinity)
Hebrew Bible is canon	Old Testament/Hebrew Bible is canon
Emphasis on sin	Emphasis on sin
Sacrifice as offering	Jesus as sacrifice and offering
Priests run temple	Priests, ministers, pastors run churches
Patriarchal organization	Patriarchal organization
Religion begins with Abraham	Religion begins with Abraham and Adam
A book is the center of faith	A book is the center of faith
Passover	Easter
Hannukah	Christmas
Division of the sexes	Division of the sexes
Created synagogue	Began in synagogue
Belief in a messiah	Belief in a messiah

We must remember that the first Christians, according to the New Testament, grew within Judaism meeting in houses or local synagogues, later called "churches."

Paul also was a hellenized Jew, which meant that he spoke Greek and appreciated the Greek way of life. Indeed, he was most successful in Greek towns in Asia, Macedonia, and Achaia. Many claim that Paul was heavily influenced by Greek philosophical thought. This may mean that while he was a Jew, he did not keep all of the laws and festivals. His letters betray influences from Gnosticism and the mystery religions. As we shall discover in our study of Paul's letters, he was also influenced by apocalyptic images.

The writer of Acts says he was a Roman citizen, which probably meant that he had more rights than the average person in the Empire (Acts 16:37; 22:28). Tarsus became a city of the Roman Empire around 42 B.C.E. and was exempt from taxes. Many people were given back their citizenship after a long political battle in the senate. Some suggested that citizenship could be bought for around 500 drachmae, or bestowed on people who had done special favors for the state. There also is some evidence that there were different levels of citizenship, from artisans to a "full" membership.

DATES OF PAUL'S LIFE

Even with specific dates of Roman officials mentioned in Acts, the actual dates of Paul's birth and death are unknown. Neither do we know the exact dates of his missionary treks, or when he wrote the letters. For years, scholars have attempted to create an elaborate picture of the history of Paul. Their conclusions are varied, but most agree to a broad chronology of the life of Paul.

Chronology of the Life of Paul

Approximate Dates	Event
4 B.C.E.	Birth of Jesus
Unknown	Birth of Paul
28–33 C.E.	Death of Jesus
32–36	Conversion of Paul
40	In Damascas after conversion
36–47	Journey to Syria and Cilicia
48–49	Jerusalem Council
49–56	Missionary journeys
49	In Corinth with Priscilla, Edit of Claudius
51-53	In Corinth, Gallio
55	In Caesarea under arrest, Festus
56	Arrest
60–64	Death of Paul in Rome
66–70	Jewish wars
65–85	Synoptic gospels
98–125	Gospel of John

FIGURE 9.2   The Damascus Gate in the old city of Jerusalem. Photo taken by Marla J. Selvidge.

Reasons for Writing the Documents

It appears Paul wrote letters and other works to many groups of people whom he converted to Christianity. Apparently, early Christians wrote to him about issues that had surfaced while building their new religion. Sometimes Paul also heard about problems from other traveling missionaries. The letters offered innovative solutions to questions, or rumors of problems. Contained also within the documents were requests for financial support, defenses of his own authority or position within Christianity, thank-you notes for funds or other types of support, and definitions or descriptions of Christian living. Paul hoped his words would unite people with differing points of view.

THE LETTERS: DATE AND AUTHORSHIP

Letters from Paul became very popular and were often read during Christian services/mass. When the rush began to collect Paul's letters from churches all over the Empire, the texts of the letters were changed in many ways. Paul's letters were collected by well-intentioned Christians near the beginning of the second century. And while we wish we had original copies of Paul's letters, we do not.

Some scholars date the letters of Paul by cross-referencing the Acts of the Apostles with known dates of Roman officials. The following chart represents a general dating of the letters. Possible dates and historical reconstructions are too numerous to summarize in this text. Consider the list of letters that follows and the approximate dates of composition. Most scholars place 1 Thessalonians as the earliest letter and Romans as the last work created by Paul.

Probably Pauline	Approx. Date	Pseudo-Pauline	Approx. Date	Not Pauline	Approx. Date
1 Thessalonians	50–60	1 Timothy	100–125	Hebrews	80–90
Galatians	50–60	2 Timothy	100–125		
1 Corinthians	50–60	Titus	100–125		
2 Corinthians	50–60	Ephesians	60–90		
Philemon	50–60	Colossians	60–90		
Philippians	50–60	2 Thessalonians	60–90		
Romans	50-60				

When you read Paul's letters, do you feel as though you cannot follow the train of thought? Do you notice that the subject under consideration is abruptly halted and then begun again somewhere else in the letter? Or perhaps you begin to read Paul and give up because you assume his work is too complicated. All of these hints suggest that the people who compiled Paul's letters did not know the exact order of the pages. For instance, in Philippians 3:1, Paul begins the topic of joy, "Finally, my brothers and sis-

FIGURE 9.3   Map of Greece, Achaia, and Asia Minor. From Clarence Larkin, *Dispensational Truth* (Philadelphia: Rev. Clarence Larkin Est., 1918).

ters, rejoice in the Lord." But the next verse begins with, "Beware of dogs..." This seems illogical. If we read a little further in Philippians 4:1, the topic of joy is continued. "Therefore, my brothers and sisters, whom I love and long for, my joy and crown, stand firm in the Lord in this way, my beloved." The intervening verses were probably misplaced, or the pages were shuffled.

Letters were written on perishable parchment and constant use would have made them quite fragile. In the haste to put together a collection or to preserve Paul's thoughts, some collectors neglected to preserve the titles of letters or the opening and closing sentences of the letters. Consequently, 1 and 2 Corinthians probably contain several letters because the transcriber did not know when one letter began and another ended. (This is similar to making notes on many cards without references. How do you know whom you are quoting and when and out of which book unless you have the proper citation at the top of the page?)

Paul's letters also were audited by the early Christian community. Interpolations or additions to letters were common during the copying process. Most transcribers added material to explain verses, but others actually added phrases to change the meaning of the texts. For instance, in 1 Corinthians 14:33b–36, women are told to be silent in the churches. This statement is totally illogical, because earlier in 1 Corinthians 11 an entire chapter is devoted to the discussion of women praying and preaching during a religious gathering. Other additions to the text portray Paul as ethnocentered when he says, "...the Jews, who killed both the Lord Jesus and the prophets, and drove us out; they displease God and oppose everything" (1 Thess. 2:15–16). This is a stereotypical view of a people. All Jews did not kill Jesus, the prophets, and so on. But some people who had a Jewish background may have done some of these things.

In studying the letters attributed to Paul, we must recognize that we do not have all of his letters; neither do we have the exact letters that he composed. We should also understand that the letters that were written were not personal philosophical treatises (with the exception of Romans). They were responses to problems and issues within the communities. We do not have the questions. All we have are the answers in the letters, and those answers sometimes are obscure.

IN THE NAME OF PAUL

Fourteen letters/documents were originally thought to have been written by Paul and therefore included in the New Testament. Scholars debate whether or not Paul actually wrote all of the letters. Most agree that Paul had a secretary or transcriber who helped him. Some letters are called Pseudo-Pauline or **Deutero-Pauline** or Pseudepigraphal and were probably written in the name of Paul.

Someone wrote the letters and claimed that Paul had written them. Paul's name was famous and would have fostered a greater acceptance of the material in the letters in communities throughout the Empire. This happens even in our time. For example, the names of famous sports people are used to sell athletic equipment. And consider Ralph Nader, consumer advocate. If he holds a press conference, almost everyone listens. Whole foundations have been created in the name of Ralph Nader, because his name stands for honesty and fairness to the consumer.

Most of us do not like the idea of someone in the Bible claiming to be someone else. It seems as though that person is untruthful. In ancient times, the practice of writing in someone else's name or using their ideas was common. *Star Wars* has returned to the big screen. Why is it so successful? One of the reasons that it reaches so many people is because it builds on popular culture, religion, and other science fiction classics. A recent letter to the editor in *Newsweek* reads in the following way:

> Star Wars is not only a cult movie but also a faith.... George Lucas's epic often reads like the New Testament recast with Luke as the light-saber-toting messiah of the Jedis,

> Darth Vader as the Devil and the supreme lord of the evil Empire, Obi-Wan Kenobi as Saint John the Baptist and the Force as the "Star Wars" holy Spirit. (Krausz 1997, 18)

And so it was with Paul's letters 1,900 years ago. Of course we have strict laws on copyright today, but in ancient times these laws did not exist.

The debate continues about whether or not Paul wrote many of the letters. Scholars analyze vocabulary and theological points of view and attempt to create a profile of Paul's beliefs. In their quest to find the original Paul, based on an elaborate scheme of argumentation that includes considering Acts as history, scholars have dated and prioritized Paul's letters. Implicit in this restructuring of Pauline ideas is a theory of theological development (or progress in beliefs) that assumes that the earlier letters represent a Paul who believed that the end was going to happen at any moment and that faith alone in Christ's saving death was the ticket to eternal life. Paul's earlier letters also have a strong emphasis on freedom to ignore the Jewish law.

Many textbooks place Pauline and Pseudo-Pauline letters in different categories. Yet all of the letters are included in the New Testament (Canon), and some letters appear to be copies or duplicates of other letters. 1 and 2 Timothy and Titus are often dated during the second century for two main reasons. The people, geography, and situations in the letters cannot be placed within the lifetime of Paul. Second, the beliefs and the content of the letters seem to be written by someone who opposes Paul's beliefs, evidenced in earlier letters. For instance, these letters place more emphasis on following the law or the strict traditions given to Timothy and Titus by the elders before them. The Christian community is also highly organized, unlikely to occur so early in the progression of an organization, with bishops, deacons, and widows. Instead of an emphasis on the living experience of a faithful life, the writer is more interested in mastering doctrines or instructions.

Scholars, in the past, have also assigned special categories to the letters. For instance, Philippians, Colossians, Ephesians, and Philemon were termed *Prison Epistles* because the idea of imprisonment is mentioned in each book (Phil. 1:12, 13; Eph. 3:1; 4:1; Col. 1:24; Philemon 1). 1 and 2 Timothy and Titus were known as the *Pastoral Letters,* because they were written to individuals who were leaders within local Christian communities.

FORM OF THE LETTERS

In communicating with churches throughout the Empire, the writer of the Pauline letters used a classical letter form that included a salutation or greeting, a word of thanks, the main reason for writing the letter or the body, and a closing that may have included a farewell wish, a prayer, instructions, or an encouragement to greet other Christians with a kiss. Paul also adds ethical guidelines in many letters. His letters are not unlike formal business correspondence today. Table 9.1 on page 190 shows how several letters fit into this basic form.

TABLE 9.1 Outline of the Structure of Ancient Letters

	1 Thessalonians	1 Corinthians	2 Corinthians	Galatians	Philippians
I. Formal Greeting					
A. Sender	1:1a	1:1	1:1a	1:1–2a	1:1
B. Recipient	1:1b	1:2	1:1b	1:2b	1:1
C. Greeting	1:1c	1:3	1:2	1:3–5	1:2
II. Word of Thanks	1:2–10 2:13 3:9–10	1:4–9	1:3–7	None	1:3–11
III. Body	2:1–3:8 (possibly 3:11–13)	1:10–4:21	1:8–9:14 10:1–13:10	1:6–4:31 3:1–4:1	1:12–2:11 4:10–20
IV. Ethical Guidelines	4:1–5:22	5:1–16:12 16:13–18	13:11a	5:1–6:10 6:11–15	2:12–29 4:2–6
V. Closing					
A. Peace Wish	5:23–24	—	13:11b	6:16	4:7–9
B. Greetings	—	16:19–20a	13:13	—	4:21–22
C. Kiss	5:26	16:20b	13:12	—	—
D. Instructions	5:27	16:22	—	6:17	—
E. Prayer	5:28	16:23–24	13:14	6:18	4:23

Excerpted and edited from Calvin J. Roetzel, *The Letters of Paul: Conversations in Context* (Atlanta: John Knox Press, 1975), 28.

SOURCES OF THE LETTERS

Nothing similar to the synoptic materials exists for Paul's works. He rarely quotes the Old Testament/Hebrew Bible directly but appears to quote or summarize several types of Christian and popular literatures in use during his lifetime. Examples of sources include the following:

A Liturgy for the Eucharist	1 Corinthians 11:23–25
Creedal statement	1 Corinthians 15:3–7
Hymn	Philippians 2:6–11
Confession	Romans 1:3–5
Love poem	1 Corinthians 13
Proverbs	1 Corinthians 15:33; Galatians 5:9
Popular slogans	1 Corinthians 15:32
List of vices (popular)	Romans 1:29–31
Old Testament quotation	Romans 3:10–18
Allusions to the Old Testament	1 Corinthians 15:27–28

The gospels in the New Testament were written after Paul's letters; thus they could not be a source for his works. Yet Paul does claim to have had a special revelation from Jesus. Since he was the preeminent missionary in the first century, he should have been aware of some of Jesus' words or stories. His letters do not concentrate on the life and teachings of Jesus, but rather on the meaning of his death. Charles B. Cousar, in *The Letters of Paul,* after a thorough comparison of the gospels with Paul's letters, finds similarities as shown in the box on page 192.

Summary of the Life and Works of Paul   Paul was a zealous and dashing young man who found a faith and believed that he had the responsibility to take it to the entire Empire. He probably journeyed throughout Asia Minor, Macedonia, and Achaia and completed his career in Rome. He wrote many documents. His words have been foundational to belief systems of Christians all over the world, for almost 2,000 years. Rather than summarize Paul's beliefs at this point in our study, we will first read and study the Pauline works. Let us proceed to a study of the letters attributed to Paul.

COMPARISON OF PAUL'S LETTERS
WITH THE GOSPELS

Pauline Letters	New Testament Gospels
Romans	
Bless those who persecute you; bless and do not curse them (12:14).	Bless those who curse you, pray for those who abuse you (Luke 6:28; Matt. 5:44).
Do not repay anyone evil for evil (12:17a).	If anyone strikes you on the cheek, offer the other also; and from anyone who takes away your coat do not withhold even your shirt (Luke 6:29; cf. Matt. 5:39b–40).
If it is possible, so far as it depends on you, live peaceably with all (12:18).	Be at peace with one another (Mark 9:50b; cf. Matt. 5:9).
Beloved, never avenge yourselves, but leave room for the wrath of God; for it is written, "Vengeance is mine, will repay, says the Lord." No, "if your enemies are hungry, feed them; if they are thirsty, give them something to drink; for by doing this you will heap coals of fire on their heads. Do not be overcome by evil, but overcome evil with good" (12:19–21).	But I say to you that listen, Love your enemies, do good to those who hate you.... But love your enemies, do good, and lend, expecting nothing in return (Luke 6:27, 35a; cf. Matt. 5:44a).
I know and am persuaded in the Lord Jesus that nothing is unclean in itself; but it is unclean for anyone who thinks it unclean. (14:14).	There is nothing outside a person that by going in can defile, but the things that come out are what defile. (Mark 7:15; cf. Matt. 15:11)
Galatians	
For the whole law is summed up in a single commandment, "You shall love your neighbor as yourself" (Gal. 5:14; cf. Rom. 13:8–10).	The first is, "Hear, O Israel; the Lord our God, the Lord is one; you shall love the Lord your God with all your heart, and with all your soul and with all your strength," The second is, "You shall love your neighbor as yourself." There is no other commandment greater than these (Mark 12:29–31; cf. Matt. 22:34–40). Translation from *The New English Bible*.

From Charles B. Cousar, *The Letters of Paul* (Nashville: Abingdon Press, 1996), 59–60.

1 Thessalonians:
The End of the World?

Now concerning love of the brothers and sisters, you do not need
to have anyone write to you, for you yourselves have been taught
by God to love one another; and indeed you do love all the
brothers and sisters throughout Macedonia.

—4:9 NRSV

For the Lord himself, with a cry of command, with the archangel's
call and with the sound of God's trumpet, will descend from
heaven, and the dead in Christ will rise first.

—4:16 NRSV

INTRODUCTION

If you knew beyond a shadow of a doubt that your life would end tomorrow, how would
it affect you? Many Christian communities throughout history have taken Paul at his
word. They also believed they were living in the last moments of time on earth. Their
world was going to end any minute. Contemplating the prospect of death changes us,
but considering the possible end to all human existence might change whole cities, even
countries.

During the nineteenth century in a blossoming America, William Miller studied
the Bible and came to the conclusion that Jesus was going to return on April 23, 1843.
Thousands of people prepared for the end. It did not come. On May 2, 1843, Miller
wrote about his great disappointment.

> Were I to live my life over again, with the same evidence that I then had, to be honest with
> God and man I should have to do as I have done. Although opposers said it would not
> come, they produced no weighty arguments. It was evidently guess-work with them; and
> I then thought, and do now, that their denial was based more on an unwillingness for the
> Lord to come than on any arguments leading to such a conclusion.
>
> I confess my error, and acknowledge my disappointment; yet I still believe that the day
> of the Lord is near, even at the door; and I exhort you, my brethren, to be watchful, and
> not let that day come upon you unawares. The wicked, the proud, and the bigot will exult
> over us. I will try to be patient. (Himes 1910, 230–31)

While Jesus did not return, the efforts of William Miller eventually resulted in a new
Christian denomination, the Seventh-Day Adventists.

Miller's dreams have been played out over and over again in countless Christian
communities. Paul believed he was living in the last moments of time, and the Thessalonians were preparing for that event. But Jesus did not return, so Paul wrote letters to
address the problems that may have resulted from their unfulfilled expectations.

193

FIGURE 9.4   William Miller. From Elder James White, *Sketches of The Christian Life and Public Labors of William Miller.* 1875 (Battle Creek, MI: Steam Press, Frontispiece. 1875).

DATE, AUTHORSHIP, LOCATION, AND AUDIENCE

Most scholars agree that 1 Thessalonians is among Paul's earliest letters (and it may be the oldest document in the New Testament), written around 50 C.E. The letter, which may be a compilation of several letters, was sent by Paul, Silvanus (Silas), and Timothy (1:1). Notice how often the letter uses "we," "our," and "us." What follows is a theoretical reconstruction of four letters sent to the Thessalonians. **W. Schmithals** attempts to resolve the out-of-place conclusions and thanksgivings in 1 and 2 Thessalonians by placing them in historical sequence.

Letter One   2 Th. 1:1–12; 3:6–16
                Letter sent after hearing disturbing news about the converts at Thessalonica.

Letter Two   1 Th. 1:1–2:12; 4:2–5:28
                Letter sent to help church protect itself from visiting preachers.

Letter Three   2 Th. 2:13–14; 2:1–12; 2:15–3:3, (5), 17f
                Letter sent because Paul heard that a fake letter from him was circulating that encouraged apocalyptic enthusiasm.

Letter Four   1 Th. 2:13–4:1
                  Letter sent after a visit by Timothy to Thessalonica.

From I. Howard Marshall, *1 and 2 Thessalonians: New Century Bible Commentary.* (Grand Rapids MI: Eerdmans, 1983), 15)

The City: Thessalonica

Thessalonica was the Roman capital of Macedonia, built on a major East and West highway across the Empire, the Via Egnatia. It was named for the half-sister of Alexander the Great, Thessalonkikeia, by Cassander early in the fourth century B.C.E. As a free Roman city during the time of Paul, it was composed of at least thirty-five towns.

Thessalonica had a full and varied religious life, which included worshipers of **Serapis**, Isis, **Zeus**, Asclepius, **Aphrodite**, **Demeter,** and **Dionysus**. A popular religion among sailors was the worship of **Cabiri**, or great gods. Around 27 B.C.E., the heads of Romans began appearing on coins, and during the first century C.E., the goddess Roma was added to the list at the temple of Caesar. Julius Caesar was acknowledged as a god and so began the beginning of a **civil religion**, sometimes termed emperor worship/imperial cult. Romans became objects of honor, standing beside the gods of the state. Archaeological evidence also concludes that there were at least two different types of synagogues in the heart of Thessalonica, one belonging to the Jews, the other to the Samaritans.

Acts and Thessalonica

According to Acts, Paul spent only three Sabbath days (two to three weeks) in a synagogue at Thessalonica with Silas (17:1–9). Their presence caused so much distress to the Jews, who were not converted, that they dragged Jason to the city magistrates claiming he was harboring dissidents (17:6–7). The locals may have charged the group with dishonoring or desecrating honorable Romans who were deified and worshiped in a civil religion. Paul and Silas escaped to Beroea under a cover of darkness (17:10). The first letter to the Thessalonians does not recall these activities but alludes to mistreatment by the Philippians (2:2).

WHY DID PAUL WRITE TO THE THESSALONIANS?

To Compliment the Thessalonians

During the first chapter, Paul nearly falls over himself describing how pleased he is with the Thessalonians. They are called "children of light" and have a good reputation in Macedonia and Achaia (2:8; 4:9). In spite of persecution, they modeled themselves after

Paul, the Lord, and the Church of God in Judea (1:6; 2:14), which some have suggested means that they were not Jews. They are now waiting for the return of Jesus (1:6). Some researchers suspect that there may have been a group of people within the community at Thessalonica, who stressed **millenialism** at the expense of all other beliefs.

New religions often generate hostility and even violence. For example, most recently, the Church of **Scientology** has been banned by the governments of Germany and France. Scientology is considered a threat to the stability of the people and the government. It is an American homegrown religion that claims to have thousands of followers. Instead of Europe sending missionaries to the New World, Americans are now going to Europe. Evidently, some Europeans do not recognize the merit of the new religion. Similarly, when Paul brought Christianity to the Thessalonians, some people were converted, but others were threatened or personally frightened and lashed out at the speaker and his friends (3:4). Scholars have theorized that these political groups could have been any one of the following: Judaizers, non-Christians, gnostics, libertines, or apocalyptic enthusiasts.

To Explain the Parousia

> "When they say, 'There is peace and security,' then sudden destruction will come upon them, as labor pains come upon a pregnant woman, and there will be no escape."
>
> —5:3 NRSV

Apparently some of the converts at Thessalonica had died (some scholars suggest they may have been martyred), and the converts wondered what was going to happen to them at the end of time (5:1–2). Paul answers their questions by creating an eschatology and describing the Parousia. He believed he was living in the last moments of the end of time. At any moment, Jesus would return and take his own with him. But Jesus did not return in Paul's lifetime.

It is possible that some of Paul's converts may have changed their entire lives based on the belief that the end of time was approaching. Throughout the history of Christianity, many religious groups have taken Paul at his word. They have quit their jobs, sold their houses, and gone to the hills, or dug underground caves, to wait for Jesus. But Jesus never returned. Paul writes to the confused Thessalonians and argues that Jesus is going to return shortly. They should not worry about people who have died, because when Jesus appears, he will first take the dead into eternity (4:16–17).

To Summarize Ethical Guidelines

Paul cannot help himself when writing letters to friends. He feels compelled to describe ethical guidelines. A selective summary of his moral opinions for the Thessalonians (chapters 4 and 5) follows:

Do not get involved with fornication (worship at other temples).

Control your body.

Do not exploit others.

Live quietly.

Mind your own affairs.

Work with your hands.

Be independent.

Welcome outsiders.

Do not drink excessively.

Respect your administrators and leaders.

Keep busy.

Encourage the depressed.

Help those weaker than yourself.

Be patient.

Do not seek retribution.

Greet each other with a kiss.

CHARACTERS:
PAUL, JESUS, AND GOD

In this very short letter, Paul reveals many facets of his life and personality. Once again, Paul defends himself and thanks the Thessalonians for their hospitality and acceptance of his words (2:1). He pulls rank on them by claiming he has the authority of the apostles, but he is happy they have followed his teaching. Some of the gossip floating around about him includes slurs and attacks against his personality. A short list of accusations that cannot easily be defended (2:3–10) includes "liar," "manipulator," "flatterer," "greedy" and "coveted the limelight."

Paul's relationship to the Thessalonians is like a father or nurse. He grieves deeply about having to leave them. They are like his own children or patients (2:7, 17; 3:10). He even sent Timothy on a fact-finding mission. Timothy reported back to Paul that all was well in Thessalonia (3:5–6).

Jesus is called "son from heaven," the Lord Jesus Christ, Lord, Christ Jesus, Lord Jesus, and Christ. Jesus was raised from the dead (1:10; 4:14), died for Paul and the Thessalonians (4:10), and will rescue both live and dead converts from the doom that is to come (4:16). Interestingly, Paul refers to God (in at least thirty-three instances) more often than to Jesus. A few phrases follow. After reading 1 Thessalonians, can you detect other references to God? Why do you think Paul placed so much emphasis on God in this very early letter?

God in 1 Thessalonians

Thessalonians	Phrase
1:1	God the Father
1:2	Thanks to God
2:3	Our God and Father
1:4	Beloved by God, he has chosen you
1:8	Faith in God
1:9	You turned to God
1:9	To serve a living and true God
2:2, 8	Our God, gospel of God
2:4	Approved by God
2:13	Word of God
2:14	Churches of God
4:5	God's trumpet
4:9	For God has destined
4:17	God in Christ Jesus
5:23	God of Peace

THE DEMONIC MYTH ABOUT THE JEWS

While Paul praises the relationship and public relations record of the Thessalonians, he inserts three verses that have fostered anti-Semitism.

> … for you suffered the same things from your compatriots as they did from the Jews, who killed both the Lord Jesus and the prophets, and drove us out; they displease God and oppose everyone by hindering us from speaking to the Gentiles so that they may be saved. Thus they have constantly been filling up the measure of their sins; but God's wrath has overtaken them at last. (2:14–16 NRSV)

In a political struggle it is not abnormal to stress the negative side of one's opponents. In Thessalonians, Paul goes beyond the negative into the realm of defamation. The Jews become a scapegoat for all of the problems Paul has encountered.

In stereotypical language, Paul demonizes the Jews, hoping for their destruction by the wrath of God. While it may be accurate to portray some Jews as obstructing Paul's missionary activities, *all* Jews in *all* time periods did not kill the Prophets and Jesus. Many scholars suggest that these verses do not belong to the original letter and may have been interpolated later, because they interrupt the logical flow of the argument. Verse 17 seems to follow the line of argumentation after verse 13, rather than the intrusion of the thanksgiving and references to the Jews in verses 14 and 16 (2:13–16).

FIGURE 9.5 Hasidic Jews carrying a copy of the Torah in Jerusalem. Photo by Melissa A. Luppens.

Summary of 1 Thessalonians: The End of the World? Paul, in about 50 C.E., wrote about his pride in the Thessalonians, although he thinks they need a refresher course in ethics. He is concerned about misunderstandings regarding the expected return of Jesus, and he assures his readers that people who have died will not be left behind. Defending himself in the face of public gossip, Paul reiterates his beliefs in God, Jesus, and the desperate future of the Jews.

2 Thessalonians:
A Second Pauline Letter?

[W]e beg you, brothers and sisters,
not to be quickly shaken in mind or alarmed,
either by spirit or by word or by letter,
as though from us,
to the effect that the day of the Lord is already here.

—2:2 NRSV

INTRODUCTION

The second letter to the Thessalonians hints at a time of anxiety, political turmoil, and public harassment. New religions are often met with fear and hostility by people outside of the faith. **Mormonism** (Church of Jesus Christ of Latter-Day Saints) faced similar problems during its formative period in the nineteenth century. The faithful were thrown off lands by gun, then imprisoned and killed. Joseph Smith was lynched by a mob who feared his popularity.

People who experience such life and death situations, feeling as though they have no control over their lives, often create apocalyptic literature. This literature projects their stress and tensions into a realm of fantasy, symbols, or a symbolic universe, where a greater force than they solves their problems. Most scholars trace the origins of Jewish apocalyptic literature to the reign of Antiochus IV and the influence of Zoroastrianism. Paul's second letter to the Thessalonians draws upon sources in this historic body of apocalyptic thought, while building its case upon the structure and contents of 1 Thessalonians.

AUTHORSHIP AND DATE

Most scholars focus more on the question of identifying the author of 2 Thessalonians than on the content of the letter. 1 and 2 Thessalonians are similar in language, style, and consideration of topics, but they are different when it comes to interpreting the events at the end of time. If Paul (Silvanus, Titus) wrote 2 Thessalonians, then scholars argue that he (they) contradicted himself regarding the events related to the predicted return of Jesus. They also wonder why Paul would write two letters on the same subject to the Thessalonians.

Those who hold to Pauline authorship claim that the letter was written soon after 1 Thessalonians in 50–51 C.E. Others who think that 2 Thessalonians is a copy written by someone else date it from the time of Nero in the 60s C.E. to the beginning of the second century C.E. Some suggest that 2 Thessalonians is a shortened and rewritten 1 Thessalonians or a combination of several letters. Others suggest that 2 Thessalonians was written first and that 1 Thessalonians corrected misconceptions. Possible authors include a friend of Paul's, a secretary, and Timothy.

REASONS FOR WRITING THE LETTER

People in Thessalonica had been experiencing hard times and possibly physical, mental, and emotional harassment. A fraudulent letter may have upset them and food may have been in short supply. Whatever the nature of their problems, some people in the congregation interpreted them as signs that the end of time was approaching. In a linear sense, some of the Thessalonian converts may have come to the end of their time by dying. A few may have claimed that the end of time already occurred and left them behind (2:1). Others quit their jobs, stopped contributing to the community, and neglected their responsibilities (3:6–12).

Paul writes to set them straight or perhaps to discredit the Thessalonians' belief about the end of time. He says that the "Day of the Lord" has not arrived. It may seem as if it has, but according to the divine plan, there must be (2:3–11) the following:

> a rebellion
>
> the appearance of the lawless one (can be seen in the work of Satan: power, signs, lying deception, refusal to love truth and be saved)
>
> the lawless one must declare himself God
>
> the lawless one will be destroyed by the Lord Jesus
>
> a delusion sent by God so the wicked believe what is false

These signs differ remarkably with 1 Thessalonians, which lists only (4:16–5:30) the following:

> cry of command
>
> archangel's call
>
> sound of God's trumpet
>
> Lord descends from heaven
>
> dead in Christ rise
>
> others caught up in the air to meet Jesus
>
> eternity
>
> like a thief in the night
>
> destruction like a woman in labor

Paul's solution to the problem of lazy converts is to abandon them. If they do not work, then they do not deserve to eat. This does not mean that the community should act in a hostile manner toward the lazy converts, but in love the community should treat them as though they did not exist. This distancing of the worshiping congregation may be an early form of **excommunication**.

IDENTITY OF THE LAWLESS ONE

The Lawless One will declare himself or herself to be God. Various theories about the identity or meaning of the Lawless One have been debated for ages. The writer could be referring to a historic person such as Nero, who harassed both Jews and Christians, or **Pompey**, who went into the Holy of Holies in Jerusalem, or **Antiochus IV**, who offered a pig on the altar, or even **Caligula**, who attempted to put his own image in a temple in 40 C.E. The Lawless One also could be a symbol for all who rebel against God, or for the ancient archenemy Satan. It may also refer to a belief within the early Church that at conversion, baptism, and during the Eucharist people took in the power of God and therefore became divine themselves. Someone may be asserting that because of these experiences and rituals, they are now *the* divine.

APOCALYPTIC FOUNDATIONS

The letters to the Thessalonians employ apocalyptic imagery but do not rely on any one particular work within Jewish or Greek literature. Matthew 24:29–35 has often been compared with 1 Thessalonians 4:15–17, but there is no way to prove that the writer of Thessalonians used it as a source. Allusions to or reminiscences of several books in the Old Testament include Psalms, Isaiah, Zechariah, Daniel, and Ezekiel. The writer also may have read **1 Enoch**, an early Jewish Apocryphal book. An excerpt from 1:1–9 follows. (Compare with the verses about the end of time in Thessalonians.)

> *And with the righteous He will make peace,*
> *And will protect the elect,*
> *And mercy shall be upon them.*
> *And they shall all belong to God,*
> *And they shall be prospered,*
> *And they shall all be blessed.*
>
> *And He will help them all,*
> *And light shall appear unto them,*
> *And He will make peace with them.*
>
> *And behold! He cometh with ten thousands of His holy ones*
> *To execute judgment upon all,*
> *And to destroy all the ungodly:*
> *And to convict all flesh*
> *Of all the works of their ungodliness which they*

> *have ungodly committed,*
> *And of all the hard things which ungodly*
> *sinners have spoken against Him.*
> (Charles 1974, 31–32)

SIMILARITIES AND DIFFERENCES OF 1 AND 2 THESSALONIANS

The second letter to the Thessalonians is based on the structure of 1 Thessalonians, yet it is remarkably different in tone, emphasis, and design. Both letters are addressed to people who have questions or have misinterpreted Paul's lectures on the second coming of Jesus. While the people in 1 Thessalonians appear to be puzzled about those who have died, 2 Thessalonians is written to converts who may be experiencing hysteria over the end of time. Their fears of the present and future, coupled with economic or social unrest, may have paralyzed their abilities to function normally. The text that follows attempts to broadly sketch the similarities and differences of the letters.

Similarities

	1 Thess.	2 Thess.
Both written by Paul, Silvanus, and Timothy	1:1	1:1
Both have two thanksgivings	1:2–10	1:3–12
Both have double conclusions	5:23	3:11
Both mention Paul's manual labor	2:9	3:8
Both encourage people to work	4:11	3:12
Both deal with eschatology	4:13–5:11	1:6–2:12
Both place Paul as a major figure	2:17–3:10	3:7–10
Thessalonians are being harassed	2:14–17	1:4, 6–7
Both contain defense of Paul	2:5, 15	3:14, 7
Both appeal to earlier teaching	5:1–2	2:5
Neither quote the Old Testament/Hebrew Bible		
Neither focus on justification by faith		
Neither address the issues of the law		

Not only are there similarities in content, but the structure of both letters is virtually the same. An edited version of **John A. Bailey**'s text comparing the two structures follows.

Identical Thessalonian Structures

	1 Thess.	2 Thess.
Address and Opening	1:1–10	1:1–12
(First Thanksgiving)	1:2–10	1:3–12

Identical Thessalonian Structures, *continued*

	1 Thess.	2 Thess.
Body of Letter	2:1–3:13	2:1–16
(Second Thanksgiving)	2:13	2:13
(Prayer or Benediction)		
Closing of Letter	4:11–5:28	3:1–18
(Teaching Section)		
(Wish for Peace)		
(Greetings)		
(Prayer)		

(From Raymond F. Collins, *Letters That Paul Did Not Write: The Epistle to the Hebrews and the Pauline Pseudepigrapha* (Wilmington DE: Liturgical Press, Michael Glazier, 1988), 219.)

While the structure and many of the topics of 1 and 2 Thessalonians are quite similar, there are considerable differences. A summary of some of these differences follows.

Differences

1 Thessalonians	2 Thessalonians
The tone is personal, warm, fresh	The tone is cool and formal
Personal	Impersonal
Issue: Time of the end unknown	Issue: Known signs before the end
Ministers should be supported	Ministers should not be supported
Stand fast in the Lord	Stand fast and hold on to traditions
Pray for survival	Pray for right action
	Paul is more authoritative and uses more commands
Personal references	No personal references

Summary of 2 Thessalonians: A Second Pauline Letter?   The converts at Thessalonica were in turmoil because of a belief that the end of time had or was about to happen. Someone (possibly Paul or someone using Paul's name) wrote a second letter to the Thessalonica between 51 C.E. and 150 C.E. Structures between the two letters are almost identical, but vocabulary, style, and specific contents differ. They both answer different questions about the parousia and detail different predicted events surrounding the return of Jesus. The letter gives directions to the lazy and unproductive by suggesting that the rest of the group abandon them if they do not change their ways.

Galatians:
A Global and Eternal Egalitarianism

But the other woman corresponds to the Jerusalem above;
she is free, and she is our mother.
—4:26

... God sent his Son, born of a woman....
—4:4

There is no longer Jew or Greek,
there is no longer slave or free,
there is no longer male and female;
for all of you are one in Christ Jesus.
—3:28 NRSV

INTRODUCTION

Galatians, one of Paul's earliest letters, reveals heated dissension within the fast-growing infant religion. This new faith had broken away from an ancient tradition of rules governing the private and public lives of its adherents. It was a faith that had created a cohesive community withstanding centuries of oppression, even exile. Traditional Jews who were converted to a belief in Jesus found it impossible to abandon their culture or lifestyle. If it had worked for them for centuries, why would it not work for others? Paul's message of freedom upset the Jewish age-old organizational structure, culture, and lifestyle.

Galatians discusses this problem by arguing that the law and circumcision were once helpful, but now they are no longer useful. Christianity, the new religion, was breaking down the old barriers. Jesus' death opened the doors to women, the uncircumcised, and especially those whose eating habits would have been considered "unclean" by traditional Judaism. The stress of change penetrates every chapter in Galatians. Even Paul feels he must reassert his authority by defending his life and choices.

LOCATION OF GALATIA

The name "Galatians" is unfamiliar to us. It sounds as though it has been taken from a science fiction movie about an alien race. Who were the Galatians? Can anyone describe them? Where did they live? These answers are not to be found in the New Testament. No one knows the exact identity of the Galatians. The letter written by Paul between 50–60 C.E. may have been directed to several congregations in a region in Asia Minor, but scholars still debate about where that region is located.

FIGURE 9.6   Photo of houses or living quarters carved in the soft rock near Görme, Turkey. This region was close to Galatia and perhaps where Christians received letters from Paul. Thousands of people lived in the rocks and underground caves in this region as a means of protection. The area is now called Cappadocia. Photo taken by Marla J. Selvidge.

A logical home for the Galatians is southern Asian Minor. According to Acts of the Apostles Paul traveled to Cilicia and Pisidia (southern Asia Minor). Yet these people were not known as the Galatians. Rome created and named Galatia, a province in Asia Minor around 25? B.C.E. This area is located generally north of where Paul is supposed to have traveled in the areas of Bithynia and possibly Pontus. Interestingly, there are many archaeological remains of ancient Christian churches in the north as well as evidence of Romans writing letters about people in Bithynia. But there is little evidence of ancient Christians in the south central part of Asia Minor. Consult Figure 9.7 for an approximate location of the old Galatia.

TOPICS OF THE LETTER

No one knows the exact reasons for sending this letter. We can attempt to reconstruct the situation by studying the letter itself which addresses several issues. We do not know if people had come to Paul with questions or reports of problems. It appears that during the early stages of Christianity, people were confused about whether becoming a Christian meant that one also had to assume all of the rules and regulations within Judaism. We have

FIGURE 9.7 Map of Galatia. From Clarence Larkin, *Dispensational Truth* (Philadelphia: Rev. Clarence Larkin Est., 1918).

read about the Jerusalem Council in the Acts of the Apostles and the idealistic stories about how early Christians worshiped at the temple and also ate together in their homes. We also have studied stories about how Peter argued that kosher rules no longer applied to new converts. Here, in Galatians, Paul discusses keeping kosher, circumcising male converts, and whether or not new converts should keep the ancient Jewish/Israelite laws. (Present-day Judaism came into existence around the sixth century B.C.E. The ancient Israelite religion may date from 1000 B.C.E. and earlier.)

Circumcision and Baptism

At first glance it would appear that Paul is writing to males in Galatia. Judaism recognized a group of worshipers as a "synagogue" only when there were ten circumcised males. Apparently Paul is very frustrated with people from the circumcision party (probably from Jerusalem) who are demanding that males be circumcised as a sign of their conversion. In chapter 5, Paul mocks the missionaries of circumcision. While the exact Greek words are difficult to translate into English, Paul portrays them as running around boasting about how many scalps (possibly the tips of penises) they had collected, "glory in the flesh or make a good showing in the flesh" (6:12). In a rather abusive tone, Paul writes, "I wish those who unsettle you would castrate themselves" (5:12).

These are earthy topics for Paul. It seems implausible that people 1,900 years ago would argue over a physical operation that is common practice today. Circumcision is not a hot topic in the twenty-first century. While some males may argue about how circumcision is done, or whether it should be done, almost all males in the United States are circumcised because of health reasons.

There is no conclusive evidence about how people knew if someone was circumcised. Clothing may have been a factor. Greek clothing in some parts of the Empire did not cover all of the body all of the time. Greeks were known to compete in athletic events in the nude. We do not know what the standards for nudity were in communities all over the Empire.

Paul is the missionary to the "uncircumcised" (2:7). What could this mean? Circumcision was a holdover from Judaism and thus centered Christianity in an androcentric or male-centered environment. If only males are members, then only males can hold office and run the local religious establishment. Paul criticizes this narrow approach and claims that during the ritual of baptism all of these preconceived ideas about a male-female patriarchal hierarchy, class structure, or ethnic background changed. He quotes a saying used at a baptismal ritual in 3:28, "There is no longer Jew or Greek, there is no longer slave or free, there is no longer male and female; for all of you are one in Christ Jesus." So the issue of circumcision is more than an issue of keeping Jewish traditions or a sign of being a member. It also is a sign that only certain kinds of males may authoritatively lead worship. Paul argues that conversion to Christianity, and with it baptism, changed this arrangement and opened up leadership to women and men from all different classes and ethnic backgrounds.

Paul's View of Jesus

The human side of Jesus does not concern Paul. It appears that he is unacquainted with the person or the sayings of Jesus, preferring to use titles such as Christ, Jesus Christ, Christ Jesus, Lord, and occasionally Son of God. For him, Jesus' crucifixion or death is of prime importance. Jesus' death justifies but also brings peace, grace, and freedom from the curse. As children of God, people are baptized in Christ and serve him. Paul has complete faith in Jesus the Messiah.

The Law and Justification (or Righteousness): Jesus' Death as a Model

The law is the center of faith for a Jew. The law describes and dictates ways of living an acceptable life. In ancient Israelite tradition, the threat of death always hung over the heads of people who did not follow the law. The story of Achan in the Hebrew Book of Joshua is about a man who lied because he did not follow the laws set down by God. For his mistake, he and his entire family lost their lives (Joshua 7). In Deuteronomy, time after time, the writer warns Israelites that disobeying the law would mean excommunication (6:18). In a tribal society, to be thrown out of a group could mean immediate death, because a person would have no food, shelter, or protection.

While he argues against using Jewish law as a mirror to assess one's life, he does not totally abandon it. The law had many purposes. It was given because people transgressed (**natural law**). It was a disciplinarian that taught people how to live and find God. Not everyone needed the law, for example, Abraham exhibited faith before the law was instituted.

Paul uses the terms *justification* or *righteousness* to describe the results of Jesus' death. The concept of justification presupposes a belief system centered around the fallibility of humans. The ancient Israelite religion, which later evolved into Judaism, instituted laws that everyone had to follow. Many of the laws were probably written to bring stability into the lives of the people in the community (whether political, social, or ethical). The ideal person followed all of the laws; thus the term *righteous* became a descriptive word for the perfect person.

Joseph Plevnik, in *What Are They Saying about Paul?* gives two examples of how people define justification. Protestants would define it in the following way: "It is a judicial act through which God, on the basis of Christ's saving death, grants to the sinner an undeserved gift of righteousness, or regards the sinner as righteous." It is received through faith. A Catholic view reads, a person who is "justified becomes really righteous, holy, transformed in the inner self and related in a new way to God" (p. 57).

Paul's view of Jesus is influenced by these ancient Israelite traditions of the righteous person. It also is influenced by a belief in "sin." A sinner is one who aims to keep the law but somehow does not. Jesus' death, according to Paul, declares that all people who believe in Him are declared innocent for all sins, crimes, and abrogations of the Jewish law. Through faith they are free to abandon the law because Jesus' death satisfied all of the sentences given for breaking the law. People can therefore stand before God as blameless and innocent of breaking the law.

CHARACTERS, GEOGRAPHY, AND POLITICAL GROUPS

Below is a list of the main characters, geographical locations, and major political groups found in Galatians. While only two women are mentioned, the issue of the status of females and their leadership within the community underlies much of the conversation Paul had with the Galatians.

Characters	Geographical Locations	Political Groups
Cephas	Arabia	James
Abraham	Damascus	Circumcision
Hagar	Syria	Spirit or Enthusiastic
Sarah	Cilicia	
Barnabas	Jerusalem	
Titus	Galatia	
James		
John		

Paul

Diplomacy or tact was not Paul's strongest point when writing to the people in Galatia. Paul's tone is vindictive and angry. At one point he calls out to the "stupid Galatians."

Certainly this is no way to win points or an argument. He is threatened by people in the community who claim that he has no authority.

Can we discover Paul's personality or person in the letter to the Galatians? It is possible. No one writes such a forceful and provocative letter such as Galatians unless he or she is deeply committed or concerned about the people. One of the most challenging things faced by parents is learning how to correct children without abusing them. Paul considers the Galatians his converts and thus wants them to succeed. And like a parent who is not always perfect or "correct" in his or her judgment, Paul may be heading into questionable territory when he calls the Galatians "idiots" (3:1).

Paul wants the Galatians to adhere to his brand of Christianity. He believes that his way, his theology, is the only acceptable theology within Christianity. This attitude has been prevalent throughout Christianity for hundreds of years. Note how many denominations, divisions, and sects exist within Christianity. All claim that their way, their belief, is more accurate or preferable.

Paul felt as though he needed to defend himself. In a heated argument, sometimes this strategy works and sometimes it does not. No one will ever know if the Galatians responded favorably to Paul. Paul told them of his background in Judaism and the fast-track life he led by climbing over the "bodies" of both men and women Christians (1:13–14). He claims that he had a special revelation (1:11) and that God had chosen him for a special mission before his birth (1:15). Acts links him with the term *apostle* only twice (14:4,14). He was accepted by the powerful traditional church in Jerusalem (2:2) and had the courage to challenge one of their leaders, Peter. He says he opposed Cephas or Peter face to face about Peter's decision to keep kosher dietary laws again (2:11–14).

Obviously, Paul was not a people pleaser (1:10). As a self-starter who had clear thoughts and directions, at times he was confrontational and at other times he felt harassed because he was misunderstood. He personally identifies with Jesus' death on the cross. "I have been crucified with Christ…" (2:19) although he did not really experience the same crucifixion.

As a zealous religious person, Paul thought his opinion was the only correct one. After studying Galatians, one wonders if Paul ever doubted his own beliefs. He argued for the inclusion of non-Jews into the new religion, but he could not broaden his own perspective to accept those who disagreed with him. Paul is so quick to point out other people's shortcomings, one wonders what shortcomings plagued his life.

Hellenistic Influences on Paul   Without a doubt, Paul was influenced by the popular movements, literature, and philosophies of the first century. Some of those Hellenistic influences were rooted in Judaism, and others in a variety of Hellenistic religions/philosophies. Paul was a Hellenized Jew; thus his culture and way of life ran very close to what are called "Gentiles" in the New Testament. The word "ethne" in Greek, commonly translated "Gentiles," means "nations." It is probably a word referring to non-Jews, especially Greek-speaking people who did not keep the Jewish dietary, purity, and sacrificial laws. The males were uncircumcised (2:9, 12). Paul argues that Gentiles should be included as full members within Christianity, but he also uses the word in stereotypical and pejorative ways, such as, "We ourselves are Jews by birth and not Gentile sinners...." (2:15). Paul appears to be denigrating the very people to whom he claims he was sent.

Paul is interested in "knowledge" and expresses it through the use of cosmic language. He believes that the Old Testament law came through angels and that the people who kept or presently follow the law in the Old Testament are "enslaved to the elemental spirits of this world" (4:3) and "... you were enslaved to beings that by nature are not gods" (4:8). He also mentions the keeping of holidays, which could refer to any religious background (4:10). Paul's opposition to denying oneself personal pleasures sounds quite similar to the Gnostic idea of flesh being evil (5:16–17).

Peter

The name Peter is rarely mentioned in Galatians. A Greek word with an Aramaic origin, meaning "rock," is mentioned in chapter 2, Cephas. Is this person named Cephas the same person we met in the gospels and Acts? Yes, according to most scholars. In Acts, we met an apostle, Peter, who had gained great powers of oratory and urged an early Christian community to abandon kosher laws. According to Acts, he was the first person to carry this news to Cornelius, a God fearer in Caesarea. But here, in Galatians, Peter vacillates. He is associating with non-Jewish Christians, eating and drinking with them. But people from the "circumcision faction" influence him to abandon his newfound friends because they are not keeping the law (2:11–14). Paul confronts and criticizes him for his hypocritical behavior.

Hagar and Sarah: She Is Our Mother

The story of Sarah, similar to the baptismal saying, underscores the radical discontinuity with the past that the new converts were experiencing. Abraham is a model of inclusive belief (3:6–9), and Sarah is portrayed as the historic model of freedom. Paul attempts to bridge the division between Judaism and Christianity by retaining and reinterpreting the stories of Jewish heroes and heroines.

The stories about Hagar and Sarah are difficult to interpret. Some have suggested that they are both types of the new Christian community. The verses are based on Genesis 16–21 and the stories of Abraham, Sarah, and Hagar. Abraham slept with a concubine, Hagar, and Ishmael was born. Meanwhile, the divine divulges to Abraham that Sarah will have a child at her advanced age of ninety years. She births Isaac. Eventually, Abraham, on the advice of Sarah, throws Hagar and Ishmael out of the house and into the desert, where they are left to die. An angel of the Lord rescues Hagar. What follows is an abbreviated list that compares the stories of Hagar and Sarah in Galatians.

Hagar	Sarah
Law	Freedom from the Law
Slave Woman	Free Woman
Child of Flesh	Child of Promise
Mt. Sinai, Arabia	
Child of Slavery	Free
Present Jerusalem	Jerusalem Above
Driven Out	
Will Not Inherit	Our Mother
Children of Slave	Isaac, Children of Free

In chapter 4, Paul argues that modern Christians are children of the free woman, Sarah. They are not slaves bound by the laws given on Mount Sinai. Their hope rests in Jerusalem, which is "above," or in heaven. Sarah, whose name is not mentioned, becomes a matriarchal model of freedom. Her life typifies the life of the new Gentile convert,... she is free, and she is our mother" (4:26).

Paul quotes Isaiah in 4:27 as he continues the argument. The verses praise childless and single women, while promising that their children will outnumber the married women. Paul may be predicting that Gentile converts will soon outnumber the traditional Jewish Christians. His argument serves as a reality check to the party of circumcision, which may soon find its numbers dwindling. He urges the party to join the free woman party and abandon their slave woman mentality.

ACTS AND GALATIANS

To understand the letters within their historical and cultural framework, scholars attempt to reconstruct history based on other texts of the New Testament. What follows is a general comparison between the stories in Acts and the claims made by Paul in his letter to the Galatians. Sometimes they agree and sometimes they do not.

Acts	Galatians
Peter breaks kosher laws. (10)	Cephas chooses to keep kosher laws. (2:11–14)
Jerusalem Council gives Paul specific guidelines on idols, fornication, blood, and strangulation. (15:19–20)	Paul claims that he was told only to remember the poor. (2:10)
Jerusalem Council accepts Paul and Barnabas. (15:1)	James, Cephas, and John recognized Paul and Barnabas. (2:9); may not be the same council.
Paul travels through Galatia. Did not stop. (16:6; 18:23)	Writes letters to people in Galatia as a friend who had visited them. (1:2–6)
Paul violently abused disciples of the Lord. (9:1)	Paul violently abused church of God. (1:13)

SOURCES AND LITERARY FORMS

Some of the sources or forms used by Paul in Galatians could have been hearsay evidence from a traveling mentor or quotes from actual letters written to Paul. There is no way to determine if Galatians or any of Paul's letters contain quotations from other undiscovered works. One can only speculate. What follows is a short list of possible resources used in creating the letter to the Galatians.

Galatians	Source/Form
1:13–2:10	Autobiography
3:28	Baptismal saying
4:27	Quotation, Isaiah 54:1; 51:1–3
3:6	Abraham in Genesis
4:21–31	Genesis 16–21
5:19	Lists of vices and virtues
6:7, 22	Parables

Many people recognize stoic influences on Paul, especially the writings of Seneca, a contemporary of Paul's who lived in Spain. Some suggest that they corresponded. See Figure 9.8.

Summary of Galatians Galatians is a letter sent to help mend dissension within a community, define the relationship of new converts to Jewish law, and underscore the egalitarian nature of the new religion. In the face of overwhelming criticism, Paul defends his career and beliefs.

To this day we do not know who received the letter to the Galatians. Their location remains a mystery. We do know that the people to whom the letter was addressed argued about proper religious lifestyles and the meaning of the death of Jesus. Some thought that all of the laws in the Old Testament, which included circumcision and eating kosher, must be followed. For Paul, Jesus' death is the center of the controversy. His Cru-

FIGURE 9.8 Ancient portrait of Seneca. From Rev. F. W. Farrar, *Seekers After God* (London: Macmillan and Co., 1886).

cifixion resulted in perfection or righteousness before God for those who believe. He argued for freedom from the old male hierarchical structures to a new type of life where all people, regardless of their race, class, or sex, were essential components in the new religion. Paul ends the letter with a hope that all of the people in the community would work toward bringing good to the "family of faith" (6:10).

Philippians:
A Love Letter to the Macedonians

For to me, living is Christ and dying is gain.

—1:21 NRSV

Let those of us who are mature be of the same mind; and if you think differently about anything, this too God will reveal to you.

—3:15 NRSV

INTRODUCTION

In times of trouble, people need each other. Paul needed the Philippians, so he sent an extended thank-you note to those he termed "saints." They had provided monetary support for him while in Thessalonica and had sent gifts to him through Epaphroditus while he was in prison. Apparently, on a trip to visit Paul, Epaphroditus became ill or was physically attacked by people who were opposed to the spread of Christianity. He nearly died. A sober and reflective Paul considers his own possible death as a mirror of Jesus' self-sacrificial love for humanity. Paul's attitude toward differences of opinion has changed in the midst of sending his unrelenting praise and love-wishes to his friends.

DATE, AUTHORSHIP, LOCATION

Timothy and Paul sent the letter to the Philippians, but researchers assume total Pauline authorship. The letter was written sometime between 56–64 from Caesarea, Rome, Ephesus, or Corinth. Scholars debate the origin of the letter because Paul seems to be in prison, but no one knows its exact location. Acts and 2 Corinthians (11:23) suggest numerous imprisonments all over the Empire.

After reading Philippians several times, it becomes obvious to the reader that the letter has several abrupt beginnings and endings, signaling that manuscripts could have been spliced together. In one paragraph, Paul uses ecstatic language to describe his love for the Philippians, and in the next he is bitterly attacking enemies. Scholars have detected several seams or conclusions in the letter, such as

3:1	Finally, my brothers and sisters ...
4:8	Finally, beloved ...
4:9	... the God of peace will be with you.
4:20	To our God and Father be glory forever and ever. Amen.
4:21	Greet every saint ...

Researchers have theorized about several different historical situations for each section of the letter. Many conclude that Philippians is a compilation of at least three letters, including editorial remarks by a scribe who collected them. There is no agreement about the exact configuration of these letters, or on how many letters were written. One possible scenario follows:

Letter One:	1:1–3:1; 4:2–9	
	Written after Epaphroditus arrived and while Paul was in prison.	
Letter Two:	3:2–4:1	
	Written after Epaphroditus recovers. Does not mention imprisonment. Focuses attack on dissenters.	
Letter Three:	4:10–23	
	A thank-you letter to be delivered by Epaphroditus.	

THE CITY OF PHILIPPI

Philippi was located on the busy Via Egnatia, which connected the Empire with Italy. It was surrounded on three sides by mountains, with a high area in the middle of the city upon which was built an acropolis. It was conquered by the Macedonians in the fourth century B.C.E. and by the Romans in 42 B.C.E. Mark Antony founded a Roman colony at Philippi for veterans. **Octavian** settled additional people from Italy in the city in 31 B.C.E. and named it Julia Augusta Philippensis. Eventually Philippi was governed by an Italian form of government and known as the first city of the region.

The religious diversity of the city has been confirmed by archaeological excavations. Among the gods and goddesses who were worshiped were Jupiter, **Mars**, Cybele, Apollo, Asclepius, Isis, and Serapis. It also had an Imperial religion or cult with religious officials who presided over deified emperors such as Julius and **Augustus**.

THE ACTS OF THE APOSTLES AND PHILIPPI

Enticed by a vision of a man from Macedonia, Paul and company, according to Acts of the Apostles, headed west toward what is now modern Greece. They passed through the port city of Neapolis, ten miles east of Philippi. Upon their arrival, they happened upon a meeting of Lydia, a successful businesswoman who later converted. She offered them a room in her house, and they accepted. Acts says very strongly, "And she prevailed upon us" (16:15).

After a few days in the city, Paul and Silas were arrested, stripped, flogged, and thrown into jail for healing a slave girl. The charge against them was, "They are Jews and are advocating customs that are not lawful for us as Romans to adopt or observe" (16:22). After a close encounter with an earthquake that opened all of the doors of the prison, the jailer freed them. Consequently, Roman magistrates escorted them to the edge of the city where they were asked to leave. Paul returned briefly to Lydia's house, and they continued on their journey to Thessalonica (see Phil. 4:16).

This tale of violence and intrigue in Philippi found in Acts of the Apostles has little in common with the letter to the Philippians. In both works, Paul is imprisoned for his religious activities. There is contact with Roman officials in both—the magistrates in Acts and the Imperial guard in Philippians (4:22). Both recognize strong female leadership within the new congregation.

REASONS FOR WRITING THE LETTER(S)

Imprisonment was not laced with opportunities for rehabilitation, exercise, or meaningful work during Roman incarceration. Little was provided by the government for prisoners. Relatives and friends had to support the prisoner with clothing, food, and medical care. Paul sent his timely letter to graciously thank the Philippians for their generous support of him while in prison and on his evangelistic trips.

Interwoven throughout this letter are expressions of Paul's love for his friends at Philippi. He stresses unity and cooperation as the basis of a solid and strong relationship. One could read these statements in several ways. Some suggest that the converts were miserably divided. Euodia and Syntyche are engaged in a personal power struggle that could be producing dissension (4:2). Yet Paul's words are gentle and sentimental, which may suggest that there is harmony among most of the people. A few of his words of care follow:

> 1:9   ... that your love may overflow....
> 2:2   ... having the same love....
> 2:12   ... beloved and long for....
> 4:1   ... whom I love and long for, beloved....

This idealism is reminiscent of the first two chapters in Acts, where Luke portrays the people "with one mind" worshiping and eating together both in the temple and in individual homes (2:46).

CHARACTERS

Friends at Philippi

This letter is addressed to the "saints" with the "bishops and deacons." The words "bishop and deacon" are used for officials within the growing Christian church. 1 Timothy 3:1–13, a second-century letter, describes the duties of these offices. Scholars do not think these particular positions existed as early as the 60s C.E. Some suggest that the words were added by a later editor. Nevertheless, the letter recognizes and respects a variety of offices and duties within the church of Philippi during the life of Paul.

Paul's relationship to the Philippians is one of trust and openness. He does not feel compelled to check off a list of ethical guidelines, as we have viewed in other letters. Paul is also willing to accept differences of opinion among converts. He admits that they can also ascertain divine information. Some of the people at Philippi may have become Christians for selfish reasons. They may have gained monetarily or politically from their association with the new faith. Paul believes their actions hurt him personally (1:12–18). Instead of denigrating these people, Paul demonstrates an open attitude by asking, "What does it matter?" (1:18). This openness to the Philippians can also be inferred from other phrases Paul uses. For instance, "to help you to determine what is best" (1:10) suggests that the Philippians do not need the guidance of Paul. They are capable of solving their own problems and determining their own future. A more mature Paul writes, "and if you think differently about anything, this too God will reveal to you" (3:15). Paul may have been a recipient of a divine message, but he admits that the Philippians also can obtain wisdom and knowledge from that same God.

Paul's tone changes in chapter 3 as he begins a tirade against people at Philippi whom he calls "dogs" (3:2). "Dogs" was a slang term for people who were not circumcised. Paul uses their own word against them. Consider the following verses:

> 3:2   Beware of dogs, beware of the evil workers, beware of those who mutilate themselves. (NRSV)
>
> 3:19 Their end is destruction; their god is their belly; and their glory is their shame; their minds are set on earthly things. (NRSV)

Scholars describe the "dogs" in terms of specific religious political parties, which include Gnostics, Jewish Christians, Enthusiasts, and Jewish Propagandists. Paul wishes for their destruction, but for his friends he promises heaven, transformation, and perhaps a new body in the next life (3:21).

Philippian converts warm Paul's heart. He is proud of their achievements and confident that their dedication to the new religion will continue. In response to their needs, Paul sends back Epaphroditus and offers Timothy's guidance.

Paul and Companions

Philippians reveals a tender and compassionate side of Paul. Timothy is a "son" and his friends and converts at Philippi are the "Beloved." He is especially thankful for the close relationship with Epaphroditus, whom he says is a "brother," co-worker, fellow soldier, messenger, and minister. He was wounded and almost died, and he is now returning to Philippi (2:25–29).

Awaiting the outcome of a trial, Paul views himself as a reflection of Jesus. While he may not want to die, he is willing to suffer death for his faith. Circumstances may be similar for the Philippians (1:30). Paul is honored to be able to suffer for his God.

In contemplating the opposition, Paul was compelled once again to defend his credentials (3:4–6). He is

> circumcised (as a child)
> a Jew
> a Pharisee
> a keeper of the law
> a persecutor of the church

In addition to his fellow workers Euodia, Syntyche, and Clement, Paul says that Timothy, who is a son, and a special friend, will be sent to Philippi soon (2:19).

LITERARY FOUNDATIONS

Hymns, Poems, Songs

Intertwined within Paul's personal words of praise, love, and affection are beautiful and thought-provoking songs, poems, and hymns that may or may not have been created by Paul. The introduction to the famous hymn about the death or incarnation of Jesus in 2:5–11 may have been a love poem or a wedding prayer (2:1–4).

> If then there is any encouragement in Christ, any consolation from love, any sharing in the Spirit, any compassion and sympathy, make my joy complete: be of the same mind, having the same love, being in full accord and of one mind. Do nothing from selfish ambition or conceit, but in humility regard others as better than yourselves. Let each of you look not to your own interests, but to the interests of others. Let the same mind be in you that was in Christ Jesus. (NRSV)

Many scholars think that subsequent verses in 2:5–11 reflect a common hymn about the death or **incarnation** of Jesus. Jesus is portrayed as a selfless entity who gave of himself by becoming a mere human slave. For his martyrdom, God the Father promoted him to a place of authority over the universe.

The concept of divine becoming human seems "normal" to a Westerner whose culture is steeped in Christian traditions. The Mediterranean world had many such stories about the union of the divine with a human, for instance, Dionysus. But this concept of incarnation was not easily defined as Christianity began to spread throughout the globe. Theologians argued about the meaning of "human" and wondered how a monotheistic God could be at the same time Father, Son, and Holy Spirit. It was humanly impossible and illogical. Later, bishops of the Church developed the idea of the Trinity, three persons in one God.

Male Metaphors or Images

In spite of all the love language used in Philippians, some scholars think that Philippians reflects primarily male experiences of Christianity. Paul is judged as ambivalent about the role of women in the new religion. Evidence for this is found in the traditional male imagery of sports, the military, and the close relationships of males. Epaphroditus is a fellow soldier (military, 2:25) and Paul is running the race to win (sports, 3:14). He refers to Timothy as "son" (2:21–22). But scholars may have missed some key information contained in the verses describing two women.

The only females who are mentioned in the letter are the squabbling Euodia and Syntyche (4:2–3). Paul's words may at first glance appear negative, yet the fact that he mentions their names means they are recognized as important people in the congregation. Paul says they were "fellow workers" who struggled with him. The image of struggling is taken from the games, where gladiators fought wild beasts. Here Paul is saying that they fought enemies together. These women are not the only friends to be given the title of "fellow worker" within the letters attributed to Paul. Consider the following list:

Phil. 2:25	Epaphroditus
1 Thess. 3:2	Timothy
Philemon	Demas, Luke, Mark, Aristarchus
Rom. 16:3	Priscilla and Aquila
Rom. 16:9	Urbanus
Rom. 16:21	Timothy

What seems to be a small, last minute thought by the writer of Philippians reveals that females were among the closest associates of Paul. "Fellow Worker" may have been one of the highest and most privileged offices within the early Christian communities.

Summary of Philippians   Philippians appears to be a composite letter written by Paul sometime towards the middle of the first century C.E. Its primary purpose was to thank the Philippians for their financial support of him during his imprisonment. Paul uses hymns and male metaphors to describe his career. Important characters include Epaphroditus, Euodia, Syntyche, and Timothy.

10

Later Pauline Documents

Romans, Philemon, 1 and 2 Corinthians

This chapter places Romans and Philemon within the context of the Roman Empire. Both letters, while addressed to a particular person or a location, were considered general letters to all Christians.

Romans: Fostering Ethnic Equality and Harmony

For I am not ashamed of the Gospel; it is the power of God for salvation to everyone who has faith, to the Jew first and also to the Greek.

—Romans 1:16 NRSV

INTRODUCTION

Romans was written to strangers whom Paul hoped to visit in the near future. Therefore, his tone is studied and disciplined and perhaps, a little defensive. He rarely gets carried away with himself, as discovered in such letters as Galatians and 2 Corinthians. He addresses issues he hopes will result in a change in the attitudes and relationships among the converts in Rome.

The letter to Romans warms the hearts of many Christians. While claiming to have fulfilled all of the demands of the ancient Israelite law by the death of Jesus, Paul, in a measure, lays down a battery of sins that have been interpreted by many Christians as the new law. Readers will struggle with understanding the language and point of view taken by Paul on many ethical issues such as same-sex relationships, submission to the government, and vegetarianism.

Paul argues for equality and harmony among all peoples throughout the Empire. He proves equality by demonstrating that everyone has sinned or missed the mark (crossed into and out of sacred space). Many of his analogies and metaphors, such as the family of God and his language of love, support the international and multiracial/ethnic view of Christianity.

AUTHORSHIP, FORM, DATE

Opinions about Pauline authorship of Romans are virtually unanimous in spite of the verse in 16:22, "I Tertius, the writer of this letter, greet you in the Lord." Tertius is concluded to be a scribe or secretary to whom Paul dictated Romans, and his/her influence is judged to be minimal. Many who argue for Pauline authorship have theorized that chapter 16 did not belong to the original letter, based on the following evidence: (1) For several hundred years, some copies of Romans circulated without chapter 16 (a fragment addressed to the Ephesians); (2) **Origen**, in his *Commentary on the Epistle to the Romans,* comments upon the missing chapters:

> Marcion,... completely removed this section (16:25ff) from this Epistle; and not this alone, but also from that place where it was written: "For all which is not based upon faith is sin" (14:23), he cut it off right up to the end. (Kümmel 1966, 222)

(3) Other copies circulated without chapters 15 and 16; (4) The "**doxology**" (16:25–27) is found in three different places in the ancient manuscripts, which suggests that Romans may have been heavily edited, and, (5) chapter 16 presupposes that Paul has many acquaintances and friends in Rome, even though there is no evidence that he visited the city.

After a meticulous study of the verses in Romans, scholars also have detected theological ideas that appear inconsistent with the remainder of Romans and other Pauline works. Verses often interrupt the logical flow of the letter. A list of questionable insertions, editions, or glosses follows:

2:16   On the day when according to my Gospel, God, through Jesus Christ, will judge the secret thoughts of all.

6:17   But thanks be to God that you, having once been slaves of sin, have become obedient from the heart to the form of teaching to which your were entrusted,

7:25b So then with my mind I am a slave to the law of God, but with my flesh I am a slave to the law of sin.

8:1   There is therefore no condemnation for those who are in Christ Jesus.

10:17 So faith comes from what is heard, and what is heard comes through the word of Christ.

(Other editing or glosses may be 1:19–21, 32; 2:1,16, 17; 3:10, etc.)

Because of the possibility of so many glosses, the abrupt change in subject matter, and the use of first-person and third-person pronouns (I and they), several theorize that Romans contains at least two different letters.

The Author, Paul

If Paul wrote the letter, he chose to reveal little about himself, inserting personal notations at the beginning and end of the letter. A summary of statements made about Paul follows.

Paul in Romans

Servant	1:1
Apostle	1:1
Teaches the Gospel of God	1:1
Sent to bring obedience of faith among Gentiles	1:5
Debtor to Greeks and Barbarians	1:14
Debtor to wise and foolish	1:14
Wanted to go to Rome but did not	1:13
Speaks the truth	9:1
Feels great sorrow for his kindred, the Israelites	9:3
Israelite, descendent of Abraham	11:1
Member of tribe of Benjamin	11:1
An apostle to the Gentiles	11:13
Recognizes that his words are strong	15:15
Minister to the Gentiles	15:16
Boasts about work	15:17
Signs and wonders accompany his teaching	15:19
Traveled from Illyricum to Jerusalem	15:19
Ambition to preach good news	15:20
Preaches where no one else has preached	15:20
Wants to avoid the conflict of interfering with someone else's converts	15:20
Unable to travel to Rome	15:22
Intends to go to Spain	15:24, 28
There is no place for him in the regions	15:23
Going to Jerusalem with monetary gift	15:28
Hopes he will be safe in Judea	15:31
Sends greetings to friends and relatives	16

Unlike other Pauline letters, Romans is more reasoned, cool, and calculating. It does not divert into tangential arguments. Paul's usual blantant defensiveness and boisterous posturing does not surface. The writing is polite, without accusing or attacking individuals for inappropriate beliefs or behavior.

Paul may even have interjected a portrait of his own vulnerability into chapter 7, but we will never know to what he was referring when he exclaimed, "Wretched man that I am! Who will rescue me from this body of death?" (7:24). This passage may also describe the struggle one faces when trying to keep the law. It reveals a frustrated individual who cannot discipline himself in order to find moral success. Using the first-person "I," Paul portrays the battle of the heart (or mind) over the body. The solution to this problem is "… to set the mind on the Spirit.… (8:6).

It appears that Paul had intended to go to Rome but never made it. For some reason, he now has the time and will come to the people shortly after he returns to Jerusalem with a gift from the converts in Macedonia and Achaia. His sights are set on Spain. Chapter 15 seems to suggest that Paul has encountered difficulties with congregations that he did not inaugurate. His goal is to travel to places where the news of Christianity may not have found its way. His fear of traveling to Jerusalem has been used by scholars to date the writing of Romans to the period just before Paul was arrested in Jerusalem and eventually taken to Rome (Acts 21:27ff).

Form and Date

The letter to the Romans fits the most basic outline of an ancient letter. But letters are written to people, and Paul usually wrote to people about issues or problems. Although Paul addresses problems in Romans, the answers seem to be general or generic and not designed for or written to individuals or a group of people. Students have theorized that Romans is not a letter. They have argued that it may be a letter essay, a diatribe, or a last will and testament, circulating to several different Judeo-Christian groups.

The content of Romans may be based on a thought-provoking teaching methodology known as **diatribe**, where the student confronts the teacher with questions and vice versa. Most agree that Romans was written in the latter part of the sixth decade C.E., or between 53–58 C.E.

THE CITY OF ROME AND READERS

Christianity began as an outlaw religion but later triumphed over the Roman Empire during the fourth century C.E. under **Constantine**, who moved his capital from Rome to Constantinople. No words can describe the splendor of ancient Rome. Travelers can still walk the streets of the forum created during the time of Augustus and stand in awe of Nero's palace, the Pantheon, the Coliseum, and the entrance to the Tiber, Ostia Antiqua. Vatican City is a visual reminder of the wealth and power that Christianity amassed during the late Middle Ages.

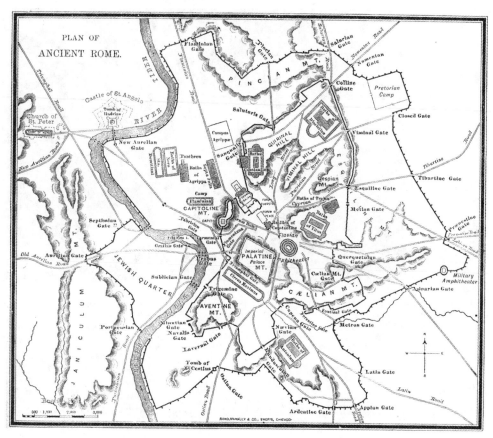

FIGURE 10.1   Plan of Ancient Rome. From Rand, McNally & Company, 1884. The Library of Congress, Washington, DC.

Rome's origins began in the eighth century B.C.E., and by 275 B.C.E., it ruled all of Italy. For the next 200 years, it conquered areas in Spain, Macedonia, and Achaia. During civil rebellions, the military assumed leadership in 60 B.C.E., with Pompey, **Crassus,** and **Julius Caesar** at the helm. Eventually, another soldier, Octavian, assumed rule in 27 B.C.E. until 14 C.E. He later took the title "Augustus" and ruled as a monarch or emperor. Augustus brought peace, and with it came time to write and rebuild cities. **Virgil**, **Horace**, and Livy penned their masterpieces during his reign. Augustus also turned the fighting machines of the military into protectors of the people.

Because Rome was the center of the Empire, it attracted all sorts of peoples from around the globe. Its religions were as diverse as its citizens. Mithras, Isis, Osiris, and Dea Syria were worshiped alongside the Jewish and Christian God.

FIGURE 10.2   Rome: The Coliseum. Photo by Marla J. Selvidge.

The Readers

It seems fairly clear that the people who first received Romans had a background in Jewish literature and tradition. Yet the letter also is addressed to non-Jews or Gentiles. No one knows the exact ethnic, social, or religious background of the converts in Rome, but scholars have created many descriptive names. They include Gentiles, converted **Diaspora Jews,** Jewish Christians, Roman Christians, and circumcised and uncircumcised Gentiles. Some of them may have originally been God fearers who converted to Christianity. Paul Minear suggests that Romans is written to several large congregations or groups living around Rome.

Ancient sources record the presence of both Jews and Christians in Rome during the first century C.E. Evidence for the presence of Jews in Rome is described by **Philo,** Josephus, and Cicero. As early as the Maccabean period, Jews may have had formal diplomatic relations with Rome. 2 Maccabees 11:34 records a letter from the Romans to the Maccabees and I Maccabees 8:17 reads,

> So Judas chose Eupolemus ... and Jason, ... and sent them to Rome to establish friendship and alliance, and to free themselves from the yoke.... They went to Rome, a very long journey; and they entered the senate chamber and spoke.... (NRSV)

Some estimate that there were as many as thirteen synagogues in Rome. Thousands of Jewish grave inscriptions were discovered in the catacombs of Rome. We know that after conquering Jerusalem, Pompey shipped as many as 50,000 Jews to Rome in 61 B.C.E. as prisoners of war. Some time later, they were released.

Suetonius, a historian of the early second century C.E., describes a riot in Rome among the Jews. Apparently, the Emperor Claudius deported Jews to keep order in Rome around 49–50 C.E. The Jews were following someone by the name of Chrestus. Scholars speculate about the identity or definition of "Chrestus." It could refer to a person, or a movement that aimed to overthrow the Roman Empire. Some suggest that Jews and Christians were fighting in the streets, whereas others suggest that Jewish Christians were against Gentile Christians. Most agree that Suetonius is referring to the same event described in Acts, listing Priscilla and Aquila as part of the exported group (Acts 18:1–2).

Later, around 64 C.E., Nero blamed Christians for a fire in Rome that he may have caused. Tacitus, a first-century historian, toward the end of his life, writes in *The Annals,*

> Therefore, to scotch the rumor, Nero substituted as culprits, and punished with the utmost refinements of cruelty, a class of men, loathed for their vices, whom the crowd styled Christians. Christus, the founder of the name, had undergone the death penalty in the reign of Tiberius, by sentence of the procurator Pontius Pilatus, and the pernicious superstition was checked for a moment, only to break out once more, not merely in Judaea, the home of the disease, but in the capital itself, where all things horrible or shameful in the world collect and find a vogue. First, then, the confessed members of the sect were arrested; next, on their disclosures, vast numbers were convicted, not so much on the count of arson as for hatred of the human race. And derision accompanied their end: They were covered with wild beasts' skins and torn to death by dogs; or they were burned to serve as lamps at night. (*Annals*, 5.15.44)

Scholars continue to debate whether or not Christians met separately from the Jews in Rome during the first century. Mark D. Nanos, in *The Mystery of the Romans,* suggests that during the first century early Christians were indistinguishable from Jews. They worshiped together. Thus Romans was sent primarily to Jews, who also accepted the Christian faith. **Ambrosiaster**, an unknown early Christian writer and author of a commentary on Romans, writes,

> It is evident then that there were Jews living in Rome ... in the time of the apostles. Some of these Jews, who had come to believe (in Christ), passed on to the Romans (the tradition) that they should acknowledge Christ and keep the law.... One ought not to be angry with the Romans, but praise their faith, because without seeing any signs of miracles and without any of the apostles they came to embrace faith in Christ, though according to Jewish rite. (Fitzmyer, 1964, 31)

REASONS FOR WRITING ROMANS

Probably the most obvious reason for writing the letter was to urge converts to practice an ethic of tolerance. Paul aims at uniting Jewish and non-Jewish or Gentile Christians.

FIGURE 10.3   Arch of Titus in Rome. Photo by Marla J. Selvidge.

Romans insists that all people are equal and have equal access before the law and God. Neither is more moral or respectable than the other. They have all missed the mark and have fallen short of the ideal.

Most of the great popular writers within Christianity view Romans as the epitome of Paul's theological thought. For them, it is a "compendium" of Christian doctrine, or the systematic doctrinal presentation of what Christians should believe. On a more personal note, Romans may also contain a confession from Paul. The first-person "I" is used in sections where Paul admits that he struggles but often fails, "For I do not do the good I want, but the evil I do not want is what I do" (7:19). And on the more practical side, Romans may have been written to gain rapport with the Romans before Paul visited them. In 15:28, Paul refers to a collection he will be taking to Jerusalem. He may be hinting that the Romans should also contribute.

THE ACTS OF THE APOSTLES AND ROMANS

Paul had not yet visited Rome, so he was writing to people he had never met (15:22, 23). If Paul did not bring the message of Jesus to Rome, then who did? Some point to Peter as the founder, but these stories are probably based on legends of the martyrdom of Peter in Rome.

The Acts of the Apostles ends with Paul's house arrest in Rome (60s C.E.), which scholars think occurred after Romans was written. When Paul arrived by ship in Puteoli, he stayed with the "brothers," presumably Jewish Christians (28:14, 16) and then continued to Rome where he began teaching the Jews (28:17). If there was a group of converts in Puteoli, who brought them the message?

The Acts of the Apostles may provide a key to the answer. During Peter's sermon in Acts 2:11, the writer lists "visitors from Rome, both Jews and proselytes" as hearing the message. Luke may be implying that their conversion was shared with others in Rome. Their reports could have resulted in many other conversions. There are also many anomalous political parties in Acts that are difficult to define. The Romans could have been members of the "Synagogue of Free" (6:9) or the "Hellenists."

CONTENT OF ROMANS

Chapters 1 through 11 describe Paul's views on the topics of equality, an ethic of tolerance for Gentiles and Jews before God, sin, the law, and living the Christian life by answering a myriad of questions. Some of those questions include the following:

2:3	Do you imagine, whoever you are, that when you judge those who do such things and yet do them yourself, you will escape the judgment of God?
2:4	Or do you despise the riches of his kindness and forbearance and patience?
2:4	Do you not realize that God's kindness is meant to lead you to repentance?
2:21	… you, then, that teach others, will you not teach yourselves?
2:21	While you preach against stealing, do you steal?
2:22	You that forbid adultery, do you commit adultery?
2:23	You that boast in the law, do you dishonor God by breaking the law?
3:1	Then what advantage has the Jew? Or what is the value of circumcision?
3:3	What if some were unfaithful? Will their faithlessness nullify the faithfulness of God?
3:8	And why not say,… "Let us do evil so that good may come?"
3:29	Or is God the God of Jews only? Is he not the God of the Gentiles also?
4:1	What then are we to say was gained by Abraham, our ancestor according to the flesh?
6:15	Shall we sin because we are not under the law but under grace?
7:7	Is the law sin?
7:13	Did what is good bring me death?

Chapter 12 includes Paul's guidelines for a moral life, and the next chapter deals with a Christian's relationship with governing bodies. Chapter 14 takes up a disagreement over food and ends with Paul's personal remarks. Chapter 15 includes the issue of the collection of monies for Jerusalem. And chapter 16 contains Paul's farewell with a list of friends.

LITERARY FOUNDATIONS

The writer of Romans draws upon Jewish traditions within the Septuagint (LXX) while employing a variety of literary strategies and images. A list of some of the literary foundations follows. (Paul quotes at least sixty-five verses from the LXX.)

Literary Foundations

Creedal fragment	1:3b-4:4:25
Strings of verses in LXX to support his argument	3:10–18; 9:25–29; 15:9–12
Songs, poems, or hymns	8:31–39; 11:33–36
Recommendation letter (Phoebe)	16:1–2
Oath	9:1–5
Chiasmus	1:17–18; 2:6–11; 6:3; 11:22
Blessing	15:13
Liturgical statement	3:25
Baptismal saying	6:4–5
Confessional	10:9
Christ sayings	12:14, 17; 13:7; 14:13, 14
Vice list	1:29–31
Rules	12:9–13

A chiasmus is a device to help students remember arguments or ideas. The story or argument follows an "ABBA" pattern. The ideas of A are repeated in the beginning and at the end. B is repeated in the middle. The following is Romans 11:22 outlined, according to the pattern.

A   Note then the kindness and

B   the severity of God:

B   severity toward those who have fallen,

A   but God's kindness toward you, provided you continue in kindness, otherwise you will be cut off.

Most teachers find that in order to communicate effectively, they must relate the topic at hand to something experienced by the student. A short list of metaphors or analogies used by Paul to enhance communication with the Roman audience follows.

A worker employed by a business	4:4
Sacrifice of an animal	5:7
Baptism	6:1–14
Servants or slavery	6:15–23
Marriage	7:1–6

Woman in labor	8:22
Potter or an artist	9:20–24
Making bread	11:16–24

Paul uses a host of literary strategies. Can you detect any other types of strategies employed by the writer?

PROMINENT CHARACTERS

Jesus: Gateway to the Beyond

Paul's view of Jesus is through the lens of his death, although he emphasizes that Jesus came in the "flesh" (1:3). Romans discusses, at length, the meaning of his sacrifice for all humanity. It is the "Gospel of his Son" (1:3, 9). That gospel fulfills the demands of law, nature, and God and will result in eternal life for the convert. Jesus was resurrected and ascended (1:4; 10:6).

While Jesus has won the future for converts, His everyday relationship pales in relationship to God. He is an intermediary (8:34) who must be worshiped (faith) in order to establish a relationship with God. He is a gateway to the beyond. Christ welcomes new converts and rescues people from death (7:24; 15:7). He is linked with the Spirit, which abides in converts (8:9). Paul views his own relationship with Christ as love. The ending of chapter 8 almost sounds like two people pledging their love for one another. Jesus is given several names in Romans. Among the titles are the following:

Son of God	1:4
Lord Jesus Christ	1:7
A Type of Adam	5:14
One Man	5:15
Spirit of Christ	8:9
Servant of Circumcised	15:8

God: Monotheistic and Patriarchal

"God" is mentioned at least 153 times compared to 66 times for "Christ." Paul's monotheistic and patriarchal God is very similar to the God of Israel or the God of the Old Testament/Septuagint/Hebrew Bible. A summary of some of the characteristics and assertions made about the Pauline God follows.

Immortal	1:23
Can be known through nature	1:19
Creator	1:25

Truthful	1:25; 3:7
Long-suffering	2:4
God is One	3:30
Giver of life/death	4:17
Cannot be separated	8:38–39
Father, our Father	6:4; 15:6
Has heirs	8:16
Judge	2:3–6

God is a father image to Paul, who is in control of his life as well as the universe. "So then he has mercy on whomever he chooses, and he hardens the heart of whomever he chooses" (9:18). God also "imprisoned all in disobedience" (11:31). Like a father, God makes judgments against those who neither pay attention to nature nor follow his law. He has a temper, and when pushed he will abandon his own when they worship other gods. Yet he is fair minded and treats each person as an equal. He is impartial, and he is a God who can be worshiped by everyone. God has not rejected the Israelites or Jews.

Paul believes that making peace with God is an ultimate goal, that peace will result in love. Chapter 12 uses the metaphor of "death to self" as a way of dedicating a life to God. Similar to Jesus, converts can also sacrifice their lives to God through their worship. And finally, in chapter 13, Paul seems to assert that God controls everyone through the power within civil structures.

The Family of God

If God is viewed as Father, then He must have a family. Throughout the letter of Romans, Paul uses images and examples from married and family life. The converts in Rome are considered the beloved of God the Father (1:7). Jesus is referred to as Son (1:9), and Abraham is an ancestor who is the father of all (4:12, 16). Paul uses the image of conceiving a child with Sarah as evidence of faith (4:19). In discussing how long a person should keep the law, he uses the analogy of marriage (chapter 7). Converts who practice living according to the Spirit are called "children" and "heirs of God" (8:17). In attempting to explain the future hope and life of a convert, Paul uses the image of a woman in the throes of bearing a child (8:22). Those who are the children of God will be adopted (8:23). Saints are members of the family or brothers of God (8:29).

In describing God's **predestination** of people, Paul again uses the story of Sarah's conception alongside Rebecca and Isaac's story of love (9:9–11). Paul's own identification of himself is through a Jewish family bloodline (11:1). And finally, the letter ends with greetings to friends, family, and those who are treasured in Rome. Intermingled in the greetings are descriptions of people counted as comrades, an extended family. Descriptions of friends include the following terms: benefactor, beloved, co-worker, compatriot, or family member. He also mentions familial relationships: mother, sister, brother, and family. In attempting to communicate important beliefs about the law and sin, Jews and Gentiles, Paul draws upon personal images that were most familiar to him within the family he knew best.

Women and Paul

Paul's language appears decidedly androcentric. The key figures in his presentation are Adam, Jesus, God, Abraham, and Moses. He mentions the names of ancient writings of Hosea, David, and Isaiah. But the main theme of Romans is that all have sinned and all can be freed from sin. All can be part of the family of God.

Circumcision   Circumcision, as we noted earlier, is no longer a male issue. Females within Judaism, because they were not circumcised, could not be counted as members of a synagogue. Paul argues that Abraham was an ancestor of those who believe but are not circumcised (4:11–12). This, of course, could refer to male Greeks/Gentiles, but it also could refer to women. The circumcised and uncircumcised are now equal members in the family of God.

Feminine Imagery and the Friends of Paul   We have already noted the images of birthing and conception used by Paul in our discussion of family. Paul continues to use feminine imagery throughout his letter. He quotes Hosea, who refers to Israel as a "her" (9:25). The female image also is applied to the Gentiles in this passage. They are now "my people" (9:25).

In typical prophetic patriarchal fashion, Paul uses feminine imagery to showcase negative or unacceptable behavior. He employs the image of an adulteress in chapter 7 to try to explain a convert's relationship to the law. The problem with this approach is that the analogy breaks down.

In ancient Israel, a woman's marriage was generally contracted by the husband. She was considered property. She had very few grounds upon which to request a divorce, and marriage did not bind people for life. It is true that within Israelite law that if a married woman slept with a married man, they were both considered adulterers and could be punished. But the burden for the divorce is with the husband, not the wife.

The point of the passage in Romans has nothing to do with making a ruling about marriage. Paul's emphasis is on fidelity to the law. It is similar to a marriage. When the law dies, as it did the moment Jesus died on the cross, then Jews are no longer bound to it. The issue is freedom from bondage (or marriage) to the law.

In addition to the characters Sarah and Rebecca previously mentioned, Paul lists nine women at the end of his letter in chapter 16: Prisca, Phoebe, Mary, Junia, Tryphaena, Tryphosa, Persis, Julia, and the sister of Nereus. This is an impressive list of females who apparently had the respect of their male companions in the early Christian communities.

The most celebrated woman is Phoebe, who is a deacon at the church in Cenchreae, a benefactor, and probably delivered the letter to the Romans. Obviously Paul is saluting an important official in Achaia who has invested some of her fortune in the Christian movement. Again, we meet Prisca, who with her husband Aquila, administers a church in their house. Paul says they risked their lives and worked diligently with him. Rufus' mother has a very special relationship with Paul. Junia is a close associate, almost family, who was a Christian before Paul was converted. She is prominent among the apostles, and she spent some time in prison with Paul. He calls Tryphena and Tryphosa "workers in the Lord," and the rest are co-workers or people who dedicated much of their lives to working with Paul.

IMPORTANT THEOLOGICAL ISSUES

Paul's Theological Vocabulary

Thousands of books have been written with the express purpose of explaining and deciphering the meaning of Romans. It is not a simple document. The writer had a strong background in Judaism which he uses to interpret the meaning of Christianity. It is impossible to understand the rhetoric of Romans without knowing the basic definitions of the following words:

Salvation	to be delivered, restored, preserved
Justification	to declare a person upright, righteous, just
Redemption	to emancipate someone, as in freeing or buying back a slave
Reconciliation	to cause to return; to change a relationship for the better
Atonement	The NRSV uses reconciliation in its place; to make peace with God; the cycle of guilt-punishment is taken away
Sanctification	to dedicate for sacred service. Some view this as perfection
Expiation	to appease God's anger; the removal of sin; to make satisfaction

Paul's View of Life

The ancients, as well as Paul (and those within Judaism), had a keen sense of the things in life that were considered sacred (perfect) or profane (human). Today, these concepts are foreign to us. When a class is asked to describe holy or sacred places in the United States, they usually suggest an altar in a church, a cemetery, the Jewish-Christian Bible, or the Quran. We do not normally view life in terms of areas controlled by the divine and space designed for the profane or human.

Religious taboos, rules and regulations, festivals, and so on were all designed to control people from stepping across the boundaries into a space that could cause them harm. Often these rules were designed to protect an individual or a group from some type of loss. Jewish law segregated people with leprosy so they would not infect others. The sabbath was probably designed to give people time off from their jobs to worship their God(s).

Breaking a rule or failing to keep a ritual meant that the person had "missed the mark" or "sinned." Something had to be done about this trespass over the lines of sacred into profane or unholy space. The ancient Israelites devised the system of sacrifices to bring the human back into good standing with the divine or the sacred. By killing an animal, contributing grain or oil, and so on, they bought redemption for themselves. They were declared justified or righteous and were reconciled with their God (see Exodus, Deuteronomy, and Leviticus).

Paul views the death of Jesus in the same terms that the ancient Israelites viewed the sacrifice of an animal. But Jesus' death meant more than an animal sacrifice. It meant that people no longer had to worry about sacred and profane space. It was gone! They did not have to worry about the minutia of the law. Their lives were now supposed to be oriented toward an eternal future that they would spend with Jesus. All of this was accomplished through a belief of the meaning of the death of Jesus.

The good news of Paul was simple, yet in trying to apply it to life, it became complicated for the early Christians. Romans logs some of these problems and attitudes toward the death of Jesus and the life of newfound Jewish-Gentile-Christians.

Equality before the Divine: God Is Not Owned by Anyone

The readers of Romans were struggling with the importance of the law, the convert's relationship to this ancient tradition, and behaviors that relegated some of the converts to a lesser status than the others. Jews and Gentiles had a long history of antisocial behavior (ethnic or cultural tension) toward one another. It is no surprise that sparks flew when they attempted to worship together. There were arguments over the meaning of "sin." Jewish law clearly outlined worship and prescribed ethical practices. New Christians entered a "gray" area where there were no boundaries.

The word "ethnos" (1:5) means little to us in the twenty-first century. Ethnos (from which we derive words such as ethnocentrism), a Greek term, referred to the masses, to people other than the Jews. It even had the negative definition of herd, such as a herd of cows. Paul also uses the word "Greek" "Hellein" (1:14) as an equivalent. Hellein was a term used for a nation, a non-Jew, or a God fearer.

"Ethnos or Hellein" could have been proud **appellations** or ethnic slurs. Consider the slurs we use in our own country. As a child, I heard people refer to my mother and father as "hillbillies." Yet they were proud to be from the close-knit honorable communities of the hill country of Kentucky and Tennessee. Hillbilly meant that they were different. Or in traveling to some Southern states, people referred to me as a "damn Yankee." Having never participated in the Civil War, the name at first surprised me.

Both "hillbilly" and "damn Yankee" were pejorative titles that reflected negatively on my geographical origin. "Greek" or "Gentile" may have been used in a similar way. Both could have been used as a slur, or as a proud appellation.

Chapters 1 and 2 describe how both Greeks or Gentiles and Jews are equally at fault in crossing the boundaries of the sacred. They have both sinned. "For there is no distinction, since all have sinned...." (3:22). This meant that regardless of who the person was or what kind of life he or she had before becoming a Christian, he or she was considered equal. All people have had the opportunity to understand the mind of the divine; thus all are responsible for following the divine. The Greeks had nature (1:18–21) and the Jews had the law. Even Abraham was justified and is now the ancestor of the uncircumcised (chapter 4).

Sin and Sins:
The Dark Side of Humans

This is a topic that causes uneasiness in people. Paul describes different types of sin and sins. In chapter 5, he traces the origin of all "sin" or trespass of the sacred to Adam (5:14). In the ancient Israelite saga, the story of Adam in Genesis occurs before the giving of the law in Exodus. When the law was given, according to Paul, it functioned like a mirror that revealed to people inappropriate activities. Jesus' death reconciled all the people who had broken the laws to a harmonious standing with the sacred. Or, explained in another way, Jesus brought humanity back to God.

Earlier in chapter 2 Paul lists the individual "sins" of both the Jews and Greeks. He seems to suggest that there are two types of sin. One is a personal choice, and the other is inherited. He also assures his audience that whether they came from a Greek or a Jewish background, the concept of sin has touched their lives. Below is a summary of how Paul plays with the idea of sin. He argues that everyone has sinned.

Greeks (Nations)	Jews
Did not honor God	Stole
Minds were darkened	Practiced adultery
Worshiped images of gods	Robbed temples
Worshiped the creature not the Creator	Broke the law
Women had unnatural intercourse	Blasphemed God's name

Same-Sex Relationships

Probably the most difficult issue or "sin" to discuss is the claim by Paul that Greeks had unnatural sexual relations. Today, these verses have been interpreted to mean homosexuality, and they are used not only to bar men and women from full participation within a Christian community but also to harass and ostracize them. Practicing homosexuals or lesbians are not allowed to serve as ministers or priests within many Christian denominations, yet others do not concentrate on the same-sex issue in these verses. They view the verses in 1:26–27 as a sin against a prescribed religious social order that enforces gender boundaries for the express purpose of producing children. They focus on the basis of the sin, which is the crossing of the boundaries of a sacred hierarchical order.

Victor Furnish, in *The Moral Teaching of Paul,* views Paul's ideas against the background of Jewish law, wisdom literature, and the cultures of Greece and Rome. Paul's attitude seems to be informed by Jewish sources (Leviticus 20:13; 18:22) that view same-sex relationships as a violation of the natural order. The belief in a natural order includes a proscribed way of males and females relating to one another. He also sees evidence of other Hellenistic influences upon Paul which linked insatiable lust with same-sex relations. The lust a male had for a female might pour over into lust for the same sex.

In attempting to interpret these verses for a modern audience, Furnish writes,

> Modern students of the subject are reluctant to speak of homosexuality and heterosexuality as mutually exclusive categories. They much prefer to speak of homosexual and heterosexual aspects in the sexual orientation of a given individual. They refer to "latent" and "active" homosexuality, and allow that the latter can manifest itself in different ways, some of them more and some of them less socially acceptable. It is also clear that homosexual behavior does not necessarily involve the sexual exploitation of another person, and that it does not necessarily take the bizarre forms that were so evident in Paul's time. (Furnish 1979, 80–81)

Like so many other statements made by Paul, we do not know exactly to what he is referring in 1:26–27. What is unnatural intercourse? Is it incest, pederasty, rape, adultery, sleeping with a menstruating woman, or bestiality? Is there only one way of making love? We could read lesbianism into this verse, but it simply does not say "lesbianism." It also seems clear that Paul is talking about men having relationships with other men in verse 27. But what kind of relationship is it?

If we read these verses in context, we begin to realize that Paul does not have a hierarchy of sins. All of the activities he lists are sins. If a person is envious, or a gossip, it is no better or worse than having a relationship with the same sex. All people and all sins are equal before God. Paul criticizes people who think that they are more "righteous" or better than others. All have sinned, all are imperfect, and Jesus' death on the cross blots out all sin and sins.

The point of all the discussion on sin is that Paul wants to bring harmony among people who think they are more righteous or morally better than others. Perhaps the Jew thinks he is morally superior because he does not have same-sex relationships, but Paul says the Jews are dead wrong. They steal, rob, and even worse, cause others to commit the greatest sin of all, to blaspheme God. We cannot fully appreciate the force of Paul's argument today because we do not have the same values and beliefs of people in the first century. To blaspheme God was close to "selling your soul to the Devil." You could not turn back once you committed this sin.

Civil Disobedience

> Let every person be subject to the governing authorities… (13:1 NRSV)

Ever wonder why people are happy when they are arrested for marching in the streets, staging sit-ins, or pouring blood on nuclear warheads? These activities are called "civil disobedience." In the United States, a major way unjust or outdated laws are changed or abandoned is through civil disobedience. A person breaks an unjust law, is arrested, and the law is taken to a court where it will be debated. Eventually, people who hope to change laws take their cases to the Supreme Court.

Chapter 13 of Romans raises a host of legal questions regarding the political positions the Romans should take in relation to their government. It appears that Paul is urging converts to allow dictators, in fact, all civil authorities, to dominate the Romans. Paul seems to be advising his readers not to protest or rebel against unjust laws or oppressors. According to Paul, all power comes from God, and God places rulers on their thrones. In addition, taxes must be paid to every ruling body that requires them. But how could this be? Are all taxes just and fair? (What about the founders of our country, who refused to pay taxes to Great Britain?)

No one has been able to reconstruct the exact historical situation of chapter 13. Some point to a time during the reign of Nero when he suspended taxation temporarily in order to reform it. Others suggest that Paul is not referring to Roman civil authorities but to religious authorities. Paul requires them to pay their assessed taxes to the synagogues. These verses may also have been written during a time of hostility and personal fear. Paul wants to protect and help converts survive. If they lie low and do not get involved in politics, life will be safer for them.

Scholars point out the problems with interpreting Paul literally by applying the advice given in Romans 13 in a universal way. Christians throughout history have interpreted Paul as setting submissive guidelines to all political authorities. That attitude has backfired and resulted in the loss of numerous lives over and over again. Christians in Germany during World War II took the passive position that they should not protest or rebel against the injustices of Hitler. Millions were killed by an oppressive and a violent government bent on conquering the world.

Health: The Politics of Food

In Corinthians, we noted that Paul's concern about eating meat offered to deities may have been a health issue. In Romans 14, Paul addresses the challenge again. Several different political views can be detected.

Politic 1:	Every kind of food is acceptable.	14:1
Politic 2:	Only vegetables are acceptable.	14:2
Politic 3:	No food on certain days.	14:6
Politic 4:	No eating of meat or drinking of wine.	14:21

Paul does not specify the context of the quarreling. The social setting of eating together may be the Lord's Supper or the Eucharist. There is an issue over what is unclean, which could refer to the kosher laws in the Torah or to the edict by the Jerusalem Council in Acts 15. Some believe in eating meat, and others do not.

There is evidence within the founding years of Christianity that some people did not eat meat. It could have been a holdover from Pythagoreanism, which subscribed to the belief that meat escalated passions in people. Vegetarianism could also have been a way of declaring that a person had changed his or her religious views to correlate with a view of the end of time where animals would be friends and not table food. We know that monks bent on reforming Christianity lived ascetic lives without the benefit of meat, and this may gradually have been adopted by Christian groups.

Whatever the exact nature of the food politics, Paul urges the people, once again, to practice a mature love. In a great Asian tradition, he asks them to consider the community as being more important than their individual rights or appetites. "We do not live to ourselves..." (14:7). "Do not, for the sake of food, destroy the word of God" (14:20). He hopes for harmony and urges them to be more open minded toward other converts and their points of view toward eating and drinking.

Summary of Romans   We have learned that Paul probably wrote the letter with the help of a secretary. His literary foundations included many different types of Greek and Hebrew literary forms and strategies. Speculation continues about the relationship of chapter 16 to the rest of the letter. Paul had never visited Rome; therefore he was writing to strangers he hoped to see shortly.

Many scholars obscure the foundational issues of unity and equality of ethnic groups (all peoples) in favor of a debate on ethics within the letter to the Romans. Romans has taken us into the highly controversial ethical issues of same-sex relationships, sin and original sin, civil disobedience, and vegetarianism, which are still hotly debated. Throughout the letter he recognizes and appreciates contributions made by women within the early years of Christianity.

While Romans has been used by many denominations (including Roman Catholicism) to lay a foundation for doctrine, it more importantly encourages loving, mature, personal relationships between all types of people. No matter what the issue, Paul encourages people to view themselves as part of the family of God.

Philemon:
A Letter of Mediation

... no longer a slave, a beloved brother ...
—Philemon 16 NRSV

INTRODUCTION

In Philemon, we will come face to face with the demonic concept of enslaving another human being. Paul's letter no longer reinforces the status quo but opens up the possibility of freedom for Onesimus and perhaps other slaves throughout the Empire.

AUTHOR AND DATE

Pauline authorship has rarely been doubted in the past 2,000 years. Some have suggested, based on a comparison with Colossians, that Archippus was Onesimus' master and that the letter to Laodicea is really the letter to Philemon (Col. 4:16), but few people hold this view. The dating of Philemon is problematic. Paul claims to be a prisoner, but the letter is closely associated with Colossians because of common characters (see Table 10.1 on page 242). Most scholars place Paul's imprisonments in Ephesus, Caesarea, and Rome at various times during the period 50–60s C.E. If Colossians is Pauline, then Philemon would have been written in the 60s C.E. If it is pseudo-Pauline, then a date toward the end of the century is more likely.

READERS AND REASONS FOR WRITING THE LETTER

While we know to whom the letter was addressed in verses 1 and 2, the rest of the letter is ambivalent about its audience. Paul writes to Philemon, Apphia (our sister), and Archippus, yet his requests are made to a "you" singular, which would suggest that he is addressing the letter to a specific person. Later in the letter he begins to use the plural form of "you," which would include more than one person (22, 25). He may be referring to all three people who appear to be administrators of a new church meeting at the home of Philemon.

Onesimus is a slave who helped Paul while he was in prison in Rome (or other places, mentioned earlier). Philemon and Paul appear to be good friends. The letter accompanying Onesimus on his way home (to Colossae?) asks Philemon to free him because of his conversion and relationship with Paul. Paul offers to repay anything that Onesimus owes.

Many questions go unanswered in studying Philemon. They include the following:

Why did he write to a church and not a person?

Was Onesimus a runaway slave?

Could he have been punished or killed for this act?

Did Philemon send him to Paul?

Was he an indentured slave?

Did he steal some money when he left Philemon?

How did he become a slave?

Was he captured or did he agree to work for Philemon in order to pay off a debt?

Where did he meet Paul?

When it says "useless" does that mean that he did not do his work or that he was not around to do work?

Was he converted? Paul implies that he is now a brother.

Does Paul want Philemon to change the legal status of Onesimus?

What kinds of laws governed slaves? Do they apply to Onesimus?

Why was this letter preserved?

Did Onesimus become the Bishop of Ephesus later in the century?

TABLE 10.1 Characters in Both Philemon and Colossians

Character	*Philemon*		*Colossians*	
Paul	1	a prisoner	1:1	an apostle
Timothy	1	our brother	1:1	our brother
Archippus	2	fellow soldier	4:17	directions to complete assigned task
Onesimus	8, 16	my child slave, beloved brother	4:9	faithful and beloved brother who is one of you
Epaphras	23	fellow prisoner	1:7	beloved fellow servant, faithful minister, messenger
			4:12	one of you, servant of Christ Jesus
Mark	24	fellow worker	4:10	cousin of Barnabas
Aristarchus	24	fellow worker	4:10	fellow prisoner
Demas	24	fellow worker	4:14	
Luke	24	fellow worker	4:14	beloved physician

SLAVERY IN THE EMPIRE AND THE PAULINE WORKS

Slavery was common during the first century. There is evidence that Augustus had as many as 4,000 slaves. According to Tacitus, slaves had few rights; they could be killed or tortured on the whim of their masters. Marriage was forbidden (in most cases), and families were often separated. Some slaves were purchased to fulfill special duties within a house, such as physician, cook, or teacher.

In studying the letters attributed to Paul, it appears that Paul taught several views on human slavery. Consider the verses in the box below.

Paul has often been accused of advocating the status quo for slaves, but Philemon demonstrates that Paul did not consistently hold rigid views about the social status of Christians. He hopes for the release of Onesimus. Theo Preiss argues,

> If Paul had wished to reinstate Onesimus in a social order which must not be changed, if
> he had juxtaposed life in Christ to an order of creation, and love to civil justice, he would

---

SLAVERY WITHIN THE PAULINE WORKS

Pauline Letters

Philemon 16	...[N]o longer a slave, a beloved brother....
1 Corinthians 7:21–24	Were you a slave when called? Do not be concerned about it.... In whatever condition you were called, brothers and sisters, there remain in God.
Galatians 3:28	There is no longer Jew or Greek, there is no longer slave or free, there is no longer male and female; for all of you are one in Christ Jesus.

In the Name of Paul? Letters

Ephesians 6:5	Slaves, obey your earthly masters with fear and trembling...
Colossians 3:11	In the renewal, there is no longer Greek and Jew, circumcised and uncircumcised, barbarian, Scythian, slave and free; but Christ is all and in all!
Colossians 3:22, 4:1	Slaves, obey your earthly masters in everything ... Masters, treat your slaves justly and fairly,...
1 Timothy 6:1	Let all who are under the yoke of slavery regard their masters as worthy of all honor, so that the name of God and the teaching may not be blasphemed.
Titus 2:9	Tell slaves to be submissive to their masters and to give satisfaction in every respect; they are not to talk back, not to pilfer, but to show complete and perfect fidelity....

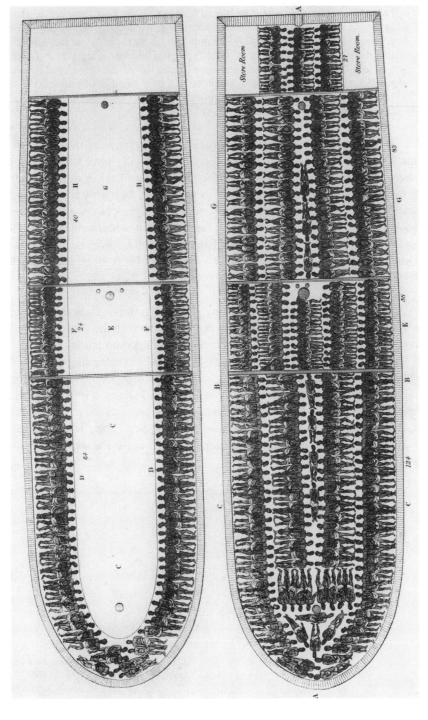

Figure 10.4 Thomas Clarkson's schematic of the slave ship Brookes drawn in 1789. Found in N.A. Stowage of the British slave ship Brookes under the regulated slave trade, Act of 1788.

have written something like, my dear Philemon, in the Lord, you are brothers and one; in the life of the world you remain each in his place socially. Above all Paul would have respected the master's right of ownership over his slave. In actual fact Paul does no such thing; fraternity, unity in Christ, seizes upon the relation of slave and master, shatters it and fulfills it upon quite another plane. Onesimus will be considered not merely as an equal, another member of the Church, he will be a member of Philemon's family, a full brother. Thus there remains no margin of paternalism, what we have is a total fraternity. (Preiss 1954, 40)

Both Galatians and Philemon advocate equality between the slaves and the free. This nonhierarchical political position could potentially have been dangerous, since most wealthy people in the Empire had acquired slaves. Paul's positive words of equality for slaves could have been viewed as **anarchist**. Certainly they had broad repercussions within Christian communities. Colossians presents two views of slavery. In baptism, there is no longer the slave or the free, but in a hierarchical household slaves must obey. Ephesians, Timothy, and Titus support the lower social status of slaves. Corinthians advises slaves not to seek freedom, probably because Paul believed that the end of time was approaching.

Summary of Philemon   Knowing what we know about slavery today, one could only wish that verses about slaves had been omitted from the Bible. Yet we will never know the positive impact they had on early Christian communities.

This short letter to Philemon raises many questions regarding Onesimus and local laws regarding slaves that may never be answered. Paul seems to advocate freeing Onesimus. Whether or not he supported the release of all slaves is impossible to ascertain. Philemon has close ties with Colossians, but no one can verify whether names were copied or if the letters were written independently. See Table 10.1. Paul demonstrates love for Onesimus, hoping for his freedom, while he twists the arm of Philemon. He offers to pay off Onesimus' debt!

1 Corinthians:
A Catalogue of Questions and Opinions

Consider your own call, brothers and sisters,
not many of you were wise by human standards,
not many were powerful, not many were of noble birth.

—1 Cor. 1:26

INTRODUCTION

The correspondence with the people in Corinth allows us to view many of the questions and difficulties encountered by a new religion. As we read 1 Corinthians, we may conclude that there is no plan or purpose to the letter. Paul's thoughts seem to wander from one issue to another, with no apparent relationship or transition. These thoughts were probably written as responses to questions sent from Chloe or rumors from Stephanas.

On the old *Tonight Show with Johnny Carson,* a comedy sketch used to be performed where Johnny would first read the answer to a question and then open an envelope with the question. This is exactly what we are doing when we read 1 Corinthians. It contains answers to questions we do not have. We must guess about the issues behind the answers. Paul may have referred to the questions or quoted them in his responses, but we have no method to determine if he did include them.

Readers of Corinthians often attempt to interpret Paul's opinions as moral commandments, which were designed for all people in all time. We must remember that Paul gives his own opinion to a specific group of people in a particular time period in history. Times change. Paul's view of the end of time colors many of his suggestions about marriage, divorce, abstinence, and celibacy and perhaps influences his opinions on other issues. Some issues seem to have little relevance for the modern reader, such as eating meat slaughtered at the temple or taking a fellow believer to court. Many of the problems in this letter are controversial, for example, women's place in the meetings, the excommunication of a member, and wearing coverings on the head. All of the aforementioned make for a fascinating and provocative study of this ancient document and its people.

DATE AND AUTHORSHIP

1 Corinthians may be the second letter (5:9) written by Paul, from Ephesus, in conjunction with Sosthenes, whom we met in Acts of the Apostles (18) sometime in the 50s C.E. The letter is directed to

the Church of God in Corinth

those sanctified in Christ Jesus, called to be saints

all those who in every place call on the name of our Lord Jesus Christ (1:1)

The first line is written to the Corinthians, but the remainder of the verse suggests that it was addressed as a general letter to all Christians. Some scholars think the line beginning with "all those" was added at a later date. Whatever the case, 1 Corinthians claims to be a letter for all converts, and within its chapters are instructional words that cut across gender, class, national, and ethnic barriers.

For about 100 years, scholars have been debating if 1 Corinthians contains one or more letters. Many agree that verses have been edited (11:3–6; 13; 14:34–35), and perhaps chapters have been moved (13). There are discrepancies about when Timothy was going to go to Corinth (4:17–21; 16:5–11). Paul describes the difficult time he had at Ephesus, as if it is in the past (15:32), yet he appears to be in Ephesus writing the letter (16:8). Topics are repeated, such as the eating of sacrificial meat (8,10), and spiritual gifts (12, 14). No consensus has occurred on whether or not 1 Corinthians is a composite letter.

THE CITY, CORINTH

In the fifth century B.C.E., Corinth was a magnificent city of about 100,000 people built in the shadow of the **Acrocorinth**, located between the mainland of Greece and the **Peloponnese**. It was known for its ship building, pottery, paintings, and bronze statues. Corinth was situated on an isthmus between the Aegean and Adriatic Seas and became the center of commerce because of its easy access from one sea to the other. Before the modern canal was built, which links the Aegean and Adriatic, ships had to go around the tip of Achaia to make their way to Rome. This was a treacherous journey because of the winds, rocks, and coral reefs. From at least the seventh century B.C.E. onward, a track or road was cut that pulled ships on ramps from one sea to another. While waiting for their ship to make the crossing, sailors, travelers, and businesspeople enjoyed Corinth.

This ancient city was completely gutted and looted by Lucius Mummis in the second century B.C.E., with no real inhabitants for the next 100 years. Julius Caesar, in 44 B.C.E., reclaimed the land and named it Colonia Laus Julia Corinthiensis. In 27 B.C.E., Augustus declared it the capital of Achaia, and it began to regain the luster of the old city; however, it was destroyed by an earthquake in the Middle Ages.

Today, travelers can visit this ancient site where archaeologists have discovered numerous shops, public paths, forums, and sacred areas. Sanctuaries to Poseidon, Aphrodite, Athena, and Artemis abound, with Roman temples dedicated to Octavia, sister of Augustus Caesar, and to Jupiter Capitolinus. There is some evidence to suggest that the city was overrun with **sacred prostitutes**. To be labeled a "Corinthian" indicated a lewd and voracious sex life.

FIGURE 10.5 Ruins of Corinth. Photo by Marla J. Selvidge.

THE ACTS OF THE APOSTLES AND CORINTH

The story of Paul in Corinth covers only a few verses in chapter 18 of Acts. After a lukewarm reception in sophisticated Athens, Paul headed southwest to Corinth, where he met Priscilla and Aquila. Silas and Timothy joined him. Frustrated with the lack of Jewish response to his preaching, Paul began teaching people in the house of Titius Justus, a god fearer who lived next to the synagogue. Crispis, an important Jew in the synagogue, also converted, as did many of the local Corinthians. The Jews were outraged by Paul's activities, grabbed him, and took him to the Proconsul Gallio. Their charge against him was, "This man is persuading people to worship God in ways that are contrary to the Law" (18:13). Gallio refused to hear the case. In retaliation for his lack of concern, they attacked Sosthenes, one of their own officials. Paul continued teaching in Corinth for about eighteen months.

1 Corinthians and Acts of the Apostles coincide at several points. Sosthenes, Aquila, and Priscilla are mentioned in both (Acts 18:17, 2; 1 Cor. 1:1, 16:19). In Acts, the writer says Paul baptized Crispis and many others (18:8), but Paul denies this in the letter. He says he baptized Crispis, Gaius, and the house of Stephanas (1 Cor. 1:16). Both books suggest that there were converts from a variety of ethnic, religious, and cultural backgrounds.

REASONS FOR WRITING THE LETTER(S): CORINTHIAN QUESTIONS

Paul had received information from "Chloe's people" that the Corinthians were forming opposing political factions (1:11). [News may also have reached him through Stephanas, Fortunatus, and Achaicus (16:17).] Paul's letter appears to have been written with the hope of uniting these factions. The remainder of the letter is devoted to answering practical questions about how to live an ethical Christian life now and in the life to come.

It is impossible to discuss all of the issues contained in Corinthians in an introductory text. Entire books have been written on individual verses. The upcoming discussion will center on selected issues that seem to have more relevance for a modern audience.

Political Parties

Corinth was a bustling city with thousands of people and a diverse population. Paul may be writing to groups, within a single congregation or several different churches, who find it difficult to agree. This is no surprise if we consider the hundreds of different Christian denominations today.

Factions were lining up along party lines based on the teachings of Paul, Apollos, Cephas, and Christ (1:12; chapters 3 and 4). Paul argues that everyone has his or her

FIGURE 10.6   Ruins of Corinth. Photo by Marla J. Selvidge.

place and gift. All have worked together to produce the Corinthian congregation. He urges unity.

The beliefs of the parties have been debated for centuries. But we do not know why these people were fighting and what the beliefs were for each group. What follows is a hypothetical scenario taken from several theories.

Corinthian Parties

The Party of Paul	Primarily non-Jews who were not circumcised. They advocated freedom from the law, inclusion, and diversity.
The Party of Cephas	Primarily traditional Jews who had converted. They advocated keeping all the law and excluding non-Jews.
The Party of Apollos	Primarily people who had followed John the Baptist and may have advocated an austere lifestyle.
The Party of Christ	Primarily militant Christians who believed that Jesus was going to overthrow Rome. Jesus would return in triumph as the Messiah or Christ to rule the world.

Immorality: Chapter 5

A man is living with his father's wife, and the Corinthians find nothing wrong with this practice. No one to date has clearly unearthed the meaning of this passage. Is the father still living, and has the son seduced the new wife? Is the son sleeping with one of the father's wives? Is this a question of an immoral sexual relationship according to Corinthian standards, or is it a challenge to the father's right to rule in his own house?

Most scholars interpret this section as being immoral, on the grounds of adultery guidelines found in the Torah. If so, then both of the offenders would be subject to stoning (Deut. 22:22–24). It is interesting to note that only the man is reprimanded. Is he a Christian/convert? Whatever the offense, Paul recommends a type of excommunication. They are to turn him over to "Satan." Does this mean that they are going to abandon him, or does it involve some type of corporal punishment? Does it imply capital punishment, that is, "the destruction of the flesh"? No one knows.

Sexual Relationships: Chapter 7:1–6

Some think Paul's attitude toward male-female relationships is strange, even abnormal. We must keep in mind when we are studying the following issues that Paul believed that the end of time was approaching. If time was going to end, then plans for the future were unnecessary. He says, "… in a moment, in the twinkling of an eye, at the last trumpet" (15:52) the end will come. His perspective is urgent! He also, time after time, acknowledges that he is human and does not have all of the answers, while offering opinions not commands (7:6).

Probably the most puzzling words for any modern person to read are, "It is well for a man not to touch a woman" (7:1). The word "touch" is a euphemism for intimacy. Why would Paul write these words? Is he asking a question or making a declaration?

If the audience was accustomed to keeping Jewish traditions, then the question from the Corinthians could have been, "Should we continue to keep the purity laws that separate men and women during a woman's menstrual period?" Paul may also have been answering the question, "Should we take vows of celibacy, since the end of time is approaching?" Another question might be, "What about having sexual relations with a cultic prostitute?" His answer is "no" to all of the possible questions.

If the question is about purity regulations, Paul does not advocate abstinence during a woman's monthly period, as required by Leviticus 12–15 (1 Cor. 7:5). Rather than a male hierarchical approach to marriage, Paul appears to be advocating an egalitarian form of monogamy (7:2) where no one has power or authority over another in a sexual relationship (7:3–4). Jewish tradition placed the male in the superior position but guaranteed the rights of food, clothing, and sex to the wife or wives (Exodus 21:10). Once again, Paul mentions "Satan" as a possible problem.

Celibacy: Chapter 7:7–8

Paul never clarifies his marital or sexual status for the audience. He merely says, "I wish that all were as I myself am" (7:7 NRSV) and implies that a wife does not travel with him (9:5). Most interpreters speculate that Paul was celibate or possibly divorced. Whatever his sexual or marital status, he does not appear to understand or appreciate marriage. He presumes that people choose marriage in order to douse the flames of passion, "For it is better to marry than to be aflame with passion" (7:8 NRSV). These verses have been interpreted in hundreds of ways, but the fact remains that Paul concludes that only passion or lack of self-control, that is, sexual attraction, is a reason for marriage. Even in ancient times, marriages were made for other reasons, such as to produce children and link fortunes, as well as for love and companionship.

Virgins and Spiritual Marriage: Chapter 7:25–38

Later, in chapter 7, Paul addresses the issue of virgins. Once again he emphasizes that it is his opinion and not a command on the topic of spiritual marriage. Scholars have suggested that there may have been couples who were in love, believing that the end of time was near, who chose to live together without having sexual relations. Paul may be addressing the question of whether or not it would be wrong to have sexual relations with the person with whom he is living. He says, "If anyone thinks that he is not behaving properly toward his virgin,… Let him marry as he wishes, it is not sin" (7:36 NRSV).

Paul urges the congregation not to make changes in their lives (7:26). He highlights the negative side of marriage; distress in the flesh (7:28); and anxiety about the world and pleasing a mate (7:33–34). Marriage is a distraction from the important things in life. There is nothing wrong with marriage or sexual relations, says Paul, but it is not the highest or best road to take, "…and he who refrains from marriage will do better" (7:38).

Proper Attire and the Place of Women at Meetings: Chapter 11:1–16; 14:34–36

For centuries, women have been wearing hats or head coverings in Christian meetings, based on a literal interpretation of 1 Corinthians 11. (Some Christian denominations do not allow women to cut their hair.) Did Paul really write about hats or wigs 2,000 years ago? No one knows what question Paul was answering in this section. Most think he is referring to a local custom. An uncovered head might have been a dishonor, or a sign of class or vocation. We know that the heads of slaves were shaved. Some Orthodox Jewish women today keep the age-old custom of shaving their heads at marriage as a sign of submission to their husbands, wearing wigs for the rest of their married lives (11:15). Could Paul be referring to this practice of shaving heads?

The language and emphasis of these verses changes direction several times, which may indicate the presence of a tampering scribe. In language reminiscent of the house laws in Ephesians and Colossians, Paul sets up a hierarchical order in the meetings (11:3–10), "… the man is the head of the woman." Men should preach/pray with their heads uncovered and women should preach/pray with their heads covered (11:5). But later, in verses 11–12, Paul prefers an egalitarian relationship.

> Nevertheless, in the Lord woman is not independent of man or man independent of woman. For just as woman came from man, so man comes through woman; but all things are from God. (NRSV)

Both of the chapters in 11 and 14 show signs of editing by a scribe or copier. In chapter 14, Paul takes up the issue of speaking in tongues, preaching, and keeping order in the meetings. He issues guidelines to people who speak in tongues (14:27–29). His personal preference is for preaching, because people can understand what is being said.

The next topic includes rules concerning women.

> As in all the churches of the saints, women should be silent in the churches. For they are not permitted to speak, but should be subordinate, as the law also says. If there is anything they desire to know, let them ask their husbands at home. For it is shameful for a woman to speak in church. (14:34–35)

These verses have been used to disqualify women from leadership positions within Christianity for centuries. Elizabeth Cady Stanton's *The Woman's Bible,* written toward the close of the nineteenth century, captures the feelings of some women about these verses.

> If it is contrary to the perfect operation of human development that woman should teach, the infinite and all wise directing power of the universe has blundered. It cannot be admitted that Paul was inspired by infinite wisdom in this utterance....The doctrine of woman,... and her subjection in consequence, planted in the early Christian Church by Paul, has been a poisonous stream in Church and State. (Stanton 1974, 2:163)

These verses raise many unanswerable questions. Is Paul giving the same advice to men as he is to women when he says in verse 14:28, "Let the men be silent in the church"? Why are woman told to be silent? Is it a local custom? The passage implies that all women are married or have a male at home. Certainly there were unmarried female converts at the meetings. And the most difficult question of all is, why does Paul give guidelines for women who are preaching in chapter 11 and then prohibit women from speaking or preaching in chapter 15? Based on Paul's egalitarian emphases in various places in his letters, many scholars suggest that the verses prohibiting women from speaking were added by a later writer and do not reflect the attitude toward women in the founding churches within Christianity. They do, however, reflect an anti-woman attitude that developed later within a highly organized patriarchal church.

The Lord's Supper and the Agape (Love) Feast

These verses probably describe the ancient practice of holding an agape, or love feast, along with the Eucharist or the Lord's Supper. It appears that the Corinthians invited less fortunate people from the community to their meetings to have a meal before they formally remembered the life and death of Jesus. Something went wrong with their community outreach. Members were arriving early and eating all of the good food before the invited guests arrived. They also were drinking the wine. In fact, they drank so much wine that they were drunk and could not properly and in an orderly fashion celebrate the life and death of Jesus. Paul also includes the famous words used to celebrate the Mass (the Eucharist, the Lord's Supper, or Communion) "... the Lord Jesus on the night when he was betrayed took a loaf of bread ... (11:23) which he received from the Lord."

Credentials of Paul

Paul is particularly vocal about his career, authority, and dedication to his calling as a minister. With tongue in cheek, he compares himself with the Corinthians in chapter 4. In chapter 9, he argues that he has the same rights as other apostles, but he does not take them, and in chapter 15 he claims that Jesus also appeared to him.

One could only guess about the nature of accusations and gossip about Paul. Perhaps he has taken divergent points of view regarding the law. People may have accused him of being ambivalent. Some may have thought he was lazy and did not deserve to be supported. Others may have been embarrassed by his casual attitude toward dress and financial success. Whatever the nature of the "gossip" about Paul, he feels compelled to set the readers straight about his relationship with them, to other apostles, and to the religion to which he has dedicated his life.

Health Issues

Today, most of us are health conscious. We carefully select the foods we eat and try to maintain an exercise program. We know that diet and physical conditioning are important to living a long and healthy life. Many of the issues discussed by Paul seem to be directed toward protecting the health of the Corinthians.

More than once, Paul refers to the body as the temple of God (3:16–17; 6:19) and indicates that it should be considered holy. Many of the issues addressed by Paul touch on the issue of preserving the body. While eating meat offered to another deity is of supreme importance to Paul as it relates to community living, there may also have been health hazards associated with eating meat that had not been fully cooked or slaughtered properly (chapters 8, 10). Paul takes up personal sexual issues that certainly would affect a person's health. Multiple partners, whether at the local temple or club, can put people at risk for all sorts of sexually transmitted diseases. He may even be addressing the issue of alcoholism in chapter 11, as people participate in the Lord's Supper.

On a psychological level, constant arguing, chaotic meetings, and fighting that results in court cases (6) can take its toll on individual as well as community health. In chapters 5 and 6, Paul makes his ethical lists for the Corinthians. He tells them not to associate with people who are

sexually immoral	fornicators
greedy	adulterers
idolaters	male prostitutes
verbal abusers	sodomites
drunkards	thieves
robbers	

Looking toward the future, Paul even describes what kind of body people will have in the resurrection (chapter 15) that will not experience death.

Summary of 1 Corinthians   Paul's responses to the questions or rumors at times seem to come from a Jewish point of view (14), at other times from a Gnostic point of view (1), and often from a Stoic point of view. He argues for a different kind of wisdom than the Corinthians have known, a wisdom that comes to them in weakness, fear, and trembling. He hopes for their success, and like a mother or father (4:14), a gardener, and even a carpenter he helps nurture and build a foundation for them (chapter 3). He wants them to preserve their marriages (7), respect the myriad of gifts displayed among the converts (12), and love each other (13) as he loves them (16:24).

2 Corinthians:
An Angry Paul and the Super Apostles

For I wrote you out of much distress and anguish of heart and with many tears,
not to cause you pain, but to let you know the abundant love I have for you.

—2:4 NRSV

The letter to 2 Corinthians is difficult to read. Instinctively, we do not want to see the hero of Acts flounder. If we have placed Paul on a pedestal, 2 Corinthians brings home the message that Paul is very vulnerable. An emotional Paul carries on about himself and his dedication to his cause in 2 Corinthians. Sparring word for word, Paul rehearses his fear of death (1:8f) and the hardships in his life. He is a man who has been given "a thorn in the flesh" (12:8) and so lives in torment. Throughout 2 Corinthians, Paul despairs over the loss of his friendship with the Corinthians and hopes that somehow he can win back their love and support.

FIGURE 10.7 The canal at Corinth.
Photo by Marla J. Selvidge.

DATE, AUTHORSHIP, AUDIENCE

The second letter is addressed to the Corinthians and to "all the saints in Achaia" (1:1). It is sent from Timothy and Paul. This letter presents the student with many inconsistencies and problems. It was apparently written about the same time as 1 Corinthians, in the 50s C.E., but scholars have been unable to date it precisely because it probably contains several letters to Corinth that are out of order. Scholars have hypothesized about elaborate historical schemes of several visits to Corinth, based on the seams and divisions within the letter. They point out the abrupt changes in subject matter and tone. In the first seven chapters, Paul defends himself. In chapters 8 and 9, he repeats himself on the subject of finances. Chapters 10 through 13 are again a defense and an attack on the Corinthians. There are questions about the "painful visit" (2:1), and Paul's references to visiting them a second or third time (13:1; 12:14). Some suggest that 6:14–7:1 is not Pauline. It may be a fragment from a letter sent to a community similar to Qumran.

PAUL AND THE CORINTHIANS

The letter(s) reveal a desperate man who is losing the love of his life. He struggles to maintain a relationship with his friends, but whatever has happened may have severed the ties. He made plans to visit them, but he changed his mind (1:5; 23). Their trust in him is fading, which is almost unbearable for Paul. His reputation has been injured, so he lashes out at his opponents. The defense is brutal and accusatory. Unlike 1 Corinthians, Paul does not answer a host of practical questions. They no longer want to hear practical advice from him. Paul's defense reveals some of the accusations or rumors against him. They include the following:

The Gossip about Paul

He is fickle in his judgment.	1:15
He is not understood by many.	1:13
He is domineering.	1:24
He is a peddler of religion.	2:16
He does not have any letters of recommendation.	3:1
He makes the process of conversion more difficult.	6:3
He is an impostor.	6:8
He has corrupted people.	10:2
He has taken advantage of people.	7:2
He has a manic personality that changes.	10:1
His personal presence is offensive.	10:10

The Gossip about Paul, *continued*

He is not a Christian.	10:7
He is inferior to super apostles.	11:5
He is a fool.	11:16
He is not an apostle.	12:12
Christ is not in him.	13:3

While Paul may love the Corinthians, 2 Corinthians is not a love letter. He describes them in the following manner:

The Gossip about the Corinthians

They are the church of god and Saints	1:1
They are unable to understand Paul	1:13
They have been offended.	2:2
They are excessive with punishments.	2:6–7
They marry or make alliances with people who are not Christian.	6:14
They excel in faith, in speech, in knowledge.	8:7
They are following a different interpretation of Christ.	11:3
They are not following Paul's ethical guidelines.	12:21

THE SUPER APOSTLES

Within the Corinthian converts are a few super apostles who have recently come from Jerusalem with letters. They have mesmerized the Corinthians with their public speaking and "signs and wonders" (12:12), offering (perhaps) more of an emotional religious experience (5:13; 12:1, 7). Scholars have given various names to these opponents, including Primitive Apostles of Jesus, Judaizers from Galatia, Jewish-Christian Wandering Preachers, Jewish-Christians, Palestinian Opponents, and Gnostics.

Their interpretation of Jesus and God differs from Paul's, but there is no discussion about their points of view. Paul views them as self-aggrandizing and showy (10:12). Being proud of their Jewish origin, they believe that their words are greater than those of Moses (3:4; 11:22). He questions their ethics and calls them servants of Satan (12:21; 11:13–15; 13:2).

FIGURE 10.8   The Temple of Appollo at Corinth. Photo by Marla J. Selvidge.

OTHER ISSUES

Interspersed among Paul's defenses are worries about how the Corinthians are treating one of their own. He wishes they would reach out and console him (2:5–11). Paul often speaks of death, and in a short paragraph he describes the new body that all Christians will receive (4:7–12). There are concerns about finances, and Paul holds up the Macedonians as model givers (chapters 8–9). He often defends Titus, which may indicate that the Corinthians (7:8; 8:6, 16, 23) also questioned his authority and authenticity as a messenger of Christ.

Summary of 2 Corinthians   Founding a new religion is always problematical, especially if the founder attempts to administer it from a distance. Paul believed his strategies and thoughts on issues were the best advice he could offer to the Corinthians. Other "super" apostles taught a different kind of Christianity, which was more to the "liking" of the Corinthians so they abandoned Paul. Paul's attempt to win back those he loved is revealed in 2 Corinthians. It appears that he failed. But no one knows the end to this story.

11

Documents Written in the Name of Paul

Colossians and Ephesians

Colossians:
The Universal and Cosmic Messiah

And let the peace of Christ rule in your hearts,
to which indeed you were called in one body.

—3:15

… [F]or in him all things in heaven and on earth were created,
things visible and invisible, whether thrones or dominions or rulers
or powers—all things have been created through him and for him.

—1:16

INTRODUCTION

Throughout the ages, Colossians has been a springboard for many controversies about the identity, nature, and purpose of the life of Jesus. In this letter, the egotistic and provocative Paul of Galatians seems sedated. A more academic, cool, and calculating person attempts to convince the readers that Jesus is still the answer and that Christianity should be the religion of choice.

Colossae and Laodicea

According to the Acts of the Apostles and the writer of the letter, Paul never visited these cities. There is some evidence that Colossae and Laodicea were destroyed in 60–61 C.E. by an earthquake. It appears that the letter was written to both of these cities. And while Laodicea rebuilt itself quickly, no one knows the fate of Colossae. Both cities were in Asia Minor. Colossae was about 100 miles east of Ephesus and eleven miles southeast of Laodicea. It was situated near the Lycus River at the foot of Mount Cadmus. No occupation is recorded after the eighth century C.E., and not much is known about the city during the first century C.E.

According to Herodotus, it was a great city of Phrygia, known to be large and prosperous until the fourth century B.C.E., located on a major trade route and known for producing wool textiles. Tax records suggest that there were as many as 7,500 Jews living in Colossae around 62 B.C.E. Coins covering several centuries depict the worship of several deities, including Artemis, Zeus, Demeter, Higeia, Athena, and Tyche. See the map (Figure 11.1) for its approximate location.

Date and Authorship

Scholars date the writing of Colossians between 60–90 C.E. The date depends on whether Pauline authorship is accepted. Logically, those who hold to the view that Paul wrote it would conclude that it was written sometime between 60–64 C.E. They presume that Colossae was not destroyed by the earthquake in 60 C.E. Others place the date later in the century, around the time of the creation of Ephesians, but perhaps before the end of the century because of its advanced or significantly different view of Jesus and the Christian communities.

Colossians may be termed a pseudepigraphal, pseudonymous, or deutero-Pauline letter because someone other than Paul wrote it in Paul's name. Whoever wrote Colossians was well versed in Paul's thoughts and views. While most students of the Bible conclude that Paul did not write this letter, they would also argue that the writer either

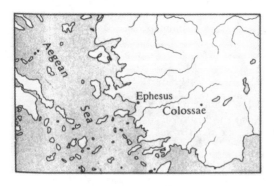

FIGURE 11.1 Map of Colossae and Ephesus. From *Harper's Bible Dictionary.* San Francisco: Harper & Row, 1985.

used Paul's letters, rewrote a smaller version of Ephesians, or had studied Paul's writings and letters.

REASONS FOR WRITING THE LETTER

To date, no one has unlocked the mysteries of Colossians. No one knows the reasons for writing the letter, nor the identity of the adversaries of the Colossians. It is clear that the letter was written as an affirmation or a recommendation for Epaphras. And it is most obvious that the theme of Colossians is the cosmic or universal Christ. One of the main points of the letter argues for the inclusion of all peoples into the mystical body of Christ, who is the head. This broad and universal view of Jesus may have been the main reason for its creation. It asserts that everyone is part of the family of Christ.

Yet most researchers assume that the letter was written to stop the encroachment of another religion(s). Scholars describe the threatening religion in various ways. Some of the adjectives include ascetic and syncretistic, with demands of ritual and moral rigorism. Competing religious political parties may include Jews (Hellenistic and traditional), Pythagoreans, Essenes or Qumran-like Christians, adherents of Mithraism, different types of Gnostics, followers of John the Baptist, or a Cerinthus who lived in the second century C.E., as well as Hellenistic mystery religions.

Cerinthus lived in Asia Minor around 100 C.E. and has been linked with the Simon Magus we discovered in Acts. Combining tenets from Judaism and Gnosticism, Cerinthus taught that the world was created by another entity other than God. The Christ (a separate being) descended at baptism on Jesus and left him before he died on the cross. Claiming that angels delivered the Jewish Laws, he made a habit of keeping all of them.

Possible Problems at Colossae

The letter itself may reveal some of the issues being tackled by the people at Colossae. A list of a few suggestions follows:

1:11	Some people may be harassed because of their faith.
2:2	There is dissension within the community. (See also 2:19; 3:13–14.)
2:4, 8	The people may be mesmerized by someone who has a very logical point of view.
2:11	There may be an argument over circumcision.
2:12	Is there a misunderstanding about baptism?
2:16	Should they observe dietary restrictions and certain rituals? (See also 2:20–22.)
2:16	Should they believe in angels and visions and practice austere measures of self-denial?
3:18f	Is the structure of the traditional family changing?

CHARACTERS

While Colossians clothes its message with a nonearthly or cosmic view of Jesus and the Church, the writer mentions several concrete people and places. Below is a selection of those people and some of the cities associated with them

People	Description	Places
Tychicus	Beloved brother, faithful minister, and servant	Laodicea
Epaphras	Faithful minister, beloved servant of Christ Jesus, one of you	Hierapolis
Onesimus	Faithful and beloved brother	Colossae
Aristarchus	Fellow prisoner	
Timothy	Our brother	
Justus	Jesus	
Nympha	Church at her house	
Luke	Beloved physician	

SOURCES AND LITERARY FEATURES

Colossians may be a compilation of many of Paul's letters and other sources. Philemon, Philippians, Romans, and Ephesians may have influenced the content of this letter. What follows are a few verses that are common to both Colossians and Ephesians. Scholars debate whether the author of Colossians copied from Ephesians or the author of Ephesians copied from Colossians.

Colossians	Ephesians
1:1–2	1:1–2
Paul, an apostle of Christ Jesus by the will of God, and Timothy our brother, To the saints and faithful brothers and sisters in Christ in Colossae: Grace to you and peace from God our Father.	Paul, an apostle of Christ Jesus by the will of God, to the saints who are in Ephesus and are faithful in Christ Jesus: Grace to you and peace from God our Father and the Lord Jesus Christ.
1:5	1:13
. . . because of the hope laid up for you in heaven. You have heard of this hope before in the word of the truth, the gospel.	In him you also, when you had heard the word of truth, the gospel of your salvation, and had believed in him, were marked with the seal of the promised Holy Spirit.

2:19

And not holding fast to the head, from whom the whole body, nourished and held together by its ligaments and sinews, grows with a growth that is from God.

4:15

But speaking the truth in love, we must grow up in every way into him who is the head, into Christ, from whom the whole body, joined and knit together by every ligament with which it is equipped, as each part is working properly, Promotes the body's growth in building itself up in love.

4:7–9

Tychicus will tell you all the news about me; he is a beloved brother, a faithful minister, and a fellow servant in the Lord. I have sent him to you for this very purpose, so that you may know how we are and that he may encourage your hearts; he is coming with Onesimus, the faithful and beloved brother, who is one of you. They will tell you about everything here.

6:21–22

So that you also may know how I am doing, Tychicus will tell you everything. He is a dear brother and a faithful minister in the Lord. I am sending him to you for this very purpose, to let you know how we are, and to encourage your hearts. (NRSV)

Other sources include the Old Testament/Hebrew Bible, a hymn to Christ in 1:15–20, and the rules governing families or household codes in 3:18–25.

THE LITERARY PAUL AND COLOSSIANS

The writer who may be using Paul's name is very concerned about the success of the community and portrays himself as a friend and integral member, even though he may never have met the Colossians. Colossians omits key Pauline ideas of personal freedom while creating cosmic concepts that are found nowhere else in the New Testament. For instance, it omits key Pauline words such as savior, spirit, justification or righteousness, justify, belief, sin, salvation, freedom, and so on. The ideas of freedom from the law and justification by faith also are missing.

The language of Colossians is indirect and convoluted. While the Paul of Galatians and Romans is direct and to the point, the writer of Colossians uses many "ands" or connectives and infinitives and seems to run on and on. An example of one sentence follows:

> And you who were once estranged and hostile in mind, doing evil deeds, he has now reconciled in his fleshly body through death, so as to present you holy and blameless and irreproachable before him—provided that you continue securely established and steadfast in the faith, without shifting from the hope promised by the gospel that you heard, which has been proclaimed to every creature under heaven. (1:21–23 NRSV)

The writer of Colossians views Jesus and the people within Christianity quite differently. We will discuss these subjects shortly.

COSMIC MYTHOLOGY

Colossians contains a distinctive vocabulary. Let's look at some of the cosmic or meta-physical (nonmaterial, abstract) vocabulary.

Chapter One

12	Saints of Light
13	Powers of Darkness
13	Kingdom of Beloved Son
15	Image of Invisible God
15	Firstborn of Creation
17	In Him All Things Hold Together

Chapter Two

2	Knowledge of God's Mystery
3	Christ ... All the Treasures of Wisdom and Knowledge
8	Elemental Spirits of the Universe
11	Spiritual Circumcision
15	Disarm the Rulers and Authorities
20	Elemental Spirits of the Universe

While Colossians may have been sent to real people with real problems, the writer uses words and concepts that fit into a metaphysical or otherworldly and futuristic language. Where are the pain, agony, and anguish of a human Jesus? The story of Jesus and his adversaries is covered with a mist. Terms are vague and the activities of Jesus are portrayed on a grand and pantheistic scale. Wisdom and mystery are vital themes. Some scholars point to Proverbs 8:22 as the foundation verse for a type of Gnosticism in Colossae, relating Jesus to Wisdom. Colossians 1:15 reads, "He is the image of the invisible God, the firstborn of all creation;..." Proverbs 8:22 claims that Wisdom was created first. "The Lord created me at the beginning of his work, the first of his acts long ago."

Jesus (as Wisdom?) seems to be part of a divine preexistent entity. He is head of the body of saints, a reflection of an invisible God, and a force pervading the universe. He is firstborn of what? Does this phrase mean he is a sovereign over the earth, the highest life form, a new life form or creation, or was Jesus a perfect human being? He is also a mediator of creation. The Deity dwells in him. Where is the personal God of the gospels or the Jesus who dies on the cross in the earlier letters of Paul?

According to the writer of Colossians, the message of Jesus is complete. It has reached everyone on earth. He was crucified, resurrected, seated at the right hand of the father, and will return in the future (1:20; 2:12; 3:1,4). Jesus has new or different enemies that are termed elemental spirits, powers of darkness, rulers, and authorities.

Those who are called saints are part of the mysterious body with Jesus at its head. They may be infused with divine energy, may experience spiritual circumcision, and may share in some type of inheritance. While Jesus is their ruler, they are holy and chosen

(1:22; 3:12). There is a universal fellowship both with local and regional churches who sing together about their experience of God (4:15–16; 3:16).

FEMALE SAINTS

The Colossian emphasis on the "body" and the universalism of Christianity seem to go beyond the need to discuss whether or not women are an integrated and important part of the early Christian community. Certainly the mention of "Nympha and the church in her house" (4:16, probably from Laodicea?) notes that foreign women did preside over congregations. Gender is not included in the baptismal saying in Colossians. Recall that "male and female" were central in the Galatian saying. Compare the verses that follow:

Galatians 3:28	Colossians 3:11
There is no longer Jew or Greek,	*In the renewal there is no longer Greek*
there is no longer slave or free,	*and Jew, circumcised and uncircumcised,*
there is no longer male and female;	*barbarian, Scythian, slave and free; but*
for all of you are one in Christ Jesus.	*Christ is all and in all!*

Of course we could conclude that equality had been reached within the Colossian churches, or we could interpret "circumcised and uncircumcised" as referring to male or female. The writer to Colossae adds barbarians and Scythians to the list. Who were the barbarians? The Jews thought everyone outside of their faith was a barbarian. Some Greeks considered themselves the only cultured race in the Empire, so barbarians were everything but Greek. The term itself was probably a racial epithet.

Scythians were a generally nomadic people who lived near the Black Sea from the seventh century B.C.E. Their empire lasted until the fourth century B.C.E. We know that they worked as mercenaries for the Babylonians and as police for the Athenians. They were well known for combat on horseback. Tombs from the fourth century B.C.E. reveal a people who had no writing system, were buried with their horses, and enjoyed art that portrayed animals fighting with one another.

The addition of these two classes of people signals that the grand universalism described by the Colossian writer did not reach everyone. In chapter 3, the writer recommends a hierarchical order within the family which mirrors the hierarchy of Christ as head and ruler of the body of Christians.

THE HOUSE LAWS OR HOUSEHOLD CODES

A hopeful egalitarianism fades as the Colossian (and also Ephesian) writer explains, "Wives be subject to your husbands,…" and "Slaves, obey your earthly masters" (3:20–25). If there is a unity, then it must be hierarchical where each person knows his or her role and must keep his or her proper place for the organization to be successful.

The Colossian message is, "Don't change and do not rock the boat! The present status is working!" In light of the subjection imposed on wives and slaves by the house laws, the omission of "male and female" from the baptismal saying in 3:11 is probably part of the Colossian design, and may mirror the birth of an early patriarchalism within a Catholic (universal) oriented church.

These practical house laws do not seem to fit into the mind-set of a Westerner who has lived in a democratic society and holds to the ideal that all people are equal. Yet the hierarchical view of family found in Colossians (and Ephesians) was widely accepted in Eastern and Middle Eastern cultures. At least five centuries before Jesus, the Chinese followed codes of conduct toward one another. They believed that there was a natural order to life and that everyone would be happy and society would remain stable if these concepts were followed. An excerpt from the Confucian *Book of Changes* follows. Does it resemble the house laws found in Colossians 3:18–4:1 and Ephesians 5:21–6:9?

The Family

The foundation of the family is the relationship between husband and wife. The tie that holds the family together lies in the loyalty and perseverance of the wife. Her place is within, while that of the husband is without. It is in accord with the great laws of nature that husband and wife take their proper places. Within the family a strong authority is needed; this is represented by the parents. If the father is really a father and the son a son, if the elder brother fulfills his position, and the younger fulfills his, if the husband is really a husband and the wife a wife, then the family is in order. When the family is in order, all the social relationships of mankind will be in order. (Serinity Young, *An Anthology of Sacred Texts By and About Women* [New York: Crossroads. 1993], 346)

Summary of Colossians   The writer to Colossae and possibly Laodicea, in the name of Paul, has created a letter for a least two Christian communities he has never met. Dates for its creation range from 60–90 C.E. When compared to other Pauline works, Colossians seems sedate and distant. Important Pauline concepts of justification by faith and freedom from the law are missing. In their place is a metaphysical portrait of the universe. Colossians describes both Jesus and the saints in cosmic terms. As a personal aside, the writer claims that he cannot visit Asia and finds himself suffering and grieving.

No one knows the exact reason for the creation of the letter. Some have suggested that competing religious traditions could have threatened the people. Others think Colossians was a general letter sent to several localities in the hope of affirming Epaphras as a minister. It may also have been sent to unify disparate groups by attempting to make them part of the family of God, a universalism.

Most scholars agree that the writer used several Pauline letters as a basis for Colossians, depending heavily on Ephesians (or vice versa). Literary forms include a hymn to Christ, baptismal sayings, household laws, and lists of acceptable and nonacceptable ethical guidelines.

The Colossian problems seem to be standard; dissension, charismatic personalities, and competing religions. Organization is a key theme with Christ as head of the body and males as head of the family. Females are theoretically relegated to a subservient position within a family, but as noted, Nympha runs a church in her home.

Ephesians:
A Predestined, Unified, and Orderly Church

Grace to you and peace from God our Father
and the Lord Jesus Christ.

—1:2

There is one body and one Spirit,
just as you were called to the one hope of your calling,
one Lord, one faith, one baptism,
one God and Father of all,
who is above all and through all in all.

—4:4–6 NRSV

INTRODUCTION

Ephesians may read like a rerun for those who have recently studied Colossians. It has the same metaphysical outlook and distant otherworldly view of Jesus. There is a heavy emphasis on unity among converts, which some have termed an early "Catholic" view of Christianity. These believers who become Christian soldiers are caught in the middle of a struggle between powers and are encouraged to battle the unseen spirits valiantly.

THE CITY OF EPHESUS AND THE ACTS OF THE APOSTLES

Ephesus is located on the southwestern shores of Turkey on the Aegean Sea. It reached its height of influence and prosperity during the first and second centuries C.E., being the fourth largest city in the Roman Empire. Paul traveled to this area several times and apparently lived in Ephesus, according to the Acts of the Apostles, for at least two years. One of his Ephesian companions, Trophimus, was responsible for Paul's arrest in Jerusalem (Acts 21–22). Ephesus is mentioned several times in other letters attributed to Paul (1 Cor. 15:32; 1 Tim. 1:3; 2 Tim. 1:18; 4:12).

The Ephesian elders were also asked to meet Paul in **Miletus**. Acts 20 describes Paul's speech, which includes an autobiography, a prediction of his death, and encouragement to the Ephesians to continue their work. He said, "Keep watch over yourselves and over all the flock, of which the Holy Spirit has made you overseers, to shepherd the church of God, that he obtained with the blood of his own Son" (20:28). This emphasis on unity and viewing the church as a single entity is also found in the letter to the Ephesians.

267

In our study of Acts, we met several important characters in Ephesus such as Priscilla, Aquila, Apollos, Sceva, Gaius, Aristarchus, Alexander, and Demetrius, a silversmith, who was threatened by Paul's success in winning converts to Christianity. As recalled, so many people became angry that a riot ensued. Earlier in the narrative the sons of Sceva, who had apparently been trying to exorcise demons in the name of Jesus, were overpowered by an evil spirit that beat them up and took away their clothes. A great feeling of fear among the witnesses resulted in the burning of magical books (Acts 18–19).

This general portrait of Ephesus by the writer of Acts seems to fit the historical records. Ephesus, whose ruins are still a major tourist site in Turkey today, was the center of the worship of **Artemis** and all sorts of magic. The religion was an important economic factor in the city, owning land and funneling all sorts of cash from worshipers who traveled to Ephesus from all over the Empire into the city coffers. A colossal statue of Artemis, located in the harbor, greeted every visitor to Ephesus. It was considered one of the wonders of the world.

While Artemis was worshiped for her powers of fertility, she was also called Savior, Lord, Queen of the Cosmos (World), and Heavenly Goddess. A prayer to Artemis in the *Acts of John*, asking her to raise a believer from the dead, follows:

FIGURE 11.2   Theatre at Ephesus, site of a riot started by Paul according to Acts of the Apostles. Photo by Marla J. Selvidge.

O Great Artemis of the Ephesians, help! Display your power upon this your man who has died. For all the Ephesians know both men and women, that all things are governed by you, and that great powers come to us through you. Give now to your servant what you are able to do in this regard. Raise up your servant Domnos. (Arnold 1989, 22)

In both Acts and the letter to the Ephesians the writers portray Ephesus as being a very diverse and international city that had huge contingents of various types of religions. Christianity struggled against this stronghold and eventually won.

DATE, AUTHORSHIP, SOURCES

Those who argue that Paul wrote Ephesians place its creation in the early 60s C.E. Others who claim it is a copy of Colossians (or vice versa) date it in the 90s C.E. Most scholars have developed numerous reasons about why Ephesians was not written by Paul. Other possible authors include Luke, Onesimus, and an elder at the church at Ephesus.

Similar to Colossians, Ephesians has no real emphasis on salvation by faith, struggle with the Jewish law, the concept of sin, or the suffering of Jesus on the cross. The

FIGURE 11.3   The ruins of Ephesus. Photo by Marla J. Selvidge.

FIGURE 11.4   The main street in Ephesus, Curetas. Photo by Marla J. Selvidge.

letter contains no personal greetings, and there appears to be no main or urgent reason for writing the letter. Scholars point to the cumbersome and deliberate style of writing that is rarely found in the accepted Pauline works (note Ephesians 1:15–23). This same type of correspondence was detected in Colossians. Some of the words used by Paul are redefined, such as "heaven, heavenly places" (1:3, 20; 2:6) and "bestowing grace" (1:6). Other words seem to be products of the second century, such as "commonwealth" (2:11), "likeness" (4:24), and "orgy or people who seduce others" (5:18).

Ephesians begins with issues that have proven unsolvable. In the earliest and best manuscripts, the phrase "to the Ephesians" is missing. In its place is an open space, where many suggest someone wrote in the name "Ephesians." There is evidence during the second century C.E. that many early church writers quoted Ephesians and therefore accepted it as authentic, but scholars from at least the sixteenth century onward have questioned Pauline authorship.

The text of the letter appears to have numerous sources. It uses Romans, 2 Corinthians, Galatians, 1 Corinthians, 1 Thessalonians, and of course there is an overwhelming amount of material common to both Colossians and Ephesians. Qumran and the writings of the people at the Dead Sea might also have influenced Ephesians, because there are many similarities in vocabulary and style of language. Numerous topics are paralleled, such as naming specific sins, a rigid hierarchy, sons of disobedience or darkness,

FIGURE 11.5
Artemis. Photo by
Marla J. Selvidge.

the concepts of light and darkness, the foolish and the wise, immersion in water or baptism, and the battle imagery at the end of the letter.

This letter, like all of the Pauline and Pseudo-Pauline letters, uses the Old Testament/Hebrew Bible as a source. There are traces of a hymn in 2:14–16 and a prayer in 1:15 and several baptismal sayings. The writer also was familiar with Gnosticism and Jewish apocalyptic literature.

FORM AND REASONS FOR THE CREATION OF EPHESIANS

Since we do not know (beyond a doubt) that Ephesians was actually addressed to the people at Ephesus, some contend that it may not have been a letter. Ephesians could have been a general introductory document for new converts. Baptismal allusions to leaving a former life and beginning a new one are found throughout the work. A few of the seemingly baptismal nuances follow:

4:22	You were taught to put away your former way of life....
4:25	...[P]utting away falsehood.....
4:31	Put away from you all bitterness and wrath....
4:24	... [C]lothe yourselves with the new self....
6:11	Put on the whole armor of God....

Ephesians may also have been a circular letter or an **encyclical**. One letter could have been written by Paul (or someone else), and then several copies made of the letter; or, one letter could have been sent to several different congregations. Some have suggested that Ephesians may have been the product of a transcriber or scribe who had collected Paul's letters and wanted to summarize his beliefs at the beginning of the works. The scribe may have created Ephesians as a type of introductory work to Paul's letters that followed.

Similar to the people of Colossae, the Ephesians may be divided and assaulted by religions that are more successful. The letter may have been written to help converts mentally battle (as escapist literature) what they perceived as evil or demonic forces. Ephesians argues that Christ has won the battle and so will they. They are part of a universal world order and are not alone.

CENTRAL THEME: ONE NEW HUMANITY

The central feature of the letter to Ephesians is its description of the saints or the church. They are called "adopted children" (1:5), "God's own people" (1:14), "Gentiles by birth, the uncircumcision" (2:11), "one new humanity" (2:15), "fellow heirs" (3:6), "beloved children" (5:1), "citizens," and "members of the household of God" (2:19).

The writer to the Ephesians continues the Colossian emphasis on universalism and unity but strengthens the notion of predestination on a cosmic level. While Jesus may have been preexistent, God is the one who brought about salvation for the people. The church has been designed by God. It is compared to a holy temple (2:20–22) and a bride without blemish (5:22–33). It has a future inheritance.

The writer characterizes the earlier lives of the saints as aliens, strangers, having no hope (2:12), and followers of the "power of the air" (2:2). They were alive but dead to the kind of life they are now living. God made this change possible. Their lives are now filled with good works, not the wrath or passions of the flesh (2:1–11). They have been marked with the seal of the Holy Spirit (1:13; 4:30) and have faith and love toward other converts (1:15).

As members of the body of Christ or the Church (1:22), they are to follow guidelines outlined by the writer (4:17–5:33) which include respecting the authority of each other, as well as structuring their families (husbands, wives, children, slaves) according to a hierarchical male-dominated order. The writer does not reiterate the Ten Commandments but gives many ethical guidelines to the saints. A list of selected rules follows:

Ephesians	Ethical Rules
4:25,26	Speak the truth. and curb your anger.
4:27,28	Throw out the Devil and stop stealing.
4:32	Be kind, tenderhearted, forgiving.
5:3,4	No fornication, impurity, greed, obscene, silly, vulgar talk.

5:12	Do not participate in secret rituals.
5:16	Use your time wisely.
5:18	Do not get drunk.

In the midst of giving ethical instructions to the saints, the writer of Ephesians includes a mythological construct that includes the Devil (4:28; 6:10), powers of the air, rulers of power, secret worlds of darkness, rulers, authorities, cosmic powers, and spiritual forces of evil (chapter 6). Saints are encouraged to put on their battle gear and engage the spirits. They are caught in the middle of a universe and a war they did not create, yet they have no choice but to do battle. Since God is in control of everything, one would hope that the armed saints would win. A popular Christian hymn, based on the mythological framework in Ephesians, follows:

Onward Christian Soldiers

Onward, Christian soldiers, Marching as to war,
With the cross of Jesus Going on before!
Christ, the royal Master, Leads against the foe;
Forward into battle, See His banner go!
Onward, Christian soldiers, Marching as to war,
With the cross of Jesus Going on before!

Most modern readers of Ephesians are mystified by the hierarchical order, the acceptance of slavery, the military metaphors, and the hostile attitude displayed toward Gentiles. Where is the gentle egalitarianism of Galatians? Paul was supposed to be a missionary to the Gentiles, but his demonizing words in chapter 4:17–19 would have enraged any non-Jew or Greek, even if they had converted.

PROMINENT CHARACTERS

In the Name of Paul, the Apostle

If Paul is writing this letter, he does not reveal very much about himself. He or she calls himself an apostle (1:1), a servant (3:7), the least of the saints (3:8), and suggests that he is a prisoner for Christ Jesus (3:1; 4:1) or in the Lord. Was the author in prison at the time of the creation of Ephesians? It is possible, but more than likely that these words are a metaphor for the writer's devotion to his god or mission. He is a member, as are his readers, of the holy body of believers chosen before the beginning of time (1:4).

Paul is under the direct guidance of God (1:1). This may have happened because of a revelation (3:1). He says he prays for the Ephesians (3:19) as if he knows them personally, but then after describing how Gentiles live futile lives, he says, "For surely you have heard about him and were taught in him, as truth is in Jesus" (4:21). If Paul had visited the Ephesians, why would he write to them asking if they had heard? Perhaps he is being sarcastic and is actually saying, "You act as though you have never heard about Jesus!"

Tychicus is the only friend of Paul's mentioned in the letter. There are vague references to saints (1:1), gentiles (2:11), holy apostles and prophets (3:5), and a general list of offices (4:11) that could refer to individual people. Paul's customary greeting and parting words, zest for life, hope of a speedy return of Jesus, and constant entourage of supporters is missing. And as many scholars suggest, Paul himself is missing from this letter.

Jesus, the Beloved and God, the Father

The cosmic Christ of Colossians has been joined by God in Ephesians. Jesus is still head of the Church (1:22) but God is now the one who seems more important. The mission of Jesus still brings redemption (1:7), but this was accomplished by God according to the plan (1:9). The writer of Ephesians views time and everything in it as being controlled by God. Thus, the idea of foreordination or predestination is a central theme. A list of some of the phrases that emphasize that time and life are under God's control follows:

1:4	Chose us before the foundation of the world.
1:5	Destined us for adoption.
1:8	Faith is the gift of God.
1:10	Plan for the fullness of time.
1:11	We have been destined.
3:7	Plan for the mystery of the ages in God.

Jesus is the Beloved (1:6), Son of God (4:13), Savior (5:23), and as Christ, was raised from the dead, ascended and descended into and from the lower parts of the earth (4:9), and sits in heavenly places (1:20). God has placed Christ in control of the Church (1:22; 5:23). And through Christ Jesus, the saints have access to the love of Christ, the fullness of God (3:10, 20).

Summary of Ephesians   Ephesus was an important port of call for Paul in the Acts of the Apostles. It was the world center for the worship of Artemis. Ephesians is a pseudo-Pauline work, which may have been an encyclical letter or a document for new converts, written between 60–90 C.E. It used several of Paul's letters as sources. The central issue of the work is its description of the saints, with an emphasis on Paul himself, the cosmic Christ, and the Father.

12

Letters Written in the Name of Paul

---

1 and 2 Timothy and Titus

For the time is coming when people will not put up with sound doctrine
but having itching ears, they will accumulate for themselves teachers
to suit their own desires....

—2 Tim 4:3 NRSV

INTRODUCTION TO THE PASTORALS

Three letters to friends of Paul have been called the "pastoral epistles" since the nineteenth century. Many have suggested that Titus was originally designed as an introduction to 1 and 2 Timothy because it contains elements from both. The contents of the pastorals deal with the structural, social, and theological problems within Christian groups. Little space is devoted to speculation or arguments about truths or philosophies. The writer of the pastorals passes on a "received" tradition, including community organizational guidelines.

An attitude of strict adherence to formal law and order pervades the pastorals. The egalitarianism of Galatians and the freedom to make choices in personal relationships found in 1 Corinthians are gone. The choices for women, widows, and single males and females are limited. Males, in order to assume high leadership positions, must be married and have children.

Love becomes a qualification for administrative positions. It has lost the gentle and forgiving nature of Philippians. Faith has become the "rule of faith" (1 Tim. 3:9). People must be "holy" in the *Faith* (Titus 1:13) which is quite different from "living by faith" (Gal. 1:20). Timothy is called a loyal child "in the faith" (1 Tim. 1:2). Faith appears to have been reduced to a set of rules and beliefs that everyone must follow, often referred to as "sound teaching," "tradition," "the Word," and "good treasure." The writer of 1 Timothy even includes those who do not follow "sound teaching" in his list, among which are killers of father or mother, slave traders, and liars (1:10–11). Disagreement was unacceptable and reprehensible to the writers of the pastorals.

> Whoever teaches otherwise and does not agree with the sound words of our Lord Jesus Christ and the teaching that is in accordance with godliness.... (1 Tim. 6:3)

In spite of their brevity, the pastorals contain as many as twenty references to geography and at least forty references to people. The foundational beliefs of the pastorals broadly agree with earlier Pauline letters but on major issues they are significantly different. There is a belief in salvation and the revelation of God through Christ, justification, and an emphasis on faith bringing eternal life. But the Greek words that are used differ considerably from the Pauline expressions. Gone is the frail Paul who defends himself and allows people to make their own personal decisions. In his place is an authoritarian legislator who believes that his rigid social plan will rescue the failing Christian groups from extinction.

AUTHORSHIP AND DATE

No one knows who wrote the letters to Timothy and Titus. Arguments line up for and against Paul. Most students claim that the letters were written by a Paulinist living sometime during the second century C.E. He or she may have used sources such as Paul's letters, Luke-Acts, and fragments of lost Pauline letters. There are major differences in language and beliefs between the Pauline letters and the disputed Pastorals. The pastorals assume a legalistic or rigid view of the gospel to which all converts must conform, whereas in the accepted Pauline letters, there appears to be a fluidity about truth because people are in the midst of creating a new religious tradition.

In reconstructing Paul's life, most scholars cannot find any time in history when Paul could have written these letters. They assume that he was killed in the sixties C.E. Timothy's ordination to a church in Ephesus and Titus' work in Crete are not mentioned anywhere else in the New Testament. They also assume that a group of converts during the first century could not have had the organizational structure outlined in these letters. Basing their analyses on early Christian writings, they suggest that the pastorals reflect images of an emerging Catholicism.

Those who support Pauline authorship point to traditions by Eusebius that Paul went on to other work in the Empire after his first imprisonment in Rome. He was arrested again many years later and executed in Rome. Luke Timothy Johnson, in *Letters to Paul's Delegates, 1 Timothy, 2 Timothy, Titus,* has recently resumed the torch for Pauline authorship. His approach is more biographically or personally oriented than literary. He argues that the pastorals reflect the Paul he has discovered. Paul encouraged order, held himself up as an example, presented ambivalent views on women within assemblies, and erected boundaries to protect converts from encroachment from other religions. He affirmed marriage and believed that there was a natural order to the universe that everyone should follow. And, finally, Johnson argues that in 1,800 years, no one questioned the authorship of the pastorals except Marcion.

Those who hold to Pauline authorship place the letters in the late sixties C.E. or after the imprisonment of Paul in Rome. Arguments for pseudonymity or a combination of sources and fragments date the pastorals in the second century C.E., 135–160. The first letter was written to Timothy in Ephesus, but no one really knows who received it. Titus was in Crete, and Ephesus is assumed to be the recipient of 2 Timothy.

FIGURE 12.1
St. Bavo's Cathedral in Ghent, Belgium, circa 1569. Photo taken by Marla Selvidge.

1 Timothy:
Implosion and The Gospel of Order

I hope to come to you soon, but I am writing these instructions
to you so that, if I am delayed, you may know how one ought
to behave in the household of God, which is the church
of the living God, the pillar and bulwark of the truth.

—1 Tim. 3:14 NRSV

INTRODUCTION

Stepping into the pages of 1 Timothy conjures up images of walking across a well-worn marble floor of a medieval gothic cathedral. As you enter the dimly lit church, the air feels damp and cool, as echoing hushed voices surround you. Looking up at the massive stone ceiling, your heart stops for a moment. The expansive structure dominates all who wander through its doors. Peering into the first letter to Timothy may give the reader a similar experience. Charismatic spontaneity and egalitarianism have given way to accepted tradition and an androcentric hierarchical structure. The wide-open doors of earlier Pauline Christianity have slammed shut.

Whoever wrote 1 Timothy believed that the Christian community was under siege, on the verge of assimilation. The writer suggested a plan to save the community from possible extinction. Perhaps the historical situation was similar to that of the ancient Jews returning to Palestine after a long exile in Babylonia-Persia. It was probably during this period that the purity laws emerged that forbade intermarriage, contracts with foreigners, and rigorous food, sex, and health regimes.

The writer's solution to the impending problem of assimilation was to set up a strong hierarchical organization of people who were well known in the community for being fair minded, authoritarian, and financially secure. Fringe groups, formerly supported by the community, were abandoned in favor of the elders. Strict guidelines concerning religious subject matter, personal relationships, and lifestyles were instituted. Many of the targets were successful religious women, in the hope of shoring up a failing weak male leadership.

REASONS FOR WRITING THE LETTER

The letter reveals the following goals of its writer:

1:18   so Timothy will be successful

3:14   so converts will know how to behave in the household of God

4:6, 12 to support Timothy

But the aforementioned are only the obvious reasons for writing the letter. Scholars have theorized about a host of other situations that would prompt such correspondence. Some contend that 1 Timothy is a code book of Christian conduct. Its broad categories, qualifications, and suggested activities set the groundwork for Christianity for the next thousand years. Whether or not it was intended to be a code book, it was certainly interpreted as such by most of Christendom.

The community seemed to be threatened internally and externally. Competing religions may have been attracting some of their most important supporters (**Alexander** and **Hymenaeus**). Some have characterized this group as being Gnostic or Jewish Gnostic. It may have influenced how people were interpreting the Torah and relating to one another. The writer warns people about listening to myths (4:7), different doctrines, and genealogies (1:4). People are talking too much! They are quarreling about who should be teachers and leaders!

1 Timothy hopes to preserve the community by purging unwanted troublemakers, reorganizing the group's functions, and reallocating funds. There are also hopes of suppressing female contributions, segregating widows, bringing slaves into line, and rescuing weak male leadership from total failure. The writer's strategy includes denigrating the perceived opposition, linking the converts to Judaic traditions, and limiting/defining the qualifications for leadership.

CHARACTERS

Timothy

Who is Timothy? Is the Timothy in 1 and 2 Timothy the same co-worker and beloved friend of Paul? We do not know. Arguments about his identity are based on scholars' views of whether or not 1 and 2 Timothy were written by Paul. If this letter is authentic, then several of Paul's letters and the Acts of the Apostles sketch a portrait of this Timothy. If it is pseudonymous, which is likely, then Timothy could be anyone, or he could represent any leader of any struggling Christian group.

According to the Acts of the Apostles, before meeting Paul, Timothy was known and respected in the communities of Lystra and Iconium. Perhaps Acts is suggesting that Timothy was a strategic contact. "Paul went on also to Derbe and to Lystra, where there was a disciple named Timothy…" (Acts 16:1). Paul persuaded Timothy to join him and to become circumcised (16:3).

Timothy remained with Paul throughout his career, taking the new religion to Philippi, Thessalonica, Athens, Corinth, and Jerusalem. He carried letters and guest lectured on behalf of Paul. The fact that two letters in his name are included in the New Testament is evidence for his success and popularity. He is listed as the co-author of Philemon, 1 and 2 Thessalonians, Colossians, Philippians, and 2 Corinthians. His name also is mentioned in Romans, 1 Corinthians and 1 Thessalonians. Descriptions of him in the Pauline letters include son, our brother, God's servant, servant of Jesus, dependable, and minister.

Timothy was the product of an ethnically diverse union of a Jew and a Greek (Acts 16:1), and 2 Timothy traces his heritage through his mother and grandmother, Eunice and Lois (1:5). The portrait of him in the letters to Timothy is not flattering and bears little resemblance to the Timothy of the Pauline letters and Acts. The letters were sent to a man who was intimidated by almost everyone, had a nervous stomach, and needed a lot of hand-holding to find success (1 Tim. 1:18; 5:23). Some suggest that the same personality deficiencies and problems are reflected in 1 Cor. 16:10–11.

> If Timothy comes, see that he has nothing to fear among you, for he is doing the work of the Lord just as I am; therefore let no one despise him. Send him on his way in peace, so that he may come to me; for I am expecting him with the brothers. (NRSV)

While others conclude that the real problem in Corinth was created by Paul, Timothy could be experiencing fallout from hostilities between Paul and community members who thought he was meddling in their affairs.

Timothy remains a supportive but shadowy figure in the life of Paul. No one knows his point of view. The letters in which he is listed as a writer have always been interpreted as Pauline, but Timothy's voice is there, in and between the lines, known yet unknown (see also 1 Thess. 3:2; Phil. 2:19–23; 1 Cor. 4:17; Rom. 16:21; and Acts 16–20).

Writing in the Name of Paul

Whoever wrote 1 Timothy included only generic remarks about the author (himself). Consider the list that follows:

Characteristics	1 Timothy
An apostle by command of God and Jesus	1:1
Appointed for service by Christ Jesus	1:12–13
Appointed a herald and an apostle	2:7
A teacher of the Gentiles	2:7
He does not write falsely.	2:7
He is coming to visit.	3:14; 4:13

If Paul did write this letter, he was a changed man, subdued and defeated, having given in to a heritage that demanded strict obedience to a religious tradition. He has lost his missionary enthusiasm and has settled on culturally conditioned answers to solve Christian dilemmas. Where is the lively, interactive faith? Where is the creative mind of Paul that we met in the Corinthian, Galatian, and Philippian correspondence?

Community Issues:
The Political Power of Widows

The following verses in 1 Timothy are difficult to read, interpret, and understand in today's environment of egalitarianism and respect for distinctive choices in careers and lifestyles.

> I desire, then,...that women should dress themselves modestly and decently in suitable clothing, not with their hair braided, or with gold, pearls, or expensive clothes, but with good works, as is proper for women who profess reverence for God. (2:8–10)

> Let a woman learn in silence with full submission. I permit no woman to teach or to have authority over a man; she is to keep silent. For Adam was formed first, then Eve.... Yet she will be saved through childbearing.... (2:11–14)

> Honor widows who are really widows. (5:3)

> Let a widow be put on the list if she is not less than sixty years old and has been married only once. (5:9)

> But refuse to put younger widows on the list; for when their sensual desires alienate them from Christ, they want to marry....Besides that, they learn to be idle, gadding about from house to house, and they are not merely idle, but also gossips and busybodies.... (5:11–13 NRSV)

Modern stories of the suppression and oppression of females find their origins in the words of 1 Timothy. Christianity has historically been hierarchical, patriarchal, and androcentric. A literal reading of 1 Timothy supports that structure and point of view. This reading has fostered and bolstered the mythical view of woman as "evil" and "contaminate." To contain her, she must be segregated and silenced.

Joanna Dewey, professor of New Testament Studies at Episcopal Divinity School, in *The Women's Bible Commentary* interprets the issue of women's place among the converts as an internal struggle for power. She suggests that the rules in 1 Timothy 2:8–15 regarding the dress and public position of women were designed not to offend men. Christian females were not allowed to challenge or offend the male power structure.

Others suggest that the writer to Timothy is drawing clear lines between women who are inside and outside of Christianity. Rules regarding speaking and attire for women were born from a struggle of competing religions, perhaps the worship of Artemis or a form of Gnosticism. This could also account for the denigrating characteristics of females in 5:13. "Besides that, they learn to be idle, gadding about from house to house; and they are not merely idle, but also gossips and busybodies, saying what they should not say" (NRSV). Temple prostitutes and priestesses might have been recognized by their apparel. They also may have been successful and attractive missionaries for their cause.

Another interpretation may be found within Gnostic creation stories. **Catherine Clark Kroeger**, president of Christians for Biblical Equality, in *I Suffer Not a Woman* reinterprets the word "authentein" in 1 Timothy 2:12, which is normally translated "rule over," as "I do not allow a woman to teach nor to proclaim herself author of man." Her research is based on Gnostic myths that describe Eve as the creator of humankind. She suggests that 1 Timothy is not denying the right of a woman to speak but is defending the Judaic-Christian belief in the male origins (Adam was first) of humankind found in Genesis.

Still others think that all of the negative verses about women in the pastoral letters and in 1 Cor. 14:28 were interpolations added by a scribe who was threatened by female leadership. The editions also could have been a planned effort of males to regain total control of an egalitarian community.

The source of the hierarchicalism also may be found within the decrees regarding marriage and the relationship of spouses issued by Augustus, Emperor of Rome, and rescinded over 300 years later. According to Jo Ann McNamara in "Wives and Widows in Early Christian Thought,"

> Through a series of laws re-issued and re-drafted throughout his principate, he aimed at the elimination of celibacy. As far as possible, he sought to have everyone married all the time, at least until they had reached the age where procreation was unlikely. Widowed and divorced persons were to be rushed into new marriages; adultery was to be punished with harsh penalties, the childless were subjected to severe legal disadvantages. (McNamara 1979, 584)

There may have been great governmental pressure to conform to the traditional, legal family structure. This emphasis on obedience to social laws goes hand in hand with the emphasis on obeying the civil authorities found throughout the pastorals.

Whatever the nature of the threat, the writer to 1 Timothy believes that Timothy must take quick action against powerful (wealthy?) women to prevent the new religion's assimilation and possible annihilation. Women's participation must be limited and defined and their charismatic activities stopped.

Defining the term "Widow" Historical evidence suggests that the term widow not only meant a woman whose husband had died but could also have been an office of celibate females. Celibacy is rare today in our culture, but in ancient times a woman lived her entire life under the domination of a male. First her father governed her and then her husband. A life of domestic childbearing and caring for children was considered the ideal career for a woman. One way to escape this cycle was to renounce marriage and live in community with other women. This renunciation brought freedom from childbearing and the freedom to pursue other meaningful activities.

The writer to Timothy may be personally or financially threatened by a group who calls themselves widows. He may have attempted to destroy the leadership, influence, and organization of these women. Evidence for this theory is found in several verses. 1 Timothy 4:3 reads, "They forbid marriage and demand abstinence from foods. . . ." This may refer to women who take vows of celibacy. The writer is also concerned about "real" widows.

> If any believing woman has relatives who are really widows, let her assist them; let the church not be burdened, so that it can assist those who are real widows. (5:16)

Some have suggested that there may have been wealthy men or women who supported, as in the following centuries within Christianity, celibate women bent on careers within Christianity. The writer may also be cutting the budget to maintain what he sees as essential services. This reduction in funds could be interpreted as a refusal to support women who are celibate.

Younger Widows Some of the suggestions regarding widows may have been made because the community was in a financial crisis. Qualifications for deacons included "not greedy for money," and for bishops, "not a lover of money." And the description of women in 1 Timothy 2 includes "expensive tastes." Previous leaders could have appropriated funds for themselves instead of managing the community resources for the benefit of everyone. Elders should be paid (5:17), but as we have seen earlier, some widows should not be paid. The writer often mentions wealth.

> But those who want to be rich fall into temptation and are trapped by many senseless and harmful desires that plunge people into ruin and destruction. (6:9)
>
> As for those who in the present age are rich, command them not to be haughty, or to set their hopes on the uncertainty of riches, but rather on God who richly provides us with everything for our enjoyment. (6:17 NRSV)

The writer may be attempting to persuade the community to personally assume more of the financial obligations of the Church. He reprimands people who are not providing for family members (5:8) but argues that financial support for destitute women should continue if the women are at least sixty years old and married only once (5:9).

Younger widows are not to receive pay at all. Some of these widows may also not be "real" widows. The writer urges them to assume a traditional life of childbearing and marriage. In other words, he tells them, "Find a husband to take care of you!" He may even be commanding them to get pregnant. "Yet she will be saved through childbearing...." (2:15)

Many have assumed that the writer did command women to have children, but others argue that the writer is making a theological point about Eve. While Eve is blamed by the author for her activities in the "apple event," he may be suggesting that it is through the bearing of a child by a woman (Mary), that all women will be saved by Jesus, her son (2:13–15).

The Men

While males seem to be the preferred group, they do not escape the writer's hierarchical and culturally conditioned traditional familial notions. In positions of leadership, they must be married. (The Roman culture demanded that both Roman and Jewish men marry and produce children.) Implicit in the descriptions of office is the notion that the leaders would be affluent, popular, and authoritarian. They were to rule their houses and children, provide for other family members, and share their riches (6:17). There may have been males who also chose a nontraditional lifestyle of celibacy. 1 Timothy would prohibit these men from assuming the role of bishop or deacon. And whoever does assume leadership must function in an atmosphere of "political correctness" by assuming a low profile before the government (2:1–3).

ORGANIZATIONAL CHART

Many scholars suggest that if a law is passed by a group of people, then someone must be breaking the law. The laws themselves are evidence that the activities prohibited are occurring. The first letter to Timothy suggests that there is some structure within the group, but that it is failing. The writer is reorganizing and redefining leadership positions within the community. A summary of the descriptive words used for each position follows.

General Job Descriptions and Qualifications

Bishop	Deacons	Female Deacons
a good reputation	serious	serious
married only once	no double-talk	not a backbiter
disciplined	not an alcoholic	objective
respected	a nonmaterialist	faithful
objective	strong beliefs	reasonable
a good teacher	must pass a test	(3:11)
sociability	gentle	
not an alcoholic	married only once	
not argumentative	good family manager	
a nonmaterialist	(3:8–12)	
good family manager		
has control of children		
a seasoned convert		
reasonable		
(1 Tim. 3:1–7)		

Elders/Presbyters	Widows on the List
should be paid	less than age sixty
teach/preach	married once
strong leadership	evidence of good works
respected	raised children
(5:1; 17–22)	sociability
	washed convert's feet
	nursed the ill
	(5:9–10)

A quick analysis of the aforementioned characteristics suggests that religious experience, education, or knowledge of beliefs or rituals are not important skills in any of the positions. Most of the positions emphasize abilities in public relations, interpersonal skills, and conflict-management strategies. Concerns include alcoholism, verbal abuse, and money. A permanent sexual relationship, that is, a patriarchal marriage, becomes an inflexible hierarchical model of the organization for the entire community.

Scholars have debated about how to interpret the phrases "one-woman man" and "one-man woman" (3:2, 12; 5:9). Many have settled on the opinion that when the verses use the quote "one-woman man," the position was clearly designed for a male who had one wife and married only once.

LITERARY FOUNDATIONS

The author of 1 Timothy seems to be aware of Paul's letters, the stories in Luke-Acts, and a host of traditional Christian material. Some of the forms and sources used include the following:

Forms and Sources of 1 Timothy

Creedal Statements	2:5–6
Hymn	3:16
Prophecies	1:18; 4:1
Prayer	1:12–17
Marriage Homily	2:13–15
Ordination Charge	6:11–16
LXX	5:18a
Luke 10:7	5:18b

Most researchers conclude that the writer did not create all of 1 Timothy, but pieced together items from many sources.

Summary of 1 Timothy   The view of the writer of 1 Timothy is inward not outward. 1 Timothy aims at preventing the assimilation or annihilation of its religious traditions. Drastic social steps are advocated. Job descriptions are given for a hierarchical organization. Men and women are encouraged to assume traditional family roles. Finances are reallocated, leaving out the celibate communities. Female leadership may have been curbed to support a blossoming androcentric church.

Paul, a changed Paul, may have written this document, but most think it was written by someone in the second century. The Timothy we meet in 1 Timothy must also be a changed man, because his personality has few of the strengths of the Timothy in Acts or other letters attributed to Paul.

2 Timothy:
A Suffering Apostle

Do not be ashamed, then, of the testimony about our Lord
or of me his prisoner, but join with me in suffering for the gospel.

—2 Tim. 1:8 NRSV

As for me, I am already being poured out as a libation,
and the time of departure has come.

—2 Tim. 4:6 NRSV

INTRODUCTION

More personal than the first letter to Timothy is 2 Timothy. In a stream-of-consciousness style, the author rambles from one subject to another. He attacks all sorts of opponents using an ineffective combination of metaphors. The letter appears to have been written during an imprisonment, which may be embarrassing to other converts. The writer is resigned to his incarceration and the physical and mental torture that comes with it. Several people and locations are mentioned, with few descriptive details.

REASONS FOR WRITING THE LETTER

Paul or the writer is in prison (in Rome?). Some of his friends have abandoned him. Is he cold, lonely, and bored? Apparently he has some personal items (a coat, books, and scrolls) stored with Carpus at Troas and hopes that Timothy will bring them to him as soon as possible (4:9–13). There is no indication of where Timothy is staying or what route he will have to take to find Paul.

Formally, the letter also may have been written to argue that the Hebrew Bible/Jewish traditions should be used as a foundation for Christian meetings. Throughout 2 Timothy, there is an emphasis on the ancient Israelite and Jewish traditions. Paul claims that his ancestors worshiped God (1:3) and recognizes the Jewish heritage of Timothy through the line of his mother and grandmother (1:5).

He reprimands local teachers by comparing them to an Old Testament/Hebrew Bible story about court magicians who battled Moses in Exodus 7:11–22. "As Jannes and Jambres opposed Moses, so these people, of corrupt mind and counterfeit faith, also oppose the truth" (3:8, NRSV). Several sources outside of the Bible mention these names, including *The Damascus Document* from the Dead Sea Scrolls and the writings of Philo, **Apuleius**, and Eusebius of Caesarea. What follows is a quote from *The Damascus Document* (CD V:17–19).

> For in ancient times there arose Moses and Aaron, by the hand of the prince of lights and Belial, with his cunning, raised up Jannes and his brother during the first deliverance of Israel.

The "truth" is no longer open to interpretation but has become a "sound doctrine" and a "good treasure" (1:14; 4:3), similar to the legal proscriptions in the Hebrew Bible. The religious readings from Timothy's childhood are considered sacred and useful to convert people to a faith in Jesus (3:14–15). But what is the identity of these writings? As far as we know, there were no written Christian books during the early years of Timothy's life. Q and a proto-Mark may have come into existence in the late 50s C.E. or early 60s. According to the Acts of the Apostles, Timothy had been a convert in the 40s C.E. A logical conclusion would be to assume that the sacred writings were from the Jewish tradition. The Scripture referred to in 3:16–17 must also be Jewish. "All scripture is inspired by God and is useful for teaching, for reproof, for correction, and for training in righteousness...." (NRSV)

PROMINENT CHARACTERS

The second letter to Timothy is basically a conversation between the author and Timothy, the recipient, but it catalogues a host of characters who are living in most of the towns visited by Paul. We have chosen to consider only a few.

The Author: In the Name of Paul

Most scholars argue that the writer of 2 Timothy is a Paulinist who used fragments of Pauline letters (1:15–18; 4:10–16) and other church materials to make his letter sound more realistic. Some suggest that it is a last testament to Paul. Whatever the case, the author presents himself as a brooding, captured missionary who is happy to be alive (1:18). He describes himself as a herald, an apostle, and a teacher (1:11), reminding the reader over and over about his sufferings and narrow escapes from death (1:8, 9, 12). Timothy, too, should follow in his footsteps of suffering. He feels abandoned and hurt because so many of his friends have left him. Unable to agree to disagree, he laments over his friendship with Hymenaeus and Philetus, who have a different interpretation of the resurrection (2:18). He knocks Alexander, an artist, who works in copper. He must have lost a major battle, because he says, "At my first defense no one came to my support, but all deserted me" (4:16).

The Winning Side

No single opposing group can be distinguished in 2 Timothy. The writer lobs disparaging words at several types of people. And, of course, a list of vices is included in the discussion. Whoever is writing to Timothy has been bested by teachers who are accommodating their pupils. One can only guess about what types of myths the writer is referring (4:4). Writing from an oppressed or a weak position, jealousy may be the cause of his remarks. Women are not listening to the writer. They seem to be star struck over others, who in the author's mind are similar to the faulty magicians Jannes and Jambres.

Luke Timothy Johnson captures the author's view of women by fantasizing that they are wealthy and looking for a little excitement in their lives. This mythic caricature projected by the writer may have been created because the only power he has over them is the power to denigrate and negate. In stereotypical language, women are viewed as being driven by their passions, unable to make intelligent decisions on their own.

LITERARY CHARACTERISTICS

The foundations of 2 Timothy are within the Hebrew Bible using quotations, allusions, and forms such as hymns, blessings, and lists, probably created by early Christian groups. Throughout the letter, the author employs many metaphors to communicate better with the audience; these include the image of a father (1:2); a soldier (2:3), and an athlete (2:5). Some of them work and some do not.

Summary of 2 Timothy   The second letter to Timothy raises many questions about the last years of Paul's life. Did he change his point of view in 2 Timothy? Or did he hold multiple views that are difficult to detect within the few Pauline documents in the New Testament? 2 Corinthians contains a brutal defense of Paul's apostleship. If Paul did not write the letter, why would someone claim to be Paul? Is that not deceptive? What did the writer gain? Why are so many negative remarks made about females in both letters? Is the antiwoman rhetoric part of the reason for the pseudonymity?

In 2 Timothy, we get a glimpse of an early Christian community and of the life of someone who wanted to continue his ministry very much. One can only hope that Paul's life did not end on such a sour and defeated note.

Titus:
A Dangerous and Stressful Assignment

I left you behind in Crete for this reason, so that you should put in order what
remained to be done; and should appoint elders in every town, as I directed you.

—Titus 1:5 NRSV

But as for you, teach what is consistent with sound doctrine.

—Titus 2:1 NRSV

INTRODUCTION

Most scholars choose to consider the pastoral letters a unit. Few take the time to consider Titus to be an independent letter. They reason that Titus is a condensation of 1 Timothy containing content from 2 Timothy and possibly Galatians, therefore its contents
have already been studied. It will be considered separately because of its distinctive
thoughts not found anywhere else in the New Testament.

PAUL AND REASONS FOR WRITING THE LETTER

The letter to Titus begins with a claim from its writer that he is a servant and an apostle for Christ who has a close relationship with a loyal child, Titus (1:1, 4). Paul, or a
person writing in his name, claims to have assigned Titus to Crete. His mission is to create an organizational structure for the communities (1:5) and to "silence" a successful
Christian (?) opposition that had chosen to keep the Jewish law. The location of the
writer is unknown, but there are hopes of a meeting with Titus in Nicopolis during the
winter (3:12).

TITUS, THE LOYAL CHILD

Similar to all of the other pastorals, the letter to Titus cannot be placed within the life
of Paul, so we do not know if Titus is the same one inferred in Acts and mentioned in
the Corinthian letters (Acts 15:2). According to these books, Titus was a close confident
of Paul's who tackled and solved problems at Corinth. Our first encounter with Titus was
in Galatians, where Paul tells the story of how he and Barnabas met with the elders in
Jerusalem early in his career (Gal. 3:1–3). Paul thought it was important to mention
that Titus was not circumcised. In 2 Corinthians, Titus is praised by Paul for his fund-

raising abilities and political expertise (2 Cor. 8:6; 7:5–16). Paul suggests that the Corinthians enjoyed his advice and company.

Little is revealed about the recipient of the letter to Titus. He is in Crete and is attempting to educate the people about the Pauline form of Christianity. The situation may be hostile. He knows Artemas and Tychicus, who may replace him (3:12), a lawyer, Zenas, and Apollos (3:13).

PROBLEMS AND ORGANIZATIONAL STRUCTURE

The situation in which Titus works is quite stressful. His goal is to bring order to the community (ies?) and harness a countermovement against the Pauline ministry. A list of a few of the major problems Titus must overcome follows:

1:5	There is a lack of organization.
1:11	People are making a profit from teaching a new religion.
1:14	Beliefs in Jewish myths and laws are dominating some members.
3:1	There may be some type of civil insurrection.

The organizational structure of elders, bishops, and so on, implies in each descriptive category that there are social problems at all levels within the community. What follows are the categories and summaries of lists of experiences or personal attributes required for each position. It appears that the structure is once again male dominated and hierarchical.

The Organizational Structure

Elders (1:5–6)	Bishop (1:7–10)	Older Men (2:1–2)	Older Women (3:1–3)
Blameless	Blameless	Temperate	Reverent in behavior
Married only once	Not arrogant	Serious	No slanderer
Children are believers	Not quick tempered	Prudent	No slave to drink
Not accused of sexual promiscuity	Not addicted to wine	Persistent	Teach what is good
Not rebellious	Not violent		Encourage younger women to love husbands
	Not greedy		
	Neighborly		
	Loves goodness		
	Prudent		
	Upright		
	Devout		
	Self-controlled		
	Understands "Word"		
	Good teacher		
	Good defender of the faith		

Younger Women (3:4–6)	**Younger Men** (3:6–8)	**Slaves** (3:9–10)
Love husbands	Self-controlled	Submit to master
Love children	Model of good work	Do not talk back
Self-controlled	Show integrity in teaching	Do not steal
Chaste	Good speech	Dedicated to master
Good manager of house		
Kind		
Submissive to husbands		

Notice that many elders are to be appointed, but only one bishop (the word is singular). Qualifications for an elder include marriage and children; neither is required for a bishop. Bishops, elders, and older men should be able to manage finances. Public displays of excessive drinking should be avoided by the bishop, older men, and women.

Younger women are given no instructions about their work within the community or in public life. The writer assumes that they will stay at home and take care of the house and children. They are to love God and submit to their husbands.

Young men are not told to love their wives or to take care of their homes. They are to control themselves and teach well. Slaves, similar to younger women, are urged to submit and remain loyal to their master. They are never to take what does not belong to them.

Literary and Theological Foundations

"Cretans were liars, brutes, and lazy gluttons" (1:12). This ethnic slur was probably taken from **Epimenides**, who lived during the seventh century B.C.E. in Crete. The writer of Titus continues his stereotypical denigration of the opposition in Crete by claiming that they are "detestable ... unfit for any good work" (1:16).

It is difficult to understand the reasons anyone would write such a demonizing letter. The writer may, once again, be threatened by the culture and prophets or teachers who are enjoying more success than he. His rigid view of ethnic origins and organizational hierarchy may be evidence that beliefs have crystallized into unarguable religious laws. Note that the writer encourages Titus to teach only "sound doctrine" (2:1). Bishops are to know the "word," preach "sound doctrine," and prove its validity to all who challenge it (1:9). If seekers will not listen to the Word, then the community must disassociate with them (3:10).

Winning over the opposition takes more than a frontal attack and flight if the opposition refuses an offer. Success takes patience, openness, and attentiveness to the social, emotional, and mental needs of a people. History has nothing to say about the success or failure of Titus in Crete.

Summary of Titus   Whoever wrote to Titus believed that the situation in Crete was on the verge of disaster. By firmly laying down social guidelines and relationships, which included submitting to authorities, the writer hoped for stability. Other strategies included verbal refutation of doctrines that did not fit into the Pauline concept of Christianity and disassociation with people who were harming the cause.

13

Struggling with a New Religion

Hebrews and James

Likewise, was not Rahab the prostitute also justified by works when she welcomed the messengers and sent them out by another road.

—James 2:25

By faith Rahab the prostitute did not perish with those who were disobedient, because she had received the spies in peace.

—Hebrews 11:31 NRSV

INTRODUCTION

Hebrews and James are two of the least-studied books within the Bible. Both appear to be written late in the first century and addressed to Jews. "To the Hebrews" was a title given to Hebrews, and James was intended for "The Twelve Tribes." Consequently, no one knows to whom the books were sent. Most consider their outlook univeral or general, written to everyone regardless of their sex, race, country, social standing, or title.

The books have many themes in common. They both attempt to use the genre of letter, and their authors are unknown. Both illustrate faith by pointing to Abraham and Rahab holding ancient Israelite traditions (LXX) as religiously authoritative. They both enjoy using metaphors from everyday life and may have originated as commentaries on particular chapters in the LXX. Scholars have detected the influence of multiple religious traditions in both texts. Each believes discipline is healthy for people and a sign of a relationship with the divine. They both tackle the sticky issues of public harassment for the new faith. Both recognize disunity and hope for harmony within the community, sharing a disdain for people who abuse power because of their wealth.

The journey that is about to begin will lead the reader into territory that is new and challenging. Hebrews and James have much to say to people who live in stressful times.

Hebrews:
A Sermon on Martyrdom

Therefore lift your drooping hands and strengthen your weak knees,
and make straight paths for your feet, so that what is lame may
not be out of joint, but rather healed.

—Heb. 12:12 NRSV

In your struggle against sin you have not yet resisted to the point of shedding
your blood. . . . Endure trials for the sake of discipline.

—Heb. 12:4, 7 NRSV

INTRODUCTION

Hebrews leads the reader through a labyrinth of argumentation. Be careful not to get lost or give up on the journey as you search its maze of tunnels. The profoundly poetic opening teases the reader to faithfully continue, when abruptly, ancient quotations intercede. Some may also have difficulty following the trail and relating to all of the references concerning the Hebrew sacrificial system. Keep on reading, however. Hebrews has many doorways and surprises.

Hebrews is unique in the New Testament. Whoever wrote the book felt compelled to prove that Jesus was superior to all Jewish traditions, people, rituals, even the angels. The argument alternates between proving the excellence of Jesus and giving practical advice for listeners or readers. (One wonders if two different sermons were intermingled.)

The local situation was dangerous. Christians had been abandoning the faith because of continued abuse by the community or government. Some died and others may have faced their own executions. The writer hopes that they will return to their faith, realizing that the abuse they have experienced is a divine form of discipline. He warns them that once they turn away, they can never "repent" or return, but if they do return, they have hopes of entering the "rest."

AUTHORSHIP, LOCATION, AUDIENCE, AND DATE

The old King James Bible begins this book with the title "The Epistle of Paul the Apostle to the Hebrews." Yet even a first-time reader will conclude that the structure, argumentation, vocabulary, and general tone of the work does not fit into a Pauline style. **Jerome**, who lived during the fourth century C.E., wrote the following about Hebrews and Paul:

> The epistle which is called the Epistle to the Hebrews is not considered his [Paul's], on account of its difference from the others in style and language, but it is reckoned, either according to Tertullian to be the work of Barnabas, or according to others to be by Luke the Evangelist or Clement afterwards bishop of the church at Rome, who, they say, arranged and adorned the ideas of Paul in his own language, though to be sure, since Paul was writing to Hebrews and was in disrepute among them he may have omitted his name from the salutation on this account. He being a Hebrew wrote Hebrew, that is his own tongue and most fluently while the things which were eloquently written in Hebrew were more eloquently turned into Greek and this is the reason why it seems to differ from other epistles of Paul. (Jerome, in Schaff and Wace, 1956, vol 3., 363.)

The elegant Greek and sophisticated vocabulary are closer to Luke-Acts, although many scholars point to similarities in content with Colossians and 1 Peter. Some compare Hebrews with the Gospel of John and wonder if there is a possible connection between the two.

In spite of all of these points of contact, the name of the author/ess of Hebrews has been lost within the pages of time. But this has not prevented scholars from speculating about who might have written this book. Some suggested writers include Epaphras, Apollos, Priscilla, Mary, the Mother of Jesus, Clement of Rome, Barnabas, Silas, and others. Almost 100 years ago, Adolph Harnack theorized that Hebrews was written by Priscilla with her husband Aquila. They were well educated, ran a house church, and hailed from Rome. The dual author theory is based on the use of "we" and "I" so often used in Hebrews (see chapters 2–13). Her name was probably erased from the title, as were many other females.

Robert Jewett, in a *Letter to Pilgrims*, describes a complicated theory that suggests that Hebrews is the lost letter to Laodicea written by Epaphras, which is mentioned in Colossians (Col. 4:16). Both Colossians and Hebrews were written to people who lived in the Lycus Valley. He finds many similarities between the two books, including the following:

Colossians	Hebrews	Similarities
2:16	13:9	Issues over food
2:16	9:1–28	Problems with religious festivals
2:18	1:4	Worship of angels
2:15	2:14	Disarming of or destroying angelic beings
1:15	1:3	An image of an invisible god
1:16	1:2	A created hierarchy
1:7	1:3	A pantheistic view of God
1:18	1:4–2:9	Christ is preeminent or superior to all

None of the above theories has been accepted by the majority of scholars. Neither can they agree on to whom the book was sent or whether or not it was a letter. It looks like a letter because it ends with a closing, but it has no return address or salutation. The contents suggests that it was a homily, speech, or sermon (a treatise) that later became an encyclical sent to many Christian groups. Note how often the writer uses words that suggest it was originally in the form of a speech. No one knows who heard or read this book for the first time. Suggestions of recipients include former Essene priests or members of Qumran, Jewish Christians outside of Jerusalem, and Gentile Christians. Locations include Rome, Alexandria in Egypt, Antioch, Corinth, Jerusalem, Ephesus, Colossae, Samaria, Cyprus, Bithynia, Pontus, and more.

Some want to place the origin of the work during the lifetime of Paul, because Timothy is mentioned at the end of the letter. They argue that it appears that the temple in Jerusalem was still functioning. Roman soldiers had not yet burned it to the ground. This would make the date of Romans prior to 70 C.E., but the Christian group described in the book was not the original eyewitness of Jesus. It seems to be of a later generation, so the dating of the book should be later. The consensus is that the writing of Hebrews took place somewhere between 70 C.E. and 120 C.E.

REASONS FOR CREATING HEBREWS

Thomas G. Long, in *Hebrews,* attempts to characterize the people who received Hebrews, from a minister's point of view.

> His congregation is exhausted. They are tired—tired of serving, . . . tired of worship, . . . tired of being peculiar and whispered about in society, tired of the spiritual struggle, . . . tired even of Jesus. Their hands droop and their knees are weak (12:12), attendance is down . . . (10:25), and they are losing confidence. The threat to this congregation is not that they are charging off in the wrong direction; they do not have enough energy to charge off anywhere. The threat here is that, worn down and worn out, they will drop their end

of the rope and drift away. Tired of walking the walk, many of them are considering taking a walk, [and] leaving the community. . . . (Long 1997, p. 3)

The people to whom Hebrews was designed were having second thoughts about their religion. They had experienced or were presently experiencing a public backlash of conversion. Some were imprisoned, and others saw their belongings stolen or destroyed (10:32–35). They had believed that the end of time was approaching, the Parousia, and they were disappointed (10:25). Some of the original founders had died (martyred?) (2:3; 13:7). There are questions about the meaning of the death of Jesus, relationship to angels, food regulations (kosher?) (13:9), and public policy issues (13:17). The price to pay for such associations with Christians was too much. As the enthusiasm of the converts cooled, they began to ignore the meetings (10:25).

Robert Jewett, in *Letter to Pilgrims,* again theorizes about the reasons for the problems among the people who received Hebrews. He suggests that the violence they had experienced pushed them away from Christianity into a religion that believed that hostile angels were now ruling the earth. They began following the Israelite rituals of sacrifice to destroy the forces and protect themselves in the future. They may even have believed that they could be transformed into powerful beings who could protect humans from the angels.

Whatever the source of the problems, the writer of Hebrews seeks to encourage and comfort these embattled converts with assurances that their God is the best and that he will not abandon them. Jesus, as a human, has suffered as they have suffered. Rituals, sacrifice, angels, and more pale in the sight of their God. The writer's emphasis on discipline and endurance of harassment, (12:1–3), his preoccupation with the sacrificial system, and his warnings about the end of time may be preparing them for or helping them to avoid their own untimely deaths (martyrdom) (6:4–6). He offers them the opportunity of entering the "rest" (chapter 4). In a run through Hebrew history, the writer champions the faithful and hopes that they too will be among the valiant who did not lose hope (Heb. 11).

COMMUNITY ISSUE: FINANCES

The writer of Hebrews may be facing a budget shortfall. If people are staying away from the meetings, then logically, so is their money. He appears to be concerned about the use of and donations of money on several fronts. He warns the readers about the love of and lust over money (13:5) and urges them to help their neighbors (13:16). Several times he mentions that priests received tithes. He may be indirectly criticizing his readers for their lack of financial support. A tithe is usually considered a sacral tax of one-tenth of a person's yearly earnings. According to Hebrews, Abraham gave Melchizedeck one-tenth of everything he owned and all the booty he collected in wars (7:2, 4). Future generations of Levites collected tithes (7:5). Did the converts who read or heard Hebrews also donate a tithe?

PROMINENT CHARACTERS

Jesus

The entire book of Hebrews revolves around the significance of Jesus' death as a perfect sacrifice for all. The writer argues that Jesus is better than angels, Moses, high priests, Melchizedek, the old covenant, the tent, and the sacrifice. Hebrews repeatedly makes the implicit comparison of Jesus to an animal chosen to be sacrificed. He is perfect, set apart, and willingly assumes (or submits to) his death. See Figure 13.1 for an artist's view of the ancient tabernacle.

The writer of Hebrews portrays a dual universe where the temple, sacrifices, and priests are only shadows of the true reality, which is in heaven with Jesus and God. Priests in ancient Israel were chosen from the tribe of Levi and later from the ancestral line of Aaron. Jesus was from the house of Judah (Heb. 7:14), which means that he did not qualify to be a priest. Yet according to the writer, his priesthood supersedes the Levites in terms of eternal effectiveness. Jesus is similar to Melchizedek. Melchizedek was a priest who had no known mother or father, no family line, and was a priest who represented all people (Heb. 7). In much the same way, Jesus administers for all, but his work is perfect and lasts forever.

We have read how Paul and others explain the meaning of Jesus' death, but the writer of Hebrews uses unique and thought-provoking descriptions. The list of terms that follows attempts to capture the significance of Jesus.

Pioneer of salvation	2:10
He has power over death.	2:11–16
Apostle and high priest	3:1
Forerunner	6:20
He has power of an indestructible life.	7:16
A guarantee of a better covenant	7:22
Holy, blameless, undefiled, exalted	7:26
Minister	8:2
Pioneer and perfecter of faith	12:2

Underlying the theme of the sacrifice and heavenly work of Jesus may be an attempt by the writer, as we have indicated earlier, to help people face their own death. Jesus is a pioneer and forerunner. He led the way to the end of this life and the hopeful beginning of another. Converts are called holy partners, partners, brothers and sisters, serving saints, and imitators (3:1, 14; 6:4, 12). All of these descriptions indicate a solidarity of purpose with Jesus. People are even urged to become perfect (6:1). Is the writer asking them to follow Jesus down the road of sacrifice and death? Is he asking them to die for their faith?

Perhaps those to whom Hebrews was intended were being arrested and imprisoned for their faith. History records that Christians died horrible deaths in coliseums with glad-

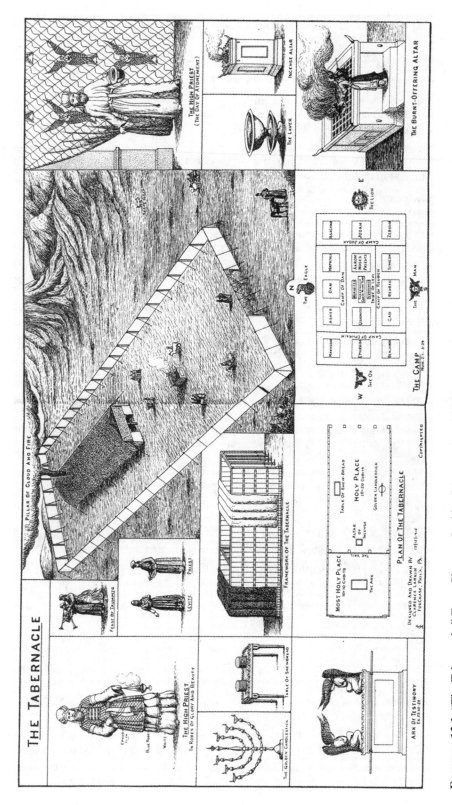

FIGURE 13.1 "The Tabernacle." From Clarence Larkin, *Dispensational Truth.* (Philadelphia: Rev. Clarence Larkin Est., 1918).

iators and wild animals. We know also of testimonies such as the *Martyrdom of Poly-carp,* where Christians believed that it was better to die than to renounce their faith. But the recipients of Hebrews appear to be renouncing their faith. They were warned several times that there was no going back. They could not repeat the act of repentance (6:4). Some of the chilling words follow:

> In your struggle against sin you have not yet resisted to the point of shedding your blood. . . . Endure trials for the sake of discipline. (12:4, 7)

> Remember those who are in prison, as though you were in prison with them; those who are being tortured, as though you yourselves are being tortured. (13:3)

> [Y]ou endured a hard struggle with sufferings, sometimes being publicly exposed to abuse and persecution, and sometimes being partners with those so treated. For you had compassion for those who were in prison, and you cheerfully accepted the plundering of your possessions, knowing that you yourselves possessed something better and more lasting. (NRSV) (10:32f)

In describing the faith of the ancestors, the writer becomes specific. Are these the stories of historic Israelites, or is the writer describing the actual situation of his listeners or readers?

> And what more should I say? For time would fail me to tell of . . . who through faith conquered kingdoms, administered justice, obtained promises, shut the mouths of lions, quenched raging fire, escaped the edge of the sword, won strength out of weakness, became mighty in war, put foreign armies to flight. Women received their dead by resurrection. Others were tortured, refusing to accept release, in order to obtain a better resurrection. Others suffered mocking and flogging, and even chains and imprisonment. They were stoned to death, they were sawn in two, they were killed by the sword; they went about in skins of sheep and goats, destitute, persecuted, tormented—of whom the world was not worthy. (Heb. 11:38 NRSV)

Whatever the actual intention of the writer, Hebrews helps readers understand that their beliefs in Jesus will last forever. Jesus will not leave them in life or in death. After one life, there is only one death. They will not have to repeat their miserable existence again (9:27).

The Living God

Hebrews argues that the very same God whom converts were presently worshiping was the impetus behind the prophets of Israel, the cultic sacrificial system, and even Melchizedek. Like a nonstop radio signal, God sends out messages to people in various ways. For instance, the Hebrew Bible is the spoken word of God, and most recently God has communicated through Jesus, his son (2:2).

The writer implores the reader to recognize that this God is living, just, peaceful, makes oaths that will never be broken, and is the one who is speaking to them now

(3:12; 9:14; 6:10; 12:25). In chapter 12, Hebrews describes Mount Zion or the City of the Living God. It includes angels, the assembly of the firstborn, spirits of the righteous, Jesus, God, and sprinkled blood (12:22–24).

Women

While some theorize that Priscilla and Aquila created Hebrews, others think Hebrews advocates a male-centered religion. They find little evidence of women in the work. Sarah, Rahab, the mother of Melchizedek, Pharaoh's daughter, and women who received the dead are females who find their way into the sermon.

Mary Rose D'Angelo, professor of the New Testament at Villanova University, thinks that the writer of Hebrews intentionally omitted the contributions of women. For example, the Hebrew Bible says that the mother of Moses hid Moses in order to protect him (Exodus 2:2). The Septuagint changes it to his "parents" hid him, but Hebrews says that his "fathers" protected him. ("Fathers" is incorrectly translated as "parents" by the NRSV Bible.) Also, in the lists of famous faithful judges, Deborah, who led the forces against Sisera (Judges 4), and Jael (Judges 4), who saved the day for everyone, are left out of the list. But Barak, who would not fight without Deborah's help, Jepthah, who sacrificed his own daughter (Judges 11), and Samson, whose life ended in utter failure (Judges 16), are immortalized.

D'Angelo also questions the all-male representation of the divine and wonders how a woman can imitate becoming a son. She is critical of the emphasis on violence as a means of discipline and correlates it with child abuse and wife beating. She suggests that the image of a male-only priesthood has been used to keep women from becoming ordained and from serving in churches for centuries.

While most of the book of Hebrews offers little advice for women, D'Angelo concludes that it does possess **androgynous** images that apply to everyone. She points to the emphasis placed on the humanity and priesthood of Jesus, which is patterned after Melchizedek. She argues that the priesthood and sacrifice have been replaced by a hope for a new transforming community.

LITERARY FOUNDATIONS

Hebrews is filled with quotations from ancient Israelite traditions. Many of them are taken from the Septuagint, but several other quotations or paraphrases differ from both the LXX and the MT or Hebrew Bible. This suggests that either the writer was quoting Scripture from memory or that there were other available versions of the Bible during the first century that did not survive into the twenty-first century. For instance, an example of a verse in the Septuagint, and the Hebrew Bible (MT), and then used by the writer of Hebrews, follows.

Psalm 22:22

Hebrew Text (MT)	Septuagint (21:23) (LXX)	Hebrews 2:12
I will tell of your name to my brothers and sisters; in the midst of the church I will praise you.	I will lift up your name to my brothers, in the midst of the church I will praise you.	I will proclaim [apostello] your name to my brothers and sisters, in the midst of the church I will praise you.

The writer of Hebrews changes the first Greek word in the sentence to reflect his new-found faith. He uses "apostello," which is a technical word for sending out people as apostles.

The Hebrews writer believes that the words of the Hebrew Scriptures came from God, Jesus, and the Holy Spirit. And those Scriptures were written with Jesus in mind. He even claims that Jesus spoke words found in the Hebrew Bible. For instance, the earlier quotation from Psalms is attributed to Jesus, along with another quote from Isaiah.

> For Jesus is not ashamed to call them brothers and sisters, saying, (1) "I will proclaim your name to my brothers and sisters, in the midst of the congregation I will praise you." And again, (2) "I will put my trust in him." And again, (3) "Here am I and the children whom God has given me." (2:12–13) (Numbers (2) and (3) are quoted from Isaiah 8:17–18.)

His method of **prooftexting** shows little concern for the historical situation or original intention of the passages in the Hebrew Scriptures. For instance, he applies Jeremiah's prophesies of a new Israel to Jesus himself in Heb. 8:8–12. Addresses to kings of Israel in Psalm 2:7 and 110:1 found in Heb. 1:5–13 are directed toward Jesus.

Almost all of the quotations from the Psalms are used to prove the identity and purpose of Jesus' life. He often takes two dissimilar Scriptures from different books and places them together, as though the source were common (see 10:37–38, taken from Isa. 26:20 and Hab. 2:3–4). While images from the Torah intertwine throughout the argument, proving Jesus more perfect than the old sacrificial system, the writer quotes more often from later Jewish writings than from the law.

Scholars have studied Hebrews in relation to Philo of Alexandria, a Hellenistic Jew who interpreted the Bible allegorically, the Dead Sea Scrolls, Stoicism, Platonism, and other Jewish and Greek mystical writings. Their goal was to determine if the writings influenced Hebrews. A consensus about whether or not Hebrews used the aforementioned as sources has not evolved.

Most scholars agree that the syncretistic age in which the writer lived helped produce his style. While Hebrews sometimes sounds like Philo, includes language about Temple worship found in the Dead Sea Scrolls, and contains a dualistic philosophy foundational to both Greek and Jewish schools, the writer is much less complicated, preferring to use simple metaphors such as farming (6:7); the home (3:6); and athletic games (12:1) as well as typology.

Jesus is viewed as a type of sacrifice, place of sacrifice, high priest, priest, and more. A type, as we discovered earlier in this text, is an interpretative method of correspondence. An event, a person, or a belief parallels others from a different time period. Sometimes we also use typology today when we speak of sports figures, actors, or even automobiles. They become types of earlier models, and we can speculate about the similarities between the two.

And finally, the masterful Greek used by the writer employs literary devices that lose their poetic power when translated into English. Entire books have been written on the writer's use of **inclusio**, alliteration, assonance, chiasm, and several other rhetorical strategies.

Summary of Hebrews   Early Christians believed Paul wrote the book of Hebrews, but its style, content, and excellent Greek point to an unknown author. It may have been written between 70–120 C.E., somewhere in the Roman Empire where people were losing their lives or facing physical abuse because of their faith.

The writer attempts to prove the superiority of Jesus to the angels, Moses, the ancient Israelite sacrificial system, and more. For him, God is living and will not abandon those who choose to worship this ancient being. Advice is given on food, money, entering the rest, and returning to the faith. Some suggest that his point of view is sexist. They wonder how females fit into an all-male view of God and religious hierarchy.

The literary foundations of Hebrews are enormous. The writer appears to be influenced by allegorical, dualistic, and mystical interpretative strategies. He prefers to use metaphors, typology, and to quote the Psalms, making changes in the text as needed. It is possible that he used a version of the Old Testament/Hebrew Bible that has been lost.

The writer of Hebrews seeks to instill in his readers/listeners a hope. They must place their faith in Jesus who, like them, has suffered. He has been sacrificed on their behalf, and that sacrifice will allow them to enter the "rest" forever.

James:
An Egalitarian Philosophy of Life

You do well if you really fulfill the royal law according to the scripture,
'You shall love your neighbor as yourself.' But if you show partiality,
you commit sin and are convicted by the law as transgressors.

—James 2:8–9 NRSV

INTRODUCTION

James presents the reader with a series of thoughts about living an equitable religious life within a community. The text must be read several times before its themes begin to emerge. Probably the most relevant theme for modern Americans is its de-emphasis on materialism. In our culture, the pursuit of money and success occupies whole lifetimes. Millions spend their time worshiping Wall Street and the Dow Jones averages.

James attacks wealthy landowners for their misuse of power. They exploit the workforce and demand their way, even if it means going to court. He is tired of the jealousy between neighbors that has resulted in murder. He reminds them of their undisciplined emotions that often are unleashed as verbal abuse on others. The deference toward the rich, who enjoy flaunting their wealth, is appalling. Instead of being friends with God, people are friends with the world. They have bought into the ideas of competition, money, and success. The results have been disastrous to community living.

James urges these self-centered people to think of others. If there is any such thing as faith, then it must be active. Reaching out to others who need help is a sign that faith is alive and working.

AUTHOR, DATE, AND RECIPIENTS

The author of James is unknown. The only clue we have to his/her identity is found within the text itself. He was a teacher (3:1), had excellent credentials in Greek language and philosophy, studied the LXX, and was familiar with wisdom, prophetical, and historical writings within ancient Judaism.

The name "James" is mentioned over forty times in the New Testament. Five distinct characters deserve consideration as possible authors.

The Author of James?

1. James, the son of Zebedee; killed around 44 C.E.   Mark 1:19; Acts 12:12
2. James, the son of Alphaeus; a disciple.   Mark 3:18

3. James, the brother of Jesus	Mark 6:3; 1 Cor. 15:7; Gal 1:19; Acts 12:17, and so on
4. James the Younger, son of Mary	Mark 15:40; 16:1; Jude 1
5. James, father of Judas; a disciple.	Luke 6:16; Acts 1:13

Most researchers agree that if the author of James is mentioned in the New Testament, it must be the brother of Jesus. He would have been well known because of his work in Jerusalem as the leader of the early Judeo-Christian community. He was the main speaker at the Jerusalem Council in Acts 12, which welcomed Paul while offering guidelines for non-Jewish converts to Christianity. Yet others argue that the Book of James offers little evidence of a personal relationship with Jesus. If James the brother of Jesus wrote James, why does he not mention Jesus' life, death, and the Resurrection?

The question of the authorship of James also depends on when the book was written and who received it. It appears to be a letter, but it is really a collection of wise sayings, interpretations, and ethical guidelines addressed to the "Twelve Tribes of the Dispersion." Who are the Twelve Tribes? Could they be God fearers? Is it a veiled reference to a new Israel or a new Christian community, or is it a letter written by a Jew to other Jews? If it is Jewish, then why is it contained in the New Testament? Some argue that the book or letter is not Christian. There are only two references to Jesus in 1:1 and 2:1, which could have been added so the book would be acceptable for Christians.

For centuries, both the Eastern and Western churches debated whether or not James was a Christian document. Many suggested that its emphasis on behavior rather than a simple faith was antithetical to the Pauline tradition, and therefore to the heart of Christian belief. And Martin Luther, in the sixteenth century, argued against its inclusion in the canon because of its legalistic approach to living a Christian life.

Those who contend that James is a Jewish work point to the use of the word "synagogue" for a meeting place (2:2); the quotation "God is One" (2:19), which indicates a radical monotheism (2:19); the view of the Old Testament law as an authority for religious living (1:25; 2:8,11, etc.); and the examples of faithful believers are all ancient Israelites (2:21–25, etc.) Most types of ethical guidelines encouraged by the writer may be found within the **wisdom** or **prophetic tradition** of Judaism. James also omits the Pauline idea of justification by faith. Work or performing social acts of kindness becomes an indicator of a person's commitment to religion.

On the other side of the argument are those who defend James as a Christian book. They point to the references to Jesus, an allusion to baptism (2:7), a belief in the second coming (5:7), and the use of a Greek word "church" for a meeting place (5:14). James includes sayings that are also found in the Synoptics. These similarities suggest that it predates the gospels. (It could also be argued that James used the Synoptics as a source, or that they both used the same source.)

Tradition suggests that the brother of Jesus died around 60 C.E. If James, the brother of Jesus, wrote the book, then it would have been pre-Pauline, which would date it in the early 40s C.E. This early date would account for the Jewish nature of the work. During the lifetime of James, as we have read in Acts, Christians worshiped in homes and at the temple. They struggled with the issues of how much of the Jewish law should be kept and what kind of lifestyles were acceptable within the new religion gathered in the name of a risen Jesus.

Yet the majority of scholars today treat James as though it were an anonymous work intended for a "catholic" or universal audience. They suggest that the dating of it could be as late as the third century C.E. but generally place its origin around the end of the first century C.E. Based on historical inquiry, scholars have determined that it is not in the Muratorian Canon; neither was it quoted by any early Christian writer until the third century C.E.

GENRE OF JAMES

The genre of James is mixed and defies definition or categorization. Although the first verse of James appears to be an introduction to a letter, it does not follow the pattern of a letter. Some have characterized it as a collection of ethical teachings or a letter-essay. Throughout the work, the writer asks multiple questions. A few follow:

2:1   [D]o you with your acts of favoritism really believe in our Lord Jesus Christ?
2:4   [H]ave you not made distinctions among yourselves, and become judged with evil thoughts?
3:13 Who is wise and understanding among you?
4:14 What is your life?
5:13 Are you among the suffering? Are any cheerful? Are any among you sick?

These questions and answers may indicate that the ancient form of a **diatribe** is being used. A diatribe was an argument between teacher and pupil, which attempted to prove a single thesis. Yet one clear thesis has not emerged in James.

REASONS FOR WRITING THE BOOK OF JAMES

If James, the brother of Jesus, knew Paul, several researchers contend that James was written to discredit Paul's view of faith. For the writer of James, internalized faith that never touches the behavior of people is not faith. Faith must have some external signs of good will and care for the community.

This James may not have known Paul, but he may have been writing to people who were internalizing their faith. They may have had a more mystical orientation to the divine or, because of economic or political fears, they may have hidden their faith. The Christian faith had not changed the way they lived their lives. The writer points out that a faith that is not known or does not move the community in a more equitable and caring direction is dead.

COMMUNITY ISSUES

Social Stratification

Conversion to a new religion can change the very basis of a town's economics. Consider the story of Artemis of Ephesus in the Acts of the Apostles. Demetrius, the silversmith, was threatened with the loss of revenues for statues of Artemis when Christianity began to become more popular (Acts 19:23–41). The people who received the Book of James were having all sorts of problems regarding money and the influence, power, and status that wealth can bring. Consider the following quotations:

1:9   Let the believer who is lowly boast in being raised up, and the rich in being brought low, because the rich will disappear like a flower in the field . . . in the midst of a busy life, they will wither away.

3:14f   But if you have bitter envy and selfish ambition in your hearts, do not be boastful and false to the truth. . . . For where there is envy and selfish ambition, there will also be disorder and wickedness of every kind.

2:6   But you have dishonored the poor. Is it not the rich who oppress you? Is it not they who drag you into court?

4:2   You want something and do not have it; so you commit murder. And you covet something and cannot obtain it; so you engage in disputes and conflicts.

4:13   Come now, you who say, "Today or tomorrow we will go to such and such a town and spend a year there, doing business and making money."

5:1f   Come now, you rich people, weep and wail for the miseries that are coming to you. Your riches have rotted, and your clothes are moth-eaten. . . . The wages of the laborers who mowed your fields, which you kept back by fraud, cry out, and the cries of the harvesters have reached the ears of the Lord of hosts. . . . You have condemned and murdered the righteous one, who does not resist you. (NRSV)

James argues for social and economic equality. There were people within the Christian community who had experienced discrimination and exploitation by the wealthy. The landowners had taken advantage of the workers and deprived them of wages. They were even taken to court. Some of these wealthy business people could also have been Christians. Affluent people wore their success on their sleeves, with brassy jewelry and expensive clothing. These flashy people were treated with more honor and respect than the people whose clothing may have needed to be washed and ironed.

Not only were people partisan, they were also greedy. This hot pursuit of economic power resulted in fights, even murder. James calls them "adulterers" because they are in love with the world and not God (4:4). Their hearts are divided, or they are double minded (1:8).

The answer to these social problems is found within the concept of group solidarity and single-minded devotion. They must be sensitive to the economic plight of others and must help them (2:15–17). This help may include food, clothing, and the typical Christian rituals of praying, singing, and anointing the sick (5:13–15). The wealthy must stop their exploitation and abuse of the poor. To those who crave economic power,

James asks that they dedicate their lives to God (4:7). To the poor, he points them to the example of Job and the hope of the end of time, the Parousia (5:7–10). He says all hardships can produce positive results in one's life (1:2f), so one should welcome them.

Conflict Management

Disputes over the accumulation and sharing of wealth have produced heated debates, according to the Book of James. People have a tendency to let their emotions control them (3:1f). Apparently, some of the teachers have misspoken on important beliefs or issues. Others have responded with abusive speech. James encourages the people to recognize that everyone is human and makes mistakes. He hopes that they will discipline their speech by practicing the wisdom of relationships geared toward gentleness and peace (3:13–18).

Egalitarian Organization

After reading the letters attributed to Paul, which outline a strong and rigid hierarchical community organization, it may be refreshing to read a book that is unconcerned with qualifications for management. Only two offices are mentioned in passing in James, that of a teacher and an elder (5:14). James described their duties without reference to gender, economic, or ethnic limitations.

LITERARY STRATEGIES

Structure

Many scholars have attempted to discover the structure or outline of James. Its apparently haphazard arrangement of material has made the task difficult. **Patrick J. Hartin**, a professor at the University of South Africa, Pretoria, in *James and the Q Sayings of Jesus,* suggests that there are four broad themes in James that are repeated throughout the book (Hartin, 1993, 29–30). What do you think?

Topical Structure of James

A   Rich and Poor
B   Doers of the Word
C   Speech
D   Wisdom
D   Wisdom
C   Speech

B   Doers of the World

A   Rich and Poor

Others suggest that there is no organization in James. Some think James was created as a commentary on Lev. 19:13–17. Can you detect similarities between the following verses and those of James?

Leviticus and James

You shall not defraud your neighbor; you shall not steal; and you shall not keep for yourself the wages of a laborer until morning. You shall not revile the deaf or put a stumbling block before the blind; you shall fear your God; I am the Lord.

You shall not render an unjust judgment; you shall not be partial to the poor or defer to the great: with justice you shall judge your neighbor. You shall not go around as a slanderer among your people, and you shall not profit by the blood of your neighbor: I am the Lord.

You shall not hate in your heart anyone of your kin; you shall reprove your neighbor, or you will incur guilt yourself. You shall not take vengeance or bear a grudge against any of your people, but you shall love your neighbor as yourself: I am the Lord. (Lev. 18:13–17 NRSV)

Most agree that James is a collection of wise sayings, paraphrases, and commentaries that do not have a central theme.

Relationship to Other Literature

James sounds similar to many other types of literature in the ancient world. Anyone who has studied classical works would find echoes of many of the themes of the literature. Scholars have done extensive studies to determine where the writer obtained the contents of James. To date, no one has uncovered a single source for James. Using the LXX as his Scripture, the writer draws ideas and phrases from Greek, Jewish, and Christian philosophies and religions. A list of some of the works that have been compared to James follows.

The Dead Sea Scrolls

Proverbs and Wisdom Literature

Greek and Roman Philosophical Literature
   (Such as: Seneca, Plato, Epictetus, Aristotle, Plutarch)

Testament of Twelve Patriarchs

1 Clement

Didache

Shepherd of Hermas

The Synoptics and Q

The Writing Prophets

1 Peter, Hebrews

Christian Influences

There is an amazing similarity between James and the Synoptics. What follows is a comparison to the Gospel of Matthew, although we could have used examples from the Gospel of Luke or Q.

James	Matthew
1:5 If any of you is lacking in wisdom ask God, who gives to all generously and ungrudgingly, and it will be given to you.	7:7 Ask, and it will be given to you, search, and you will find; knock, and the door will be opened to you.
4:12 There is only one lawgiver and judge who is able to save and to destroy. So who, then, are you to judge your neighbor?	7:1 Do not judge, so that you may not be judged.
5:12 Above all, my beloved, do not swear, either by heaven or by earth or by any other oath, but let your "Yes" be yes and your "No" be no, so that you may not fall under condemnation.	5:34f But I say to you, Do not swear at all, either by heaven, for it is the throne of God, or by the earth. . . . Let your word be 'Yes, Yes,' or 'No, No'; anything more than this comes from the evil one.
3:18 And a harvest of righteousness is sown in peace for those who make peace.	5:9 Blessed are the peacemakers, for they will be called children of God.

James also appears to have knowledge of other books in the New Testament, including Romans, Galatians, Ephesians, Colossians, Hebrews, and 1 Peter.

Judaism and the Ancient Israelite Traditions

There are many similarities between James and the wisdom and prophetic traditions within the ancient Hebrew Scriptures. A select list of similar topics found in Proverbs follows.

James	Proverbs
1:26 If any think they are religious, and do not bridle their tongues but deceive their hearts, their religion is worthless.	12:18 Rash words are like the sword thrusts, but the tongue of the wise brings healing.
2:12 So speak and so act as those who are to be judged by the law of liberty.	15:1 A soft answer turns away wrath, but a harsh word stirs up anger.
5:9 Beloved, do not grumble against one another, so that you may not be judged.	18:2 A fool takes no pleasure in understanding, but only in expressing personal opinion.

Luke Timothy Johnson, in *The Letter of James,* finds many similarities between James and the prophetic tradition in the Old Testament. A list of their common topics found in James and verses found in Isaiah, Jeremiah, Amos, Hosea, and Ezekiel follows.

> Suffering has benefit.
> Condemning the rich.
> The fleeting moments of life.
> Religion is visiting orphans, widows, and the sick.
> No friendship with the world.
> Adultery is a symbol of separation or breaking the covenant with God.
> Return or convert to a friendship with God.

Greek Philosophy and Religions

Throughout the book of James, we learn of religious beliefs, attitudes, and behaviors. Some of that tradition was drawn from popular Greek religion and philosophy. Note how often the writer refers to nature.

> 3:6   Cycle of nature
> 3:5   Forest fire
> 4:14 Mist
> 1:6   Wind tossed like a wave in the sea
> 1:17 Looks to the lights, astronomical (see also "hosts" in 5:4)

Rather than referring to Christianity or Judaism, James addresses the topic of a nondescript "religion." "Religion that is pure and undefiled before God, the Father, is this: to care for orphans and widows in their distress, and to keep oneself unstained by the world" (1:26). This phrase is so general that it could have originated with many different religious traditions. We have already discussed James' love for nature, but note also his interest in athletic games, riding horses, sailing, and metallurgy.

PROMINENT CHARACTERS

James believes that God is a positive force in the lives of his readers and implies that they have direct access to God. How they treat their neighbors is a reflection of their relationship with God. They have a special connection with their Creator who has placed the "Word" inside of them (1:18; 1:21; 4:5). This friendship is maintained if they do not make friends with the world (4:4). Wisdom or the ability to act out faith in a way that benefits everyone finds its source in God (1:5). Disrespect for God is played out in verbal abuse of and arrogance toward others (2:5–6; 3:9). All that is good comes from God (1:17), and people should consider his wishes when planning the future (4:13f).

The only other characters mentioned in James include Abraham, **Job**, Rahab, and **Elijah** the prophet. Job is used as an example of endurance (5:11), and Elijah demonstrates the power over nature when a human is in touch with the divine (5:17). Abraham and Rahab are listed as examples of people whose behavior announced their faith (2:21, 25).

Sharyn Dowd, associate professor of the New Testament at Lexington Theological Seminary, in *The Women's Bible Commentary,* summarizes some of the popular Jewish legends about Rahab that are not found in the Scriptures.

> Legend had it that she was exceptionally beautiful, that she was a prophet, that she married Joshua, and that among her descendants were Jeremiah and Ezekiel. She was regarded as the archetypal convert to Yahwism. (Dowd 1993, 369)

Although Abraham is considered the founder of Judaism, he was actually the first convert. Both he and Rahab represent certain types of outsiders who performed unusual acts of faith or trust that merited their use by James.

Summary of James   James presents the reader with many great ideas but little organizational form. It was probably written by someone using the name of James. Dates of composition range from the 40s C.E. to 250 C.E. Many question whether the book is Christian, claiming Jewish sources and points of view.

James fits no particular form in ancient times, but some have suggested that it is either a letter-essay or a diatribe. We do not know to whom this book was addressed, so there is no consensus on the goals of the writer. Some think it is a sermon based on Leviticus 19. People to whom James was written may have had an internalized faith or may have been facing public harassment for their faith. Their choice was to "hide" their faith, and James disagrees with their choices. Many suggest James was writing to combat Paul's emphasis on "faith" only. James believes that faith must result in concrete benefits to others.

Unlike the radical concept of egalitarianism taught in Acts 2, James believes that the wealthy and healthy should voluntarily help others. He hopes for the birth of an egalitarian attitude and organization.

James has affinities with Jewish, Christian, and Greek religious writings. The God of James could be the God of any religion. He is viewed as a best friend who cares about the welfare of others

14

Documents to Friends
in Far-Away Places

1 and 2 Peter and Jude

May grace and peace be yours in abundance.

—1 Peter 1:2 NRSV

INTRODUCTION

The books—1, 2, Peter, and Jude—have traditionally been categorized as **catholic** Epistles because their messages seemed to be designed for a worldwide audience. While all three authors claim to have personal contacts with Jesus, those assertions seem doubtful. All of the books were written to people who were in trouble, so the reading may not be as uplifting as some of the other letters we have studied.

Some of the readers, even the writers, were suffering physically, emotionally, and mentally because of their faith. Local congregations were feeling growth pains, and with it, the indecisiveness and tension that accompany change. Should they maintain authoritarian and hierarchical traditions, or should the organization be more congregational (or democratic)? There were questions about the efficacy of baptism, about how to hold love feasts, about the future and where it would leave people, and about personal sexual relationships. New popular teachers were reinterpreting the traditions of the apostles. A rigorous ascetic discipline may have been replaced by an emphasis on personal freedom. The issue of finances or revenue was a sticking point. While the problems appear real for the recipients, the letters often couch recommendations or criticisms in metaphorical or symbolic language. Even noncanonical fables, unfamiliar to modern audiences, are quoted in 2 Peter and Jude. We can only guess at the meanings and hope that we have faithfully re-created their messages.

1 Peter:
Suffering, Sacrifice, and Baptism

Resist him, steadfast in your faith, for you know that your
brothers and sisters in all the world are undergoing the
same kinds of suffering.

—1 Peter 5:9 NRSV

But rejoice insofar as you are sharing Christ's sufferings, so that
you may also be glad and shout for joy when his glory is revealed.

—1 Peter 4:13 NRSV

INTRODUCTION

The forcefulness of Peter's message may be lost on the majority of Americans. For
most people in our country, it is almost impossible to identify with the readers of 1 Peter.
Christians in the United States are not faced with giving up their lives for their faith.
Rather, they are the majority religion that often dictates to the minority or the alien.
They are comfortable, highly visible, and wage considerable power in local and na-
tional politics. This was not the case for the readers of 1 Peter.

The context of 1 Peter suggests that people are miserable because of their faith.
Peter attempts to console them by relating their suffering to Jesus' own human sacrifice.
His death images the sacrifices performed by ancient Israelites. Using apocalyptic
rhetoric, Peter reminds people that he knows of their "fiery ordeal" and the nearness of
the end of time (4:7, 12).

Intertwined in Peter's words of prediction and consolation are references to baptism. For him, it is a remedy for the violence they are experiencing in their lives. Baptism has changed the readers. They have a new birth and should never look back. They
are purified and preserved for eternity. While Peter may be discussing baptism as we
know it, an initiation ritual by water, he also may be using it as a symbol or metaphor
for martyrdom.

AUTHORSHIP, DATE, LOCATION

When we read 1 Peter, are we hearing the voice of Peter the friend, student, and companion of Jesus? We know that Matthew indicated that Peter would receive the keys
to the Kingdom of God from Jesus (16:18–20), but all of the gospels agree that Peter

wavered in his faith just before Jesus was killed (Mt. 26:69f; Mk. 14:66f; Luke 22:55f; Jn. 18:25ff). In Acts, Peter becomes a new man with great speaking and leadership abilities (Acts 2). He and James, the brother of Jesus, become pillars of the new Jerusalem Church (Acts 15). Once again, in Galatians, we meet the vacillating Peter (or Cephas) who cannot make up his mind about the issue of food customs (2:11f). Now, in 1 Peter, we meet an apostle who writes in a commanding tone that Christians should not waver but should remain in the faith they have chosen.

The author of 1 Peter claims to be an apostle of Jesus, yet there are no indications that the writer had a personal relationship or personal knowledge of Jesus. He may have heard of problems in the churches, but he also has no personal relationships with anyone to whom he wrote. The sophisticated level of Greek language skills used by the writer does not fit the story and profile we have of Peter the fisherman. Later we will discover that 1 Peter uses numerous other New Testament works.

Those who claim that the apostle Peter wrote the book point to Silvanus in 5:12 as a possible transcriber or secretary. Others suggest that the writer was a member of a Petrine school who wrote in the name of the founder. He or a group of people within the Petrine community also may have created 2 Peter and Jude. Most claim that 1 Peter is an anonymous or a pseudonymous product by someone who used the famous name of Peter to gain acceptance of the work.

Dating the book is based on whether or not scholars believe that the apostle Peter wrote it. If Peter did write it, then it is dated around 60 C.E. If he did not, then dates range from the late first century to the early second century C.E. In dating the work later in the first century, most point to the use of the word "Babylon" as a code word for Rome (5:13), which was not used until after 95 C.E.

1 Peter was written to "exiles of the dispersion in Pontus, Galatia, Cappadocia, Asia, and Bithynia" (1:1). Consult the map (Figure 14.1) to locate these areas in Asia Minor. The geographical locations may either be territories or provinces. Observe that the Southern provinces to which Paul traveled are not listed, and Bithynia and Pontus are separated for an unknown reason. Who are these people, and why are they called "exiles of the Dispersion"? I Peter suggests that they were the following:

1:14, 18; 2:9; 4:3	Gentiles?
2:7–8	Jews?
2:12, 15; 3:1, 16	Evangelists
4:12	going through a fiery ordeal
1:8; 2:6	experiencing conversion
2:9	a chosen race
2:9	a royal priesthood
2:9	a holy nation
2:9	God's own people

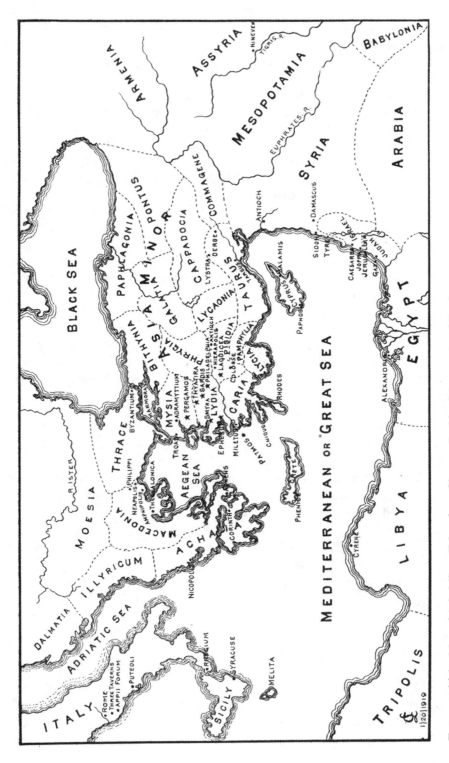

FIGURE 14.1 Map of Asia Minor. Taken from Clarence Larkin, *Dispensational Truth* (Philiadelphia: Rev. Clarence Larkin, Est., 1918).

We assume that the recipients of this book were Christians. John H. Elliott, in *A Home for the Homeless,* claims that out of 8.5 million people in this region of the Empire, less than 1 percent were Christian, or 80,000, whereas there were 1 million Jews, or over 10 percent. Perhaps "aliens" is a word that denotes the scarcity of followers of Jesus. As a minority religion dispersed throughout the vast mountainous regions of Asia Minor, they may have felt as though they were indeed aliens who were very alone. During the first century C.E., it took many weeks of travel to reach Jerusalem, Ephesus, or Rome, where Christianity flourished.

1 Peter also describes his readers as "sojourners, visiting strangers, or pilgrims" (1:17; 2:11). Are these words also figurative, or do they point to a specific strata of society during Roman times? According to Elliot, it was not uncommon for people who migrated to provinces within the Empire to be considered aliens. In some areas, laws were passed that limited their participation in communal affairs, which included voting, purchasing property, and marriage.

1 Peter reveals that the community consisted of free people, slaves, women who were married to non-Christians, men who were married to Christian women, elders, and recent converts (2:16,18; 3:1, 7; 5:1, 5). In the list of house laws in chapters 2–5, the wealthy or slave owners are not mentioned, which has led some scholars to speculate that the person who wrote 1 Peter owned slaves or that very few, if any, of the Christians were wealthy.

REASONS FOR WRITING 1 PETER

The writer of 1 Peter includes some of the reasons for writing the book in 5:12. "I have written this short letter to encourage you and to testify that this is the true grace of God." Why would the Christians in Asia Minor need to be encouraged? We know little about the historical situation of this area during the first century C.E. We do know that conflict arose between Rome and the new Christian religion toward the end of the first century C.E. in Pontus and Bithynia. **Trajan**, who was the Roman Emperor during 98–117 C.E., answered Governor **Pliny's**, letter regarding how such Christian cases should be handled. He wrote,

> The method you have pursued, my dear Pliny, in sifting the cases of those denounced to you as Christians is extremely proper. It is not possible to lay down any general rule which can be applied as the fixed standard in all cases of this nature. No search should be made for these people; when they are denounced and found guilty they must be punished; with the restriction, however, that when the party denies himself to be a Christian, and shall give proof that he is not (that is, by adoring our Gods) he shall be pardoned on the ground of repentance, even though he may have formerly incurred suspicion. (Kee 1984, 95)

We do not know whether or not the situation described by Trajan occurs during the same historical time frame of 1 Peter. The problems seem to be quite similar.

According to 1 Peter, social stability in the provinces and within Christian groups was deteriorating. Some scholars suggest that there may even have been a Christian group advocating a revolution against Rome. People appear to have been on the edge of personal disaster. After becoming Christian, some had lost their identity, given up their family ties, and were alienated or disenfranchised by the rest of the community. Those who chose to continue living with relatives discovered that their choice of faith created domestic conflict at home.

Some of the new converts could not take this pressure and abandoned the faith because of personal friendships, harassment by local officials, and possible physical harm. Some may have been arrested for legitimate reasons; others had been detained for their beliefs. Because of the general loneliness and public abuse, people returned to their former relationships, lifestyles, and beliefs.

The writer of 1 Peter sends this book to people who need to be loved and supported in their new faith. It may also have been created in an attempt to diffuse a politically or religiously explosive situation. Some converts may have believed that their lives were controlled by the government or unseen spiritual forces. Consequently, they felt impotent and feared the loss of their lives. This tension could have produced a very volatile situation.

Peter wants them to know that they are part of the family of God through baptism, which began in time past and will continue into eternity (4:7). They will never be alone, and they do not have to face the future alone. The trouble they are experiencing is not new. As far back as the prophets, people suffered similar kinds of problems for their faith. The stress and hardships in the lives of the prophets meant that they had chosen the right path for their lives. The writer implies that it will never be easy to be a Christian. He asks the readers to consider the death and suffering of Jesus and its results. The anguish they are suffering should be welcomed and is a sign that they have made the right choice, he says.

PROMINENT CHARACTERS

Jesus: A Suffering Model

1 Peter unexpectedly carries on the great tradition of Pauline faith in the resurrection. There is a Pauline emphasis on suffering with Christ, a call for separation from past community life, and a hope for a high ethical standard. Based on what we know about Peter, if he had actually written this letter, there should have been more of an emphasis on how Jesus met the requirements of ancient Israelite law and prophecy.

In 1 Peter, Jesus becomes the ideal or model human being. It was in the divine plan for Jesus to suffer and die on behalf of future followers. He accomplished the goal and was rewarded for it (3:22). Those who follow Jesus may suffer in similar ways and receive comparable rewards. What follows are a few of 1 Peter's statements about the suffering human model, Jesus.

1:1	Christians are sprinkled with the blood of Jesus.
1:19	Jesus ransoms people through his blood.
2:4	People offer spiritual sacrifice through Jesus.
3:18	Jesus suffered for sins in order to bring people to God.
3:19	Jesus was put to death in the flesh and made alive in the spirit.
4:1	Jesus suffered in the flesh.

God: The Loving Father

The God of 1 Peter sounds much like the ancient patriarchal God of the Israelites. God has been in control from the beginning of time. His plan for the salvation of humankind through Jesus, like the sacrifices in the Old Testament/Hebrew Bible, is staged within the history of humanity. The responsibility for humanity began in time past, when the divine plan for the suffering and death of Jesus was created (1:10–12). Jesus' human death, intercessory abilities, and future work were designed to bring people to God. This holy, monotheistic God has accepted his role in life as a protector and parent of his children (3:15; 1:17). As a loving shepherd, he takes care of the souls of people (2:25).

Women and the Household Laws

We have encountered many hierarchical household laws in our previous studies. Some contend that the laws were a way of appeasing Roman officials who attempted to force Christians to fit into the Roman familial model. They may suggest that the groups were organized differently, perhaps more democratic and egalitarian. The Roman government showed preferential treatment toward married people. They were rewarded by the tax system for having children. 1 Peter carries on the strict family organizational structure, similar to the Confucian ideals of filial piety, where all submit to the more powerful person above them in the hierarchical structure. Peter asks everyone to "Honor the Emperor" (2:17).

1 Peter includes suggestions for slaves, wives, husbands, elders, and younger converts. Missing from the list are slaveholders, children, and parents. In typical patriarchal rhetoric, Christian women are told to submit to their non-Christian husbands and to dress plainly (3:1–6). Their attitude and demeanor may be a way of winning over their spouse to Christianity (3:1).

The Old Testament rationale given for these pronouncements is a misinterpretation of the story of Abraham and Sarah. The writer of 1 Peter, using the LXX, says that Sarah called her husband "Lord." But this misses the whole point of the story. Throughout the narrative about Hagar and Ishmael, Sarah is in control. She commands Abraham. In the Hebrew Bible (MT), God speaks to Abraham about Sarah's command to cast out the woman slave and her child. It reads, "Whatever Sarah says to you, do as she tells you. . . ." (Gen. 21:12). In addition, 1 Peter's reference to "Holy Women" in ancient times has no parallel in the Old Testament/Hebrew Bible.

In the classical tradition, 1 Peter also continues the common myth about the inferiority of females, ". . . paying honor to the woman as the weaker sex. . . ." (3:7). No explanation is given regarding what is "weaker." Does Peter believe females are physically, intellectually, emotionally, historically, and politically weaker? Many have used this verse to perpetuate the damaging myth that women are weaker than men in all respects and therefore must be reared and sheltered like children. One hundred years ago **Elizabeth Cady Stanton** reacted to this quotation in the following way:

> The Apostles, having given such specific directions as to the toilets of women, their hair, ornaments, manners and position, in the Church, the State and the home, one is curious to know what kind of honor is intended for this complete subordination. Man is her head, her teacher, her guardian and her Saviour. What Christ is to him, that is he to the weaker vessel! It is fair to infer that what he has done in the past he will continue to do in the future. Unless she rebels outright, he will make her a slave, a subject, the mere reflection of another human will. (Stanton 1974, 2:175)

Slaves are treated in much the same manner as women. They are not encouraged to free themselves but to submit to their masters, even if they are physically abused (2:20). They should suffer in silence. According to Sharyn Dowd, in *The Women's Bible Commentary,* these words also have been applied to women and children who have been physically abused by spouses and fathers. 1 Peter has been used to argue, in the name of God, for the rights of an abuser and historically, even in our own country, for the slaveholder. This would be an excellent time to discuss how these verses have been employed and interpreted. Unfortunately there is not enough space in this book to summarize all of the harm that has been done to people by the misuse of the above texts.

LITERARY FOUNDATIONS

Genre

1 Peter begins, ends, and is organized like an ancient letter that may have been circulated during Passover or Easter. (Note the numerous times the word "suffer" is mentioned.) But many argue that it is not a letter. For them, it is an apologetic tract designed to explain why Christians have to experience public abuse and civil trials. It could also have been a homiletical **midrash** (or sermon) based on 1 Peter 1:10–12. Others note that it has too many commands (or **imperatives**) to be a personal letter. It may have been an encyclical. Below are a list of some of the commands:

1:13	Prepare your minds.
1:13	Discipline yourselves.
1:17	Live in reverent fear.
1:22	Love one another deeply from the heart.

2:13   Accept the authority of every human institution.

2:17   Honor everyone.

2:17   Love the family of believers.

2:17   Fear God.

2:17   Honor the Emperor.

Because of its heavy emphasis on baptism, some suggest that 1 Peter was a sermon given to new converts who had recently been baptized (see 1:3–4:11). Baptism was viewed as the creation of a new person, a symbol of change. The old person was washed away in the water, and the new person emerged. For Peter, it was a permanent change that protected the person from outside evil forces and inside tendencies to stray away from the religious path. 1 Peter captures the imagery of that change.

> And baptism, which this prefigured, now saves you—not as a removal of dirt from the body, but as an appeal to God for a good conscience. (3:21 NRSV)

Other allusions to baptism include the following:

1:3   He has given us a new birth (resurrection from the dead).

1:15–16   Be holy yourselves.

1:22   Now that you have purified your souls . . .

1:23   You have been born anew.

Scholars note the constant emphasis on leaving or separating from the old life and becoming "holy" (1:16), which could indicate that 1 Peter might have been created as an ordination sermon for an ascetic religious group such as Qumran. Why would readers be asked to abstain from all sensual desires? "Beloved, I urge you as aliens and exiles to abstain from the desires of the flesh that wage against the soul" (1 Peter 2:11).

The argument over whether or not 1 Peter is a genuine letter may find its origins in the composite nature of the work. Some scholars suggest that 1 Peter contains two or three sermons or letters. The two-letter theory suggests that the first letter ends with the "Amen" in 4:11. "Suffering" appears as though it may happen in the first letter, but in the second letter, beginning in 4:12, suffering is already occurring in the lives of the readers. The first letter also contains many allusions to baptism, and the second does not.

The Old Testament (LXX and MT) and the Book of Enoch

1 Peter draws upon multiple religious traditions in the LXX, the New Testament, 1 Enoch, and popular beliefs. Peter believes that the foundations of Christianity began with the ancient prophets, patriarchs, and matriarchs of the Old Testament/Hebrew Bible.

He alludes to or quotes from the Pentateuch, Psalms and many of the Prophets, especially Isaiah. Using Israelite terminology, 1 Peter draws upon images found in the Torah and the prophets to describe new Christians—they are a chosen race, a holy nation, and a royal priesthood (Ex. 19:16; Isa. 43:20–21), and they are sprinkled with the blood (1 Pet. 1:1).

In a curious defense of suffering, 1 Peter refers to the story of Noah (3:20) as a type of baptism for Christian converts. Noah went through the storms and was rescued. Now they have experienced baptism, which will "save" them (3:21).

In the same paragraph about baptism, 1 Peter says Jesus "went and made a proclamation to the spirits in prison" (3:19). Who are the spirits, and where is the prison? Most researchers agree that Peter has evoked the themes found in a noncanonical book, 1 Enoch. Some people believed that angels or spirits were powerful beings who could control the earth and the universe. The fate of humans rested on the whims of the angels. 1 Peter is probably claiming that Jesus is in control of everything, even the angels.

Enoch tells the story about the origins and destiny of the angels, as well as their influence on humans. 1 Enoch 10:4–6 reads in the following way:

> And again the Lord said to Raphael: 'Bind Azazel hand and foot, and cast him into the darkness: and make an opening in the desert, which is in Dudae, and cast him therein. And place upon him rough and jagged rocks, and cover him with darkness, and let him abide there for ever, and cover his face that he may not see light. And on the day of the great judgement he shall be cast into the fire. And heal the earth which the angels have corrupted, and proclaim the healing of the earth. . . .' (*The Book of Enoch* in Charles 1982, 37 or 10:4–7 and 67:2–69.)

The New Testament

Several studies have compared 1 Peter to the rest of the New Testament and have suggested that the writer used the Pauline letters, the gospels, James, Hebrews, and Acts as sources. If this letter were written by Peter, the eyewitness, there would have been no need to use Paul's letters as resource material. What follows is a comparison of a couple of the same ideas found in 1 Peter and Romans.

1 Peter	**Romans**
1:13–19 Therefore prepare your minds for action; discipline yourselves; set all your hope on the grace that Jesus Christ will bring you when he is revealed. Like obedient children, do not be conformed to the desires that you formerly had in ignorance. Instead, as he who called you is holy, be holy yourselves in all your conduct; for it is written, "You shall be holy, if I am holy."	12:1–2 I appeal to you therefore brothers and sisters, by the mercies of God, to present your bodies as a living sacrifice, holy and acceptable to God, which is your spiritual worship. Do not be conformed to this world, but be transformed by the renewing of your minds, so that you may discern what is the will of God—what is good and acceptable and perfect.

1:21 Through him you have come to trust in God, who raised him from the dead and gave him glory, so that your faith and hope are set on God.

4:24 ... they are now justified by his grace as a gift, through the redemption that is in Christ Jesus. (NRSV)

Hymns, Confessions, and Metaphors

1 Peter also employs many fragments of hymns and confessions. Based on the text, scholars have attempted to re-create an original confession from which the writer was working. According to Gerhard Krodel, in *Hebrews, James, 1 and 2 Peter, Jude, Revelation*, it may have looked like the following:

> He was put to death in the flesh,
> he was made alive in the Spirit,
> he went to Heaven,
> subjected to him were angels, authorities, and powers. (1977, 67)

In almost every chapter, 1 Peter uses common experiences and metaphors to explain his point of view. Consider the metaphors of a parent (1:17); nature (1:24), and a nursing baby (2:2).

Summary of 1 Peter   1 Peter probably was written as a circular letter by a well-meaning Christian late in the first or early in the second century C.E. No one really knows who received the letter, but it was addressed to most of Asia Minor. The readers could have been resident aliens or made to feel like aliens because of their recent conversion to Christianity. They were certainly not wealthy and many were married to people who had not converted.

While 1 Peter appears to be a letter, it may also have been an apologetical tract, a baptismal sermon, or a midrash. Some suggest that at least two or three different works have been combined in 1 Peter.

The readers are in danger. Possible riots, death, and turmoil at home are facts of life. Family and community life have been disrupted by the new faith. Government or community leaders are abusing Christians. Some have gone to jail. 1 Peter writes to calm people's fears by giving them hope in Jesus and a secure future. Baptism will save them. Jesus is the role model to follow in the present circumstances. He suffered and won, and so will they. God is always watching and controlling things from a distant place.

In a quest for peace, the writer proposes traditional solutions to family solidarity and relationships to the state. His answer is "submit"! He may be hoping that passive behavior will result in a peaceful solution to the violence Christians are experiencing.

While 1 Peter claims to have been written by the apostle Peter, the writer uses a host of religious resources that include several Books in the New Testament, the Book of Enoch, and the Old Testament/Hebrew Bible. Peter may be building a sermon based on an early Christian creedal statement. Metaphors permeate his work.

One wonders what happened to the readers who were gazing at death's door. Did they survive? Was a revolution ignited? Did Christianity continue, or was it destroyed by the local authorities?

2 Peter:
Apostolic versus Individual Interpretation

These people, however, are like irrational animals mere creatures
of instinct, born to be caught and killed.

—2 Peter 2:12 NRSV

INTRODUCTION

2 Peter may give us an ancient view of how denominations or breakaway sects within
Christianity begin to form. 2 Peter was written by a person who claimed to represent
apostolic knowledge and authority, the only acceptable view of Christianity. Some of
the readers of 2 Peter were challenging that authority. They felt they had the right and
responsibility to interpret the traditions and scriptures from their own points of view. No
one knows if the recipients of 2 Peter ever broke away from the apostolic church, but
chances are they did. And when they broke away, they began to legitimate their own way
of living, believing, and performing rituals.

AUTHOR, DATE, READERS, GENRE

2 Peter's author claims to be "Simeon or Simon Peter, servant and apostle of Jesus
Christ" (1:1) and supports that claim with the following evidence:

1:14	His death is approaching so he is writing to the readers.
1:16	He was an eyewitness of his majesty.
1:18	He heard the voice of God when he was on the mountain with the Son.
1:21	He indirectly claims that his words are from God. He does not give them a private interpretation.
2:2	His ability to predict the future which includes false teachers.
3:10–13	His ability to predict events occurring to the universe.
3:15	He is a friend, a brother of Paul's.

But few scholars think the apostle Peter actually wrote 2 Peter. It is too impersonal.
While Jesus is mentioned, the central ideas of his death, resurrection, and physical return at the end of time are absent. 2 Peter refers to Paul's writings, but the writer does
not appear to have a relationship with him or with anyone to whom this work was sent.
Most of his images or metaphors are transcendent or mystical (rather than specific

everyday life experiences) such as the holy mountain (1:8); eternal kingdom of our Lord (1:11); and waterless springs and mists (2:17).

2 Peter has little similarity with 1 Peter. Commonalties with 1 Peter include the greeting, references to Noah, and the prophets. Scholars have demonstrated that 2 Peter had knowledge of several of the Pauline letters, Enoch, probably copied from Jude, and was influenced by Epicurean and Stoic philosophies.

Some suggest that 2 Peter was written by the same Petrine school that created 1 Peter, but most consider the work anonymous or pseudonymous. Someone probably wrote in Peter's name using his fame as a lever to convince readers of his message. No one knows when it was written. Dates range from 90 C.E. to the late second century C.E. 2 Peter was not accepted by most of the Christian community as being authentic until the fourth century C.E.

No one knows who first received 2 Peter. Some have suggested that it was bound for the same areas in Asia Minor as 1 Peter. The letter itself gives few hints about its readers. They appear to have been people who were converted to a traditional form of Christianity but who now were following a newer interpretation, which prompted the writing of this letter (1:1). It may have been sent from Rome.

Genre

The discussion about the genre of 2 Peter is still on the table. It presents itself as a letter, but many claim that it is a homily. Some think that it is a solemn decree from a divine benefactor. Others want to call it literary fiction, based on the stories it uses and its relationship with Jude. Jerome H. Neyrey thinks it is an apology that defends five issues: the parousia, prophecy and interpretation, divine judgment, the word about judgment, and the delay of the judgment. Most place the book within the realm of a Last Will and Testament. Examples abound in both the Old and New Testaments; people such as Jacob, Moses, Joshua, Samuel, Jesus, and Paul are credited with last testaments.

PURPOSE OF THE WORK

The View of the Writer

The reasons for writing this letter can be viewed from several perspectives. There is the view of the writer, the view of the people who are labeled "false teachers," and the view of the people to whom the letter was written. From the view of the writer, 2 Peter was written:

1:14	To give the last will and testament of Peter.
3:7	To stop the spread of a perceived heresy that will ruin the future for believers.
2:1	To warn the readers about false teachers who will exploit and teach them traditions that differ from the original founders of Christianity, the apostles.

3:5–13	To protect the erosion of cherished beliefs in the control of history by God, his ability to reward and punish, and the future Parousia.
2:3	To protect the readers from the loss of their money.
1:18	To reaffirm the traditions and authority of the apostles.
2:20	To correct a view that suggests that traditions or prophecies can be individually interpreted. There is an official point of view.
1:5–6	To summarize accepted Christian values and ethics.
3:17	To maintain the devotion of the readers to the traditional faith.

The writer thinks the teachers are spreading fabrications, and he attempts to shock the readers by his characterization of them as ignorant (3:16); depraved (2:10); slanderers (2:10); and more. The writer believes that he represents authority and stability, which is everything that they are against.

The View of the Teachers

The converts have been waiting for the end to come, and they are still waiting. How can anyone live on the "edge" just waiting for the rest of their lives? Instead of being disillusioned or disappointed, these Christians began to debate the issue. It seemed to them that God was very slow and that it did not appear that anything was going to happen (3:9). What if the parousia had already come? Maybe the ancient apostles, like Paul, did not mean the literal end of time. Maybe it was a metaphor for something else. Perhaps there is no judgment. If there is no end of time, then we are living according to a strict ethical code that means nothing, and it is making our lives miserable. Should not a good and gracious God want to make us happy?

The View of the Readers

Some of the readers could have been the teachers. The congregation may have been donating money to the new teachers (2:3) and probably stopped the donations to the group the writer represented. They searched Jewish traditions and Paul's works to answer their questions. Some were among the older converts who were still following their interpretations of the beliefs and ethics of the original evangelists.

Younger or newer converts questioned the practicality of some of the teachings and began to reinterpret the traditions. The younger converts viewed people such as the writer of Peter suspiciously. They wondered why the older converts were so rigid and isolationist. They were afraid to plan for the future. Perhaps it was time for them to step out into the real world where real Christians had to live. It had become increasingly difficult to maintain a normal life while attempting to follow the old ways. Younger converts were beginning to exert influence and may have won over the entire congregation to their way of thinking.

The Debate

The writer of 2 Peter defends his point of view by raising questions, quoting beliefs by the teachers, and then refuting them. A list of issues and how the writer responds to them follows.

1. Issue 1: There is no Parousia and no hope for the future.

    2 Peter affirms that the reader's point of view is narrow. It may seem as though it has been a long time to wait, but in God's eyes a thousand years may be one day (3:8). The end is coming, and it will be more violent than anyone can imagine. Everything will be destroyed by fire (3:10), and a new home for the believers, the heavens, and earth will be recreated (3:3, 13).

2. Issue 2: God is not in charge of the universe.

    God created the universe (3:5) and has brought judgment on people in the past. For example, study the stories of the angels, Lot, Noah, and Balaam (2:4–16). God has the power to reorient the cosmic order and recreate a world that has abandoned him. He will judge the good and evil.

3. Issue 3: Anyone can interpret scripture.

    Interpretation must come from God. The apostles had a divine experience on the mountain and thus were capable of interpreting the messages from God. You did not experience the mountain and may not explain the message (1:16–21). Others who interpret scriptures will only lead you away from, not toward the truth.

4. Issue 4: Freedom

    2 Peter assures readers that when they converted they received a faith and became part of the divine nature (1:2–5). They are part of God and they should know that that experience will bring them freedom at the end of time. But the freedom desired by the readers has little to do with theology. They may have been following all sorts of regulations that had little meaning for them. They wanted the freedom to form their own beliefs and ethics (2:19). The experience of life was more pressing than the idea of freedom in the future.

PROMINENT CHARACTERS

It is impossible to find the name of a female character in 2 Peter. Females may be included in the use of the word "brethren," which is usually translated "brothers and sisters" by the NRSV (1:10; 3:1, etc.). The wording of 1:21 has different variants, so females may be among the ancient prophets. Females may be referred to indirectly when the author of 2 Peter assaults the false teachers for their sensual desires, lack of self control, and adultery (2:10; 2:14; 2:2).

Jesus

Little is said about Jesus' life and death. Peter serves him (1:1), and Jesus is given the honorific title of "Lord," a benefactor. He, with God, is a patron of the church. The following summary highlights significant characteristics of Jesus.

1:1	He is a Savior.
1:11	He has an eternal kingdom.
1:14	He has spoken to the author about his impending death.
2:9	He rescues the godly and punishes the unrighteous.
23:2	He spoke commands through the apostles.
3:9–10	He is involved with the events of the end of time as a judge and a thief.

Characters Who Were Judged by God

In chapter 2, Peter attempts to persuade his audience that God has been at work in history. He refers to angels, Noah and the flood, Lot and Sodom and Gomorrah, and Balaam, son of Bosor. Those who are unfamiliar with Jewish traditions may miss the meaning of chapter 2 because they do not know the background of these characters.

Noah and the Flood (Genesis 6–9)   According to Genesis, all of the people on the earth were corrupt, accept Noah and the animals. They had not abandoned God. Noah was told to build an ark, into which he took his family and two of every kind of animal, bird, and so on. God flooded the earth with rain for forty days and killed all of the inhabitants. Noah's family and the rest of the zoological group survived.

Lot and Sodom and Gomorrah (Genesis 18–19)   God had determined that he was going to destroy the city of Sodom. Abraham argued with God, hoping he could save the city. God agreed that if he could find ten righteous people in the city he would not destroy it. The story turns to Lot, who is in Sodom and visited by angels. In the evening, the males of the city want to have sex with the angels, presumably male. A miracle prevents them from fulfilling their desires. The next day, Lot and his family are told to leave the city. Sodom and Gomorrah are destroyed by fire.

Balaam, Son of (Beor) Bosor (Numbers 22:21–35)   Officials from Moab had come to Balaam, asking him to curse Israel for taking their land. Balaam did not follow the advice of God, so on his way to meet the people of Moab, his donkey spoke to him. The donkey had seen the angel of the Lord three times in the path, and Balaam had hit the donkey because it would not keep on walking down the path.

The Angels   This story about angels being thrown into Tartarus may find its origins in the story about the sons of God who had sex with the daughters of men (Genesis 6:1–5), or within the embellished stories about angels found in 1 Enoch.

LITERARY FOUNDATIONS

Jude

The similarities between 2 Peter and Jude are remarkable. Studies suggest that nineteen of the twenty-five verses in Jude have parallels in 2 Peter. Most theorize that 2 Peter copied from Jude, because some of the verses only make sense if they are read within the context of Jude. Others suggest that both could have been using the same source or written by the same author. Compare the verses in the box below, as well as 2 Peter 2:1–3:3 with Jude 5b–19.

2 Peter	Jude
1:2 May grace and peace be yours in abundance in the knowledge of God and of Jesus our Lord.	2 May mercy, peace, and love be yours in abundance.
2:5 and if he did not spare the ancient world, even though he saved Noah, a herald of righteousness, with seven others, when he brought a flood on a world of the ungodly;	5 . . . afterward destroyed those who did not believe.
2:12 These people, however, are like irrational animals, mere creatures of instinct, born to be caught and killed. They slander what they do not understand, and when those creatures are destroyed, they also will be destroyed.	10 But these people slander whatever they do not understand, and they are destroyed by those things that, like irrational animals, they know by instinct.
1:12 Therefore I intend to keep on reminding you of these things, though you know them already and are established in the truth that has come to you.	5a Now I desire to remind you, though you are fully informed.
3:2–3 that you should remember the words spoken in the past by the holy prophets, and the commandment of the Lord and Savior spoken through your apostles. First of all you must understand this, that in the last days scoffers will come, scoffing and indulging their own lusts.	17–18 But you, beloved, must remember the predictions of the apostles of our Lord Jesus Christ; for they said to you, "In the last time there will be scoffers, indulging their own ungodly lusts."
3:14 Therefore, beloved, while you are waiting for these things, strive to be found by him at peace, without spot or blemish;	24 Now to him who is able to keep you from falling, and to make you stand without blemish in the presence of his glory with rejoicing. (NRSV)

Jude informs the interpretation of 2 Peter, for example, 2 Peter 2:11, "whereas angels, though greater in might and power, do not bring against a slanderous judgment from the Lord," makes little sense until Jude 9 is read.

> But when the archangel Michael contended with the devil and disputed about the body of Moses, he did not dare to bring a condemnation of slander against him, but said, "The Lord rebuke you!" (NRSV)

Pauline Works

The writer of 2 Peter claims to have known Paul but acknowledges that his works are difficult to interpret. "There are some things in them hard to understand, which the ignorant and unstable twist to their own destruction, as do the other scriptures" (5:16). According to Jerome H. Neyrey, professor of the New Testament at the University of Notre Dame, the writer of 2 Peter probably had read 1 Corinthians, Romans, and 1 Thessalonians. He finds the following common themes between the Pauline works and 2 Peter: Both describe inheriting the divine nature, list Christian virtues, discuss false prophets who do not believe that there will be a judgment at the end of time, and tackle the issue of freedom from the law and God's judgment.

Jewish Writings

The foundational myth for 2 Peter is built upon a monotheistic and patriarchal view of a God who is the creator. This God is in control of the universe and time and occasionally enters human history through the work of Jesus and the Holy Spirit. There is a respect for tradition, whether in written form or voiced through a prophet/apostle. Like his Jewish ancestor, the writer believes in living by a standard of conduct.

2 Peter shows familiarity with Old Testament stories such as Noah and Balaam, as well as the traditions about the prophets. While there are many allusions to the Hebrew Bible or the LXX, only three quotations are employed from Proverbs, Psalms, and Isaiah (see 2:22; 3:8; 3:13).

Greek Religions and Philosophy

Most researchers comment on the unique Greek vocabulary used by the writer of 2 Peter. Words such as "tartarus," or hell (2:4), the virtues of goodness, self-control, endurance (1:5–7), arguments over myths (1:16f), and the mystical experience of participating in the divine nature (1:4) are only some of the popular views among the Greeks of being religious. Some of the language, such as tartarus, might have brought to mind the myth of the **Titans** in **Hesiod's** writings, in much the same way that mentioning "hyperspace" today makes Americans think of Star Wars.

Several scholars suggest that the false teachers in 2 Peter were really followers of a popularized form of Epicureanism. Jerome Neyrey (1993) outlines their beliefs in *2 Peter, Jude*. Pleasure and the freedom from pain and fear were the primary goals of Epicureans. They reasoned that even God should be spared pain, and so taught that God did not judge humans. They believed that the earth was not created by a divinity or rationale entity. Its origins were a matter of chance. A divinity does not control the earth or humans. This would destroy freedom. There is no evidence that the just and the unjust are rewarded or punished. This procrastination or laziness on the part of the divine merits a disbelief in the divine control of the universe. There is no need for *divination* or prophecy, because there is no plan to the universe. Everything happens by chance. Death has no meaning. Epicurus said, "Death is nothing to us; for that which is dissolved is devoid of sensation, and that which is devoid of sensation is nothing to us" (Laëtius 1905, 10:31, 3, or p. 474).

Summary of 2 Peter   2 Peter may have been written by a Petrine school, but most scholars assume it is pseudonymous. Dating could be as early as 90 C.E. or as late as the third century C.E. No one knows who received the first work. Some suggest the Christians in Asia Minor.

The book of 2 Peter, probably a testament, was written by a person who claimed apostolic authority. He knew of people who were denying that there would be a judgment at the end of time. His letter assaults Christians for interpreting the Scriptures/traditions from their own point of view, predicting utter disaster for them but hope for other Christians who do not deviate from apostolic teachings.

While no female characters are featured, the writer draws stories from the ancient Israelite traditions, which include Noah, Lot, Balaam, and the sons of God (angels). Jesus is present at the beginning and end of time, but nothing is mentioned about his death on the cross.

2 Peter is influenced by the Pauline writings and ancient Hebrew traditions. Using a popular Hellenistic vocabulary, 2 Peter appears to be combating the encroachment of Epicureanism. It has much in common with Jude. The writer may have used Jude as a source (or vice versa), or they both could have used the same source in creating their works.

Jude:
Wandering Stars and the Faith

They are waterless clouds carried along by the winds; autumn trees
without fruit, twice dead, uprooted; wild waves of the sea, casting
up the foam of their own shame; wandering stars, for whom
the deepest darkness has been reserved forever.

—Jude 12–13 NRSV

INTRODUCTION

Jude, similar to 2 Peter, may also be writing to a community that is in transition. New people have become part of the Christian group. Rituals and beliefs are changing. This threatens the writer, who holds onto the faith of the saints and the predictions of the apostles. In a violent rhetoric designed to scare the readers, Jude lashes out at the popular new intruders, wishing eternal destruction upon them. He does not advocate action by the group but leaves their ultimate judgment in the hands of God. He hopes for love, unity, and mercy for those who are caught in the middle.

AUTHOR, DATE, READERS, GENRE

The writer of the book of Jude (or Judas) claims to be the brother of James (1). There are at least five different characters with the name Judas mentioned in the New Testament.

> Who is Judas?
> 1. Judas, brother of Jesus (Mark 6:3).
> 2. Judas, a person who housed Paul (Acts 9:11).
> 3. Judas Iscariot, who betrayed Jesus.
> 4. Judas, son of James (Luke 6:16).
> 5. Judas, sometimes called Barsabas (Acts 15:22).

James probably refers to the brother of Jesus, because it appears that he is well known by the readers, therefore Judas is also the brother of Jesus.

Scholars disagree about whether or not Jude was written by a relative of Jesus. They claim that there is too much evidence suggesting that it was written long after Judas died, pointing to references about the apostles' teaching and the solidified belief system. Faith is a body of literature, not a human activity, yet there are some today who maintain that Jude is one of the earliest documents contained in the New Testament and that it was actually written by a close relative of Jesus. There also are legends about the cousins of Jesus who were instrumental in influencing Rome to stop its persecution of Christians.

The geographical location of the recipients remains a mystery. Suggestions include Palestine, Alexandria, or Syria. Dates of creation range from 54 C.E. to 160 C.E. because of the anonymous nature of the writing and the inclusion of stories from noncanonical works. Christians debated for hundreds of years about whether or not Jude should be included in the New Testament. Today, it is the least studied of all of the New Testament literature, ignored by most of **Protestantism**.

The people to whom the Letter of Jude is addressed are referred to as "beloved." We know that they are Christians, and it appears that the Church has been in existence for a long time. They hold regular **love feasts**, which were part of the Eucharist, Communion, or Lord's Supper. Their historical background includes knowledge of Jewish Scriptures, both canonical and noncanonical.

Genre

Jude looks like a letter, with its opening and closing, but most scholars think it was some type of encyclical essay. It also has been referred to as a diatribe, **midrash**, or **discourse**. Some contend that there is no organizational structure to Jude. Others detail an intricate schemata, based on multiple inclusios. Most agree that the letter follows a line of argumentation, which accuses the intruders (denounces them) and then offers a story from the ancient religious traditions that is explained in reference to the group threatening the writer (predicts punishment). For example,

4	Accusation or Denouncing "For certain intruders have stolen in among you, people who long ago were designated for this condemnation as ungodly, who pervert the race of our God into licentiousness and deny our only Master and Lord Jesus Christ."
5–7	Appeal to Ancient Religious Traditions (5) Noah (Old Testament/Hebrew Bible) (6) Angels (1 Enoch or Old Testament/Hebrew Bible) (7) Lot and Sodom and Gomorrah (Old Testament/Hebrew Bible)
8	Application to Readers (also an accusation) "Yet in the same way these dreamers also defile the flesh, reject authority, and slander the glorious ones." (NRSV)
9–10	Punishment

Reasons for Writing the Book

Jude is written by an author who is threatened and in turn wants to retaliate against the readers and intruders. "Intruders," or possibly itinerant preachers/teachers, have taken the congregation by storm. Their teachings and style of Christian living does not fit into the "norm" of the faith (Jude 3). They are dividing the Christians (Jude 19). Instead of negotiating with the popular new group, the writer hurls insults at them. We do not know if the accusations are true or merely hyperbole. Neyrey (1993, 37–38) studied the vocabulary describing both intruders and readers in Jude. What follows is an adaptation of his comparison.

Readers	Intruders
holy	godlessness
await mercy	await judgment
in fear	fearless
unblemished	defiled/stained
pray in the Spirit	do not have the Spirit
build up	divide
stand before God	stumble
are saved	are destroyed
honor God	challenge God

Scholars over the past 1,900 years have taken Jude's lead and assigned various hypothetical (heretical) labels to the "intruders," which include Docetists, **Carpocrations**, **Marcosians**, early **Gnostics**, **Essenes**, Judaizers, and **Edessans**. Some of thes people may have believed that the Kingdom of God had already come into their lives; there was no future parousia. They may also have believed that faith in the new religion allowed them to be completely free from any moral restraints. The letter could also have been directed against Paul or a misguided Pauline group. Today we still do not know where the Christians lived, nor do we know the mysterious origins of the intruders threatening the writer.

Some of the other problems associated with the intruders included nontraditional love feasts (Jude 12), abuse of speaking in tongues (Jude 16), the worship of angels (they consider themselves superior to angels?) (Jude 8), loss of revenues or greed (Jude 11b, 16), a brash approach to faith (Jude 16), denial of the parousia (Jude 17), claims of personal revelation (Jude 8), anti prayer (Jude 19), and of course, the popularity of the intruders (Jude 16). Solutions to the problems included remembering the faith of the saints and apostles (Jude 3, 17), praying (Jude 20), remembering that the intruders will be judged by God (Jude 6–22), and practicing love by being merciful to the people who are caught in the middle of this political fight (Jude 2, 22).

LITERARY FOUNDATIONS

Jude chose characters as foils or examples of people who received a negative judgment from God in order to prophesy a violent future for the intruders. The writer draws examples from Jewish traditions, canonical and **noncanonical**, as well as other legends that have been lost over time. Jude is the only New Testament book to quote an Apocryphal work, 1 Enoch, in an authoritative way (14–15) (compare Enoch and Jude, which follows). Remember that the translations were made by different people (and possibly from different languages), which can account for some of the differences.

Jude 14	**Enoch 1:9**
See, the Lord is coming with ten thousands of his holy ones, to execute judgement on all, and to convict everyone of all the deeds of ungodliness that they have committed in such an ungodly way, and of all the harsh things that ungodly sinners have spoken against him. (NRSV)	And behold! He cometh with ten thousands of His holy ones, To execute judgement upon all. And to destroy all the ungodly. And to convict all flesh; of all the works of their ungodliness which they have ungodly committed. And of all the hard things which ungodly sinners have spoken against Him. (1 Enoch 1:9, translated by R. H. Charles)

Jude also includes an affirmation in a belief in angels as significant political entities (Jude 6, 9). The quotation "hating even the tunic defiled by their bodies" (Jude 22) has a ring of magic to it. Can cloth defile anything?

Metaphors

Jude uses chaotic, violent, and dangerous-sounding metaphors to describe his opponents, such as "irrational animals" (10); "blemishes" (12), wild waves (13) and wandering stars (13). This strategy is probably created because of the apocalyptic mind-set of the reader. As we noticed earlier in 2 Thessalonians and will discuss in depth in the Book of Revelation, apocalyptic literature is created by people who are threatened, who feel as though they are not in control of the situation, such as the writer of Jude. They are powerless to make any changes, so they throw their hopes and dreams into the hand of the divine, who ultimately will rescue them or make "things right." The author of Jude is confident that on the last day of the end of time, he will be vindicated.

Summary of Jude   Jude is probably an anonymous or a pseudonymous letter sent to an unknown congregation somewhere in the Roman Empire. It is an attack against intruders who have brought new ways of thinking and practicing religion to his Christian community. He assaults their personalities, strategies, beliefs, and ways of relating to others.

Like the ancient prophets who couched Israel's waywardness in sexual terms (e.g., see Hosea), Jude also may be doing the same. Many scholars want to focus on what they call the "libertine" side of the intruders. They explore the possible accusations of homosexuality and promiscuity. All of these accusations about the intruders may be a form of scapegoating. What was the real problem for the readers of Jude?

It appears that they were all Christians, but they began taking different positions on rituals, beliefs, and relationships with others. The writer hoped to curb the changes that were happening in the group. He felt that the intruders had too much power over the church, but he could do nothing about it but stand on the sidelines and preach doom. He stops short of advocating a revolution, but he hopes people will learn to love each other and work together.

15

Conflict and Christianity

1, 2, 3 John and Revelation

Whoever says, "I am in the light," while hating a
brother or sister, is still in darkness.

—1 John 2:9 NRSV

INTRODUCTION

As we begin the study of 1, 2, 3, John, and Revelation, we enter a space charged with
tension. All four books ridicule, slander, and demonize their opponents. Their messages
originated within mature Christian communities that were experiencing change. Some
of those changes were interpreted as threats to the viability of the groups. Elements and
themes common to all four works include the following:

- They are associated with a writer named John.
- They are traditionally called letters, but literary critical studies suggest that 1 John and
  Revelation may not be letters.
- They are concerned with the identity of Jesus, economic issues, and political struggles
  within Christian communities.
- Their faith is rooted in dualism, which can see only two sides of an issue.
- Family relationships are important to all.
- They are familiar with Old Testament/Hebrew traditions.
- They are unconcerned with the resurrection of Jesus.
- They all fear people who believe differently than themselves.

- They are concerned with hospitality and the rules concerning food.
- Both 2 John and Revelation portray strong female images.
- All of the books are mysteries, because we know nothing about the authors or to whom the letters were written. We can only speculate.

Some scholars have suggested that the Gospel of John, the Johannine letters, and Revelation were written by the same hand. They point to vocabulary and agreement on theological issues. There is a close relationship among the Johannine letters. Seventy percent of the words in 3 John and 86 percent of the words in 2 John also are found in 1 John, indicating origins by the same writer or group of people. Yet most scholars today tend to assign different dates and writers to Revelation and the Gospel of John. They admit that the writers of the Johannine letters and Revelation must have read or studied the Gospel of John.

Tread softly and quietly as we pace through these books. The authors are quite persuasive. Readers may automatically take their points of view. When possible, try to imagine being a member of the group being attacked. How would you feel? Try to keep an open mind.

1 John:
Love Your Friends

They went out from us, but they did not belong to us. . . .

—1 John 2:18 NRSV

INTRODUCTION

After reading 1 John, most us may want to head for a copy of *Newsweek* or *Time,* where we can obtain summaries of world events in a few sentences. Unlike the writer of 1 John, the news magazines aim at clarity, with the hope of saving time for the reader. 1 John had other ambitions. It repeatedly states its point of view. The main theses of 1 John could probably be summarized in the following hypothetical press release:

Christian Beliefs Divide Local Congregation

Local Christian group argues over the Messiah, ethics, sin, the end of time, and more! Slanderous charges have been leveled at the breakaway group! Negotiations are at a standstill!

AUTHOR, DATE, READERS

Many ancient writers conclude that John, the son of Zebedee (Mark 3:17), and John, the beloved disciple in the Gospel of John (John 19:26), are the same person, and that that person wrote the Johannine letters. Some modern scholars still hold to this position. **Papias**, an early church writer, suggested that there were legends about two "Johns." **Eusebius**, in *Ecclesiastical History*, quotes Papias and then makes his own comments about John.

Papias

But if I met with any one who had been a follower of the elders any where, I made it a point to inquire what were the declarations of the elders. What was said by Andrew, Peter or Philip. What by Thomas, James, John, Matthew, or any other of the disciples of our Lord. What was said by Aristion, and the presbyter John, disciples of the Lord; for I do not think that I derived so much benefit from books as from the living voice of those that are still surviving.

Eusebius

Where it is also proper to observe the name of John is twice mentioned. The former of which he mentions with Peter and James and Matthew, and the other apostles; evidently meaning the evangelist. But in a separate point of his discourse he ranks the other John, with the rest not included in the number of apostles, placing Aristion before him. He distinguishes him plainly by the name of presbyter. So that it is here proved that the statement of those is true, who assert there were two of the same name in Asia, and that there were also two tombs in Ephesus, and that both are called John's even to this day. (Eusebius 1973, 125 or 3:39)

1 John does not claim to have been written by anyone named John. The name may have been assigned to it late in the second century. We know that all three letters were not accepted and used on a regular basis by Christian writers until the fourth century C.E.

Second and third John were written by an "**elder.**" Some theorize that the "elder" in 2 and 3 John is actually the author of 1 John. Most researchers today conclude that 1 John was written by a group of people who had studied the Gospel of John and may even have studied with the author of John. These people or the Johannine school created the letters of John. Note some of the following verses that suggest joint authorship:

1:1   *We* declare to you what was from the beginning . . .

1:4   *We* are writing . . .

2:2   He is the atoning sacrifice for *our* sins . . .

Using the Gospel of John as a source, the Johannine school must have created 1 John after studying the gospel. Note the similarities between 1 John 1–4 and John 1:1–18.

1 John 1:1–4

We declare to you what was from the beginning, what we have heard, what we have seen with our eyes, what we have looked at and touched with our hands, concerning the world of life—this life was revealed, and we have seen it and testify to it, and declare to you the eternal life what was with the Father and was revealed to us—we declare to you what we have seen and heard so that you also may have fellowship with us; and truly our fellowship is with the Father and with his Son Jesus Christ. We are writing these things so that our joy may be complete. (NRSV)

John 1:1–18

In the beginning was the Word, and the Word was with God, and the Word was God. He was in the beginning with God. All things came into being through him, and without him not one thing came into being. What has come into being in him was life, and the life was the light of all people. The light shines in the darkness, and the darkness did not overcome it.

There was a man sent from God whose name was John. He came as a witness to testify to the light, so that all might believe through him. He himself was not the light, but he came to testify to the light. The true light, which enlightens everyone, was coming into the world.

He was in the world, and the world came into being through him; yet the world did not know him. He came to what was his own, and his own people did not accept him. But to all who received him, who believed in his name, he gave power to become children of God, who were born, not of blood or of the will of the flesh or of the will of man, but of God.

And the Word became flesh and lived among us, and we have seen his glory, the glory as of a father's only son, full of grace and truth. . . . From his fullness we have all received, grace upon grace. The law indeed was given through Moses; grace and truth came through Jesus Christ. No one has ever seen God. It is God the only Son, who is close to the Father's heart, who has made him known. (NRSV)

Rudolph Bultmann, in *The Johannine Epistles* (1973), gives the theory another twist. He suggests that 1 John was created from a previous fragment or fragments, possibly Gnostic, and then edited by a Johannine group to make it fit into traditional Christian beliefs. Others have suggested similar theories but claim that the original source that was rewritten had Jewish origins.

Date and Readers

Dating for the Gospel of John is in the 90s C.E., which places the writing of 1, 2, and 3 John into the late first century and early second century between 90 and 150 C.E. The people to whom 1 John is addressed are Christians who have separated from the older, more established group. Some suggest that they were located in the same geographical area as the readers of the Book of Revelation. (We will discuss this shortly.) This book may originally have been intended for Smyrna, Ephesus, Syria, or another city in Asia Minor.

Genre

1 John does not claim to be a letter. It has no opening or closing. Some believe they have found traces of letters. Bultmann (1973) suggests that 1:5–2:27 was an independent letter and 5:13 ends another letter, but there is no agreement among scholars. Consequently, there has been no end to the speculation about its organization and genre. It has been classified as a tractate, an instructional booklet, a manifesto, a summary of sermons, edited letters or works, and a collection of fragments from documents within Gnosticism.

REASONS FOR THE WRITING OF 1 JOHN

They went out from us, but they did not belong to us; for if they had belonged to us, they would have remained with us. But by going out they made it plain that none of them belongs to us. (2:19–20 NRSV)

A Christian group has lost some of its members. The unfortunate situation is charged with hostile feelings accompanied by slanderous remarks made by people on both sides.

The remaining members are angry about the beliefs and actions of their former friends. To preserve the fragile unity within the community, a third party, aligned with those who remain in the Church, has written 1 John.

The writer repeats many reasons for writing 1 John. They include the following:

1:3	to foster friendship
1:4	to create a more joyful situation
1:5	to give them a message
2:1	to keep the people from sinning
2:8	to remind them of a commandment
2:12–14	to address children, fathers, young people about the faith
2:26	to correct misconceptions about Christianity
5:13	to assure readers that eternal life is waiting for them

Issues Dividing the Christians

The groups hold to a number of different beliefs, among them the disagreement over the identity and work of Jesus, the concept of sin, and social responsibility. The writer feels compelled to define the person and role of Jesus. This may suggest that the dissenting group believed the opposite. The following discussion illustrates *possible* scenarios of some of the beliefs.

Issue 1: Identity and Work of Jesus

Verses	Beliefs of Remaining Group	Beliefs of Dissenting Group
1:1	Jesus was real.	Jesus was only a ghost or a spirit.
1:2	Jesus is eternal coming from the Father, that is, He is divine.	Only God is divine. Jesus was important but is not on the same level as the Father. Or, they may have argued that they were just as divine as Jesus because they have the Spirit.
1:3	Christians have a relationship with both Father and Son.	Christians have a relationship with God, but Jesus is not his Son.
2:1	Jesus is perfect and pleads our case to the Father.	There are other intercessors who can plead our case. Jesus is not effective, he is dead.
2:2	Jesus was offered as a sacrifice for the sins of the whole world.	There are many ways to erase sin. How could this one man's death reach the whole world? Or, what is sin? We do not accept your definition of sin.

Verses	Beliefs of Remaining Group	Beliefs of Dissenting Group
2:3	A Christian is one who keeps the commandments of Jesus.	Jesus did not give commandments, Moses did.
4:2	People who believe that Jesus came in the flesh as a human are from God.	Flesh is evil. How could the divine inhabit this mortal and corruptible body? It is not logical.
4:14	Jesus is the savior of the world.	How can Jesus be a savior to people he did not even know? Is the whole world Christian?
5:1	Jesus is the Christ.	Jesus is not the messiah. The Messiah may still be coming.

The dissenting group could not accept the beliefs in Jesus as a human who sacrificed his life for the sake of the whole world. He was not divine, nor was he the Son of God. This argument over Jesus was not new. We have read several stories in the gospels about questions concerning the identity of Jesus, and Paul centered most of his letters on the meaning of the death of Jesus. Controversies concerning the interpretation of Jesus' life and death monopolized the time of clerics and politicians for several hundred years. The Holy Roman Catholic Church debated the definition, person, and relationship to the Father and the Spirit in ecumenical councils, the most famous being the Council of Nicea in 325 C.E.

The problem of sin appears to be presented in an illogical manner by the writer. The readers are told that all people sin. If all people sin, then how can Christians be without sin? It is possible that the writer is defending his own belief that everyone sins because the dissenters teach that sin is an allusion? It is difficult to know exactly when the writer is giving his own point of view or attacking his opponents.

Issue 2: Sin

Verses	Beliefs of Remaining Group	Beliefs of Dissenting Group
2:1	All people sin.	Sin is an allusion, or sin permeates the universe. Humans do not commit sin. Or, again, what is sin?
2:5	Christians can be perfect.	There is no such thing as a perfect person, especially in this mortal body.
3:9	All who abide in Jesus do not sin.	There is no such thing as sins. If there was then it is illogical that one person could erase those sins.

Verses	Beliefs of Remaining Group	Beliefs of Dissenting Group
4:12	Christians are perfect because God dwells in us.	How could an omnipotent God live in a human being? God is too great and too complex to reside in humans.
5:18	Christians do not sin.	Okay if there is sin, then prove it!
5:17	There is a sin that cannot be forgiven, a mortal sin.	How can one sin affect the rest of time? Why would anyone want to believe in a religion that dooms people?

The dissenting group did not adhere to the principles of sharing wealth. Raising funds for religious groups can create problematic situations. People do not like to part unwillingly with their money, much less their own lives. Whatever happened among the Christians produced disastrous personal situations. Hate divides. It has been at the root of family, religious, and national wars. It appears that both parties share this emotion of hate.

Issue 3: Social Responsibility

Verses	Beliefs of Remaining Group	Beliefs of Dissenting Group
1:7	Our religion informs our living on a daily basis.	Religion should not dictate how people live. People are free to make their own choices.
2:9	Hate is not a product of Christianity. Christians do not hate each other.	People must hate the things that can destroy them.
3:16	Love requires personal sacrifice, even one's own life.	We are not willing to die for anyone. We want to live.
3:17	We should share our material wealth with those who are less fortunate.	We cannot give up the money we have earned just to help others. They can go to work too!

Issue 4: The End of Time

The writer of 1 John slanders his opponents with labels such as "antichrists" and "deceivers" (2:18, 26). Most people associate the idea of the "antichrist" with the Book of Revelation and the predictions of the end of time in 2 Thessalonians (Rev. 12–14; 2 Thess. 2:1–12). In these books, the images of the "dragon" and the "lawless one" take on mythological tones and are often interpreted as characterizations of the "antichrist." Yet the Greek word for "antichrist" is only used in 1 and 2 John (7), referring to those who differ with the accepted beliefs in Jesus. They are leaders of the separatist movement.

1 John strategically uses the concept of the end of time to threaten or frighten his opponents. The writer hopes that the readers will remain dedicated to Jesus (2:28; 4:17) because there is an adventure waiting for them in the future (3:2). At the same time, he believes that true Christians are presently participating in the life of the divine. They have passed from death to life (3:14; 5:11–13). Eternal life is just around the corner for some.

LITERARY FOUNDATIONS

Dualism: Children of God and Children of the Devil

The writer of 1 John adopted the dualistic outlook of the Gospel of John. All of his arguments are divided in half, or have only two sides. In the writer's mind, the separatists are either with or against us. There is no middle ground, no negotiating. The writer (or writers) believes that he has a corner on the truth, and former friends have now aligned themselves with the Devil. Friends of God are called "Children of God," and those who believe differently are called "Children of the Devil." A short summary of some of the characteristics of each group follows.

Children of Devil	Children of God
belong to the world	in God
evil	good
hate	love
walk in darkness	walk in light
liars	truth speakers
hates brothers and sisters	loves brothers and sisters
will pass away	will live forever
lawlessness	righteous
sinful	do not sin
like Cain	born of God
murderers	lay down their own lives for each other
make God a liar	testimony in their hearts
no life	eternal life
under power of evil one	evil one does not touch them

Metaphors

The image of family, with its idealistic close ties and commitments, is employed in all three of the Johannine letters. God is the Father who loves his children. Both 2 and 3 John are addressed to children (1 Jn. 1:1; 2 Jn. 4). Love is essential if there is to be a harmonious relationship. 1 John also uses images of a lamp, a lamb, a king, and an army.

The Pastorals and the Johannine Letters

While scholars do not think the Johannine authors used 1, 2 Timothy and Titus (the pastorals) as a source, they think they are similar documents with similar purposes written at about the same time in history. Both emphasize holding on to a historic belief system. They urge people to follow commandments. They write in order to keep the faith and avoid divisions and arguments. They are both experiencing separatist movements and suggest how readers can avoid sin.

CHARACTERS

While the writer of 1 John defends the humanity and work of Jesus, God the Father is always in the background of the story. "God" is mentioned over fifty-five times in 1 John. This is significant compared to the Gospel of John, which is at least nine times larger and employs "God" only eighty-three times. God's love and spirit are infused into Christians and his son Jesus. He is the one in control of time, the universe, and the judgment. A few of the statements made about God in 1 John follow.

1:5	God is light.
3:1	Christians are called "Children of God."
3:9	Whoever is born of God does not commit sin.
3:17	God loves.
4:2	There is a Spirit of God.
4:12	No one has seen God.
4:15	God dwells in Jesus.
4:21	Whoever loves God loves others.
5:11	God gives eternal life.

While Jesus is an important character, we have summarized 1 John's view of him in the preceding "Issues." Other characters include the Spirit, the Children of God, the Children of the Devil, and Cain. While 1 John quotes no passages from the Hebrew Bible, the writer does employ an Old Testament story about Cain to illustrate how Christians should live in harmony.

Summary of 1 John   No one knows who wrote 1 John. Any number of people by the name of John have been suggested, along with the elder who wrote 2 and 3 John. 1 John has close affinities with both of the other letters, and especially the Gospel of John. Most scholars believe that all of the aforementioned are products of the Johannine school. Students may have known the original author of the Gospel of John and then copied his style.

Toward the end of the first century C.E., many Christian groups had forgotten their first taste of the new religion. Jesus did not return, as predicted. The disciples of Jesus were gone, and the image of a suffering cross was not very appealing. While there had always been differences of opinion, new interpretations of Jesus began to grow stronger. The discipline, social awareness, and responsibilities of the old ways began to fade.

1 John was written in the midst of these changes. Hoping to hold on to Christians who wanted to abandon the traditional ways, the writer beats the love drum with one hand. With the other hand, he indicts and slanders the same people. He singles out leaders he calls antichrists and deceivers. He is shocked that the separatists believe that Jesus was not human and that his death meant nothing to the entire world. Perhaps some within the community believed that since they had the Spirit of God, they too were perfect, without sin. The writer seems to affirm this point of view. It is odd that John never mentions the resurrection of Jesus.

FIGURE 15.1   The Resurrected Jesus. The Chora Church, Istanbul. Jesus is resurrecting Adam and Eve from their graves. Photo taken by Marla J. Selvidge.

2 John:
A Qualified Love

The elder to the elect lady and her children, whom I love in truth. . . .

—2 John 1, NRSV

INTRODUCTION

Second John couches his criticisms of people with whom he disagrees in the language of love. It is one thing to verbally attack opponents; it is another to withhold food and shelter from them. Yet, in love, this is the message of the elder. No one knows if his directions caused economic hardships for traveling missionaries. It is possible that it did.

AUTHORSHIP AND RECIPIENTS

Second John is a personal letter written to a woman who is administering a church somewhere in the Roman Empire. Suggestions usually begin with Ephesus and remain in Asia Minor. While some scholars have suggested that 2 John was written to a woman who ran a church in her house, most agree that the words, "elect lady and her children" are not to be interpreted literally. The lady is a metaphor for a community of Christians.

While most scholars view "lady" (a feminine form of the word "lord") symbolically, there is nothing in history that would suggest that this letter was not written to a woman. Indeed, the elder could be writing about a personal love for the woman. It is not difficult to imagine Aquila and Priscilla or a similar couple administering churches in different locations in the Empire. For example, **George and Margaret Fell Fox**, the founders of **Quakerism** in the seventeenth century, lived separate lives because of their missionary zeal. Note also that the elder sends wishes from another congregation or woman, the elect sister (13).

As suggested earlier, many scholars identify the elder in 2 and 3 John as the author of 1 John. Some even attempt to argue that 2 John was written first and that 1 John was the last letter. No one really knows the identity of the writer or the order in which the letters were written. Some suggest that he had no official capacity. Perhaps he was a secretary for the women running the churches.

ISSUES FACING THE ELECT LADY

Apparently there were people who visited the elect lady's church who taught that Jesus was not a human being (2 John, 7). The elder calls them antichrists. There is no way to uncover the exact content of their beliefs. The elder urges the elect lady not to allow them to stay in her home or house church (2 John, 10). One wonders how such a policy would be administered. Did people question everyone who came to their doors? Or did they know most of the itinerants? Forced verbal assent to a fixed doctrine has proved dangerous throughout history. From the witch trials in the Middle Ages, to the messianic beliefs of the Third Reich, to the McCarthyism of our own country, separating people into labeled groups has resulted in the loss of many lives. The elect lady, if she followed the elder's advice, was heading into the mouth of a dragon.

3 John:
Financing the Missionaries

Beloved, you do faithfully whatever you do for the friends,
even though they are strangers to you. . . .
—3 John 5, NRSV

INTRODUCTION

Third John is another personal letter written by the elder to Gaius. He expresses his love for him in the same manner he did for the elect lady in 2 John. Who is Gaius? No one really knows his identity. A Gaius, a Macedonian, is one of the people dragged by the Ephesians to the theatre in Acts (Acts 19:29). Another Gaius from Derbe is listed with Paul as he made his journey west (Acts 20:4). An unidentified Gaius appears to be taking care of Paul while writing the letter to the Romans (Rom. 16:23). And, finally, Paul is thankful that he baptized Gaius in Corinth (1 Cor. 1:14).

REASONS FOR WRITING THE LETTER

This letter was written to clear up financial responsibilities, to complain about Diotrephes, and to introduce Demetrius. Apparently there were problems with supporting itinerant preachers or missionaries. The writer hopes Gaius will welcome into the church the preachers who are strangers. These people, who have dedicated their lives, also should be provided with monetary gifts and supplies for their journeys (3 John, 5–8).

Diotrephes has refused to help the itinerants, and he excommunicates anyone who will help them. He may represent a breakaway group, or the elder himself could be heading a separatist movement. Note the use of "us" in verse 10. The elder is offended by Diotrephes' refusal to open his house and does not like the gossip he has heard about himself. He hopes that he will set things straight in the future.

And, finally, Demetrius is introduced. He is truthful, and a host of people will verify his character (3 John, 11–12). Demetrius may have been the courier of the letter.

Summary of 2 and 3 John   Scholars have created many theories about the congregations behind these letters and the seqence in which they were written, which we have not discussed in this chapter. These speculations are grounded in the vocabulary of the letters without the benefit of evidence from other historical sources. 2 and 3 John represent mature Christian groups in the process of change. In 2 John, people were questioning the ancient traditions about Jesus. The elder feared that their beliefs would destroy his community, so attempted to keep them at a distance.

3 John also deals with Christian hospitality. This time the elder requests Gaius to open his heart and his wallet for the missionaries. Diotrephes appears to be following the exact instructions given to the elect lady by the elder. He will not support itinerant missionaries, or those who associate with them.

Whatever the exact nature of the disagreements, the Johannine letters reflect real, not ideal, Christian groups that were attempting to solve problems that were dividing them in many ways. It also supports the notion that the interpretation and meaning of the life of Jesus was a dynamic process that began and continued in early Christian communities.

Revelation:
Politics of the Last Resort

Come, gather for the great supper of God, to eat the flesh of kings, the flesh of
captains, the flesh of the mighty, the flesh of horses and their riders—flesh of
all, both free and slave, both small and great.

—Revelation 19:19 NRSV

They will hunger no more, and thirst no more; . . .
and God will wipe away every tear from their eyes.

—Revelation 7:16–17 NRSV

INTRODUCTION

An unforgettable speech was made by **Martin Luther King Jr**. in Washington, D.C.
in 1963. It follows:

> I have a dream that one day this nation will rise up and live out the true meaning of its
> creed; I have a dream that one day even the state of Mississippi, a desert state sweltering
> with the heat of injustice and oppression, will be transformed into an oasis of freedom
> and justice. . . .
>   I have a dream that one day every valley shall be exalted, every hill and mountain
> shall be made low, the rough places will be made plains, and the crooked places will be
> made straight, and the glory of the Lord shall be revealed, and all flesh shall see it to-
> gether. (McGriggs 1978, 166–68)

His hope, born out of anguish, focused on a future when God would make peace
among people of differing skin tones. In 1963, it looked as if God was the only one
who could solve the race-relation problems in the United States. Indeed, only a few
years later, riots broke out in Watts and Detroit. Entire blocks of houses were looted and
burned to the ground. In the South, hundreds of people were beaten or jailed as they
marched, demanding equal justice for all.

During times of social crises like these, apocalyptic literature makes its way to the
surface, giving people hope that times will change, or become better. King placed his
hopes in an omnipotent God who could free his people from the chains of inhuman
treatment. He was re-creating a genre of literature read by thousands and perhaps millions of people through the centuries. Apocalyptic literature has assured people that
an omnipotent force will rescue them from the distress in their lives. All they have to
do is wait.

The appeal of apocalyptic literature may also lie within its almost impenetrable
mysterious symbols and story lines. Students of the New Testament have wrestled

for centuries with the tragic, obtuse, and sometimes repulsive stories in Revelation. Almost every major scholar seeks the key or the ultimate answer to unleashing the mysteries of the text. Some approach the text mystically, reverently assuming that the writer has some important message hidden between the lines or in the stories themselves. Secretly, some scholars wish for a direction, an arrow, a way to predict or understand themselves or the future. Practically, researchers also know that only the writer of Revelation has the power over his or her own created symbolic universe.

This ambivalent attitude toward a book that advocates violence as a solution to a religio-political power struggle remains in the canons of biblical inquiry and scholarship. Its legitimacy has often been questioned. Its influence on our culture may indirectly have promoted and institutionalized violence and terrorism.

While some may look to the Book of Revelation for consolation, or as a prediction for the future, they may also discover prejudice and injustice. **D. H. Lawrence**, a famous fiction writer, makes his own assessment of the Book of Revelation in *Apocalypse*.

> What we realize when we have read the precious book a few times is that John the Divine had, on the face of it, a grandiose scheme for wiping out and annihilating everybody who wasn't of the elect, the chosen people, in short, and of climbing up himself right on the throne of God. With nonconformity, the chapel people took over to themselves the Jewish idea of the chosen people. They were 'it,' the elect, or the 'saved.' And they took over the Jewish idea of the ultimate triumph and reign of the chosen people. From being bottom dogs they were going to be top dogs: in Heaven. (Lawrence 1982, 6).

And there are people, even today, who would agree that violence and killing are part of the Christian faith. If the world is going to be won for God, then a little shed blood is acceptable.

As we begin the study of the Book of Revelation, we will tread softly upon its pages, understanding that its roots in social crises make it an ideal vehicle for the expression and outlet of feelings of envy, resentment, and desire for revenge. We will explore possible interpretations of Revelation, also knowing that no one has found the key to unlock its meaning.

THE APOCALYPSE

The contents of Revelation reveal a seer who claims to have had a vision from God. He describes a titillating blood-and-guts adventure story of combatants who are struggling for power over the earth. His God is on the winning side. His God uses whatever means is necessary to win. All forces who oppose his God are accused and doomed to a hideous annihilation. No one survives the violent power of the writer's God except those who agree with his point of view. In the end, even the heavens and the earth must be destroyed to make room for a new, pure universe under a theocratic rule (Rev. 20).

Revelation is an apocalypse. "Apocalypse" is taken from the Greek word "apokalupsis," meaning to "reveal or uncover." What is an apocalypse and what does it mean to be apocalyptic? Apocalyptic literature falls under the category of **eschatological** writings. These writings are often called prophetic because they appear to predict the future. Unlike many prophetic writings in the Old Testament/Hebrew Bible, which involve people in the solution of a problem, the Book of Revelation assumes that the ultimate power or answer to the author's dilemma is in the hands of an almighty God (a radical monotheism). In other words, apocalyptic literature suggests that humans cannot change or control history by their decisions or actions. God is in control, and God does what God chooses.

Apocalypses are created by people who are distressed. They are powerless people who feel oppressed by a force greater than themselves. Their lives are so miserable that they feel as though they can do nothing to remedy their situation. This distress can be real or imagined. Their only hope in escaping their oppression is placed in a superhuman force that often comes in the clouds on a white horse to rescue them.

There are many theories about the origins of apocalyptic literature. While some would assign a Christian origin to the contents of Revelation, others see it as an extension of a popular Jewish or Greco-Roman literature influenced by Zoroastrianism, and in existence for centuries. Apocalyptic Jewish literature seems to have become popular during the barbarous reigns of the Seleucids under Antiochus IV and continued through the Roman domination in Palestine.

Recognizing an Apocalypse

D. S. Russell suggests a wealth of common components of apocalyptic literature in his book *The Method and Message of Jewish Apocalyptic* (1976). Some of those characteristics include the following:

1. a messianic kingdom (messianism)	A kingdom ruled by a God-appointed liberator.
2. a combat myth	A story about the inevitable and age-old struggle of good against evil.
3. transcendentalism	The belief in the superiority of the intuitive or spiritual over the empirical and scientific.
4. dualism	The belief that two gods exist, one a force for good, the other force for evil, competing for control of the universe.
5. numerology	The study of the meanings of numbers and their influence on life.
6. primordiality	A belief that something is the first in time, or that one must return to the original state.
7. determinism	A belief that history is governed by a cause.
8. symbolism	The use of animals and angels to symbolize opponents.

The Jerome Biblical Commentary attempts to describe apocalyptic literature found in the Hebrew Bible, noting that the socio-political results of such literature have resulted in war.

> Apocalyptic can be briefly characterized as . . . [the] development of prophetic style in which heavenly secrets about a cosmic struggle and eschatological victory are revealed in symbolic form and explained by angels to a seer who writes down his message under the pseudonym of some ancient personage . . . [W]e recognize that apocalyptic found its home within the nascent Christian community of the 1st century A.D. Extreme apocalyptic contributed to the great Jewish revolts of A.D. 60–66 and 132–35. These led to dreadful defeat and near despair. Judaism thereafter abandoned the hope of an imminent breakthrough of Yahweh's world kingdom and based her religion upon the minute practice of the law. Christianity considered herself to be the eschatological triumph of God in Christ Jesus, transforming the world into a new kingdom of the spirit and thereby fulfilling the ancient prophecies. (R. Brown, 1968, 1:343)

Apocalyptic literature forces the reader to reach beyond his or her ordinary experience into a symbolic and mythological arena of numbers, heavenly signs (sun, stars, moon), dreams, visions, and secret angels (messengers) bearing wisdom. Human space is divided into good and evil, light and dark, and God and the monster. The use of symbols forces readers to operate on two levels at the same time. On one level they move in a fantastic universe of angels and monsters, prostitutes and virgins, stars and temples, dragons and warriors, Christ and the antichrist. On another level exists the possibility of real conflict with real people that is taking place in real history.

AUTHORSHIP, DATE, AND ORIGINAL READERS

The Book of Revelation claims that a person named John received a vision through an angel from Jesus Christ. This John was a Christian who was a prisoner or an exile on an island, Patmos, just off the coast of Ephesus (1:1, 4, 9; 22:8). Which John was he?

> John the son of Zebedee?
> John the Beloved in the Gospel of John?
> John, the elder from Ephesus (author of the Gospel of John or the Johanine letters)?
> John the Baptist?
> Another unknown John?
> Anonymous? Could John be a code name for something else?

No one really knows who wrote the book. Some want to date Revelation early in the first century C.E., so they argue for John, the son of Zebedee. He knew Jesus, so this raises his status and reliability as a writer. John the Baptist could have been a likely candidate because he was also known to Jesus. He came out of the desert and taught many of the same themes that are found in Revelation, for example, the image of the Lamb of God, a prediction of the coming Messiah, and baptism by fire. Others find similarities in vocabulary and thought between the Gospel of John and the Johannine letters. They place the creation of Revelation late in the first century.

If the content of Revelation was created in response to the killing and torturing of Christians for their faith, we may be able to locate it within the reigns of Nero or **Domitian**. Nero was known for an uprising against the Jewish Christians in Rome in the 60s, but toward the end of the reign of Domitian, around 96 C.E., people in his own household were accused of atheism against the state and brought to trial. We have already discussed the harassment of Christians in Pontus and Bithynia by **Pliny**, so we know people were being jailed for their faith in communities throughout the Empire toward the end of the first century C.E. Revelation could have been written any time between 64 and 100 C.E.

AN ENCYCLICAL?

While Revelation does not begin as a letter, it contains mini-letters to the seven churches in Asia including Ephesus, Smyrna, Pergamum, Thyatira, Sardis, Philadelphia, and Laodicea. (See figures 15.2 and 15.3 to locate possible recipients.) Presumably Christians in these cities were the first readers of Revelation. Most people conclude that it was designed as a circular letter. Among other suggested forms are prose narrative, drama, fantasy, liturgy, myth, and prophecy. Several scholars find seams in the work, and thus suggest that the author was working with Jewish or Hellenistic sources. **J. Massyngbaerde Ford**, a professor at the University of Notre Dame, in *Revelation* (Ford 1975, 3), suggests a novel redaction of the work with three distinct editions.

Part 1	Letters to the Churches	Rev. 4–11	Written by John the Baptist before he died and before Jesus' career.
Part 2	The Apocalypse	Rev. 12–22	Written by Jewish disciples of John the Baptist, perhaps as late as 70 C.E.
Part 3	Personal Notes and Hopes	Rev. 1–3; 22:16a, 20b, 21	Added by a later disciple of John the Baptist.

Many scholars disagree with Ford's conclusion that Revelation is an early Jewish document. They think the writer was familiar with Jewish apocalypses but created his own Christian interpretation of Jesus. Some students accept Ford's speculations about the divisions and later editions of Revelation. A popular outline of the Book of Revelation follows.

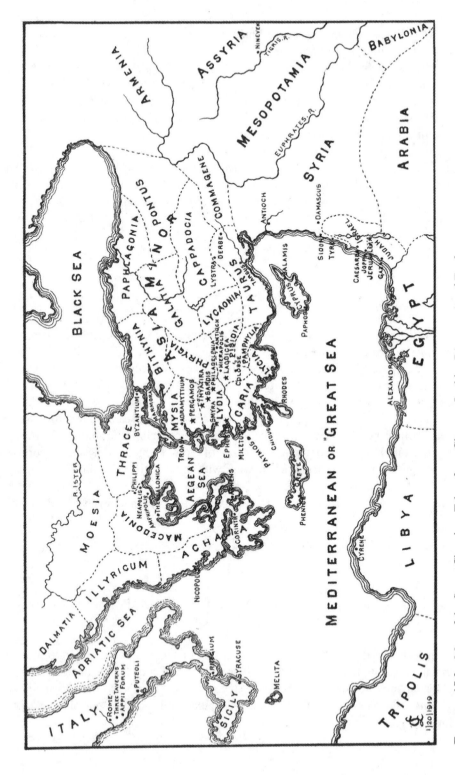

FIGURE 15.2 Map of the Seven Churches. Taken from Clarence Larkin, *Dispensational Truth* (Philadelphia: Rev. Clarence Larkin, Est., 1918).

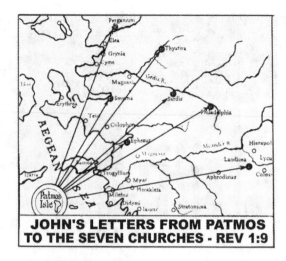

JOHN'S LETTERS FROM PATMOS TO THE SEVEN CHURCHES - REV 1:9

FIGURE 15.3 The Seven Churches. Taken from J.T. Marlin, The Seven Churches of Asia. (Nashville, TN: Williams, 1980).

Outline of the Book of Revelation

1:1–20	Introduction	
2–4	Letters to Seven Churches	
4–22	The Future	
	Seven Seals	4–8
	Seven Trumpets	8–11
	The Dragon and the Lamb	12–14
	Seven Bowls	15–16
	Judgment of Babylon	17–19
	Coming of Christ and the End of the Universe	19–22
22	Epilogue	

REASONS FOR WRITING THE BOOK OF REVELATION

Obviously the writer is experiencing the stress of some type of physical, mental, economic, or emotional harassment. Perhaps people are being jailed or losing their lives for their faith. By analyzing the first seven letters, we may find hints of crises within the Christian groups.

At Ephesus, the threat comes from people who claim to be apostles but are not. Evidently people have abandoned teachings from the original apostles in favor of the newer teachers (Revelation 2:1–7). In Smyrna, there are problems with people who are affluent and seem to be pretending to be Jews (Rev. 2:8–11). In Pergamum, people are being killed for their faith. John takes a position against eating meat offered to another God and accuses people of fornication. Perhaps they are Christians by day and worship another God at night? They are following the Nicolaitans, possibly a Gnostic sect.

FIGURE 15.4   Library of Celsus in Ephesus, Turkey. Photo taken by Marla J. Selvidge.

In Thyatira, the writer is challenged by a teacher he labels "Jezebel." She encourages people to eat meat offered to other Gods (Rev. 2:18–29). Again, the female leader of the community differs with the more conservative John. Paul allowed the eating of any meat. In some way Jezebel is aligned with Satan. The writer is not specific. Sardis seems to have lost its enthusiasm for the faith (Rev. 3:1–6). In Philadelphia the Christians could be harassed by a local synagogue (Rev. 3:7–13). The Christians at Laodicea seem to be happy with their prosperous lives. John wishes that the Laodiceans would be more dedicated to the faith (Rev. 3:14–22).

Whatever the nature of the crisis in the life of the writer, he thinks it merits a sermon about the end of time. He showers his readers with fire from heaven and a prediction of the destruction of the earth and their enemies. Describing a paradise in the midst of a battle between the forces of God and the beast, John offers his audience hope.

INTERPRETING THE APOCALYPSE

Scholarly and popular interpretation and representations of Revelation are immensely diverse. After reading the book several times, most of us still feel as though we are in a fog. What does it mean? The challenge is still waiting for a scholar to accurately categorize and describe all of the ways in which the Book of Revelation has been interpreted. In the following paragraphs, we will attempt to summarize a sampling of the interpretative approaches.

Popular Use of Revelation

The sights, sounds, and mythic stories found in Revelation have permeated Western culture for almost 2,000 years. Literature, art, movies, popular songs, and television programs have been inspired by the words of Revelation. Consider Michaelangelo's "Last Judgment" in the Sistine Chapel, Handel's "Messiah," Dante's *Divine Comedy*, and Daniel Berrigan's *Beside the Sea of Glass*. Medieval churches were built based on images of the new city of Jerusalem in Revelation.

Before we entered the twenty-first century we heard from many who predicted that the world was coming to an end. Even governments feared the effects of Y2K on global security systems. From the threat of a nuclear holocaust in *The Late Great Planet Earth* to the fear of the death star in the original *Star Wars* series, Revelation is a daily part of our lives. From the Lone Ranger to Superman to the threat of annihilation by the Dominion in *Star Trek, Deep Space Nine*, we seem to always be faced with the possibility of extinction. Politicians also understand the power of apocalyptic language and use it to manipulate Congress and the public. Consider the following, which is only one of the hundreds of apocalyptic statements made by President George Bush during the Persian Gulf War of 1990:

> Out of these troubled times, our fifth objective—a new world order—can emerge: a new era—freer from the threat of terror, stronger in the pursuit of justice, and more secure in the quest for peace. An era in which the nations of the world, East and West, North and South, can prosper and live in harmony. A hundred generations have searched for this elusive path to peace, while a thousand wars raged across the span of human endeavor. Today that new world is struggling to be born, a world quite different from the one we've known. (*Weekly Compilation of Presidential Documents* 1990, 1358)

Revelation has spawned hundreds and perhaps thousands of utopian communities such as the Cathars, **Shakers**, **Oneida Perfectionists**, Seventh-Day Adventists, **Owenites**, and more. For instance, in Estero, Florida, during the nineteenth and early twentieth centuries, the **Koreshan Unity Settlement** lived in the shadow of the end of time. They created an entire city plan based on their views of the future New Jerusalem. Mother **Ann Lee** founded a celibate Christian community, the Shakers, in the eighteenth century in New England, based on her own heavenly vision of the end of time. Revelation has given hope to those living under apartheid in South Africa or a militarist dictatorship in Central America. It has propelled countless missionaries into backwoods communities in the hope of bringing people back to Christianity before the day of doom.

SCHOLARLY APPROACHES

The function of the Apocalypse in the lives of the oppressed is hotly debated. Is it madness? Was it written by a paranoid person? Was it a kind of therapy that suspended the reader's experience of oppression? Was it used to persuade community members from engaging in violence themselves? If God were going to eventually vindicate them, then why should they take up arms against their oppressors? Or was it a document that helped solidify the hatred of an enemy launching a holy war? Is it written in code? If so, was it a blueprint for overthrowing Rome? Was it a secret document that was used to indirectly threaten or coerce oppressors? Was it directed to Christians as well as to those who opposed the religion? Was it designed to give hope and provide a sort of catharsis for people who were losing their lives for their faith? In summary, the Book of Revelation may

- offer hope to the hopeless;
- serve the psychological function of relieving tension between opponents and for the oppressed, providing the reader with a rest from stress;
- provide the ideological framework or rallying cry needed to launch or stop a holy and "just" war;
- unite a group of people to solve a domestic or international crisis.

Revelation assures readers that regardless of what violence they are experiencing in the present, the future is controlled by God. That future includes the extinction of their opponents and an eternal paradise.

Many students attempt to rescue the Book of Revelation. They recognize its vehement language as something positive. **Adela Yarbro Collins** has developed several theories that place the origins of Revelation within an oppressed, minority community that is seeking to protect itself in the first century C.E. She views the violence and massive destruction in the narrative as a way or means of overcoming a crisis of identity and economic deprivation. The violence enacted in the stories may be a transference of aggression. She reasons that Christians have ethical options in their lives, and one of those choices is murder. Revelation becomes a catharsis or a way of overcoming cognitive dissonance. Collins invites her readers to a postcritical reading of the text, which still has meaning for the twenty-first century.

Sean Freyne recognized a similar violent psycho-strategy used by the authors of Matthew and the Gospel of John. He labels it the "Rhetoric of Vituperation," or vilification. The community transfers its fears into a verbal rhetoric of aggression. Thinking about the destruction of the enemy may produce "hope."

Because of the repetition of numbers and similar actions by the characters, many scholars have wondered if Revelation has one basic theme of punishment of the opposition and reward for the faithful, which is repeated again and again. They suggest that Revelation does not progress in a linear manner, that it is one short story that keeps making the same cyclical point.

Historical-Critical Approach

The most obvious answer to the question, "What does it mean?" is found by asking another question, "What did it mean to the author and Revelation's first readers?" While

HISTORICAL LINKS

Revelation	Event
6:6 . . . and I heard what seemed to be a voice in the midst of the four living creatures saying, 'A quart of wheat for a day's pay, and three quarts of barley for a day's pay. . . .'	Economic Recession of 68 C.E.
8:7 The first angel blew his trumpet and there came hail and fire, mixed with blood, and they were hurled to the earth; and a third of the earth was burned up, and a third of the trees were burned up, and all the grass was burned up.	Storms of 67–69 C.E.
8:8 The second angel blew his trumpet, and something like a great mountain, burning with fire, was thrown into the sea.	Refers to Thera, a volcanic island.
See also the following verses:	
8:10	Falling of a meteorite supposedly responsible for polluting drinking water.
8:12	Eclipses or a storm on January 10, 69 C.E.
9:2	A volcano on Puteoli.

this information is probably lost forever, researchers attempt to recreate the historical times in which the book was written. If the book was written to actual people with actual problems, then there might be a link with documents found in history. Some scholars link specific verses with actual events, as shown in the box above.

Many want to assign the number "666" to Nero, or give names to popular Christian leaders to Jezebel and the false prophets at Ephesus. Jezebel has been equated with the wife of a bishop, Asiarch, or the Chaldean Goddess Sibyl.

Bruce Malina, a professor of biblical studies at Creighton University and author of *On the Genre and Message of Revelation: Star Visions and Sky Journeys*, believes that he has found the historical key that unlocks the meaning of Revelation. He thinks that the author of Revelation was looking up at the sky when he had his visions. The constellations and planets were the basis for images in the Book of Revelation. Malina calls it ancient astral prophecy. Messages were received from sky servants (angels).

The Book of Revelation presents an Israelite interpretation of the sky by an astral prophet who accepts Jesus as Messiah and as Cosmic Lamb. We find in the work the normal astronomic cast of characters including constellations, stars, falling or otherwise, sun and moon, as well as the cosmic abyss in the southeastern sky. All this pertains to the cosmic furniture, so to say. But we also find reference to the distinctive tradition of Israel as contained in its sacred writings and its sacred lore. (Malina 1995, 51)

Malina's research on the sociology of people during the first century led him to conclude that the average person did not look into the future to find answers. They looked back to the traditions of the elders. Revelation is therefore an account of the stories of the ancients, with a new spin. It deals with God's punishment of Israel and the elimination of evil by a cosmic renewal.

Source Criticism

Source-critical studies also look back into history to determine what sources were used by the writer. Anyone who has read Daniel and Zechariah in the Old Testament/Hebrew Bible will hear their echoes in Revelation. Some scholars claim that there are over 500 allusions to the Old Testament found in Revelations. A few are shown in the following box.

ALLUSIONS TO THE OLD TESTAMENT

Revelation

1:7	He who is coming on the Clouds	Dan 7:13	I saw one like a human being coming with the clouds of heaven.
1:8	Alpha and Omega (first and last)	Isa. 41:4	I, the Lord, am first, and will be the last.
2:7	Tree of Life	Gen. 2:9	. . . the tree of life also in the midst of the garden.
2:29	Morning Star	Isa. 14:12	O Day Star, son of Dawn!
3:9	I am the one who reproves and disciplines all those he loves.	Prov. 3:12	. . . for the Lord reproves the one he loves, as a father the son in whom he delights.
4:8	Holy, Holy, Holy is the Lord God Almighty.	Isa. 6:3	Holy, holy, holy is the Lord of hosts;

The following is an excerpt from Daniel 7:13–14 (NRSV). Does it sound familiar?

I saw one like a human being coming with the clouds of heaven. And he came to the Ancient One and was presented before him. To him was given dominion and glory and kingship, that all peoples, nations, and languages should serve him. His dominion is an everlasting dominion that shall not pass away, and his kingship is one that shall never be destroyed. (NRSV)

Another example of apocalyptic literature, taken from the *Sibylline Oracles,* follows:

> After these things, in succession came another race of men, late of fulfillment, the youngest, bloodthirsty, indiscriminate, in the fourth generation. They shed much blood, neither fearing God nor respecting men. For a raging wrath and grievous impiety was indeed inflicted on them. Wars and slaughters and battles cast some to the nether world, though they were miserable impious men. Others the heavenly God himself later removed from his world in wrath, draping them around with great Tartarus, under the base of the earth. (Charlesworth 1983, 337)

The Dead Sea Scrolls (circa 165 B.C.E. to 70 C.E.) also reveal a Jewish religious community that had hopes for a liberator who would lead the charge; at the same time, Michael, with the other angels, would battle and win against the sons of darkness. The people at Qumran believed that someday they would rule the world. They explored the hope of a powerful God who would overthrow enemies and set up a new kingdom.

Literary Criticism

A literary critical approach considers many questions that include the genre, myth, characters, symbols, organizational structure, and author's point of view or redaction(s). Revelation also can be viewed as a powerfully persuasive document that uses all sorts of **rhetorical** devices. It employs many different forms of literature, including,

Hymns	4:1–11; 5:9–12
Doxologies	1:6; 4:9; 5:13b–14
Thanksgivings	11:1–17–18
Oracles of Doom	12:12
Curses	22:18–20

Ancient Mediterranean and Babylonian mythological stories probably influenced the creation of the following myths in Revelation:

Combat	19:11–22:9
The Sacred Marriage	19:6–10
War of the Angels and the Dragon	12:7–9
The Divine City	21:9–22:5

Some have even suggested that everything mentioned in Revelation is in a special code (or symbol) referring to something else. Whether or not it is in a special code, in a way it is in a code we cannot break. We do not understand nor do we have the experiences of the person who wrote Revelation. We are lost because we can never be immersed in the culture of the first century.

Consider the immense changes that occurred in our vocabulary with the invention of the computer and the appearance of *Star Wars*. We all use metaphors related to the computer to explain everyday activities. For instance, we say someone has come "on-line." Instead of figuring tax returns, we "compute" them. A "mouse" is no longer just a mouse. We even have new words, such as cyberspace, Internet, surfing, and more.

If *Star Wars* had not impacted our lives in hundreds of ways, would we understand the meaning of the following terms? Are we comfortable using the language of computers or science fiction to describe our lives and perhaps history?

STAR WARS VOCABULARY

Galactic Empire	Hyper-Space
Death Star	Light Speed
Wookie	Main Reactor
Imperial Slugs	Darth Vader
Blast Shield	Set for Stun
Escape Pod	Scanning Crew
Droids	Chewie
Tractor Beam	The Force
Yoda	Energy Field
Transport	Tatooine
Parsecs	Speeder

In much the same way, we cannot penetrate the mind of the author. Is a lion or a lamb really a lion or a lamb, or something else?

Allegorical is a time-honored interpretative strategy used for dealing with Scriptures that are difficult to understand. It assigns universal truths or ideas to the characters and stories (this is very close to defining Revelation as a code). Every part of the book has some symbolic referent or meaning. For example, the beast may become a symbol of evil destroyed. The Woman Clothed with the Sun becomes a symbol for Mary, the mother of Jesus, or for the Church. The destruction of the earth and heavens may represent the belief that good will always triumph over evil.

Dispensationalist

Throughout history, many have concluded that Revelation was written to predict the end of history. Its pages are searched for clues or signs of when the end will occur. During the late nineteenth century and early twentieth century in the United States, Christians began to focus on interpretations concerning events leading to the thousand-year reign of Christ (20:6). The debate among many Evangelical groups continues about when Christians will be taken to heaven. Will it be before Armageddon? Will it be before the reign of Christ or premillennial? Will it be after the reign of Christ or postmillennial, or will it be during the battle of Armageddon or the tribulation, mid-tribulation?

Dispensationalism had its roots within a movement begun by **John Nelson Darby** in England among the Plymouth Brethren. **C. I. Scofield** took Darby's ideas and incorporated them into his own annotated bible, the *Scofield Reference Bible*. He divided history into dispensations or time periods that ran from the story of creation in Genesis to the end of the world in Revelation. The last time period or dispensation is the "Fullness of Time" or the "Millennium" in which he answers the questions about Christians and the millennium. Figure 15.5 on page 367 is a chart devised by Clarence Larkin in 1913 that graphically depicts the dispensation.

In general, Scofield's schemata suggested that Christians were presently living in the time of the Church. This would end with the rapture, which would take Christians alive and dead to heaven. The rapture would precipitate a tribulation, then a thousand-year reign, and finally a new heaven and earth. As the future unfolds, even today, some Christians are continually looking for the signs that will signal to them that the drama of history is about to end.

CHARACTERS OR SYMBOLS

It would be impossible to discuss all of the characters found in the Book of Revelation. We have chosen to focus on a few of the women characters.

Portraits of Women

Revelation may do more than perpetuate prejudice, intolerance, and injustice. It also may perpetuate a tolerance for violence, terrorism, and pornography. The writer justifies the annihilation of the other in order to bring into existence a new social order. He advocates revolution (religious, social, cultural), not based on informed choice but on the ashes of others. He unabashedly advocates the total destruction of a people who are in power.

No one has established a direct link between the violence in our culture and the Book of Revelation. Yet if we read this book carefully and with an open mind, we may find stories and ideas that jar us out of our comfortable easy chairs. Over the centuries, could readers have drawn the conclusion that all "evil" or "evil forces" stem from women? Does the author personify the myth of Eve? Could the annihilation of the earth in Revelation 20 represent the final alienation and annihilation of Mother Earth?

Jezebel   The hope of exacting vengeance on one's enemy creates a captivating drama in the Book of Revelation. In grotesque militant language, the writer portrays the

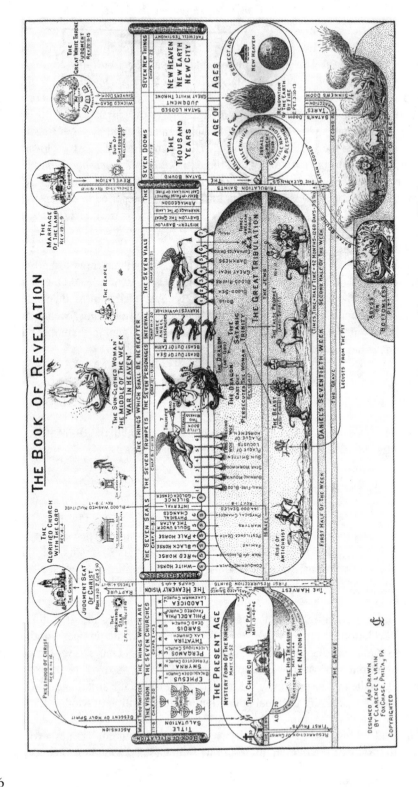

FIGURE 15.5 Dispensational Chart "The Book of Revelation." From Clarence Larkin, *Dispensational Truth.* (Philadelphia: Rev. Clarence Larkin Est., 1918).

violent demise of all forces or powers that oppose his point of view. Some of those forces are portrayed as female conspirators.

The writer creates stories that attack powers that control his life. Some of the images/symbols in those stories portray vivacious, intelligent women who, unlike the author, control not only congregations but also empires. Other female images feature beautifully dressed women who have no control over themselves, their offspring, or their environment.

Memories of these portraits (stories/images/characters/metaphors) may languish in Jewish, Mesopotamian, Hellenistic, Persian, Roman, and Egyptian mythologies. While interpreters may also search for historical figures in the stories about Jezebel (chapter 2), the Great Prostitute (chapter 17), the Woman Clothed with the Sun (chapter 12), Babylon the Great (chapter 18), or even the Bride (chapter 21), the writer's referent will always remain illusive.

The writer's first portrait of a woman feeds upon a malicious myth about an ancient Sidonian queen. In a voice claiming divine right from the Son of God (Rev. 2:18), the writer indicts a popular woman who wields both personal and intellectual power over the people and possibly over the writer. He labels his opponent "Jezebel" (1 Kings 16:21), and with that name conjures up feelings about an ancient Jezebel who challenged the forces of Yahweh and ultimately paid the price with her life (1 Kings 18:21–46). She is a teacher, a prophetess, and a leader in the community of Thyatira (Rev. 2:20). He aims at conversion through the use of terror (Rev. 22:7, 10, 18, 19).

In grueling epithets, he characterizes Jezebel's control in terms of mental, emotional, and physical/sexual activities. She uses her superior talents to persuade the people to follow her religious beliefs and practices. The writer labels Jezebel's dynamic curriculum "that teaching" (Rev. 2:24), which may be the same as "the deep things of Satan" (Rev. 2:24). The writer does not seem to know the content of that knowledge. Jezebel's teachings, apparently, are important to those who listen. People willingly allow her to carry out religious activities. Most do not challenge her in Thyatira (Rev. 2:24).

While Jezebel is in control, the writer assures the reader/listener (perhaps the servants) (Rev. 2:20) that whoever follows her will be severely punished. She will be punished for her religious activities and her adulteries (Rev. 2:22). Similar to the prostitute of Babylon, (Rev. 18:23) the dragon (Rev. 12:9), the beast (Rev. 13:14), false prophets (Rev. 19:20), and satan (Rev. 20:8), the writer claims that Jezebel deceives (Rev. 2:20) people. She does not need to use "signs" (Rev. 19:20) or "magical acts" (Rev. 18:23). She reaches the people through her teaching abilities.

The writer believes that Jezebel should be punished for her success. He threatens her with violence from the Son of God, "whose eyes are like blazing fire" (Rev. 2:18). In a powerful visual metaphor, he laughs at her accomplishments by characterizing her church as a bed of seduction, which ultimately becomes her prison. Yet she will not repent. She will not change her mind or her ways. But she is not alone. Throughout the apocalypse, people who oppose John's point of view refuse to repent, even when faced with a torturous, scorching death or life in darkness (Rev. 16:9,11). For example,

> The fourth angel poured his bowl on the sun, it was allowed to scorch them with fire; they were scorched by the fierce heat, but they cursed the name of God who had authority over these plagues, and they did not repent . . . (16:8–9 NRSV)

Since the writer cannot intimidate, change, or move Jezebel, he threatens, "I will strike her children dead" (Rev. 2:23). Ironically, in chapter 12 the dragon also uses the same tactic on the Woman Clothed with the Sun. He seeks to devour "her child" (Rev. 12:4–5).

The portrait of a Jezebel-like woman may be designed to frighten the readers (the community) into assenting to him or his religious point of view. In any case, while Jezebel may be performing and teaching religious activities that the writer negates, she remains in power. The writer is unable to control or change the dynamic leader in any way. He predicts power or authority (Rev. 2:26) for those who do his will or follow his teachings to the end, but the writer can only wish for the woman's demise. He never actually describes or witnesses Jezebel's downfall, although he does, in general, describe the ultimate annihilation of all opposing forces (Rev. 19).

The Woman Clothed with the Sun: An Impotent Goddess   This story takes place somewhere outside of the earth's atmosphere. The writer spins an unusual story about a conflict between a dragon and a Woman Clothed with the Sun. Scholars have written thousands of pages attempting to equate this woman with Mary, the mother of Jesus. Most scholars find the roots for this story in myths about ancient Mediterranean goddesses.

The dragon is so unsavory that he preys on the vulnerability of the woman while she is having a child. Poised to devour her newborn, he is foiled when God (who also is present at the birth) snatches the male child to heaven. The woman flees the scene with the aid of wings to the desert. The dragon pursues her and tries to drown her, but she is miraculously saved by the earth, which swallows the water. The enraged dragon is temporarily stopped. In the future he will make war with the rest of her offspring (Rev. 12:1–6; 13–17).

This woman is described in powerful and incandescent words. She is "a great and wondrous sign" (NEB) who is "clothed with the sun" (Rev. 12:1). John's apparition came to him in a similar burst of light, "His face was like the sun shining in all its brilliance" (Rev. 1:16). She is aligned with the moon and the stars. (Stars were thought of as living beings.) She stands on the moon and wears a crown of twelve stars (Rev. 12:1). But she has met her match in the battle that ensues. Her position in the heavens and her glistening attire fool the reader. She showcases power but is unable to protect herself or her child; she is a helpless goddess.

The writer's view of this woman is ambivalent. She appears to have her own place in the desert/hideout (Rev. 12:17). Her stature is majestic and supernormal, but she exhibits no supernatural powers. The moon is at her feet and there are stars for her crown, but she possesses no armament and no strategies to fight the dragon.

XXIII

THE TRIBULATION

FIGURE 15.6 "Woman Clothed with the Sun." From Clarence Larkin, *Dispensational Truth.* (Philadelphia: Rev. Clarence Larkin Est., 1918).

She cannot make her own decisions. She is powerless to alleviate her pain or save her child or herself. God takes the child away from her, indicating great plans for it—but not for her. Both the earth and God must provide assistance. They give her a means and a place of escape and protect her from the elements.

While she appears to have a relationship with the heavens, the stars, and the moon, her most important attributes appear to be her abilities to bear children (Rev. 12:17). This portrait of an impotent Goddess presents a humiliating picture of one who seems to have power but is in the end incapable of protecting herself, her child, or her offspring. Like a beautiful jewel, her power is only in refracted light.

The impotent Goddess may be a reflection of the writer's feelings about himself. Like so many other vulnerable Christians, he is in the same position as the woman, bearing an important message but unable to change history. He, like the woman, is only one member cast in a violent intergalactic future. In conflicting, passionate responses to an extremely oppressive religio-political power, the writer portrays ambivalent images of women. All of the images are strained characterizations of powers he cannot control, powers that are manipulated by and succumb only to an intergalactic divine energy.

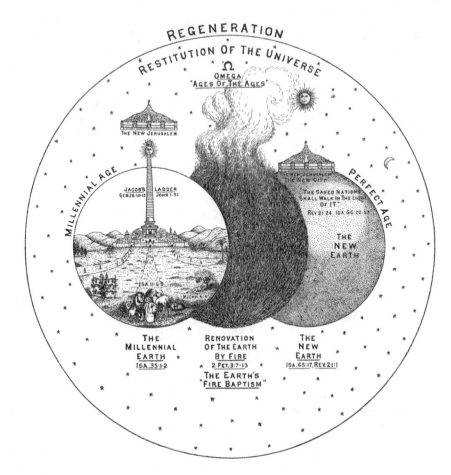

FIGURE 15.7 "Regeneration, Restitution of the Universe." From Clarence Larkin, *Dispensational Truth*. (Philadelphia: Rev. Clarence Larkin Est., 1918).

THE MYTHOLOGICAL BATTLE

The author of Revelation has created a many-tiered universe, with wars in heaven, armies of God, and powers of satan, the beast, and the devil on earth and in hades. In a war, neither side can afford to allow the other side to use superior armament. Throughout Revelation, both God and the beast use similar strategies in the battle. A closer look at Revelation will reveal that it may be God who uses more violent tactics than the Beast. Consider the comparisons in the box on page 371.

Comparison of Tactics Used by the Forces of Good and Evil

God and the Forces for Good		Satan and the Forces for Evil	
2:22	Strike children dead	12:4	Attempt to devour son
6:4	Cause people to slaughter one another	2:14	A stumbling block before people
6:6	Cause economic recession	13:7	Make war on the saints
6:8	Kill, cause famine and pestilence		
6:13	Moon turns to blood, stars fall from sky, sky vanishes	13:3	Perform great signs, fire from heaven
8:12	Destroy part of moon, stars, light	13:15	Killed those who did not worship the beast
7:4	Mark is placed on forehead of servants	13:7	Place a mark on the forehead
14:1	Name of Father on the forehead of 144,000		
8:8	Kill sea creatures and ships		
8:10	Destroy waters		
16:3	Kill everything in sea		
16:4	Turn river to blood		
9:3	Send locusts		
9:5	Torture people who will wish they were dead	2:10	Throw people into prison as a test
14:9	Torment with fire. No rest.		
16:2	Cause sores		
16:8	Scorch people		
16:9	Create sores that cause people to gnaw their tongues		
18:7	Burn harlot with fire		
9:18	Part of humanity killed	6:9	Slaughter souls
11:13	7,000 killed in earthquake	11:7	Kill two witnesses
14:20	Blood flowed like wine press	17:6	Drunk with the blood of saints
8:7	Cause hail, fire, blood	18:24	Killed prophets and saints
16:19	Cause earthquakes, split city, plagues, hailstones, level mountains		
19:18	Eat flesh of kings	12:4	Attempt to eat son

Analyze these notations about the forces of good and evil. Does one force have more power than the other? Are there certain areas each force controls? Describe their battlefield.

Summary of Revelation   The phrase "politics of the last resort" explains the mood of Revelation. There appears to be no human way to solve the impending or present crises. God has been forced to take the "last resort." There are no negotiations, accommodations, or other virtuous points of view. The writer believes he has received the truth, and those who do not agree with him will experience "the last resort."

No one has uncovered the identity of the author of John. It could be any number of Johns mentioned in the Bible or famous people in history. Revelation was probably written during the last part of the first century. It contains prophecies that effect the entire globe and letters written to seven churches in Asia Minor. Each community is assailed for failing to meet standards. The author also describes a fierce battle that results in the suffering of humanity. Has God abandoned his people? John assures the reader that God is in control of history and that their suffering will soon end.

The genre of apocalypse is difficult to describe and define. It is a literature that seeks to reveal something hidden or mysterious, containing elements such as a liberator from God, a fight against evil forces, a hope for the future, and numerous symbols of animals, people, and numbers. Apocalyptic writings may have contributed to the escalation of actual physical conflicts, such as the Jewish wars.

The Book of Revelation serves many psychological, social, ideological, and religious purposes. It can unite people to solve a problem or begin a revolution. It can relieve stress in individuals and entire nations. It can also be used to manipulate people into supporting unpopular war efforts. The themes and struggles within Revelation have been adopted in literature, film, art, music, and architecture. Utopian communities have lived in anticipation of entering the heavenly city.

Scholars and casual readers differ immensely over what method should be used to interpret Revelation. It may be allegory, astral prophecy, or a series of stories that repeat the same theme. Sources for the stories are found throughout the Mediterranean and Middle Eastern literatures. Some scholars spend their time looking at symbols, characters, and other literary aspects of Revelation, while others believe its words are actual prophecies about to blossom in our own lifetimes.

We have chosen to analyze women characters by studying passages about Jezebel and the Woman Clothed with the Sun. The writer's attitude is ambivalent. He portrays Jezebel and the Harlot as popular, powerful, and successful. The Woman Clothed with the Sun is passive when under siege. She and her son are preserved only because of the mighty hand of God, which is portrayed in much the same way as the forces of evil. In fact, Revelation creates an image of God who excels in torture and abuse.

Revelation ends on a note of triumph and peace. The war is over. Satan is chained. The Beast is under arrest, and the Harlot is destroyed. The heavens and earth have been replaced with something new. God has won!

Glossary

By Annette L. Farbolin,
Student Assistant
to the Center For Religious Studies,
Central Missouri State University

Acrocorinth the hill above the city of Corinth. It supported the temple to Aphrodite and was used for military purposes.

Acts of John a Greek romance of the fifth century C.E., written by Prochorus, which centers on the journeys of John of Patmos and the miracles he performed.

Adonai derived from the Hebrew word for "Lord." Jews did not pronounce the name "Yahweh," so they used the word "Adonai." The word "Jehovah" results from reading the consonants of Yahweh with the vowels of the substitute word Adonai.

Adventist a person holding to the belief that Christ's second coming, or advent, and the last judgment will soon occur, bringing about a new age.

Aetiological Legend a myth that tells the origin or cause of something; also known as an etiology.

Agape "love feast" and community meal during which the Eucharist was sometimes celebrated. The feast represented respectful and unselfish love for the church community and helped feed the poorer members of the church.

Alexander a Christian living in Ephesus, considered a false teacher by Paul; see **Hymenaeus**. Alexander was also a son of Simon Cyrene (Mark 15:21, 1 Timothy 1:20); a member of a high priestly family (Acts 4:6); and a Jew from Ephesus (Acts 19:33).

Alexander the Great (356–323 B.C.E.) ruler of Macedonia who defeated the Persians and created an empire that stretched from Greece to Egypt and Western Asia. His empire fostered the growth of Greek language and culture (Hellenism) throughout the known world.

Alexandria Egyptian seaport founded by Alexander the Great in 332 B.C.E. It was the Hellenistic center of learning in the ancient world and had a museum and two great libraries.

The museum library was damaged when Caesar besieged Alexandria, and it was destroyed during the civil war under Roman Emperor Aurelian. The second library was demolished by Christians. Alexandria also was famous for its lighthouse, which was considered one of the wonders of the world.

Allegory an extended metaphor; a story in which people, things, and happenings have a hidden or symbolic meaning. Allegories are used for teaching or explaining ideas or moral principles. Many of the early church writers interpreted the New Testament allegorically. They saw moral principals in almost every passage.

Alves, Rubem A. Brazilian social scientist, theologian, and professor at Campinas State University who wrote *What Is Religion?* and *Tomorrow's Child.*

Ambrosiaster a name given to the unknown author of a commentary on the letters of Paul the Apostle; the epistles were originally attributed to Ambrose, but most scholars agree that he did not write them.

Analytic pertaining to the separation of a whole into its parts and an examination of those parts; to be investigative.

Anarchist a person who believes that law and government should be destroyed so that individuals can be free from the oppressive institutions of the state. Society would be ordered by voluntary agreements between people, since humans are considered good by nature. An anarchist could also be a person who rebels against any established rule or custom. An exponent of anarchism was Zeno of Citium.

Androcentric male centered; of the perspective that the male is the model human and the center of the universe, while the female is "other." This view arises out of male control of culture that excludes females, claiming that they are inferior and subordinate.

Androgyny female and male characteristics in one being.

Angelou, Maya a writer, poet, performer and civil rights activist who wrote *I Know Why the Caged Bird Sings, And Still I Rise,* and *On the Pulse of Morning: The Inaugural Poem.*

Anna a Jewish woman portrayed in the Gospel of Luke who is called a prophetess and was present when Mary and Joseph took Jesus to the Temple.

Anointing the ritual application of oil to announce or recognize a new king; to eliminate disease or demons; to introduce divine power; to prepare for a ceremony or a sacrament; to bid farewell to the ill or dying.

Anthropologists those who study human behavior, beliefs, and language, including humanity's cultural and biological development.

Anti-Semitism this term arose from an ethnic ideology that sought to separate Jews from Germans. Today, it can mean any hatred or antagonism toward Jews or Judaism.

Antioch in Syria ancient city on the Orontes river twenty miles from Seleucia and the Mediterranean. It was an influential Roman capital of the province of Syria and a center of commerce and culture. Antioch is famous because the term *Christian* was coined in this city. Christians came to Antioch to escape persecution. The missionary Paul began and ended two journeys there.

Antiochus Epiphanes IV son of Antiochus the Great, who usurped the throne in 175 B.C.E. after his brother was assassinated. He wanted to Hellenize the Seleucid Empire, so he prohibited all Jewish rites and rededicated the Temple in Jerusalem to Zeus. This campaign against the Jews resulted in the Maccabean Revolution.

Antony, Mark (83–32 B.C.E.) Roman general who aligned himself with Julius Caesar in a civil war with Pompey and expected to become emperor after Caesar's assassination. However, he was rivaled by Octavian and became part of a triumvirate with Octavian and Lepidus. After an affair with Cleopatra, he was finally defeated by Octavian.

Aphrodite   Greek goddess of love and beauty who was married to Hephaestus (Vulcan). According to Greek legends, she had many affairs and became the mother of Aeneas by Anchises. The Romans identified her with Venus.

Apocalypse of Peter 5   an apocalypse composed around 125–150 C.E. that describes the messiah Bar Kokhba. Some early Christians accepted it as canonical, but others, such as Jerome and Eusebius, did not.

Apocalyptic   meaning "revelation" of or pertaining to prophetic literature produced by people who believe they are oppressed (real or imagined). They predict future deliverance by cosmic forces, often involving the destruction of the world and/or coming disasters. Apocalyptic literature is known for its use of symbolism, dualism, superhuman beings, and a negative view of history.

Apocrypha   "hidden" in Greek. A category of writings usually noncanonical, of unknown origin, or merely considered unorthodox and esoteric. Usually they are the books not included in the Hebrew or Christian Bible. Jewish, Protestant, and Roman Catholic religious bodies differ in what they consider Apocryphal and their treatment of Apocryphal literature.

Apollo   an ancient Greek god associated with healing, vegetation, herds and flocks, beauty, courage, wisdom, culture, and purification. He had a famous oracle and cultic center at Delphi and is the son of Zeus.

Apollonius of Tyre   an anonymous romance from the second or third century C.E. that focuses on Apollonius, his wife, and his daughter.

Apostle   one who is sent by another, especially a Christian missionary Jesus commissioned, as in the Twelve Apostles or disciples. The New Testament contains stories about both male and female apostles.

Appellations   names, titles, or classifications that describe a person or thing.

Apuleius   (124–170? C.E.) Roman rhetorician, philosopher, and poet. He wrote *Metamorphoses* or *The Golden Ass,* which contains information about the mysteries of Isis and Osiris.

Archaeologists   those who study the material remains of archaeological digs in order to reconstruct the past and understand historic or prehistoric people and their cultures.

Aretalogies   ancient stories or narratives about divine people, such as Jesus or Isis, who perform supernatural tasks and sometimes teach moral philosophies.

Aristarchus   a Jewish Christian from Macedonia who traveled with Paul and was imprisoned with him.

Aristotle   (384–322 B.C.E.) Greek philosopher and pupil of Plato. He founded his own school and wrote on a variety of subjects, including metaphysics, politics, and ethics. He is famous for the argument for the existence of an "unmoved mover."

Artemis   a mother-goddess (not related to the virgin hunting goddess of Greece and Rome) worshiped throughout Asia Minor, Greece, and Rome. One of her statues at Ephesus was a wonder of the ancient world.

Ascetic   practicing self-discipline or self-denial, especially for religious reasons. Sometimes ascetic practices would lead people to cut off parts of their bodies, live in caves, or sit on poles for many years. Ascetic practices often drew attention to social, cultural, political, religious, and ethical problems or inequities.

Asklepios   ancient God of healing from Asia Minor who became one of the most popular deities in the Hellenistic world.

Assumption of Moses an apocalyptic work that had been combined with *Testament of Moses* and does not exist in its full form today. It tells a story about a quarrel between Michael and Satan over the body of Moses.

Atman a Hindu word for the "self" or "soul" of each individual.

Attis Phrygian god of vegetation and the consort of the mother-goddess Cybele. His festival, at the spring equinox, celebrates renewal after death. After being adopted by the Romans, he became a sun god who offered immortality.

Audience (or readers) the group of people to whom a writing or speech is addressed or merely the person who reads or hears the literature.

Augustine (354–430 C.E.) Christian theologian, bishop of Hippo, and prolific writer, best known for his *Confessions.* His ideas influenced Western culture and Christianity, and he is best known for popularizing the concept of "original sin."

Augustus (63 B.C.E.–14 C.E.) Gaius Julius Caesar Octavius was also known as Octavian. He was adopted by his uncle, Julius Caesar, and became the first Roman emperor. His reign was marked by peace, advances in culture, and stable government. The senate gave him the title of Augustus to honor his contributions to the Roman state.

Aum Shinrikyo "the true teaching of Aum," or "teaching of the truth." A modern Japanese religion known for its messianic and apocalyptic outlook. It blends Hindu, Buddhist and yogic teachings. It is thought that some of its members were responsible for numerous murders and a nerve gas attack on a Tokyo subway in March 1996.

Bacchanal a celebration in honor of Bacchus (Dionysus) or a devotee of Bacchus; see **Dionysus**.

Bailey, John A. a professor in the Department of Near Eastern Studies at the University of Michigan. He has written many books, including *Traditions Common to the Gospels of Luke and John* and *Ministry of the Church in the World.*

Baptism a common initiation ritual, usually involving water or blood, that could signify unity, a new life, a new covenant, or an enlightenment.

Bathsheba the wife of Uriah the Hittite, one of King David's military captains. She was desired and seduced by King David, who saw her bathing on a roof top. David made Bathsheba his queen after he arranged for the death of her husband. She became the mother of Solomon.

Beatitudes sayings of blessedness pronounced by Jesus in the Sermon on the Mount that illustrate ideals of Christian living. Similar blessings also are found in the Gospel of Luke. The word translated as "beatitude" also can be translated as "happy."

Beguines a loosely organized lay sisterhood, begun in the twelfth century, that did not adhere to permanent vows or a full conventual life, yet stressed continence, obedience, and charity. Beguines held a wide variety of beliefs, such as mysticism, illuminism, antinomianism, and Joachimism. Today there are approximately one dozen beguinages in Belgium and Holland.

Bishop from the Greek word "episcopos," meaning overseer or guardian; an early Christian office or function sometimes equated with "elder" that became an ecclesiastical title and office in the later church.

Bithynia an area in Northern Asia Minor that later became a Roman province.

Book of Kells a manuscript of the gospels dated to 800 C.E. that is famous for its intricate illuminations. It once belonged to the Abbey of Kells but is now housed at Trinity College in Dublin.

Brahma the Hindu creator God and ultimate reality who forms a trinity with Vishnu the preserver and Shiva the destroyer.

Brown, Raymond E. educator and priest in the Roman Catholic Church. His numerous publications include *The Birth of a Messiah, Mary in the New Testament,* and *The Community of the Beloved Disciple.*

Bultmann, Rudolph K. (1884–1976) Christian theologian and New Testament scholar. He was influenced by existentialism and demythologization and helped found form criticism of the synoptic gospels. His many books include *What Is Theology?, Faith and Understanding,* and *Theology of the New Testament.*

C.E. (Common Era) This inclusive abbreviation is used with dates and is an alternative for A.D. (Anno Domini, "In the year of our Lord").

Cabiri early fertility gods and smiths of the underground who later became the focus of popular mystery rites and were called "great gods" by the Greeks. Some reports suggest that Zeus and Dionysus were worshipped as the Cabiri; others mention three or four deities.

Caesar, Julius (100–44 B.C.E.) a general and statesman who accumulated unusual power and offices and ruled as dictator of the Roman Empire from 49 B.C.E., until he was assassinated.

Caesarea Roman seaport in Palestine that was originally a small Phoenician town founded by Straton, King of Sidon, in the fourth century B.C.E., but it was rebuilt under Herod in 9 B.C.E. It was the ancient Roman capital of the region and the seat of the Roman governor of Judea; also known as Caesarea Maritima and Caesarea Palestinae.

Caligula (12–41 C.E.) Gaius Julius Caesar Germanicus nicknamed Caligula after the military boots he wore as a child. He was adopted by Tiberius and became a cruel and insane Roman emperor. He enforced emperor worship by turning Jewish places of worship into cultic shrines and threatening to place his image in the Jerusalem Temple. He and his family were later murdered and succeeded by Claudius.

Calvin, John (1509–1564 C.E.) French Protestant reformer who believed in predestination, salvation of the elect by God's grace, and a strict moral code.

Campesino a farmer or farm worker who lives in a rural area.

Canon a collection of books and/or writings that a religious body considers divinely inspired, sacred, and authoritative; rule.

Carpocrations followers of the Gnostic teacher Carpocrates, who lived during the second century C.E. He was influenced by Platonism and taught that all creation was evil and came from an unknown first principle. He claimed that in order to be reincarnated, a state of perfect hate must be achieved by despising all laws. He also advocated complete sexual freedom.

Catechumen a person who is being taught the doctrines of Christianity in preparation for baptism.

Cathars the Cathari or "the pure" were twelfth-century Christians who had no doctrinal unity, although most believed in a dualism where the principles of good and evil fought an endless war on earth. Their beliefs were related to Gnosticism, Manichaeism, Docetism, Monarchianism, and Hinduism. They were ascetics who thought matter was evil. They rejected many Roman Catholic ideas, including the power of clerics and the Sacrament. The Cathari were destroyed by the Inquisition and the Albigensian Crusades.

Catharsis a general process of purification that can be therapeutic, magical, or protective; especially a purging or release of emotions.

Catholic "universal." This term can be applied to the Western division of the Church after it split in 1054 C.E. Catholicism also is distinguished from the Protestant movement of the sixteenth century. "Roman Catholic" refers to those who hold the Bishop of Rome (the Pope) as the highest church authority.

Celibacy abstaining from marriage.

Centurion the commander of 100 men in the Roman army. A centurion was well paid and would receive many rewards for his military service.

Cerinthus a Gnostic teacher of Asia Minor who lived around 100 C.E. He believed that the world was created not by God but by a separate power. He also believed that Jesus was human and separate from the Christ spirit and that only Jesus suffered the Crucifixion.

Character a person, animal, god, or thing represented in a play, story, novel, or gospel. The combination of characteristics that makes a person or thing distinct.

Church and State the concept that religion and government should be separate from each other. It is related to the first amendment of the United States Constitution, which guarantees that neither shall interfere with the free exercise of the other.

Cicero, Marcus Tullius (106–43 B.C.E.) Roman statesman, orator, and writer who was exiled from Rome after he was consul. He returned and joined Pompey in the Roman civil war against Caesar. Because he supported the senate, he was executed by Antony following the assassination of Caesar.

Circumcision removal of the foreskin of the penis, which can symbolize entrance into puberty, marriage, or a religious community (as in the case of the Jews).

Civic Religion rituals, beliefs, myths, and symbols that unite a city, state, or country; see **Emperor Worship**.

Claudius (10 B.C.E.–54 C.E.) Tiberius Claudius Drusus Nero Germanicus was the grandson of Augustus and the nephew of Tiberius. He expelled those who were following "Chrestus" from Rome in 49–50 C.E.

Clement of Rome a saint and pope whose pontificate is usually placed in the last decade of the first century. According to Irenaeus, he was the third pope after St. Peter, and his martyrdom is legendary. Many works are attributed to him, but only his *First Epistle to the Corinthians* is authentic.

Cleopas one of the two disciples who met Jesus on the road to Emmaus in Luke 24.

Coelestius (Caelestius or Celestius) an attorney and a monk from Great Britain who lived during the fifth century C.E. and followed Pelagius. He was condemned by several church councils from Carthage to Ephesus because he did not believe in original sin and argued against infant baptism.

Collins, Adela Yarbro a professor of the New Testament and chair of the Department of New Testament and Early Christian Literature at the University of Chicago. She has written many books, including *The Apocalypse, Is Mark's Gospel a Life of Jesus?*, and *Cosmology and Eschatology in Jewish and Christian Apocalypticism.*

Commentary comments, explanations, annotations, or treatises on religious writings. A commentary can be critical, homiletical, or devotional.

Confucian a term describing the philosophy taught by K'ung Fu'tzu (551–479 B.C.E.), also known as Confucius. Confucius taught a code of ethics and stressed correct personal behavior, along with duty toward society. Many schools of thought arose from Confucius' teachings. His thought provides the foundation for Chinese education.

Constantine the Great (280?–337 C.E.) Flavius Valerius Aurelius Constantius was the Roman emperor who issued the Edict of Milan in 313 C.E. that legalized Christianity. He moved the capital of the Roman Empire to Byzantium, which he renamed Constantinople, and founded the Church of St. Peter in Rome. He consented to be baptized into Christianity while on his deathbed.

Council of Trent the nineteenth general council of the Roman Catholic Church, held from 1543 to 1563 C.E., where the canon of Scripture was defined. The Council was called because many wanted reform to stop the abuses of the clergy. The churchmen who attended not only defined the doctrines of the Roman Catholic Church but condemned Protestant doctrines.

Crassus, Marcus Licinius (115?–53 B.C.E.) a wealthy Roman politician and military leader who raised an army to defeat a large slave revolt led by Spartacus. He was a member of the first triumvirate with Pompey and Julius Caesar.

Crusades eleventh- to thirteenth-century military expeditions by the Church. The object of most of the Crusades was to recover the Christian "Holy Land" from Muslims and Jews.

Cybele a mother-goddess of Asia Minor, worshipped in conjunction with her lover Attis. Her religion spread to Greece by the fifth or seventh century B.C.E. and to Rome in the third century B.C.E., where she was known as "Magna Mater" or Great Mother. She often is represented standing or sitting between two lions or leopards.

Cynicism Greek philosophical school founded by Diogenes of Sinope. Cynics were critical of society's excesses and stressed virtue, self-sufficiency, and asceticism.

Danker, Frederick a Lutheran minister and Professor of exegetical theology who wrote *Multipurpose Tools for Bible Study* and revised the second edition of *A Greek-English Lexicon of the New Testament.*

Daphnis and Chloe a romance from the third century C.E., usually attributed to Longus, that centers on two lovers and their adventures. It also is known as the *Lesbiaca.*

Darby, John Nelson (1800–1882) an ordained minister who was not satisfied with the religious denominations available to him. He and other Christians united and called themselves the Brethren. They wanted to return to a simple, early form of Christianity. Darby believed in dispensationalism, the presence of Christ at religious gatherings, and regular Bible study.

Decipher to discover the meaning of something difficult to understand and translate it into understandable language.

Demas a fellow worker of Paul who also was imprisoned with him. Later, he left Paul and went to Thessalonica.

Demeter Greek mother-goddess of marriage and agriculture, especially of grain. She was the mother of Persephone (Kore or Proserpina) who was kidnapped and taken to the underworld. Her mysteries or rituals at Eleusis celebrated the cycles of rebirth. The Romans identified her with Ceres.

Denomination a religious body with a specific name, organization, and belief system within Protestantism.

Deutero-Pauline those writings attributed to Paul but probably not written by him; see **Pseudo-Pauline**, **Pseudonymous**, and **Pseudepigrapha**.

Dewey, Joanna professor of New Testament Studies at Episcopal Divinity School who contributed to *The Women's Bible Commentary.*

Dialect a distinctive language within a major language. A group variation of a language often called, "the vernacular." Examples in the United States include a Southern drawl, or the new "Ebonic" language.

Diaspora the dispersion or scattering of any religious people from their homeland. The Jewish dispersion began with the Babylonian exile of 587 B.C.E.

Diatribe a bitter, abusive criticism or a denunciation used by Cynics to reprimand students and the general public.

Diogenes of Sinope (412?–323? B.C.E.) founder of the Greek philosophical school of Cynicism whose nickname was "the dog." He was an ascetic who rejected all of society's conventions and wrote many dialogues and tragedies.

Dionysus Greco-Roman god of wine, vegetation, the underworld, and ecstasy, whose followers (called Maenads or Bacchae) worshipped in the countryside. The majority of his followers were female. They often wore animal skins and carried decorated poles during rituals in which they would have visions and eat raw flesh. Dionysus often would appear as an animal in these ceremonies and commune with his followers.

Discourse communication of thoughts and ideas by using speech or writing, especially a long and formal discussion of a certain subject, as in a dissertation, treatise, or sermon.

Docetism the belief that Jesus was not human and that he only appeared to have died on the cross.

Dogma formal and authoritatively affirmed doctrines, tenets, and beliefs.

Domitian, Titus Flavius (51–96 C.E.) the son of Vespasian and brother of Titus, who became a Roman emperor in 81 C.E. He tried to enforce religious and moral standards, which made him hostile to Jews and Christians. After hearing of a conspiracy, he began a reign of terror that lasted until he was assassinated.

Doublet the repetition of the same idea. For example, a story that grew out of or alongside an original story. This literary form often appears in the gospels and Acts of the Apostles, especially when parables or miracle stories are employed.

Doxology a standardized prayer or hymn that praises God; see **Kaddish.**

Drachma a Greek unit of measurement, or a silver coin. In New Testament times, a drachma was equal to a day's wage, and four drachmas were equal to a shekel.

Dualistic (Dualism) the idea that there are only two ultimate principles or causes in the world, such as good and evil or soul and body.

Edessans pupils and teachers of the School of Edessa in Turkey (modern Urfa). It was an Antiochene and Nestorian school and was an important center of early Christianity until it was closed in 489 C.E. by the Council of Chalcedon. Many of its students went on to become Persian bishops. They believed Jesus was two persons or had dual natures: divine and human. They did not believe Mary could be the Mother of God, since she gave birth to a human only.

Elder a presbyter, leader, or teacher in a Christian church.

Elijah a Hebrew prophet of Israel who lived during the ninth century B.C.E. The Book of Kings spins a story about his conflict with Jezebel and of being taken to heaven.

Elizabeth a friend or relative of Mary who gave birth to John the Baptist. She may have descended from a priestly family.

Elohim a general word for "God" and a plural form of "El."

Emmaus a village whose site is still unknown. Jesus traveled with two disciples, Cleopas and another, who were on the road to Emmaus in Luke 24.

Emperor Worship/Imperial Cult the honoring of dead heroes/heroines and living rulers or their wives that developed in Greece during the third and fourth centuries B.C.E. The imperial cult became an official part of Roman religion when Julius Caesar was deified after his death in 44 B.C.E. Emperor worship developed into the worship of a living or dead Roman emperor who was capable of supernatural deeds that benefited the community; see **Civic Religion**.

Encyclical a single letter addressed generally to one audience but circulated to many other locations or congregations.

Enigma a statement, circumstance, or thing that is perplexing or cannot be solved.

Enoch, 1, a series of revelations or writings, no older than the second or fourth century B.C.E., which includes a discussion of the cosmos, world judgment, myths about Enoch's journeys, an angelogical section, and a historical section.

Epaphras a Colossian, fellow worker, and prisoner with Paul.

Epicureanism philosophical school founded by Epicurus. Epicureanism was popular from 300 B.C.E. to 200 C.E., and it stressed materialism, hedonism, and escapism. Epicurus was concerned with obtaining happiness in this earthly life, since it was the only life he recognized.

Epimenides a religious teacher and prophet from Crete who lived around 500 or 600 B.C.E. Many works are attributed to him, including a history of Crete and writings on religious mysteries.

Eschatology the study of the end of time, the future, or the last things.

Esoteric that which is difficult to understand or can only be known by those who are initiated; secret.

Essenes an ascetic and apocalyptic Jewish community, circa 164 B.C.E.–78 C.E. that stressed radical obedience to the law; see also **Qumran** and **Zadokites**.

Eucharist The Mass or Lord's Supper; a ritual that involves sharing and consuming wine and bread. Some Christians believe that the bread or "host" and wine are the actual blood and body of Jesus. Others view it as a symbol or remembrance of Jesus.

Eusebius (260–339 C.E.) a Christian theologian and historian who became Bishop of Caesarea and wrote a history of Christianity entitled *Church History.*

Evangelicalism a conservative religious philosophy or political point of view common among many denominations within Protestantism. Evangelicals stress proclaiming the gospel, biblical authority, personal religious experience, human sinfulness, and the necessity of a new birth. They differentiate themselves from fundamentalists.

Excommunication the separation of a person from the religious community to punish him or her.

Exegesis critical analysis or explanation of text, especially the Bible, using principles of hermeneutics.

External Evidence information that comes from sources outside of the Bible that proves, disproves, or helps illuminate biblical passages.

Extracanonical something outside of the general canon; those writings that are not widely accepted as part of the Books collected in the Old Testament or Hebrew Bible and New Testament. See Canon.

Facsimile an exact reproduction or copy.

Feminist Criticism varying methods of criticism that focus on the final form of the text and examine it to determine its point of view regarding women, children, racial, and ethnic minorities. The condition of women's lives, female characters in the Bible, and lost works by women are taken into account, along with the androcentric and patriarchal character of Scripture in the effort to support the equality of women.

Feminists adherents to the view that women should have political, economic, and social equality with men.

Filial Piety devotion, respect, and honor for parents, often manifested in rituals dedicated to ancestors.

Foreordination see **Predestination**.

Ford, J. Massyngbaerde a professor and theologian at Notre Dame University who has written many books, including *A Trilogy on Wisdom and Celibacy, Jesus and Violence in Luke,* and *We Are Easter People.*

Fox, George and Margaret (Fell) George Fox (1624–1691) was a founder of the Religious Society of Friends, also known as Quakers. He and his wife, Margaret Fell Fox (1614–1702), believed that each person had an inner light that helped them reach religious truth. George Fox began as an itinerant preacher (among other things) and was jailed because he spoke against established churches. After Margaret was converted, her home in England became a center of Quakerism; see **Quakerism.**

Freyne, Sean professor of Hebrew, biblical, and theological studies at Trinity College of the University of Dublin who wrote *Galilee, Jesus, and the Gospels.*

Galatia an interior division of Asia Minor that became a Roman province that included Phrygia, Pisidia, Lycaonia, and the cities of Iconium, Lystra, Derbe, and Antioch. Although the exact location of the region named Galatia has varied through time, the province spanned the area between the Black Sea and the Mediterranean.

Galilee Roman province in northwestern Palestine where Jesus lived and preached according to the gospels.

Genre a literary form or category with a specific style. Writers within the New Testament used many different types of literary forms to convey meaning, that is, letter, narrative, apocalypse, gospel, miracle story, parable, and so on.

Gentiles "nations" in Greek; people who are not Jewish.

Gnosis spiritual, esoteric, syncretistic, allegedly superior, and mysterious knowledge that is gained through self-illumination, revelation, or initiation into a secret tradition.

Gnosticism a philosophy that is syncretistic, views matter as evil, and stresses escapism through Gnosis. Many Gnostic groups focused on the Goddess Sophia (Wisdom or Knowledge), calling her the Great Mother, World Soul, God's Female Soul and Source of His Power, the Spirit of Female Wisdom and the Spouse and Mother of God. Other groups worshipped a bisexual being called Father/Mother or thought that Christ, God, and Sophia merged into one. During the early years of Christianity, this type of Gnosticism merged with Christianity and attracted many women, becoming one of the more popular forms of Christianity.

God Fearers non-Jews who believed in the one God of the Jews and attended synagogue but did not adhere to the purity laws. They usually were uncircumcised.

Gospel Old English "godspel" or good story/news.

Gutenberg Bible "Mazarin Bible," the first book to be printed mechanically by using a printing press. It was printed by Johann Gutenberg in 1456 and was based on the Latin Vulgate.

Hagiography stories about the saints of the Roman Catholic Church found in narratives, legends, and biographies.

Harmonize to bring into an agreement; to blend ideas from different sources into a single whole.

Hartin, Patrick J. professor at the University of South Africa, Pretoria, who wrote *James and the Q Sayings of Jesus.*

Heaven a Christian belief of an eternal state or a place of complete happiness, rest, and union with God that can only be attained after death.

Hebrew Bible sacred scriptures of the Jewish people containing twenty-four books, which include the Torah (Pentateuch), the Nevi'im (Prophets), and the Ketuv'im (Writings); also known as the Old Testament, Hebrew/Jewish Scriptures, Torah, Tanakh, Holy Books/Writings, and First Testament.

Hellenism the word used to describe the influence of Greek culture on other cultures. Greek culture, language, and philosophy spread throughout the Empire after Alexander the Great conquered most of the known world.

Heretics those who hold views that are in opposition to the politically correct beliefs of the people who are in power within a religion.

Hermeneutics the principles of interpretation used in the determination of the meaning of a text in Scripture.

Herod Antipas a son of Herod the Great. He ruled Galilee from 4 B.C.E. to 39 C.E. and was married to Herodias. She was once the wife of his half-brother, Philip.

Herod the Great (73?–4 B.C.E.) Idumean governor of Galilee who was crowned King of Judea in 37 B.C.E. by the Romans. He began many building projects during his lifetime, including a palace that was later named Masada and the Temple in Jerusalem, which was not completed during his lifetime.

Hesiod a Greek poet who lived around 700 B.C.E. who wrote the *Theogony,* which describes the origin of the universe, the lives of the gods, and how they came to power.

Heterogeneity the quality of being composed of different or miscellaneous parts.

Hierarchy (Hierarchical) a group of persons or things that is organized in order of rank, grade, class, or other characteristic, making some persons or things subordinate to others; a system of church government.

Historical Criticism method of criticism that looks at the historical setting in which the Bible was written. It considers the social conditions, data on governments, peoples, and cultures, and seeks external evidence to support the Bible.

Holiness Groups religious groups that arose from the Holiness movement of the nineteenth century. They protested the show of wealth, much like the Puritans, and advocated long hair for women, no jewelry, and long skirts. They emphasized the work of the Holy Spirit in their lives, believing that they could be perfect.

Holy Spirit "breath" or "wind" in Hebrew and Greek. This term occurs only in the New Testament and is used to mean the manifestation of God. The term is central to Christian theology and denotes the presence of God in a person's spiritual experience.

Homophile from the word "to love the same," a homosexual or someone who supports the well-being and rights of homosexuals.

Horace (65–8 B.C.E.) Quintus Horatius Flaccus was a Roman author and poet famous for his *Satires, Epodes, Odes, Epistles,* and *The Art of Poetry.*

Hymenaeus a Christian living in Ephesus whom Paul or a pseudonymous writer considered to be a false teacher (1 Timothy 1:20); see **Alexander.**

Iconoclastic relating to the use of religious images or icons in worship. Iconoclasts are those who oppose the veneration of religious images and thus destroy them.

Ideology a system of belief that tries to explain and change the world; a doctrine, opinion, and/or way of thinking.

Imperatives rules, duties, or commands.

Impiety lack of reverence for what is determined sacred by a group.

Incarnation "becoming flesh"; the act of a God or spirit taking on a human form.

Inclusio a passage of Scripture in which an opening phrase, a verse, or a word is repeated at the end.

Indulgences remission of worldly punishment by God for a sin, given by the Church through absolution or suffrage. During the time of Martin Luther, indulgences were sold to finance the building of St. Peter's Basilica in Rome, Italy.

Initiates those who have been accepted into an organization or have been allowed to participate in secret knowledge. Often the initiation involved secret rituals such as baptism or the reception of Sacraments.

Inquisition a trial system created in the thirteenth century C.E. It was established by the Papacy and controlled by the Franciscans and Dominicans. It was headed by a tribunal that hunted, tried, punished, and tortured those that disagreed with the Catholic point of view. Nonreligious leaders took control of this trial system in Spain, where it was used against Jews, Muslims, and Protestants.

Internal Evidence information that comes from Books within the Bible that proves, disproves, or helps illuminate biblical passages.

Interpolate to alter a piece of literature by adding material to the text.

Inversion the reversal or alteration of the natural order or meaning of words.

Isis ancient Egyptian goddess who was queen of the dead and wife of Osiris. Her popular mystery cult was followed during the Greek and Roman Empires.

Israelites the Hebrew people who descended from Jacob and lived in the ancient kingdom of Israel. They considered themselves the chosen people of Yahweh; see **Jewish.**

Jamnia biblical city in Palestine that was the center of Jewish learning after the fall of Jerusalem in 70 C.E. Some theorize that the canon of the Hebrew Bible and the Palestinian Talmud were collected and edited at Jamnia.

Jerome (340?–420? C.E.) born Eusebius Hieronymus Sophronius, he was a monk, scholar, and prolific writer who is best known for his Latin translation of the Bible, the *Vulgate.*

Jewett, Robert a minister, theologian, and professor of Bible studies at Garrett Evangelical Theological Seminary in Illinois. Among his many books is *The Captain America Complex: The Dilemma of Zealous Nationalism.*

Jewish of the Jews or Judaism; a nation or an ethnic group; see **Israelites.**

Jewish Apocrypha parts of the Septuagint that are not found in the Hebrew Bible but are given authoritative value; see **Apocrypha.**

Jewish Scriptures see **Hebrew Bible, Torah,** and **Talmud.**

Job The Book of Job contains the story of the man who was the subject of a wager between God and Satan. He endured much suffering but did not lose his faith in God.

Johnson, Luke Timothy professor of New Testament studies at Candler School of Theology at Emory University who has written several books, including *Letters to Paul's Delegates: 1 Timothy, 2 Timothy, Titus.*

Joppa ancient Palestinian seaport also known as Jaffa, or Haifa today.

Josephus, Flavius (37–100 C.E.) a Jewish general, historian, and an apologist who wrote *The Jewish Antiquities,* which contains a history of the Jewish people.

Judea geographical term for an area where the tribes of Judah and Benjamin settled after they returned from Babylon, including the city Jerusalem. This word also could designate all of Palestine or a Roman territory in Palestine.

Jupiter the sovereign Roman deity who ruled over aspects of the atmosphere, politics, law, and contracts. He is identified with the Greek Zeus and Jove. As Jupiter Capitolinus, he ruled over the Roman games, and his temple was built on Capitoline hill in ancient Rome.

Justification to bring a person into a right relationship with God, God's acceptance and pardoning of sinners, or to declare a person innocent of a wrongdoing or breaking the law.

Kaddish a doxology or formula of praise to God recited after the reading of Scripture and by mourners after the death of a close relative; see **Doxology.**

King James Version (Authorized Version); an English translation of the Bible that was proposed by the Puritan John Reynolds at the Hampton Court Conference in 1604. It was published in 1611 with the authorization of King James I. A group of scholars used the Bishop's Bible, along with other versions, to create this standard version for English-speaking Protestants.

King, Martin Luther Jr. (1929–1968) an American civil rights leader, Baptist minister, and orator. He founded the Southern Christian Leadership Conference and employed a philosophy of nonviolence to advance the rights of black Americans, for which he was awarded the Nobel Peace Prize. He authored several books and famous speeches, such as "I Have a Dream," before he was assassinated.

Kinsperson a person's relative through descent, marriage, or blood; or the people in one's family, clan, or residence who share common interests and obligations. People often organize their societies based on kinship, including economic, political, and religious groups. A kinsperson also could be a close friend with no family ties.

Koine "common" in Greek; the everyday language used throughout the Greek world during the Hellenistic and Roman periods; the language of the New Testament.

Koreshan Unity Settlement a utopian community founded by Cyrus Tweed in the 1880s. The group worked for sexual, spiritual, and social equality and believed that God was both female and male. Their property is now a park in Florida, devoid of Koreshans.

Kroeger, Catherine Clark founder of Christians for Biblical Equality and professor of classical and ministry studies at Gordon-Conwell Theological Seminary who coauthored *I Suffer not a Woman* and coedited *Women, Abuse, and the Bible.*

"L" refers to sources or materials used only by the writer of the Gospel of Luke; they are not used by other synoptic gospel writers.

Lawrence, D.H. (1885–1930) an English author who wrote novels, short stories, poetry, dramas, and non-fiction. He is famous for his *The Rainbow, The Plumed Serpent,* and *Lady Chatterley's Lover.* Many of his works were based on a moral system that called for complete freedom of expression. Some of his books were banned in the United States because of their sexual content.

Lectionary a book that generally contains readings from the Old Testament/Hebrew Bible and New Testament that is used to plan liturgies for every day of the year.

Lee, Ann (1736–1784) while living in England, she joined a Quaker group known as the Shaking Quakers. She began to advocate celibacy, taught that Christ would return as a female, and took over the leadership of the group. Her followers called her "Mother Ann" because she claimed to have a vision of Christ. Later, she established a community in America called the United Society of Believers in Christ's Second Appearing, also known as the Shakers; see **Shakers**.

Legion a division of the Roman army.

Levi a tax collector and son of Alphaeus, mentioned in the Gospel of Luke, who left his post to follow Jesus. This character is often identified with Matthew in the Gospel of Matthew. Levi also is mentioned in the genealogy found in Luke.

Liberation Theology the interpretation of the Bible in a way that promotes the social and political freedom of those who experience poverty and political and social oppression. Jesus is viewed as the liberator, and violence may be an acceptable method of obtaining freedom in this life.

Literal the ordinary/denotative meaning of the actual words of a text or statement that does not go beyond the meaning intended by the author.

Literary Criticism method of criticism that determines the literary character or development of the Books of the Bible by examining the final form of the text for its genres, rhetoric, literary structures or features, such as plot, character, timing, and setting, as well as the meaning for the individual reader.

Literary Form genre or style of writing such as the parable, law, narrative, letter, apocalypse, and so on.

Livy (64? B.C.E.–17? C.E.) Titus Livius was a Roman historian about whose life we know little. He wrote a history of Rome that some suggest is inaccurate.

Lord a common title similar to the use of "Mr." today. In ancient times it was used to describe the emperor of Rome, Greek and Roman deities, Jesus, and the Jewish monotheistic God.

Lord's Supper see **Eucharist**.

Love Feasts see **Agape**.

Luther, Martin (1483–1546 C.E.) a German, Protestant reformer who believed in the authority of Scripture and justification by faith.

LXX see **Septuagint**.

"M" refers to sources or materials used only by the writer of the Gospel of Matthew; they are not used by the other synoptic Gospel writers.

Macedonia an area north of Greece in the Balkan Peninsula once ruled by Philip of Macedon. His son, Alexander the Great, expanded the empire and began the Hellenization of most of the known world.

Maenads women and men, also called Bacchae, who worshipped Dionysus in the mountains. They wore animal skins and carried decorated poles during their rituals in which they would have visions and often kill a fawn or kid with their bare hands and devour it. They worshipped and communed with Dionysus, who could appear as a bull or goat.

Magnificat the song of praise found in the Gospel of Luke and sung by either Mary or Elisabeth.

Malina, Bruce a professor of theology at Creighton University in Nebraska who has written many books, including *The Social World of Jesus and the Gospels*.

Mandaean Texts the abundant literature of the Mandaeans, including ritual books, commentaries, discourses, and legends. Mandaeans exist today in Iraq and Iran and are influenced by Christian, Jewish, Iranian, Babylonian, and Gnostic thought. Some of their texts are the *Ginza,* also known as the *Treasure,* the *Canonical Prayerbook,* and the *Book of John.*

Marcan Priority or Priority of Mark the theory that the Gospel of Mark is the primary source of Matthew and Luke because most of Mark is found in both. It is suggested that Matthew and Luke used Mark as a source and adapted its material for their own purposes.

Marcion (85–160 C.E.) founded an independent Christian church in the second century C.E., which rivaled the Orthodox Church. He rejected Judaism and its influence on Christianity and thought that the God of the Hebrew Bible was different from the God of love, revealed through Jesus. Marcion edited the New Testament, rejecting much of it, and assembled his own canon. This may have had an impact on the development of the Christian canon.

Marcosians the followers of a Gnostic, Marcus, who taught in the Rhône Valley of Southern Gaul in the second century C.E. Our knowledge of them comes from Irenaeus, who called Marcus a charlatan who used magic to deceive women into being his prophetesses.

Mark 6:45–8:26: The Great Omission the part of the Gospel of Mark that is not used by the writer of the Gospel of Luke.

Mars originally an agricultural divinity, he became the Roman god of war identified with the Greek Aries.

Martyr from the Greek word "to witness"; a person who commits suicide, is murdered, or suffers because of his or her beliefs.

Masada a mountain fortress built by Herod the Great on the shore of the Dead Sea. It was designed to protect him from Cleopatra or invading armies. In 74 C.E., Jewish Zealots chose to commit suicide here rather than to face imprisonment or slaughter by the Romans. Today, Masada is considered a symbol of opposition to oppression. Every Jewish soldier ascends Masada and takes a vow never to let Israel fall into enemy hands again.

Masons "freemasons" are members of a fraternal religious organization that has a system of moral teachings, degrees of membership, rites, symbolism, a tradition of secrecy, and a historical association with political movements.

Mass see **Eucharist**.

Matthew the anonymous author of the Gospel of Matthew.

Messiah a term meaning "anointed," transliterated "Christos" in Greek. The messiah is the liberator of the Jewish people, an actual or a future king of Israel who would bring about a new age. For writers of the New Testament, Jesus was this Messiah, or Christ.

Metaphor a figure of speech in which a term is used to represent something else; a symbol.

Midrash exegesis or interpretation of biblical text with the aim of making it relevant to the reader and to teach or advise.

Miletus an ancient Greek city of Southwest Asia Minor. It was a major trading hub and port, but it now lies five miles inland due to changes in the land. It was captured by Alexander the Great in 334 B.C.E., and Paul stopped there on his third missionary journey. He sent for the elders of Ephesus and was forced to leave an ill companion there.

Millenialism a belief that Jesus will rule the earth for 1,000 years. There are a variety of beliefs about this period of time, including the idea that the millennium will conclude with a final judgment and the establishment of the Kingdom of God.

Minyan a group of ten (male) Jews in Orthodox Judaism and ten males or females in Reform or Conservative Judaism. This is the minimum number of people who must be present to conduct a worship service.

Mithraism an Indo-European religion centering around the God Mithra. It spread to Greece and Rome, where it became a mystery religion popular among soldiers. Mithraism had degrees of initiation, elaborate symbolism, and rituals such as baptism in blood. The faithful believed that their souls would pass through seven spheres until they reached heaven, where they would experience life after death. It had much in common with Christianity, which included a Mass, a wine and bread remembrance ceremony, and a rising and dying God.

Mithras an Indo-Iranian deity who was worshipped as a defender of justice. Later, he was identified with the sun and became the center of a widespread mystery religion whose rituals like the Taurbolium took place in cave-like buildings. Many suggest that Mithraism competed with and influenced early Christianity. See Mithraism.

Moabite person from the region of Moab, which is east of the Dead Sea and west of the Arabian desert. Ancient Israelites despised the Moabites, probably because they represented a political and economic threat to prosperity. Genesis records an incestuous story about the births of Edom and Moab in Genesis 19:30–38.

Moltmann-Wendel, E. a professor and theologian in Tubingen, Germany, who wrote *The Women around Jesus, God–His and Hers,* and *Liberty, Equality, Sisterhood.*

Monotheists those who believe that there is a single Divinity.

Mormonism common name for the Church of Jesus Christ of the Latter-day Saints, founded by Joseph Smith Jr. in 1830. Mormons accept the Book of Mormon as revelation and believe that their president is a vehicle for continuous revelation from God. They practice baptism for the dead, observe dietary laws, and believe that they can become like God as they progress in the afterlife. Mormons practiced polygamy in the past and have a strong sense of community.

MT (Masoretic Text) a text of the Hebrew Bible that was produced by Jewish scholars called Masoretes; or the standard and accepted Hebrew Bible developed by Tiberian Masoretes around 1,000 C.E. The Hebrew alphabet contains no vowels, therefore, the Masoretes developed a system of vowel signs that were in conjunction with the consonants.

Multicultural Interpretation or Use considering several different cultures or cultural identities when interpreting or using a writing, speech, and so on.

Muratorian Canon "Muratorian Fragment"; the earliest known list of New Testament writings dating to the second century C.E.

Mysia an ancient region in Northwest Asia Minor, along the Hellespont and Aegean, which included the cities of Troas, Adramyttium, Assos, and Pergamum.

Mystery a mystery religion that usually has secret rites, rituals, and knowledge that can only be known by initiated worshipers.

Myths a story that communicates faith in the sacred and sometimes deals with phenomena, origins of the world/ humans/ nature of the world, and gods/heroes/heroines. Myths organize a person's beliefs about self, nature, the divine, and a host of ethical values.

Nag Hammadi books dated to the fourth century C.E. that were found near an Egyptian village in 1945. They were influenced by Gnosticism and early Christianity and are considered monastic and ascetic.

Narrative Criticism method of analysis that is opposed to the historicizing and theologizing of the text. It studies the narrator, implied reader, real readers, real author, and the real world; sometimes equated with reader response criticism.

Natural Law laws or principles that appear to be governing human behavior that are based on nature.

Nazareth the town in lower Galilee that was the home of Mary, Joseph, and Jesus.

Nero (37–68 C.E.) Lucius Domitius Ahenobarbus, later known as Nero Claudius Caesar Drusus Germanicus. He became the emperor of Rome after being adopted by Claudius. He was very cruel to the followers of Chrestus during his reign, accusing them of arson after a devastating fire in Rome. After hearing of a revolt of his generals, he committed suicide.

New Testament a "New Covenant or Agreement"; twenty-seven different writings produced by people within early Christianity.

Niddah "banishment"; the act of cloistering a woman during her menstrual period and at childbirth.

Noncanonical books that have not been included as authoritative by either Roman Catholics or Protestants; see **Canon.**

Octavian (27 B.C.E.–14 C.E.) Gaius Julius Caesar Octavius was the first Roman emperor; see **Augustus.**

Old Testament see **Hebrew Bible.**

Omniscient having absolute, transcendent, and infinite knowledge; an attribute of a Deity.

Oneida Perfectionists a communal group in Oneida, New York, founded by John Humphrey Noyes. Perfectionists believed that Christ's second coming had already occurred, so they attempted to live a life of perfection on earth without sin and selfishness, which Noyes called "Bible Communism." They believed that they were living in the Kingdom of God on earth and so created communal property and complex marriages. They disbanded in 1880, but a corporation was formed that became famous for its silverware.

Onias, Temple of Onias, a high priest built a temple for the Jews in Leontopolis.

Opaque obtuse; hard to understand.

Oracles a message, directly from a deity or through a medium, in response to a question; also a sacred place where such divination occurs.

Oral Transmission a process by which the stories and sayings of a culture are passed down through the generations.

Origen (185–253 C.E.) an ascetic teacher and early church writer. He believed in the equality of all spirits who became human as they were separated from God. The spirit's goal was to reunite with or become like God. He also tried to synthesize Christian beliefs and Greek philosophy. Origen wrote *Commentaries on the Holy Scriptures, Homilies,* and *Hexapla.* After being ordained in Palestine by the bishops of Jerusalem and Caesarea, the bishop of Alexandria excommunicated him.

Owenites followers of Robert Owen (1771–1858) who lived in a community called New Harmony that he established in Indiana. He wanted to free people from what he believed were the evils of private property and irrational systems of religion and marriage. Owen also believed that the factory system of the Industrial Revolution caused human suffering and shaped people's characters in a negative way. His ideas of social reform influenced many of the later labor movements.

Paleolithic meaning "Old Stone Age"; generally, an era in human culture where stone tools were used and pottery and agriculture were unknown.

Palestine geographical area including modern Israel and part of Syria. It was once occupied by the kingdoms of Israel and Judah and is also known as "Canaan" or the "Holy Land."

Pantheism the idea that a Deity is in everything, or all is the Deity.

Pantheon a magnificent Roman temple dedicated to famous dead heroes, heroines, gods, and goddesses. This term also could refer to the heroes, heroines, gods, and goddesses themselves.

Papias known only from fragments of his *Exposition of the Lord's Logia,* which is quoted in the writings of Irenaeus and Eusebius. He lived during the second century C.E. and is famous for his statements about Mark and Matthew.

Parousia the hope of the second coming of Christ.

Passion the trial, harassment, and Crucifixion of Jesus.

Patriarchal father rule; pertaining to a social organization in which a male (father or eldest male) is recognized as the head of the family, tribe, or government; characterized by descent traced through males. The term is used to describe government, rule, or domination by males; see **Androcentric**.

Paul (?4 B.C.E.–?64 C.E.) a missionary of the first century C.E. who is considered a saint and an apostle by some Christians. He is the author of many letters in the New Testament.

Pauline the term applied to those writings in the New Testament that are attributed to Paul and are characteristic of his teachings. Although there is some disagreement about the authorship of these writings, Paul is thought to have written Romans, 1 and 2 Corinthians, Galatians, Philippians, Philemon, and 1 and 2 Thessalonians; other disputed Books include Colossians, Ephesians, 1 and 2 Timothy, and Titus.

Pelagius (350?–429? C.E.) an ascetic monk who was exiled by the Roman Catholic Church because he taught that there was no such thing as original sin. He wrote the *Tract on the Trinity* and *Eclogarum Liber* and commentaries on the letters of St. Paul.

Pella a Hellenistic town near the Jordan River in Palestine where many Jewish Christians fled to escape persecution after the Jewish wars of 66–70 C.E.

Peloponnese the peninsula of Southern Greece named after Pelops.

Pentateuch from the Greek word meaning "five." The first five books of the Hebrew Bible/Old Testament also termed the Torah.

Perea a term describing the land west of the Jordan River; Transjordan.

Philistines sea peoples from the Aegean region who migrated to Palestine in the first part of the twelfth century B.C.E. and competed with the Israelites for land and power in the region. Palestine received its name from the Philistines.

Philo of Alexandria (13 B.C.E.–50 C.E.) a Jewish philosopher and theologian who led a delegation of Jews to the Emperor Caligula to obtain exemption from having to worship the Emperor; his writings include *Apology of the Jews* and *Allegory of the Sacred Law.*

Philosophy from the Greek word "to study" or "to love" wisdom; the analysis of beliefs about conduct, thought, knowledge, and the nature of the universe.

Phrygia a region in West Central Asia Minor, situated between the North Aegean and the River Halys. The territory included the cities of Antioch, Iconium, Laodicea, Colossae, and Hierapolis. It was once a very important center of Christian life and activity.

Pierce, Ronald W. professor of biblical studies and theology at Talbot School of Theology who has contributed to many journals, including the *Journal of the Evangelical Theological Society* and *Trinity Journal.*

Piety reverence or devotion, especially to the divine.

Pilate, Pontius a Roman procurator of Judea, Samaria, and Idumaea from 26–34 C.E.

Pilgrim, Walter E. a Lutheran minister and professor of theology at Pacific Lutheran University in Tacoma, Washington. He has written many books, including *When the Future Be-*

comes a Threat, Good News to the Poor: Wealth and Poverty in Luke-Acts, and *The Amer-ican Poor.*

Plato (427?–347 B.C.E.) a Greek philosopher who studied under Socrates, founded the Athen-ian Academy and taught "idealism." He believed that there were two worlds: This world was an object of perception, while the other was a real and an unchanging world of forms. These forms, such as beauty itself and justice itself, are patterns that are imposed on pre-existing matter by the creator God. Plato also believed that immortal humans were rein-carnated in a progression toward connection with these forms.

Platonism the philosophy of Plato and his school, or the teachings of later philosophers who changed or used Plato's doctrines. Platonism went through many stages. Old Academy Platonism separated the body from the soul and thought that the soul was immortal. It also proposed that there was an intelligible world of forms, along with a world perceived by the senses. After the Middle Academy came the New Academy Platonists, who did not believe in the possibility of certain knowledge as Middle Platonists did. Middle Platon-ists also thought that there was a first principle and many levels of being. Neo-Platonists thought that the first principle was "the One" instead of Intellect. Each form of Platon-ism was distinguished by different beliefs, but they were all reinterpretations of Plato's original ideas.

Pliny the Younger (61?–114? C.E.) a Roman writer and lawyer named Publius Caecilius Se-cundus who was adopted by his uncle, Pliny the Elder, and took his name. He wrote many letters, the most famous of which was addressed to the Emperor Trajan. Pliny asked Tra-jan for advice concerning the official treatment of Christians.

Pluralism a policy of favoring the preservation of distinctive groups (religious, ethnic, cultur-al) within a nation or society.

Plutarch (46–127? C.E.) a Greek writer who is responsible for a collection of biographies of Greek and Roman political and military leaders called *Parallel Lives.* He also wrote *Morals,* which was a collection of writings on various subjects. He was a priest of Apollo, and his philosophical views were based on Plato and influenced by Pythagoreans, Peripatet-ics, and Stoics.

Polycarp of Smyrna (69–156 C.E.) a church official and writer who was bishop of Smyrna and a friend of John, the son of Zebedee. Polycarp is considered a saint by the Roman Catholic Church because of his death as a martyr.

Pompey (106–48 B.C.E.) Gnaeus Pompeius was a Roman military leader who conquered Jerusalem while intervening in a civil war, but he did not loot the Temple or prohibit Jewish worship. Later, he formed a triumvirate with Crassus and Caesar.

Predestination the belief that God has planned all events in the past, present, and future, in-cluding every person's destiny.

Promulgate to communicate through publishing, open declaration, formal proclamation, or public teaching.

Prooftexting using a verse in the Bible that is out of context in order to give evidence for an argument or to prove a point of view.

Prophetic Tradition (within Judaism) the literature of the Bible in which Prophets criticize the morals of the people, the policies of government, and institutionalized religion. Prophet-ical works of the Bible include the Books of *Joshua, Ruth, Isaiah, Ezekiel, Hosea,* and *Malachi.*

Protestants those who belong to a diverse movement that protested the injustices within the Roman Catholic Church. The movement led to the Reformation during the sixteenth century.

Proto-Mark hypothetical writings or oral traditions about Jesus that were used as a source for and later incorporated into the Gospel of Mark.

Protos a Greek word meaning first in time, status, or a series.

Pseudepigrapha "false writings"; a term that designates writings outside of the Bible that are attributed to important figures found within the Bible; see **Pseudo-Pauline**, **Pseudonymous**, and **Deutero-Pauline**.

Pseudo-Pauline this term is usually applied to the New Testament writings that are often attributed to Paul but probably were not written by him. Although there is some disagreement, the writings generally include 2 Thessalonians, Colossians, Ephesians, 1 and 2 Timothy, and Titus; see **Deutero-Pauline**, **Pseudonymous**, and **Pseudepigraphal**.

Pseudonymous a fictitious name used by a writer to conceal his/her identity; see **Deutero-Pauline**, **Pseudepigrapha**, and **Pseudo-Pauline**.

Publican ancient Roman tax collector or the representative of the imperial procurator of Judea who collected public tolls, revenues, and so on. Jews thought that Jewish Publicans were traitors and sinners, so they were held in very low esteem.

Purity Laws the Jewish idea that purity, holiness, or cleanliness is needed in order to approach God. Therefore, acts of sin or contact with things considered unclean require a period of separation, ritual washing, and sometimes sacrifice. The entire "kosher" ritual system is based on the notion of keeping people "clean" or "ritually prepared" for worship with a deity.

Pythagoreans the select followers of Pythagoras who held a secret doctrine that numbers were the basic elements of reality and the "first unit" was the principle of the universe. They wore white, had dietary prohibitions, and believed in the transmigration of the soul. They also believed that the soul was imprisoned in the body, which seeks to unite itself with the world soul.

"Q" abbreviation for "Quelle," which means "source" in German; also known as the "Logia" or "sayings" of Jesus; a theoretical source for the Gospels of Matthew and Luke. "Q" is not found in the Gospel of Mark.

Quakerism the common name for the Society of Friends that believes each person has an inner light—and is a part of God. This inner light is a person's only authority and leads her or him to a right relationship with God. Quakers reject institutionalized religion and refuse to take part in military service and oaths. They were attacked and persecuted until the Toleration Act of 1689 was passed in England. Today, their governance is egalitarian and their name is often synonymous with the peace movement; see **George and Margaret (Fell) Fox**.

Qumran the place on the northwest shore of the Dead Sea where an ascetic community once lived until the first century C.E. They produced the Dead Sea Scrolls, which describe an expected messiah. They thought that with the help of God they would someday rule the world; see **Zadokites** and **Essenes**.

Rahab An innkeeper of Jericho whose house was on or near the city wall. She hid Caleb and Joshua. Her family was allowed to escape when the city was destroyed by the ancient Israelites.

Reader-oriented Criticism also known as reader-response criticism; a method of criticism that focuses on the roles of the reader and author. It distinguishes between the actual reader (or author) and the implied reader (or author). The implied author manipulates or controls the actual reader into becoming the ideal/implied reader.

Recapitulation a brief summary at the end of a speech, discussion, or piece of writing.

Redaction Criticism a method of criticism that interprets writings by looking at the author's own theological themes and interpretations, plus the perspectives and goals of the editor(s) who used various traditions, forms, and sources to create the final written form of a work.

Redeemer a person who sacrifices self in order to deliver others from the consequences of sin.

Redemption to buy back; the act of God forgiving the sinful or rescuing the faithful; especially the event of Jesus sacrificing his life as a ransom for the lives of sinners.

Reincarnation the belief that the soul or self can be reborn over and over again, taking various new forms that can propel a person toward or away from the divine or ultimate reality.

Resurrection Appearance the appearance of Jesus to people after his death.

Rhetoric the ability to speak or write effectively about any subject in order to persuade others.

Roman Catholic a member of the Western Catholic Church as opposed to being a member of the Eastern Orthodox Church.

Roman Procurator an ancient Roman officer who managed the financial affairs of Roman provinces that had problems or civil strife. The procurator often had the administrative powers of the emperor or a governor.

Rosicrucians members of a secret fraternity of the seventeenth and eighteenth centuries that stressed understanding of ancient and secret knowledge. They believed in general reformation and magic, and promised initiates insight into the nature of life and a new paradise. They were influenced by Kabbalism, alchemy, and astrology. The life and teachings of their legendary founder, Christian Rosencreutz, was described in *Fama Fraternatis* and *Confessio Fraternatis.*

Russell, D. S. (David Syme) a Congregationalist minister, principal, and lecturer of Old Testament languages and literature who lives in England and wrote *Between the Testaments, The Jews from Alexander to Herod,* and *Daniel: An Introduction to Jewish Apocalyptic.*

Ruth widow from Moab (non-Jew) and daughter-in-law of Naomi, who later married Naomi's relative, Boaz the Bethlehemite. Her marriage secured economic security for Naomi and produced an heir to the land belonging to Boaz. According to the Scriptures, she also became the ancestress of David and Jesus.

Sacred Prostitutes cultic functionaries that celebrated human sexuality as a divine gift and whose rituals provided for the continuing fertility of nature.

Salvation protection or preservation from harm, sin, or death.

Samaria an ancient Palestinian district or the capital of the Kingdom of Israel; its inhabitants were called Samaritans, and they were often in conflict with the Jews after the return from Babylon. Samaritans were despised by Jews because they did not worship in Jerusalem or keep purity regulations.

Samaritans the people who live(d) in the territory of Samaria and maintain a unique identity apart from the Jewish people but who claim to be direct descendants of the Israelite tribes.

Sannyasin one who renounces his or her possessions, name, and caste to wander, seeking liberation from the cycle of rebirth (samsara); generally found within Hinduism and Buddhism.

Savior a person who rescues another from danger or destruction; often used to describe rulers, leaders, and divinities such as Aesclepius, Isis, and Jesus.

Schmithals, Walter minister and professor who wrote many articles and books, including *An Introduction to the Theology of Rudolph Bultmann* and *Gnosticism in Corinth: An Investigation of the Letters to the Corinthians.*

Schüssler-Fiorenza, Elizabeth biblical scholar with a feminist critical and biblical-historical approach. She attempts to reconstruct the history of women in early Christianity using historical-critical, rhetorical-critical, and feminist-critical methods. Among her many books is *In Memory of Her.*

Scientology, Church of a religion founded in 1952 by L. Ron Hubbard, who authored *Dianetics.* Scientologists believe that to liberate their souls or "thetans," they must become free of "engrams," which are defense mechanisms that lead to self-defeating behaviors.

Scofield, Cyrus I. (1843–1921) a pastor and popular speaker who was influenced by the ideas of John Nelson Darby and the Plymouth Brethren. He edited the *Scofield Reference Bible,* which had a dispensational framework.

Scribe a professional scholar, copyist of manuscripts, or letter writer. In the Hebrew tradition, scribes studied the law and could be either a Pharisee or Sadducee.

Sect a sociological category referring to a religious group protesting against or breaking away from a parent body.

Sectarian an adherent of a particular religious denomination that has distinguished itself from another established group; a breakaway group.

Seneca, Lucius Annaeus (5? B.C.E.–65 C.E.) a Roman politician, philosopher, Stoic, and teacher who wrote the *Dialogues, Epistle to Lucilius,* and *Epistles of Paul and Seneca.*

Septuagint "LXX"; a Greek translation of the Hebrew Bible, which is said to have been translated by seventy Jewish scholars, but probably was assembled by many Hellenistic Jews at different times after 250 B.C.E. The LXX was used by early Christians.

Serapis an Egyptian god of the underworld who was a combination of Apis (the sacred bull) and Osiris. His religion spread to Greece and Rome, where he was a god of healing, navigation, and fertility.

Seventh Day Adventists a church influenced by the teachings of William Miller about Christ's second coming, which was later organized by the prophetess Ellen Gould White. Adherents accept her visions and writings as inspired, along with those of present-day prophets. They observe Saturday as the day of worship, vegetarianism, and abstention from "worldly dress or amusement."

Shakers a communal group known as the United Society of Believers in Christ's Second Appearing. They were led to America by Mother Ann Lee, who they thought was Christ reincarnated. Shakers were spiritualists who believed in revelation and healing and interpreted the Bible literally. They also practiced celibacy. Their distinct worship service was based on meditation, song, and frenzied dance, which gave them their popular name of the "Shaking Quakers"; see **Ann Lee**.

Sibylline Oracles oracles attributed to Sibyls (prophetesses) that were written and collected over the centuries. Some of the oracles were of Greek, Jewish, and Christian origin and served as political propaganda that outlined world history, predicted Jewish victory over their enemies, and described a messiah.

Sicarii a militant, Jewish revolutionary group, also known as Zealots, who conquered the mountain fortress, Masada. They protected themselves from the Romans until 74 C.E., when they committed suicide rather than face slaughter or capture; see **Zealot**.

Simeon the man who offered a prayer for and blessed the infant Jesus in the Temple in the Gospel of Luke, chapter 2.

Social Stratification a system of social inequality found in the form of class, estate, and caste stratification that ranks people according to their wealth, circumstance of birth, religion, gender, race, power, or status.

Sociological Criticism method of criticism that uses modern theories about human behavior, social institutions, practices, and so on to interpret the social world of the Bible.

Sophia "wisdom"; related to God/Yahweh/Elohim. Some consider Sophia another name for the Holy Spirit, a Gnostic deity, one of the Aeons, the spirit of God, or one who coexists with God and assisted in creation. Some have compared Sophia to Jesus.

Source Criticism method of criticism that attempts to identify the sources used in creating a text.

Sproul, Barbara C. a professor and director of the program in religion at Hunter College of the City University of New York. She edited *Primal Myths: Creation Myths Around the World.*

Stanton, Elizabeth Cady (1815–1902) women's rights leader who organized the world's first women's rights convention with the help of Lucretia Mott in 1848. She published *The Women's Bible* and coauthored *The History of Woman Suffrage.*

Stereotypical that which is conventional, oversimplified, and fixed; as in an idea or a belief that does not take individuality or criticism into account; a person, group, event, or issue that typifies or conforms to an unvarying pattern or manner.

Steward a manager or trustee who is responsible for the possessions that are entrusted to him or her.

Stoicism a Greek philosophical school, popular from 300 B.C.E. to 200 C.E. and founded by Zeno. Stoicism went through many changes, but stressed virtue, reason, and indifference to the world and its emotions. Later, Stoicism abandoned apathy in favor of a more social agenda. Early Christian writers were influenced by Stoicism.

Suetonius Gaius Suetonius Tranquillus was a Roman historian, lawyer, and scholar who wrote biographies of famous Romans called *Lives of Illustrious Men* and *Lives of the Caesars.*

Supplicant a person who asks humbly and earnestly; one who prays, asking for help from the divine.

Symbol a term derived from Greek meaning "to bring together" or "compare"; an outward sign representing a hidden meaning or an abstract idea through association or convention. Religious symbols may reveal or provide access to the sacred.

Synonym a word having the same or similar meaning as another.

Synoptic Problem the problem of understanding the close relationship among the synoptic gospels (Matthew, Mark, and Luke).

Tacitus, Publius Cornelius (55–120? C.E.) a Roman historian who wrote the *Annales* and the *Historiae,* which covered the events from the death of Augustus to the death of Domitian.

Talmud Jewish writings, including the Mishnah (oral law, tradition, and teaching) and Gemara (commentary on the Mishnah), which developed during the founding years of Christianity. There are two forms of the Talmud: the Jerusalem/Palestinian and the Babylonian.

Tamar Canaanite woman who was married to Judah's first two sons. She disguised herself as a prostitute and had relations with Judah when he tried to withhold his third son from her. She became pregnant by Boaz and bore Perez and Zerah, who were ancestors of David and Jesus. In the Book of Kings, Tamar was the daughter of David. She was tricked and raped by her half-brother, Amnon. Later, she was avenged by her full brother, Absalom.

Taurobolium baptism in the blood of a sacrificed bull, as practiced by some mystery religions, including Mithraism.

Testament an agreement or a covenant, as in the Old and New Testaments.

Textual Criticism analytical method that compares various ancient manuscripts and versions of the Bible from the early centuries of the Christian era in an attempt to reconstruct the best and most original texts.

The Twelve the people chosen by Jesus who were with him from the beginning. All of the lists of The Twelve that are found in the gospels are different. Some of The Twelve founded the early Christian church after his death. In the Gospel of Mark, "The Twelve" is a term for people who fail Jesus.

Theocracies governments that are run or influenced by God, gods, or those claiming to have the divine authority of a god or gods.

Theology from the Greek words "God" and "study of"; the interpretations of, study of, and conversation about any religious tradition; the systemization of beliefs.

Theophany a manifestation of the divine to a person in the form of a direct message, a dream, a vision, or an angel.

Theophilus Greek for "friend or beloved of God." The Gospel of Luke and the Acts of the Apostles were dedicated to this person, but his or her identity is unknown.

Thucydides (460–400 B.C.E.) a Greek statesman and historian who wrote a history of the Peloponnesian War.

Titans the twelve children of Uranus (sky) and Gaia (earth) who were defeated by Zeus in a battle for control of the universe.

Titus (39–81 C.E.) a Roman general who destroyed Jerusalem in 70 C.E. and held a long siege at Masada. In 79 C.E., he succeeded his father, Vespasian, and became the emperor of Rome.

Tolbert, Mary Ann professor of religious studies who wrote *Sowing the Gospel*. She is interested in studying early Christian documents in the context of ancient and modern literature and literary theory.

Torah (the Pentateuch or Law) the first five books of the Old Testament/Hebrew Bible.

Traditions a set of cultural customs, beliefs, written materials, or legalisms that are handed down from generation to generation.

Trajan (53–117 C.E) Marcus Ulpius Traianus became a Roman emperor after he was adopted by Nerva. He was very popular with the people, the army, and the senate, and his military expertise helped him expand the Empire to its fullest height. His letter to Pliny provides valuable information about the way Christians were treated in his time.

Translate to move from one place to another, as in the relics or remains of a saint; a transference into heaven without death; also, to change the text of one writing into another language.

Translation the act of taking words found in one language and transferring or equating them in another language or a simpler form.

Transliteration to change letters or words into corresponding characters of another language or alphabet, or to write the words of one language in symbols of another; not a translation.

Troas a port city of Mysia in Northwest Asia Minor, near the city of Troy. Many routes to places such as Ephesus and Athens radiated from Troas.

Tunic a straight shirt, skirt, or gown worn by ancient Greeks and Romans.

Utopia past or future ideal of a perfect place, state, society, or situation.

Vestal Virgins young female virgins that were chosen to become priestesses to attend to the fire of Vesta, the Roman goddess of the hearth, for approximately thirty years.

Via Egnatia a Roman road that stretched from the cities of Apollonia and Dyrrachium through Pella and Thessalonica and ending at the Hebrus River.

Victor of Antioch Bible interpreter of the fifth century, famous for his commentary on the Book of Jeremiah and the Gospel of Mark.

Virgil (70–19 B.C.E.) Publius Vergilius Maro was a Roman poet and author of the epic *Aeneid.*

Von Harnack, Adolph (1851–1930) German historian, theologian, and scholar who contributed to the development of form criticism and the demythologizing approach. He wrote within the series *Texts and Examinations of the History of Old Christian Literature, The History of Dogma,* and *Mission and Expansion on Christianity in the First Three Centuries.* He was interested in studying how Greek culture influenced the development of Christianity.

Waldensians a sect of Christians which developed after 1170 C.E. that stressed obedience to God before obedience to humanity and a life similar to that of Jesus' on earth, including poverty. They preached against the wealth and laxity of the clergy, purgatory, indulgences, fasting, and the cult of the saints. They also preached and practiced the teachings of the gospels, thought that anyone could preach, accepted women preachers, and borrowed some beliefs from the Cathari. Eighty Waldensians were burned in 1211 C.E. as a result of Pope Innocent III's crusade against heretics.

"We" Passages the term referring to passages in the Acts of the Apostles in which the writer switches from the third person singular or plural of "he" or "they" to the first person plural of "we."

Wicca Anglo-Saxon word meaning "bend" or "shape," or an Old English term designating a male witch or wise man; benevolent witchcraft often linked with healing and practiced by covens that preserved ancient knowledge. In modern times, this term refers to the entire religion of white or good witchcraft within a framework of female spirituality.

Wisdom (within Judaism) literature that is written in many forms, such as riddle, proverb, and fable. It often deals with the knowledge one must gain in order to lead a happy life in harmony with fellow humans and the world. It usually consists of rules that govern daily life, virtues to be cultivated, and vices to avoid. Biblical wisdom literature usually includes Job, Proverbs, Ecclesiastes, Ecclesiasticus, the Wisdom of Solomon, the Wisdom of Ben Sira (Sirach), Deuteronomy, and a poem in Baruch. See Sophia.

Witches negative appellation of successful women; women who were thought to have supernatural powers and the ability to manipulate nature. They generally were thought to have made an arrangement with the Devil or spirits. Women often were falsely accused and killed for being witches because they were a threat to religious systems and governments.

Womanist a feminist of color who believes that feminist analysis must link gender with race, class, and culture because it should include all women, thereby eliminating gender stereotypes, class prejudice, and white male dominance.

Yahweh also known as the Tetragrammaton. It is a name for God, meaning "lord." Jews would not pronounce the sacred name, therefore, they used the Hebrew term *Adonai.*

Zadokites (Dead Sea People) the Zadokites, or Essenes, were Jewish ascetics who lived in communities near the Dead Sea from approximately 200 B.C.E. to 100 C.E. The Dead Sea

Scrolls, discovered in 1948, contain copies of most of the Books of the Hebrew Bible and several other works that create rules for the community and a constitution for the world. They believed that they would some day rule the world with the help of the divine; see **Essenes** and **Qumran**.

Zealot a Jewish revolutionary, including (but not limited to) a member of a nationalistic party formed during the Roman occupation of Palestine; see **Sicarii**.

Zechariah the husband of Elisabeth and the father of John the Baptist. He was unable to speak after the angel Gabriel told him that he would have a son in his old age.

Zeus an ancient sky god of Greece considered the supreme ruler of men and gods; associated with mountains, rain, and thunderstorms. He was the son of Kronos and Rhea, brother to most of the Olympian gods, husband to numerous wives, and father of many gods and mortals. The Romans identified him with Jupiter.

Zoroastrianism an early form of monotheism and the religion formed by Zarathustra (Zoroaster) who reformed ancient Persian religion. He replaced ceremonies centering on animal sacrifice and daeva (demon) worship with worship of Ahura Mazda (Wise Lord) and a fire ritual.

Works Consulted

CHAPTER 1

Alves, Rubem. *What Is Religion?* New York: Orbis Books, 1984.

Amador, J. D. *Academic Constraints in Rhetorical Criticism of the New Testament: An Introduction to a Rhetoric of Power.* Sheffield, UK: Sheffield Academic Press, 1999.

Bettenson, Henry. *Documents of the Christian Church.* New York: Oxford University Press, 1975.

Black, David Alan, and David S. Dockery. *New Testament Criticism and Interpretation.* Grand Rapids, MI: Zondervan Publishing House, 1991.

Brown, Raymond, Joseph A. Fitzmyer, and Roland Murphy, eds. *The Jerome Biblical Commentary.* Upper Saddle River, NJ: Prentice Hall, 1968.

Cameron, Ron. *The Other Gospels. Non-Canonical Gospel Text.* Philadelphia: Westminster Press, 1982.

Cartlidge, David R., and David L. Dungan, eds. *Documents for the Study of the Gospels.* Minneapolis, MN: Fortress Press, 1980.

Ellis, E. Earle. "The Making of the New Testament Documents," Biblical Interpretation Ser. Brill Academic, 1999.

Fredriksen, Paula. *From Jesus to Christ: The Origins of the New Testament Images of Jesus.* New Haven, CT: Yale University Press, 2000.

Gabel, John B., and Charles B. Wheeler. *The Bible as Literature. An Introduction,* 2d ed. New York: Oxford University Press, 1990.

Grant, Robert M. *A Short History of the Interpretation of the Bible.* New York: Macmillan, 1966.

Holladay, Carl R. *Biblical Exegesis. A Beginner's Handbook.* Atlanta: John Knox Press, 1973.

Hanson, Paul D. *The Dawn of Apocalyptic.* Philadelphia: Fortress Press, 1975.

Harrington, Daniel J. *Who Is Jesus? Why Is He Important? An Invitation to the New Testament.* Ashland, OH: Sheed & Ward, 1999.

Klein, Ralph W. *Textual Criticism of the Old Testament. From the Septuagint to Qumran.* Philadelphia: Fortress Press, 1974.

Küng, Hans and Jurgen Moltmann, eds. *Conflicting Ways of Interpreting the Bible,* New York: Seabury Press, 1980.

McKenzie, Steven L., and Stephen R. Haynes. *To Each Its Own Meaning. An Introduction to Biblical Criticisms and Their Application.* Louisville, KY: Westminster, 1993.

Metzger, Bruce M. *The Canon of the New Testament. Its Origin, Development, and Significance.* Oxford: Clarendon Press, 1987.

Osiek, Carolyn. *Philippians and Philemon,* New Testament Commentaries Ser. Nashville, TN: Abingdon, 2000.

Pagels, Elaine. *The Gnostic Gospels.* New York: Vintage, 1981.

Pilgrim, Walter E. *Uneasy Neighbors: Church and State in the New Testament.* Minneapolis, MN: Augsburg Fortress, 1999.

Powell, Mark A., ed. *The New Testament Today.* Louisville, KY: Westminster John Knox, 1999.

Schüssler-Fiorenza, Elizabeth. *Bread Not Stone. The Challenge of Feminist Biblical Interpretation.* Boston: Beacon Press, 1984.

———, ed. *Searching the Scripture. A Feminist Introduction.* New York: Crossroad, 1993.

Simon, Richard. *A Critical History of the Old Testament.* English translation from the French. London: 1682.

Sproul, Barbara C. *Primal Myths. Creating the World.* New York: Harper and Row, 1979.

Tate, W. Randolph. *Biblical Interpretation. An Integrated Approach.* Peabody, MA: Hendrickson, 1991.

Templeton, Douglas A. *The New Testament as True Fiction: Literature, Literary Criticism, Aesthetics.* Sheffield, UK: Sheffield Academic Press, 1999.

Ting, K.H. *Voices from the Margin. Interpreting the Bible in the Third World,* R.S. Sugirtharajah, ed. New York: Orbis Books, 1991.

Wortham, Robert A. *Social-Scientific Approaches in Biblical Literature.* Lewiston, KY: Edward Mellen Press, 1999.

CHAPTER 2

Arrowsmith, William, trans. "The Bacchae," In *Euripides: The Complete Greek Tragedies.* Chicago: University of Chicago Press, 1959.

Benko, Stephen. *Pagan Rome and the Early Christians.* Bloomington: Indiana University Press, 1986.

Braver, George C., Jr. *Judea Weeping. The Jewish Struggle Against Rome from Pompey to Masada.* New York: Thomas Y. Crowell, 1970.

Brown, Raymond E., et al., eds. *The Jerome Biblical Commentary.* Upper Saddle River, NJ: Prentice Hall, 2000.

Downey, Glanville. "Unroman Activities: The Ruling Race and the Minorities." *Anglican Theological Review,* 58 (1976): 432-443.

Eastland, Terry, ed. *Religious Liberty in the Supreme Court. The Cases That Define the Debate over Church and State.*, Grand Rapids, MI: Wm. B. Eerdmans, 1995.

Engelsman, Joan Chamberlain. *The Feminine Dimension of the Divine.* Philadelphia: Westminster Press, 1979.

Euripides. William Arrowsmith, trans. Chicago: University of Chicago Press, 1959.

Eusebius. *Ecclesiastical History,* 2 Vols, The Leob Classical Library. Edited by J. E. Oulton and H. J. Lawler. New York: Putnam's Sons, 1966.

García, Florentino Martínez. *The Dead Sea Scrolls Translated. The Qumran Texts in English,* 2d ed. Translated by Wilfred G. E. Watson. Leiden: E. J. Brill, 1996.

Gaster, Theodore H. *The Dead Sea Scriptures. With Introduction and Notes.* Garden City, NY: Anchor Books, 1976.

Godwin, Joscelyn. *Mystery Religions in the Ancient World.* San Francisco: Harper and Row, 1981.

Graetz, Heinrich. *History of the Jews.* Philadelphia: Jewish Publication Society of America, 1893.

Grant, F. C. "The Economic Background of the New Testament." In *The Background of the New Testament and Its Eschatology,* W. D. Davis and D. Daube, eds. New York: Cambridge University Press, 1964, pp. 113-114.

Josephus. *Jewish Wars,* Books IV-VII. Translated by H. St. J. Thackeray, The Loeb Classical Library Series. Cambridge, MA: Harvard University Press, 1968.

Kee, Howard Clark. *The Origins of Christianity. Sources and Documents.* Upper Saddle River, NJ: Prentice Hall, 1973.

Kraemer, Ross S. *Maenads, Martyrs, Matrons, Monastics. A Sourcebook on Women's Religions in the Greco-Roman Period.* Philadelphia: Fortress Press, 1988.

Martin, Luther H. *Hellenistic Religions. An Introduction.* New York: Oxford University Press, 1987.

Meyer, Marvin W. *The Ancient Mysteries. A Sourcebook.* San Francisco: Harper and Row, 1987, pp. 1-14.

Meyer, Marvin W. *The Mithras Liturgy.* Society of Biblical Literature Texts and Translation. No. 10. Missoula, MT: Scholars Press, 1976.

Nearing, Scott. *War. Organized Destruction and Mass Murder by Civilized Nations.* New York: Garland Publishing, 1971, p. 55.

Pagels, Elaine. *The Gnostic Gospels.* New York: Vintage, 1981.

Parkes, James. *A History of Palestine from 135 A.D. to Modern Times.* New York: Oxford University Press, 1949, p. 45.

Prudentius. *Peristephanon X,* 1011-1050. In John Ferguson, *The Religions of the Roman Empire.* New York: Cornell University Press, 1970.

Rajak, Tessa. *Josephus: The Historian and His Society.* Philadelphia: Fortress Press, 1983.

Ramm, Bernard. *Protestant Biblical Interpretation: A Textbook of Hermeneutics.* Grand Rapids, MI: Baker Books, 1999.

Robinson, James M., ed., *The Nag Hammadi Library.* New York: Harper Collins, 1990.

Safrai, S., and M. Stern, eds., *The Jewish People in the First Century. Geographical, Political History, Social, Cultural, and Religious Life and Institutions.* Philadelphia: Fortress Press, 1976.

Scroggs, Robin. "Early Christian Communities as Sectarian Movement." In *Christianity, Judaism, and other Greco-Roman Cults.*, Vol 2, edited by Jacob Neusner. Leiden: E. J. Brill, 1975.

Selvidge, Marla J. *Notorious Voices. Feminist Biblical Interpretation, 1500-1920.* New York: Continuum, 1996.

———. *Woman, Violence, and the Bible.* New York: Mellen Biblical Press, 1996.

Smallwood, E. Mary. *The Jews Under Roman Rule. From Pompey to Diocletian,* Leiden: E. J. Brill, 1976.

Sugirtharajah, R.S. *Asian Biblical Hermeneutics and Postcolonialism: Contesting the Interpretations.* Sheffield, UK: Sheffield Academic Press, 1999.

Tacitus. *The Annals of Tacitus.* Translated by Henry Furneaux, rev. H. F. Pelham and C. D. Fisher. Oxford, UK: Clarendon Press, 1907.

———. *History.* Translated by Alfred John Church and William Jackson Brodribb; Moses Hades, ed. New York: Modern Library, 1942.

Vickers, Michael. *The Roman World.* New York: Peter Bedrick Books, 1989.

Wentz, Richard E. *Religion in the New World. The Shaping of Religious Traditions in the United States.* Minneapolis, MN: Fortress, 1990.

Wilkinson, L. P. *The Roman Experience.* New York: University Press of America, 1974.

CHAPTER 3

Allison, Dale C. *Jesus of Nazareth: Millenarian Prophet.* Minneapolis, MN: Augsburg-Fortress, 1998.

Boer, Harry R. *The Four Gospels and Acts. A Short Introduction.* Grand Rapids, MI: Wm. B. Eerdmans, 1982.

Brown, Robert McAfee. *Unexpected News. Reading the Bible with Third World Eyes.* Philadelphia: Westminister, 1984.

Bultmann, R. *The History of the Synoptic Traditions.* New York: Harper and Row, 1963.

Cameron, Ron. *The Other Gospels. Non-Canonical Gospel Texts.* Philadelphia: The Westminster Press, 1982.

Cartlidge, David R., and David L. Dungan. *Documents for the Study of the Gospels.* Philadelphia: Fortress Press, 1980.

Childs, Hal. *The Myth of the Historical Jesus and the Evolution of Consciousness.* Atlanta: Society of Biblical Literature, 2000.

Crossan, John Dominic. *Sayings Parallels: A Workbook for the Jesus Tradition.* Philadelphia: Fortress Press, 1986.

———. *The Historical Jesus: The Life of a Mediterranean Jewish Peasant.* Minneapolis, MN: Fortress Press, 1991.

Funk, Robert. *The Acts of Jesus. The Search for the Authentic Deeds of Jesus.* San Francisco: Harper-San Francisco, 1998.

Girzone, Joseph F. *Jesus, His Life and Teachings: As Recorded by His Friends Matthew, Mark, Luke, and John.* New York: Doubleday, 2000.

Hedrick, Charles W. *When History and Faith Collide: Studying Jesus.* Peabody, MA: Hendrickson Publishers, 1999.

Karman, James. "If We Try to Blunt the Edge of a Great Idea to 'Protect' our Students, Education Suffers." *The Chronicle of High Education.* 22, March 23, 1981: 64.

Kee, Howard Clark. *Jesus in History. An Approach to the Study of the Gospels.* New York: Harcourt Brace Jovanovich, 1977.

Johnson, Luke Timothy. *The Real Jesus: The Misguided Quest for the Historical Jesus and the Truth of the Traditional Gospels.* San Francisco: HarperSan Francisco, 1996.

Longstaff, Thomas R. W., and Page A. Thomas. *The Synoptic Problem: A Bibliography 1716-1988*, Macon, GA: Mercer University Press, 1988.

MacRae, George W., and Eldon J. Epp. *The New Testament and Its Modern Interpreters.* Philadelphia: Fortress Press, 1987.

Nickle, Keith F. *The Synoptic Gospels. An Introduction.* Atlanta: John Knox Press, 1973.

Scroggie, W. Graham. *A Guide to the Gospels.* London: Pickering and Inglis, 1967.

Stonehouse, Ned B. *Origins of the Synoptic Gospels. Some Basic Questions.* Grand Rapids, MI: Baker Book House, 1979.

Theissen, Gerd. *Sociology of Early Palestinian Christianity.* Philadelphia: Fortress Press, 1977.

———, and Annette Merz. *The Historical Jesus : A Comprehensive Guide.* Translated by John Bowden from *Der historische Jesus: Ein Lehrbuch.* Minneapolis, MN: Fortress, 1998.

Wansbrough, Henry. *Jesus and the Oral Gospel Traditions.* Sheffield, UK: Sheffield Academic Press, 1991.

Weaver, Walter P. *The Historical Jesus in the Twentieth Century, 1900-1950.* Harrisburg, PA: Trinity Press International, 1999.

CHAPTER 4

Bynug-Mu, Ahn. "Jesus and the Minjung (Crowd) in the Gospel of Mark." In R. S. Sugirtharajah, ed. *Voices from the Margin. Interpreting the Bible in the Third World.* Marynoll, NY: Orbis, 1991, 85-103.

Carrington, Philip. *The Primitive Christian Calendar.* Boston: Cambridge University Press, 1952.

Christ, Carol P., and Judith Plaskow, eds. *Womanspirit Rising: A Feminist Reader in Religion.* New York: Harper and Row, 1979, pp. 25-42.

Eusebius. *The Ecclesiastical History.* Edited by J. E. Oulton and H. J. Lawlor, 2 vols, The Loeb Classical Library. New York: C. P. Putnams, 1966.

García, Florentino Martínez. *The Dead Sea Scrolls Translated. The Qumran Texts in English*, 2d ed. Translated by Wilfred G. E. Watson. Leiden: E. J. Brill, 1996.

Juel, Donald H. *The Gospel of Mark.* Nashville, TN: Abingdon, 1999.

Kealy, Sean P. *Mark's Gospel. A History of Its Interpretation.* New York: Paulist Press, 1982.

Kee, Howard C. *Community of the New Age: Studies in Mark's Gospel.* Philadelphia: Westminster Press, 1977.

MacDonald, Dennis Ronald. *The Homeric Epics and the Gospel of Mark.* New Haven, CT: Yale University Press, 2000.

Martinez, Florentino Garcia, *The Dead Sea Scrolls Translated.* The Qumran texts in English. New York: E.J. Brill, 1996.

Mesters, Carlos. "How the Bible Is Interpreted in Some Basic Christian Communities in Brazil." In *Conflicting Ways of Interpreting the Bible,* Hans Küng and Jürgen Moltmann, eds.New York: Seabury Press, 1980, pp. 41-42.

Rhoades, David, and Donald Michie. *Mark as Story: An Introduction to the Narrative of Gospel.* Philadelphia: Fortress Press, 1982.

Schaff, Philip, and Henry Wace, eds. *St. Augustine. Selected Lessons of the New Testament.* vol. 6, A Select Library of the Nicene and Post-Nicene Fathers of the Christian Churches, Grand Rapids, MI: Wm. B. Eerdmans, 1956, 1978, and 1979.

Selvidge, Marla J. *Daughters of Jerusalem.* Scottdale, PA: Herald Press, 1987.

Weeden, Theodore J. *Mark: Traditions in Conflict.* Philadelphia: Fortress Press, 1971.

Whiston, William. trans., *The Works of Flavius Josephus.* Grand Rapids, MI: Associate Publishers, 1972, p. 582.

CHAPTER 5

Anderson, Janice Capel. "Matthew: Gender and Reading. " In *Semeia: The Bible and Feminist Hermeneutics,* 28 (1983):7.

Bacon, B. W. *Studies in Matthew.* London: Henry Holt, 1930.

Bornkamm, G., G. Barth, and H. J. Held. *Tradition and Interpretation in Matthew.* Philadelphia: Westminster Press, 1963.

Brown, Raymond E. *The Birth of the Messiah.* New York: Image Books, 1979.

Donfried, K. P. "The Allegory of the Ten Virgins (Matt. 25:1-13) as a Summary of Matthean Theology." *Journal of Biblical Literature,* 93 (1974):415-428.

Howell, David B. *Matthew's Inclusive Story. A Study in the Narrative Rhetoric of the First Gospel.* London: Sheffield Academic Press, 1990.

Kingsbury, Jack Dean. *Matthew. Proclamation Commentaries.* Philadelphia: Fortress Press, 1977.

Monk, Robert C. *Exploring Religious Meaning,* 4th ed. Upper Saddle River, NJ: Prentice Hall, 1994.

Neusner, Jacob, William S. Green, and Ernest S. Frerichs. *Judaisms and Their Messiahs at the Turn of the Christian Era.* Boston: Cambridge University Press, 1987.

Schaberg, Jane. *The Illegitimacy of Jesus. A Feminist Theological Interpretation of the Infancy Narratives,* New York: Seabury Press, 1985.

Scroggie, W. Graham. *A Guide to the Gospels.* London: Pickering and Inglis, 1967.

Selvidge, Marla J. *Daughters of Jerusalem.* Scottdale, PA: Herald Press, 1987.

———. *Woman, Violence, and the Bible.* New York: Edwin Mellen Press, 1996.

Senior, Donald. *What Are They Saying about Matthew?* New York: Paulist Press, 1983.

Simon, Arthur. *Bread for the World.* New York: Paulist Press, 1975.

Swidler, Leonard. *Woman in Judaism: The Status of Women in Formative Judaism.* Lanham, MD: Scarecrow Press, 1976.

Thompson, W. G. *Matthew's Advice to a Divided Community.* Rome: Biblical Institute Press, 1970.

Waetjen, Herman C. "The Genealogy as the Key to the Gospel According to Matthew." *Journal of Biblical Literature,* 95 (1976): 205-230.

Swartley, Willard A. *Slavery, Sabbath, Ware and Women: Case Issues in Biblical Interpretation.* Scottsdale, PA: Herald Press, 1983.

CHAPTER 6

Boer, Harry R. *The Four Gospels and Acts. A Short Introduction.* Grand Rapids, MI: Wm. B. Eerdmans, 1982.

Cardenal, Ernesto. *The Gospel in Solentiname.* New York: Orbis, 1976.

Cassidy, Richard J. *Jesus, Politics, and Society. A Study of Luke's Gospel.* New York: Orbis, 1983.

Cassidy, Richard J., and Philip J. Scharper, eds. *Political Issues in Luke-Acts.* New York: Orbis, 1983.

Craddock, Fred B., Lloyd R. Bailey, and Victor P. Furnish, eds. *The Gospels.* Nashville, TN: Abingdon, 1981.

Conzelmann, Hans. *The Theology of St. Luke.* Philadelphia: Fortress Press, 1961.

Danker, Frederick W. *Luke. Proclamation Commentaries.* Philadelphia: Fortress Press, 1976.

Ford, J. Massyngbaerde. *My Enemy Is My Guest. Jesus and Violence in Luke.* New York: Orbis, 1984.

Gowler, David B. *Host, Guest Enemy, and Friend: Portraits of the Pharisees in Luke and Acts.* New York: Peter Lang Publishing, 2000.

Jervell, Jacob. *Luke and the People of God. A New Look at Luke-Acts.* Minneapolis, MN: Augsburg, 1972.

Jewett, Paul K. *Man as Male and Female: A Study in Sexual Relationships from a Theological Point of View.* Grand Rapids, MI: Wm. B. Eerdmans, 1975.

Jordan, Clarence. *The Cotton Patch Version of Luke and Acts. Jesus' Doings and Happenings.* New York: Association Press, 1969.

Moltmann-Wendel, Elizabeth. *The Women around Jesus.* New York: Crossroads, 1982.

Neyrey, Jerome H, *The Social World of Luke-Acts.* Peabody, MA: Hendrickson, 1991.

Nickle, Keith F. *The Synoptic Gospels. An Introduction.* Atlanta: John Knox Press, 1973.

Pilgrim, Walter E. *Good News to the Poor:Wealth and Poverty in Luke-Acts.* Minneapolis, MN: Augsburg, 1981.

Scroggie, W. Graham. *A Guide to the Gospels.* London: Pikering and Inglis Ltd., 1967.

Schüssler-Fiorenza, Elizabeth. *In Memory of Her. A Feminist Theological Reconstruction of Christian Origins.* New York: Crossroad, 1983.

Selvidge, Marla J. *Daughters of Jerusalem.* Scottsdale, PA: Herald Press, 1987.

Talbert, Charles H., ed. *Perspectives on Luke-Acts. Perspectives in Religious Studies 1978.* Danville: Association of Baptist Professors of Religion, 1978.

———. *The Gospel of Luke and the Acts of the Apostles.* Nashville, TN: Abingdon Press, 2001.

Tyson, Joseph B., *Luke-Acts and the Jewish People. Eight Critical Perspectives.* Minneapolis, MN: Augsburg, 1988.

———. *Images of Judaism in Luke-Acts.* Columbia: University of South Carolina Press, 1992.

Wahlberg, Rachel. *Jesus According to Women.* New York: Paulist Press, 1975.

The Works of Flavius Josephus. Antiquities of the Jews, Book XVIII, Chap. 3.3. Translated by William Whiston. Grand Rapids, MI: Associate Publishers, 1972.

CHAPTER 7

Ashton, John. *Understanding the Fourth Gospel.* Oxford: Clarendon Press, 1993.

Bacon, B. W. *The Fourth Gospel in Research and Debate. A Series of Essays on Problems Concerning the Origin and Value of the Anonymous Writings Attributed to the Apostle John.* New York: Moffat, 1910.

Barrett, C. K. *The Gospel According to St. John. An Introduction with Commentary and Notes on the Greek Text.* London: SPCK, 1978.

Bauer, W. *Orthodoxy and Heresy in Earliest Christianity.* London: SCM, 1972.

Brodie, Thomas L. *The Quest for the Origin of John's Gospel. A Source-Oriented Approach.* New York: Oxford University Press, 1993.

Brown, Raymond E. *The Community of the Beloved Disciple. The Life, Loves, and Hates of an Individual Church in New Testament Times.* New York: Paulist Press, 1979.

———. *The Gospel According to John.* Garden City, NY: Doubleday, 1966, 1970.

Brown, Raymond E., Karl P. Donfried, and John Reumann, eds. *Peter in the New Testament.* Minneapolis, MN: Augsburg, 1973.

Bruns, J. Edgar. *The Christian Buddhism of St. John.* New York: Paulist Press, 1971.

Bultmann, R. *The Gospel of John, A Commentary.* Translated by, G. R. Beasley-Murray. Oxford: Blackwell, 1971.

Cassidy, Richard J. *John's Gospel in New Perspective. Christology and the Realities of the Roman Power.* New York: Orbis Books, 1992.

Colwell, E. C. *John Defends the Gospel* Chicago: Willett, Clark, 1936.

Conway, Colleen M. *Men and Women in the Fourth Gospel: Gender and Johanine Characterization.* Atlanta: Society of Biblical Literature, 1999.

Culpepper, R. A. *The Johannine School: An Evaluation of the Johannine-school Hypothesis Based on an Investigation of the Nature of Ancient Schools.* Missoula, MT: Scholars Press, 1975.

de Jonge, Marinus. *Jesus: Stranger from Heaven and Son of God.* Edited and translated by John E. Steely. Missoula, MT: Scholars Press, 1977.

Freed, Edwin D. *Old Testament Quotations in the Gospel of John.* Leiden: E. J. Brill, 1965.

Furnish, Victor Paul. *The Love Command in the New Testament.* London: SCM, 1973.

Gardner-Smith, P. *Saint John and the Synoptic Gospels.* Cambridge: University Press, 1938.

Goodenough, E. R. *By Light, Light. The Mystic Gospel of Hellenistic Judaism.* Amsterdam: Philo, 1969.

Hamman, Adalbert, ed. *The Mass. Ancient Liturgies and Patristic Texts,* New York: Alba House, 1967.

Harner, P. B. *The "I Am" of the Fourth Gospel: A Study in Johannine Usage and Thought.* Philadelphia: Fortress Press, 1970.

Jonas, H. *The Gnostic Religion. The Message of the Alien God and the Beginnings of Christianity.* Boston: Beacon, 1958.

Karris, Robert J. *Jesus and the Marginalized in John's Gospel.* Collegeville, MN: Liturgical Press, 1990.

Käseman, E. *The Testament of Jesus. A Study of the Gospel of John in the Light of Chapter 17.* G. Krodel. Philadelphia: Fortress Press, 1968.

Kee, Howard Clark. *The New Testament in Context. Sources and Documents.* Upper Saddle River, NJ: Prentice Hall, 1984.

Kostenberger, Andreas J. *Encountering John: The Gospel in Historical, Literary and Theological Perspective.* Grand Rapids, MI: Baker Books, 1999.

Lussier, E. *God is Love. According to Saint John.* New York: Alba House, 1977.

Manscheck, Clyde L., ed. *A History of Christianity. Readings in the History of the Church.* Grand Rapids, MI: Baker Books, 1964.

Martyn, J. L. *History and Theology in the Fourth Gospel.* Nashville, TN: Abingdon Press, 1979.

Mohammed, Ovey N. "Jesus and Krishna." In *Asian Faces of Jesus*, edited by R. S. Sugirtharajah. New York: Orbis Books, 1993, pp. 9-24.

Mussner, F. *The Historical Jesus in the Gospel of St. John.* Translated by W. J. O'Hara, New York: Herder and Herder, 1967.

Parkes, J. *The Conflict of the Church and the Synagogue. A Study in the Origins of Antisemitism.* London: Soncino, 1934.

Petersen, Norman R. *The Gospel of John and The Sociology of Light. Language and Characterization in the Fourth Gospel.* Valley Forge, PA: Trinity Press International, 1993.

"Reinterpreting John. How the Dead Sea Scrolls Have Revolutionized Our Understanding of the Gospel of John." *Bible Review,* 9 (1993): 18-25, 54.

Ringe, Sharon H. *Wisdom's Friends: Community and Christology in the Fourth Gospel.* Atlanta: Westminster John Knox, 1999.

Sandmel, S. *Anti-Semitism in the New Testament.* Philadelphia: Fortress Press, 1978.

Schneiders, Sandra M. "Women in the Fourth Gospel and the Role of Women in the Contemporary Church." *Biblical Theology Bulletin,* 12 (1982): 35-45.

Schüssler-Fiorenza, Elisabeth. *In Memory of Her: A Feminist Theological Reconstruction of Christian Origins.* New York: Crossroad, 1983.

Scroggie, W. Graham. *Guide to the Gospels.* London: Pickering and Inglis, 1967.

Sloyan, Gerard S. *John. Interpretation. A Bible Commentary for Teaching and Preaching.* Atlanta: John Knox Press, 1988.

———. *What Are They Saying about John?* New York: Paulist Press, 1991.

Smith, D. Moody. *The Theology of the Gospel of John,* New York: Cambridge University Press, 1995.

———. *John.* Abingdon New Testament Commentareis Ser. Nashville, TN: Abingdon Press, 1999.

Watkins, Henry William. *Modern Criticism Considered in Its Relation to the Fourth Gospel.* London: John Murray, 1890.

Whitacre, Rodney A. *Johannine Polemic. The Role of Tradition and Theology.* Chico, CA: Scholars Press, 1982.

Witherington, Ben III. *John's Wisdom. A Commentary on the Fourth Gospel.* Louisville, KY: Westminster John Knox Press, 1995.

CHAPTER 8

Aho, James A. *Religious Mythology and the Art of War. Comparative Religious Symbolisms of Military Violence.* Westport, CT: Greenwood Press, 1981.

Barnstone, Willis. *The Other Bible.* San Francisco: Harper and Row, 1984.

Barrett, C. K. *Luke the Historian in Recent Study.* London: Epworth Press, 1961.

———. *The Acts of the Apostles.* Books International, VA, 1999.

Bettenson, Henry. *Documents of the Christian Church.* New York: Oxford University Press, 1963.

Borg, Marcus J. *Conflict, Holiness, and Politics in the Teachings of Jesus,* Studies in the Bible and Early Christianity, No. 5. New York: Edwin Mellen Press, 1984.

Bovon, Francois. *Luke the Theologian: Thirty-Three Years of Research.* Allison Park, PA: Pickwick Publications, 1987.

Brawley, Robert L. *Luke-Acts and the Jews: Conflict, Apology, and Conciliation.* Atlanta: Scholars Press, 1987.

Brown, Robert McAfee. *Religion and Violence. A Primer for White Americans.* Philadelphia: Westminster Press, 1973.

Cadbury, Henry J. *The Making of Luke-Acts.* London: SPCK, 1958.

Cassidy, Richard J. *Society and Politics in the Acts of the Apostles.* Maryknoll, NY: Orbis Books, 1987.

Conzelmann, Hans. *The Theology of St. Luke.* Philadelphia: Fortress Press, 1982.

Dibelius, Martin. *Studies in the Acts of the Apostles.* New York: Charles Scribner's Sons, 1956.

Esler, Philip. *Community and Gospel in Luke-Acts.* Cambridge: Cambridge University Press, 1987.

Evans, Craig, and Donald A. Hagner, eds. *Anti-Semitism and Early Christianity. Issues of Polemic and Faith.* Minneapolis, MN: Fortress, 1993.

Fitzmyer, Joseph A. *Luke the Theologian. Aspects of His Teaching.* New York: Paulist Press, 1989.

Flender, Helmut. *St. Luke: Theologian of Redemptive History.* Philadelphia: Fortress Press, 1967.

Garrett, Susan R. *The Demise of the Devil. Magic and the Demonic in Luke's Writings.* Minneapolis, MN: Fortress Press, 1989.

Gasque, W. Ward. *A History of the Interpretation of the Acts of the Apostles.* Peabody, MA: Hendrickson, 1989.

Haenchen, Ernst. *The Acts of The Apostles. A Commentary.* Philadelphia: Westminster Press, 1971.

Harnack, Adolph. *The Acts of the Apostles.* Translated by J. R. Wilkinson. New York: G. P. Putnam's Sons, 1909.

Hemer, Colin J. *The Book of Acts in the Setting of Hellenistic History.* Tübingen, Germany: J.C.B. Möhr, 1989.

Hengel, Martin. *Acts and the History of Earliest Christianity.* Philadelphia: Fortress Press, 1980.

———. "The Geography of Palestine in Acts." In *The Book of Acts in Its Palestinian Setting.* Grand Rapids, MI: Wm. B. Eerdmans, 1995, pp. 28-75.

Hill, Craig C. *Hellenists and Hebrews. Reappraising Division within the Earliest Church.* Minneapolis, MN: Fortress Press, 1992.

Jervell, Jacob. *Luke and the People of God.* Minneapolis, MN: Augsburg, 1972.

———. *The Unknown Paul: Essays on Luke Acts and Early Christian History.* Minneapolis, MN: Augsburg, 1984.

Kee, Howard Clark. *Good News to the Ends of the Earth. The Theology of Acts.* Philadelphia: Trinity Press, 1990.

Krodel, Gerhard. *Acts.* Philadelphia: Fortress Press, 1981.

Kümmel, Werner Georg. *Introduction to the New Testament.* Translated by A. J. Mattill, Jr. New York: Abingdon Press, 1965.

Lentz, John Clayton, Jr. *Luke's Portrait of Paul.* New York: Cambridge University Press, 1993.

Lüdemann, Gerd. *Early Christianity According to the Traditions in Acts.* Minneapolis, MN: Fortress Press, 1989.

The Original African Heritage Study Bible, King James Version. Nashville, TN: James C. Winston Publishing Company, 1993.

O'Toole, Robert F. *The Unity of Luke's Theology. An Analysis of Luke-Acts.* New York: Michael Glazier, 1984.

Perkins, Pheme. *Peter. Apostle for the Whole Church.* Columbia: University of South Carolina Press, 1994.

Pervo, Richard I. *Profit with Delight: The Literary Genre of the Acts of the Apostles.* Philadelphia: Fortress Press, 1987.

———. *Luke's Story of Paul.* Minneapolis, MN: Fortress Press, 1990.

Pilgrim, Walter E. *Good News to the Poor: Wealth and Poverty in Luke-Acts.* Minneapolis, MN: Augsburg, 1981.

Powell, Mark Allan. *What Are They Saying About Acts?* New York: Paulist Press, 1991.

Richter, Reimer Ivoni. *Women in the Acts of the Apostles. A Feminist Liberation Perspective.* Minneapolis, MN: Fortress Press, 1995.

Ruether, Rosemary Radford. *Faith and Fratricide. The Theological Roots of Anti-Semitism.* New York: Crossroads, 1974.

Samartha, Stanley J. "The Cross and the Rainbow: Christ in a Multireligious Culture." In *Asian Faces of Jesus,* R. S. Sugirtharajah, ed. New York: Orbis, 1993, pp. 117-119.

Sanders, Jack. *The Jews in Luke-Acts.* Philadelphia: Fortress Press, 1982.

Selvidge, Marla J. "Acts of the Apostles. A Violent Aetiological Legend." In *Woman, Violence, and the Bible.* New York: Mellen Press, 1996, pp. 95-109.

Soards, Marion L. *The Speeches in Acts. Their Content, Context, and Concerns.* Louisville, KY: Westminster John Knox, 1994.

Talbert, Charles H. *Luke and the Gnostics: An Examination of the Lucan Purpose.* Nashville, TN: Abingdon Press, 1966.

———. *Literary Patterns, Theological Themes, and the Genre of Luke-Acts.* Missoula, MT: Scholars Press, 1974.

Tannehill, Robert C. *The Narrative Unity of Luke-Acts.* Philadelphia and Minneapolis: Fortress Press, 1986, 1989.

Tyson, Joseph. *The Death of Jesus in Luke-Acts.* Columbia: University of South Carolina Press, 1986.

Witherington, Ben III, ed. *The Book of Acts.* Cambridge: Cambridge University Press, 1996.

———. *History, Literature, and Society in the Book of Acts.* New York: Cambridge University Press, 1996.

Vielhauer, Philip. "On Paulinism of Acts." In *Studies in Luke–Acts,* edited by Leander Keck and J. Martyn. Phildelphia: Fortress Press, 1980, pp. 33-50.

CHAPTER 9

Beker, J. Christiaan. *Paul the Apostle. The Triumph of God in Life and Thought.* Philadelphia: Fortress Press, 1982.

Bornkamm, Günther. *Paul.* Translated by D. M. G. Stalker. New York: Harper and Row, 1971.

Brown, Joanne Carlson, and Carole R. Bohn, eds. *Christianity, Patriarchy, and Abuse. A Feminist Critique.* Cleveland: Pilgrim Press, 1989.

Brown, Raymond E. *The Churches the Apostles Left Behind.* New York: Paulist Press, 1984.

Charles, R. H., trans. *The Book of Enoch.* London: SPCK, 1982.

Clabeaux, John J. *A Lost Edition of the Letters of Paul. A Reassessment of the Text of the Pauline Corpus* attested by Marcion. Washington, DC: Catholic Biblical Association, 1989.

Collins, Raymond F. *Letters that Paul did not Write. The Epistle to the Hebrews and the Pauline Pseudepigrapha.* Wilmington, DE: Michael Glazier, 1988.

Cousar, Charles B. *The Letters of Paul.* Nashville, TN: Abingdon Press, 1996.

Craddock, Fred B. *Philippians. Interpretation. A Bible Commentary for Teaching and Preaching.* Atlanta: John Knox Press, 1985.

Davies, W. D. *Paul and Rabbinic Judaism. Some Rabbinic Elements in Pauline Theology.* Philadelphia: Fortress Press, 1980.

Doty, William G. *Letters in Primitive Christianity.* Minneapolis, MN: Fortress Press, 1973.

Engberg-Pedersen, Troels, ed. *Paul in His Hellenistic Context.* Minneapolis, MN: Fortress Press, 1995.

Farrar, F. W. *Seekers After God.* London: Macmillan, 1886.

Furnish, Victor Paul. *The Moral Teaching of Paul.* Nashville, TN: Abingdon Press, 1979.

———. *1 Thessalonians, 2 Thessalonians.* Nashville, TN: Abingdon Press, 2000.

Grayston, Kenneth. *The Letters of Paul to the Philippians and to the Thessalonians.* New York: Cambridge University Press, 1967.

Hallman, David G. ed. *Ecotheology: Voices from South and North.* New York: Orbis Books, 1994.

Hanson, Anthony Tyrrell. *Studies in Paul's Technique and Theology.* Grand Rapids, MI: Wm. B. Eerdmans, 1974.

Himes, Joshua. *A Brief History of William Miller the Great Pioneer in Adventual Faith.* Boston: Advent Christian Publication Society, 1910, pp. 230-231.

Jewett, Robert. *The Thessalonian Correspondence: Pauline Rhetoric and Millenarian Piety.* Philadelphia: Fortress Press, 1986.

———. *Paul. The Apostle to America. Cultural Trends and Pauline Scholarship.* Louisville, KY: John Knox, 1994.

Keck, Leander E. *Paul and His Letters.* Minneapolis, MN: Fortress Press, 1979.

Keck, Leander E., and Victor Paul Furnish. *The Pauline Letters.* Nashville, TN: Abingdon Press, 1984.

Kern, Philip H. *Rhetoric and Galations.* Cambridge, MA: Cambridge University Press, 1999.

Krausz, Tibor. "The Second Coming." *Newsweek,* February 17, 1997: 18.

Krodel, Gerhard, ed. *The Deutero-Pauline Letters. Ephesians, Colossians, 2 Thessalonians, 1-2 Timothy, Titus.* Minneapolis, MN: Fortress Press, 1993.

Lührmann, Dieter. *Galatians. A Continental Commentary.* Minneapolis, MN: Fortress Press, 1992.

Maccoby, Hyam. *The Mythmaker. Paul and the Invention of Christianity.* New York: Harper and Row, 1986.

Malherbe, A. *Paul and the Thessalonians.* Philadelphia: Fortress Press, 1987.

———. *The Letters to the Thessalonians.* New York: Doubleday, 2000.

Marshall, I. H. *1 and 2 Thessalonians.* Grand Rapids, MI: Wm. B. Eerdmans, 1983.

Morland, Kjell Arne. *The Rhetoric of Curse in Galatians. Paul Confronts Another Gospel.* Atlanta: Scholars Press, 1995.

Newsom, Carol A., and Sharon H. Ringe, eds. *The Women's Bible Commentary.* London: SPCK, 1992.

Neyrey, Jerome H. *Paul, In Other Words.* Louisville, KY: Westminster John Knox Press, 1990.

O'Connor, J. Murphy, and James H. Charlesworth. *Paul and the Dead Sea Scrolls.* New York: Crossroad, 1990.

Plevnik, Joseph. *What Are They Saying about Paul?* New York: Paulist Press, 1986.

Puskas, Charles. *The Letters of Paul. An Introduction.* Collegeville, MN: Liturgical Press, 1993.

Richard, Earl J. *First and Second Thessalonians.* Collegeville, MN: Michael Glazier, 1995.

Roetzel, Calvin J. *The Letters of Paul, Conversations in Context.* Atlanta: John Knox Press, 1975.

Rosner, Brian S., ed. *Understanding Paul's Ethics.* Grand Rapids, MI: Wm. B. Eerdmans, 1995.

Segal, Alan F. *Paul the Convert.* New Haven, CT: Yale University Press, 1990.

Sevenster, J. N. *Paul and Seneca.* Leiden: E. J. Brill, 1961.

Smith, Abraham. *Comfort One Another. Reconstructing the Rhetoric and Audience of 1 Thessalonians.* Louisville, KY: Westminster John Knox Press, 1995.

Thurston, Bonnie. *Reading Colossians, Ephesians and 2 Thessalonians.* New York: Crossroad, 1995.

Wiles, Virginia. *Making Sense of Paul: A Basic Introduction to Pauline Theology.* Peabody, MA: Hendrickson, 2000.

Young, Serinity, ed. *An Anthology of Sacred Texts By and About Women.* New York: Crossroad, 1993.

Ziesler, John. *Pauline Christianity.* New York: Oxford University Press, 1983.

CHAPTER 10

Baker, Bill. *2 Corinthians*, NIV Commentary Ser. Joplin, MO: College Pr. Pub., 1999.

Bartchy, S. Scott. *First Century Slavery and the Interpretation of 1Corinthians 7:21.* Missoula, MT: Society for Biblical Literature, 1971.

Beardslee, William A. *First Corinthians. A Commentary for Today.* St. Louis, MO: Chalice Press, 1994.

Best, Ernest. *The Letter of Paul to the Romans.* Cambridge: Cambridge University Press, 1967.

Bettenson, Henry, ed. *Documents of the Christian Church.* New York: Oxford, 1975.

Black, Matthew. *Romans.* In *The New Century Bible Commentary.* Grand Rapids, MI: Wm. B. Eerdmans, 1989.

Bristow, John Temple. *What Paul Really Said About Women.* San Francisco: Harper and Row, 1988.

Brooten, Bernadette J. *Women Leaders in the Ancient Synagogue. Inscriptional Evidence and Background Issues.* Chico, CA: Scholars Press, 1982.

Bruce, F. F. *The New Century Bible Commentary. 1 and 2 Corinthians.* Grand Rapids, MI: Wm. B. Eerdmans, 1980.

Byrne, Brendan. *Romans.* Collegeville, MN: Michael Glazier, 1996.

Campbell, William S. *Paul's Gospel in an Intercultural Context.* New York: Peter Lang, 1992.

Charles, R. H. *The Book of Enoch.* London: SPCK, 1974.

Chueng, Alex T. *Idol Food in Corinth: Jewish Background and Pauline Legacy.* Sheffield, UK: Sheffield Academic Press, 1999.

Clark, Elizabeth A. *Women in the Early Church.* Wilmington, DE: Michael Glazier, 1983.

Donfried, Karl P. *The Romans Debate.* Rev. and expanded edition. Peabody, MA: Hendrickson, 1991.

Donfried, Karl P., and I. Howard Marshall. *The Theology of the Shorter Pauline Letters.* New York: Cambridge University Press, 1993.

Fisk, Bruce N. *1 Corinthians.* Interpretation Bible Study Ser. Louisville, KY: Presbyterian Pub., 2000.

Fitzgerald, John T. *2 Corinthians.* Abingdon New Testament Commmentaries Ser. Nashville, TN: Abingdon Press, 1999.

Fitzmyer, Joseph A. *Romans. The Anchor Bible.* New York: Doubleday, 1964.

Furnish, Victor Paul. *The Moral Teaching of Paul.* Nashville, TN: Abingdon Press, 1979.

———. *The Theology of the First Letter to the Corinthians.* New York: Cambridge University Press, 1999.

Gaventa, Beverly Roberts. "Mother's Milk and Ministry in 1 Corinthians 3." In *Theology and Ethics in Paul and His Interpreters. Essays in Honor of Victor Paul Furnish,* Eugene H. Lovering, Jr. and Jerry L. Sumney, eds. Nashville, TN: Abingdon Press, 1996, pp. 101-113.

Getty, Mary Ann. "God's Fellow Workers and Apostleship." In *Women Priests: A Catholic Commentary on the Vatican Declaration,* Arlene and Leonard Swidler, eds. New York: Paulist Press, 1977, pp. 442-445.

Gillman, Florence M. *Women Who Knew Paul.* Collegeville, MN: Michael Glazier, 1992.

Guerra, Anthony J. *Romans and the Apologetic Tradition. The Purpose, Genre, and Audience of Paul's Letters.* Cambridge: Cambridge University Press, 1995.

Harrisville, Roy A. *1 Corinthians.* In *Augsburg Commentary on the New Testament.* Minneapolis, MN: Augsburg, 1987.

Hayter, Mary. *The New Eve in Christ. The Use and Abuse of the Bible in the Debate about Women in the Church.* Grand Rapids, MI: Wm. B. Eerdmans, 1987.

Hooker, Morna D. "Authority on Her Head: An Examination of 1 Cor. 11:10." *New Testament Studies,* 10 (1963), 410-416.

Jones, Amos. "Paul's Message of Freedom." In *The Bible and Liberation. Political and Social Hermeneutics,* Norman K. Gottwald and Richard A. Horsley, eds. New York: Orbis Books, 1993, pp. 505-530.

Kümmel, Werner Georg. *Introduction to the New Testament.* A. J. Mattill, Jr., trans. New York: Abingdon Press, 1966.

Linzey, Andrew, and Tom Regan, eds. *Animals and Christianity. A Book of Readings.* New York: Crossroad, 1988.

Loades, Ann, ed. *Feminist Theology. A Reader.* Louisville, KY: John Knox Press, 1990.

Lohse, Eduard. *Colossians and Philemon.* Philadelphia: Fortress Press, 1971.

MacDonald, Margaret Y. "Early Christian Women Married to Unbelievers." *Studies in Religion/Sciences Religieuses.* 19 (1990): 221-234.

MacHaffie, Barbara J. *Her Story. Women in Christian Tradition.* Philadelphia: Fortress Press, 1986.

Martin, Ernest D. *Colossians, Philemon.* Scottsdale, PA: Herald Press, 1993.

Martin, Ralph P. *Colossians and Philemon.* Grand Rapids, MI: Wm. B. Eerdmans, 1981.

Minear, Paul S. *The Obedience of Faith. The Purposes of Paul in the Epistle to the Romans.* Naperville, IL: Alec R. Allenson, 1971.

Murphy-O'Connor, Jerome. *The Theology of the Second Letter to the Corinthians.* New York: Cambridge University Press, 1991.

Nanos, Mark D. *The Mystery of the Romans.* Minneapolis, MN: Fortress Press, 1996.

Newsom, Carol A., and Sharon H. Ringe, eds. *The Women's Bible Commentary.* Louisville, KY: Westminster John Knox Press, 1992.

Parvey, Constance. "The Theology and Leadership of Women in the New Testament." In *Religion and Sexism. Images of Woman in the Jewish and Christian Traditions,* Rosemary Radford Ruether, ed. New York: Simon and Schuster, 1974, pp. 117-149.

Pieris, Aloysius. "Towards an Asian Theology of Liberation: Some Religio-Cultural Guidelines." In *Asia's Struggle for Full Humanity: Towards a Relevant Theology,* Virginia Fabella, ed. New York: Orbis Books, 1980.

Pinches, Charles, and Jay B. McDaniel. *Good News for Animals? Christian Approaches to Animal Well-being.* New York: Orbis, 1993.

Preiss, Theo. *Life in Christ. Studies in Biblical Theology.* Translated by Harold Knight. Chicago: Alec R. Allenson, 1954.

Samartha, Stanley J. "Hindu-Christian Funeral." In *Frontiers in Asian Christian Theology. Emerging Trends,* edited by R. S. Sugirtharajah. New York: Orbis Books, 1994, pp. 179-182.

Schüssler-Fiorenza, Elizabeth. "The Apostleship of Women in Early Christianity." In *Women Priests. A Catholic Commentary on the Vatican Declaration,* Arlene and Leonard Swidler, eds. New York: Paulist Press, 1977, pp, 135-140.

———. "Women in the Early Christian Movement." In *Womanspirit Rising. A Feminist Reader in Religion,* Carol P. Christ and Judith Plaskow, eds. San Francisco: Harper and Row, 1979, pp. 84-92.

Soards, Marion L. *1 Corinthians,* Vol. 7. New International Biblical Commentary Ser. Peabody, MA: Hendrickson, 1999.

Souter, A. *A Study of Ambrosiaster.* Cambridge: Cambridge University Press, 1905.

Stanley, Christopher D. *Paul and the Language of Scripture. Citation Technique in the Pauline Epistles and Contemporary Literature.* Cambridge: Cambridge University Press, 1992.

Stanton, Elizabeth Cady, ed. *The Woman's Bible.* Seattle, WA: Jane T. Walker, 1974, 2:163.

Tacitus. *The Annals.* John Jackson, trans. Cambridge, MA: Harvard University Press, 1925, Vol 5, 15:44.

Tetlow, Elisabeth M. *Women and Ministry in the New Testament.* New York: Paulist Press, 1980.

Torjesen, Karen Jo. *When Women Were Priests. Women's Leadership in the Early Church and the Scandal of Their Subordination in the Rise of Christianity.* San Francisco: Harper San Francisco, 1993.

Walters, James C. *Ethnic Issues in Paul's Letter to the Romans. Changing Self-Definitions in Earliest Roman Christianity.* Valley Forge, PA: Trinity Press, 1993.

Winegard, Robert. *Paul and the Corinthians.* Life Letters Of Paul Ser. Nashville, TN: Abingdon Press, 2000.

Wire, Antionette Clark. *The Corinthian Women Prophets. A Reconstruction through Paul's Rhetoric.* Minneapolis, MN: Fortress Press, 1990.

Witherington, Ben III. *Women in the Earliest Churches,* Society for New Testament Studies Monograph Series 8, Cambridge: Cambridge University Press, 1988.

CHAPTER 11

Arnold, C. E. *Ephesians. Power and Magic.* New York: Cambridge University Press, 1989.

Barth, Markus. *Ephesians.* In *The Anchor Bible,* 2 vols. New York: Doubleday, 1974.

Bassler, Jouette. *Divine Impartiality: Paul and a Theological Axiom.* Chico, CA: Scholars Press, 1982.

Beker, J. Christiaan. *Paul the Apostle. The Triumph of God in Life and Thought.* Philadelphia: Fortress Press, 1982.

Bettenson, Henry, ed. *Documents of the Christian Church.* Oxford: Oxford University Press, 1963.

Bornkamm, Günther. *Paul.* D. M. G. Stalker, trans. New York: Harper and Row, 1971.

Brown, Raymond E. *The Churches the Apostles Left Behind.* New York: Paulist Press, 1984.

Clabeaux, John J. *A Lost Edition of the Letters of Paul. A Reassessment of the Text of the Pauline Corpus.* Washington, DC: Catholic Biblical Association, 1989.

Collins, Adela Yarbro, ed. *Feminist Perspectives on Biblical Scholarship.* Chico, CA: Scholars Press, 1985.

Collins, Raymond F. *Letters That Paul Did Not Write. The Epistle to the Hebrews and the Pauline Pseudepigrapha,* Wilmington, DE: Michael Glazier, 1988.

Cousar, Charles B. *The Letters of Paul.* Nashville, TN: Abingdon Press, 1996.

Davies, W. D. *Paul and Rabbinic Judaism. Some Rabbinic Elements in Pauline Theology.* Philadelphia: Fortress Press, 1980.

Doty, William G. *Letters in Primitive Christianity.* Minneapolis, MN: Fortress Press, 1973.

Engberg-Pedersen, Troels, ed. *Paul in His Hellenistic Context.* Minneapolis. MN: Fortress, 1995.

Farrar, F. W. *Seekers After God.* London: Macmillan, 1886.

Furnish, Victor Paul. *The Moral Teaching of Paul.* Nashville, TN: Abingdon Press, 1979.

Hanson, Anthony Tyrrell. *Studies in Paul's Technique and Theology.* Grand Rapids, MI: Wm.B. Eerdmans, 1974.

Hengel, Martin. *The Pre-Christian Paul.* Philadelphia: Trinity Press International, 1991.

Jewett, Robert. *Paul. The Apostle to America. Cultural Trends and Pauline Scholarship.* Louisville, KY: John Knox, 1994.

Keck, Leander E. *Paul and His Letters.* Minneapolis, MN: Fortress Press, 1979.

———, and Victor Paul Furnish. *The Pauline Letters.* Nashville, TN: Abingdon Press, 1984.

Keesmaat, Sylvia C. *Paul and His Story: (Re)Interpreting the Exodus Tradition.* Sheffield, UK: Sheffield Academic Press, 1999.

Kiley, Mark. *Colossians as Pseudepigraphy.* Sheffield, UK: JSOT Press, 1986.

Krodel, Gerhard, ed. *The Deutero-Pauline Letters. Ephesians, Colossians, 2 Thessalonians, 1-2 Timothy, Titus.* Minneapolis, MN: Fortress Press, 1993.

Lincoln, Andrew T., and A. J. M. Wedderburn. *The Theology of the Later Pauline Letters.* New York: Cambridge University Press, 1993.

Lohse, Eduard. *Colossians and Philemon.* Philadelphia: Fortress Press, 1971.

Maccoby, Hyam. *The Mythmaker. Paul and the Invention of Christianity.* New York: Harper and Row, 1986.

————. *Paul and Hellenism.* Philadelphia: Trinity Press, 1991.

Martin, Ernest D. *Colossians, Philemon,* Scottsdale, PA: Herald Press, 1993.

Martin, Ralph P. *Colossians and Philemon.* Grand Rapids, MI: Wm. B. Eerdmans, 1981.

Miranda, Jose Porfirio. *Marx and the Bible. A Critique of the Philosophy of Oppression,* John Eagleson, trans. New York: Orbis, 1974.

O'Connor, J. Murphy, and James H. Charlesworth. *Paul and the Dead Sea Scrolls.* New York: Crossroad, 1990.

Neyrey, Jerome H. *Paul, In Other Words,* Louisville, KY: Westminster John Knox Press, 1990.

Newsom, Carol A., and Sharon H. Ringe, eds. *The Women's Bible Commentary.* London: SPCK, 1992.

Plevnik, Joseph. *What Are They Saying about Paul?* New York: Paulist Press, 1986.

Preiss, Théo. *Life in Christ. Studies in Biblical Theology.* Harold Knight, trans. Chicago: Alec R. Allenson, 1954.

Puskas, Charles. *The Letters of Paul. An Introduction.* Collegeville, MN: Liturgical Press, 1993.

Rhoads, David. *The Challenge of Diversity. The Witness of Paul and the Gospels.* MN: Fortress Press, 1996.

Roetzel, Calvin J. *The Letters of Paul. Conversations in Context.* Atlanta: John Knox Press, 1975.

Rosner, Brian S., ed. *Understanding Paul's Ethics.* Grand Rapids, MI: Wm. B. Eerdmans, 1995.

Schnackenburg, Rudolf. *Ephesians. A Commentary.* Helen Heron, trans. Edinburgh: T&T Clark, 1991.

Segal, Alan F. *Paul the Convert.* New Haven, CT: Yale University Press, 1990.

Souter, A. *A Study of Ambrosiaster.* Cambridge: Cambridge University Press, 1905.

Sevenster, J. N. *Paul and Seneca.* Leiden: E. J. Brill, 1961.

Young, Serinity, ed. *An Anthology of Sacred Texts by and about Women.* New York: Crossroad, 1993.

Tacitus. *The Annals.* John Jackson, trans. Cambridge, MA: Harvard University Press, 1925, Vol 5, 15:44.

Thurston, Bonnie. *Reading Colossians, Ephesians and 2 Thessalonians.* New York: Crossroad, 1995.

William, David J. *Paul's Metaphors: Their Context and Character.* Peabody, MA: Hendrickson, 1999.

Ziesler, John. *Pauline Christianity.* New York: Oxford University Press, 1983.

CHAPTER 12

Agrippa Von Nettesheim, Heinricus Cornelius. *The Glory of Women; or, a Treatise Declaring the Excellency and Preheminence of Women above Men Which Is Proved Both by Scripture, Law, Reason, and Authority, Divine and Humane.* London: Robert Ibbitson, 1652. For a discussion of his work, consult Marla J. Selvidge, *Notorious Voices. Feminist Biblical Interpretation 1500-1920.* New York: Continuum, 1996.

Bassler, Jouette M. *1 Timothy, 2 Timothy, Titus.* Nashville, TN: Abingdon Press, 1996.

Dewey, Joanna. "1 Timothy." In *The Women's Bible Commentary,* Carol A. Newsom and Sharon H. Ringe, eds. London: SPCK, 1992.

Dibelius, Martin, and Hans Conzelmann. *The Pastoral Epistles. A Commentary on the Pastoral Epistles.* Philadelphia: Fortress Press, 1972.

García, Florentino Martínez. *The Dead Sea Scrolls Translated. The Qumran Texts in English,* 2d ed. Wilfred G. E. Watson, trans. Leiden: E. J. Brill, 1996.

Hanson, Anthony Tyrrell. *The Pastoral Letters.* Cambridge, MA: Cambridge University Press, 1966.

Johnson, Luke Timothy. *Letters to Paul's Delegates. 1 Timothy, 2 Timothy, Titus.* Valley Forge, PA: Trinity Press International, 1996.

Keener, Craig S. *Paul, Women and Wives. Marriage and Women's Ministry in the Letters of Paul.* Peabody, MA: Hendrickson, 1992.

Kroeger, Catherine Clark, and Richard Clark Kroeger. *I Suffer Not a Woman. Rethinking 1 Timothy 2:11-15 in Light of Ancient Evidence.* Grand Rapids, MI: Baker Books, 1992.

Kümmel, Werner Georg. *Introduction to the New Testament.* New York: Abingdon Press, 1966.

MacDonald, Margaret Y. *The Pauline Churches. A Socio-historical Study of Institutionalization in the Pauline and Deutero-Pauline Writings.* Cambridge, MA: Cambridge University Press, 1988.

MacHaffie, Barbara J., ed. *Readings in Her Story. Women in Christian Tradition.* Minneapolis, MN: Fortress Press, 1992.

McNamara, Jo Ann. "Wives and Widows in Early Christian Thought." *International Journal of Women's Studies,* 2 (1979): 575-592.

Oden, Thomas C. *First and Second Timothy and Titus.* Louisville, KY: John Knox Press, 1989.

Roetzel, Calvin J. *The Letters of Paul. Conversations in Context.* Atlanta: John Knox Press, 1975.

Stanton, Elizabeth Cady. *The Woman's Bible.* New York: European Publishing Company, 1898. Reprint: Seattle, WA: Coalition Task Force on Women and Religion, 1974. For a discussion of this work, consult Marla J. Selvidge, *Notorious Voices. Feminist Biblical Interpretation 1500-1920.* New York: Continuum, 1996.

Swidler, Arlene, and Leonard Swidler. *Women Priests. A Catholic Commentary on the Vatican Declaration.* New York: Paulist Press, 1977.

CHAPTER 13

Attridge, Harold W. *The Epistle to the Hebrews.* Philadelphia: Fortress Press, 1989.

Buchanan, George Wesley. *To The Hebrews.* In *Anchor Bible.* New York: Doubleday, 1972.

Chester, Andrew, and Ralph P. Martin. *The Theology of the Letters of James, Peter, and Jude.* New York: Cambridge University Press, 1994.

D'Angelo, Mary Rose. "Hebrews." In *The Women's Bible Commentary,* Carol A. Newsom and Sharon H. Ringe, eds. Louisville, KY: John Knox Press, 1992, pp. 364-367.

Dibelius, Martin. *James. A Commentary on the Epistle of James.* Philadelphia: Fortress Press, 1976.

Dowd, Sharon. "James," in *The Women's Bible Commentary,* Carol A. Newsom and Sharon H. Ringe, eds. London: SPCK, 1992.

Gordon, Robert P. *Hebrews.* Sheffield, UK: Sheffield Academic Press, 2000.

Hartin, Patrick J. "Exegesis and Proclamation." *Journal of Theology for South Africa,* 84 (1993): 57-63.

Hurst, L. D. *The Epistle to the Hebrews. Its Background of Thought.* New York: Cambridge University Press, 1990.

Hartin, Patrick J. *James and the Q Sayings of Jesus.* Sheffield, UK: Sheffield Academic Press, 1991.

Jewett, Robert. *Letter to Pilgrims. A Commentary on the Epistle to the Hebrews.* New York: Pilgrim Press, 1981.

Johnson, Luke Timothy. *The Letter of James.* In the *Anchor Bible.* New York: Doubleday, 1995.

Jordan, Clarence. *The Cotton Patch Version of Hebrews and the General Epistles.* New York: Association Press, 1973.

Kee, Howard Clark. *The New Testament in Context. Sources and Documents.* Upper Saddle River, NJ: Prentice Hall, 1984.

Krodel, Gerhard, ed. *The General Letters.* Proclamation Commentaries. Minneapolis, MN: Fortress Press, 1995.

———, ed. *Hebrews, James, 1 and 2 Peter, Jude, and Revelation.* Proclamation Commentaries. Philadelphia: Fortress Press, 1977.

Kümmel, Werner Georg. *Introduction to the New Testament.* New York: Abingdon Press, 1966.

Lindars, Barnabas. *New Testament Theology.* New York: Cambridge University Press, 1991.

Long, Thomas G. *Hebrews. Interpretation, A Bible Commentary for Teaching and Preaching.* Louisville, KY: John Knox Press, 1997.

Peterson, David. *Hebrews and Perfection. An Examination of the Concept of Perfection in the Epistle to Hebrews.* New York: Cambridge University Press, 1982.

Reicke, Bo. *The Epistles of James, Peter, and Jude.* In the *Anchor Bible.* New York: Doubleday, 1964.

Scholer, John M. *Proleptic Priests. Priesthood in the Epistle to the Hebrews.* Sheffield, UK: JSOT Press, 1991.

Selby, Donald J., and James King West. *Introduction to the Bible.* New York: The Macmillan Company, 1971.

Sidebottom, E. M. *James, Jude, 2 Peter.* In the *New Century Bible Commentary.* Grand Rapids, MI: Wm. B. Eerdmans, 1982.

Tamez, Elsa. "The Scandalous Message of James: The Angle of Praxis." In *The Bible and Liberation: Political and Social Hermeneutics,* edited by Norman K. Gottwald and Richard A. Horsley. New York: Orbis Books, 1993, pp. 531-532.

———. *The Scandalous Message of James. Faith Without Works Is Dead.* New York: Crossroad, 1990.

CHAPTER 14

Bauckham, Richard. *Jude and the Relatives of Jesus in the Early Church.* Edinburgh: T&T Clark, 1990.

The Book of Enoch, Charles, R.H., trans. London: SPCK, 1982.

Chester, Andrew, and Ralph P. Martin. *The Theology of the Letters of James, Peter, and Jude.* New York: Cambridge University Press, 1994.

Dear, John. *The God of Peace.* New York: Orbis Books, 1994.

Elliott, John H. *A Home for the Homeless. A Sociological Exegesis of 1 Peter, Its Situation and Strategy.* Philadelphia: Fortress Press, 1981.

———. *1 Peter: A New Translation with Introduction and Commentary.* Doubleday, 2000.

Freedman, David Noel. *Anchor Bible Dictionary.* New York: Doubleday, 1992, Vols. 3 and 5.

Kee, Howard Clark. *The New Testament in Context. Sources and Documents.* Upper Saddle River, NJ: Prentice Hall, 1984.

Krodel, Gerhard. *Hebrews, James, 1 and 2 Peter, Jude, Revelation.* Philadelphia: Fortress Press, 1977.

Kümmel , Werner Georg. *Introduction to the New Testament.* New York: Abingdon Press, 1965.

Laërtius, Diogenes. *The Lives and Opinions of Eminent Philosophers*, trans. C. D. Yonge. London: George Bell and Sons, 1905, 10:31,3 or p. 474.

Newsom, Carol A. and Sharon H. Ringe, eds. *The Women's Bible Commentary.* London: SPCK, 1992.

Neyrey, Jerome H. *2 Peter, Jude.* In the *Anchor Bible.* New York: Doubleday, 1993.

Pilch, John J. "'Visiting Strangers' and 'Resident Aliens.'" *Bible Today,* 29 (1991), 357-361.

Reicke, Bo. *The Epistles of James, Peter, and Jude.* In the *Anchor Bible.* New York: Doubleday, 1964.

Sidebottom, E. M. *James, Jude, 2 Peter.* In the *New Century Bible Commentary.* Grand Rapids, MI: Wm. B. Eerdmans, 1982.

Stanton, Elizabeth Cady. *The Woman's' Bible,* Seattle, WA: Coalition Task Force on Women and Religion, 1974. Originally published in 1898.

Stone, Michael E., ed. *Jewish Writings of the Second Temple Period. Apocrypha, Pseudepigrapha, Qumran Sectarian Writings, Philo, Josephus.* Philadelphia: Fortress Press, 1984.

Van Den Heever, G. "In Purifying Fire: World View and 2 Peter 3:10," *Neotestamentica,* 27, 1 (1993), 107, 110-115.

CHAPTER 15

Alves, Rubem. *Tomorrow's Child; Imagination, Creativity, and the Rebirth of Cultuer.* New York: Harper and Row, 1972.

Barr, David L. "Elephants and Holograms: From Metaphor to Methodology in the Study of John's Apocalypse." *SBL Seminar Papers,* 25 (1986), 400-411.

Beck, T. *The Apocalypse of John.* Grand Rapids, MI: Baker Books, 1991.

Benson, Ivan M. "Revelation 12 and the Dragon of Antiquity." *Restoration Quarterly,* 29, 2 (1987), 97-102.

Boesak, Allan A. *Comfort and Protest. The Apocalypse from a South African Perspective.* Philadelphia: Westminster Press, 1987.

Boring, M. Eugene. *Revelation. Interpretation. A Bible Commentary for Teaching and Preaching.* Louisville, KY: John Knox Press, 1989.

Briggs, Robert A. "A Jewish Temple Imagery in the Book of Revelation." In *Studies in Biblical Literature.* New York: Peter Lang Publishing, 1999.

Brown, Raymond E. *Jerome Biblical Commentary.* Upper Saddle River, NJ: Prentice Hall, 1968.

Bultmann, R. *The Johannine Epistles.* Philadelphia: Fortress Press, 1973.

Bush, George, "Address Before a Joint Session of the Congress on the Persian Gulf Crisis and the Federal Budget Deficit." *Weekly Compilation of Presidential Documents,* September 11, 1990, p. 1358.

Carey, Greg. "Elusive Apocalypse." *Studies in the Biblical Hermenuetics.* Macon, GA: Mercer University Press, 1999.

Charles, R. H. *The Revelation of St. John.* Edinburgh: T & T Clark, 1929.

Charlesworth, James H. *The Old Testament Pseudepigrapha. Apocalyptic Literature and Testaments.* New York: Doubleday, 1983.

Collins, Adela Yarbro. *The Combat Myth in the Book of Revelation.* Missoula, MT: Scholars Press, 1976.

———. "Coping with Hostility." *Bible Today,* 19 (1981): 327.

———. "The Revelation of John. An Apocalyptic Response to a Social Crisis." *Currents in Theology and Mission,* 8 (1981): 12.

———. *Crisis and Catharsis. The Power of the Apocalypse.* Philadelphia: Fortress Press, 1984.

———. "Vilification and Self-definition in the Book of Revelation." *Harvard Theological Review,* 79 (1986): 316-317

———. "Women's History and the Book of Revelation." *SBL Seminar Papers,* 26 (1987): 80-91.

Court, John M. *Myth and History in the Book of Revelation.* Atlanta: John Knox Press, 1979.

Culpepper, R. Alan. *1,2,3 John.* Atlanta: John Knox Press, 1985.

Daly, Mary. Gyn-Ecology. *The Metaethics of Radical Feminism.* New York: Beacon Press, 1978.

Drane, John. *Revelation. The Apocalypse of St. John.* New York: St. Martins, 1999.

Dworkin, Andrea. *Our Blood. Prophecies and Discourses on Sexual Politics.* New York: Harper and Row, 1976.

Dyer, Charles H. "The Identity of Babylon in Revelation 17-18." *Bibliotheca Sacra,* 98 (1987): 327-331.

Edinger, Edward. *Archetype of the Apocalypse: A Jungian Study of the Book of Revelation.* LaSalle, IL: Open Court, 1999

Eusebius. *The Ecclesiastical History of Eusebius Pamphilus.* Grand Rapids, MI: Baker Book, 1973, p. 125 or 3:39.

Faley, Roland J. *Apocalypse Then and Now: A Comparison to the Book of Revelation.* Mahwah, NJ: Paulist Press, 1999.

Freedman, David Noel, ed. *Anchor Bible Dictionary.* New York: Doubleday, 1992.

Ford, J. Massyngberde. *Revelation.* In the *Anchor Bible.* New York: Doubleday, 1975.

Freyne, Sean. "Vilifying the Other and Defining the Self. Matthew's and John's Anti-Polemic Focus." In *To See Ourselves as Others See Us,* Jacob Neusner, ed. Chico, CA: Scholars Press, 1985, pp. 118-119.

Grayston, Kenneth. *The Johannine Epistles.* In the *New Century Bible Commentary.* Grand Rapids, MI: Wm. B. Eerdmans, 1984.

Hanson, Paul. *Dawn of Apocalyptic.* Philadelphia: Fortress Press, 1975.

Hopkins, M. "The Historical Perspective of Apocalypse 1-11." *Catholic Biblical Quarterly,* 27 (1965), 44.

Klassen, W. "Vengeance in the Apocalypse of John. An Apocalyptic Response to a Social Crisis." *Catholic Biblical Quarterly,* 28 (1966), 310.

Krodel, Gerhard, ed. *The General Letters. Hebrews, James, 1-2 Peter, Jude, 1-2-3 John.* Minneapolis, MN: Fortress Press, 1995.

Kümmel, Werner Georg. *Introduction to the New Testament.* New York: Abingdon Press, 1966.

Lawrence, D. H. *Apocalypse.* New York: Viking Press, 1982.

LeFrois, B. J. "The Mary-Church Relationship in the Apocalypse." *Marian Studies,* 9 (1958), 89.

Majka, Frank. "Of Beasts and Christians." *Bible Today* (1984), 284.

Malina, Bruce J. *On the Genre and Message of Revelation. Star Visions and Sky Journeys.* Peabody, MA: Hendrickson, 1995.

Malina, Bruce and John J. Pilch. *Social-Science Commentaries on the Book of Revelation.* Minneapolis, MN: Augsburg-Fortress, 2000.

McGriggs, Lee Augustus. *The Odyssey of Martin Luther King, Jr.* Washington, DC: University Press of America, 1978.

Morgan, Robin. *The Demon Lover. On the Sexuality of Terrorism.* New York: Norton, 1989.

Newsom, Carole A., and Sharon H. Ringe, eds. *The Women's Bible Commentary.* Louisville, KY: Westminster John Knox Press, 1992.

Paulien, Jon. "Recent Developments in the Study of the Book of Revelation." *Andrews University Studies,* 26, 2 (1988), 159-170.

Peake, Arthur S. *The Revelation of John.* London: Holborn Publishing House, N.D.

Pilch, John J. *What Are They Saying about the Book of Revelation?* New York: Paulist Press, 1978.

Pippin, Tina. *Death and Desire. The Rhetoric of Gender in the Apocalypse of John.* Louisville, KY: Westminster John Knox Press, 1992.

Russell, D. S. *The Method and Message of Jewish Apocalyptic.* Philadelphia: Westminster Press, 1976.

Schüssler-Fiorenza, Elisabeth. "Apocalyptic Gnosis in the Book of Revelation and Paul." *Journal of Biblical Literature,* 4 (1973).

———. *The Book of Revelation. Justice and Judgmen.,* Philadelphia: Fortress Press, 1985.

———. "Followers of the Lamb. Visionary Rhetoric and Social-Political Situation." In *Discipleship in the New Testament,* F. Segovia, ed. Minneapolis, MN: Fortress Press, 1985, 162. Also found in *Semeia,* 36 (1986): 123-46.

Selvidge, Marla J. *Woman, Violence, and the Bible.* New York: Edwin Mellen Press, 1996.

Smith, D. Moody. *First, Second, and Third John.* Louisville, KY: John Knox Press, 1991.

Stanley, John E. "The Apocalypse and Contemporary Sect Analysis." *SBL Seminar Papers,* 25 (1986): 416.

Strecker, Georg. *The Johannine Letters. A Commentary on 1,2, and 3 John.* Linda M. Maloney, trans. Minneapolis, MN: Fortress Press, 1996.

Turner, William L. *Making Sense of the Revelation: A Clear Message of Hope.* Macon, GA: Smyth & Helwys, 2000

Vorster, W. S. "Genre and the Revelation of John: A Study in Text, Context, and Intertext." *Neotestamentica,* 22 (1988): 111-123.

Watson, Duane F. "Amplification Techniques in 1 John: The Interaction of Rhetorical Style and Invention." *Journal for the Study of the New Testament,* 51 (1993): 99-123.

Williams, Michael E. *Daniel and Revelation.* Nashville, TN: Abingdon Press, 1999.

Worth, Ronald H., Jr. *The Seven Cities of the Apocalypse and Greco-Asian Culture.* Mahwah, NJ: Paulist Press, 1999.

Young, Serinity. *An Anthology of Sacred Texts By and About Women.* New York: Crossroad, 1993.

Index

Compiled by Julie Kendall,
Student Assistant to the Center for Religious Studies